SpringerWienNewYork

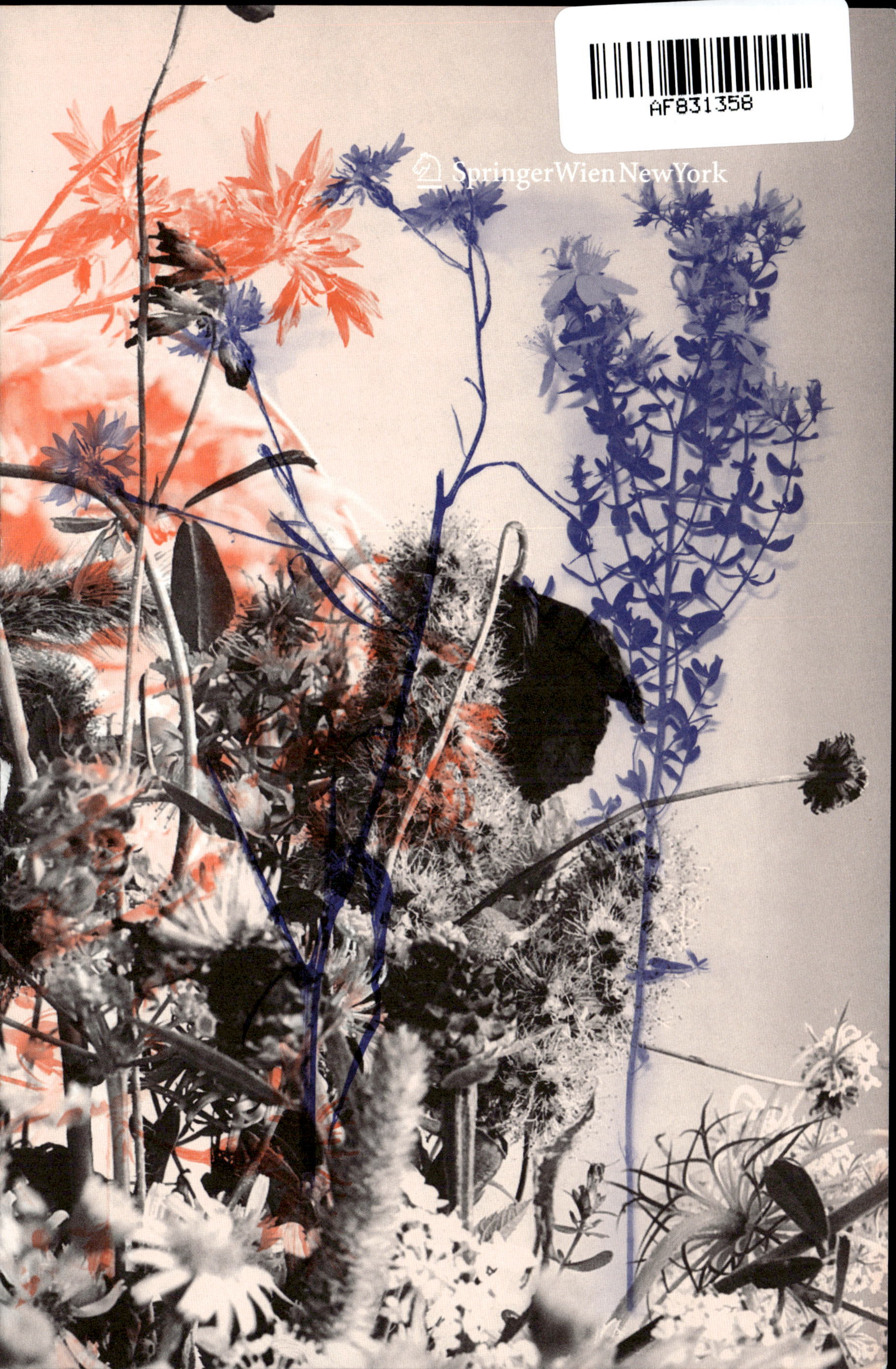

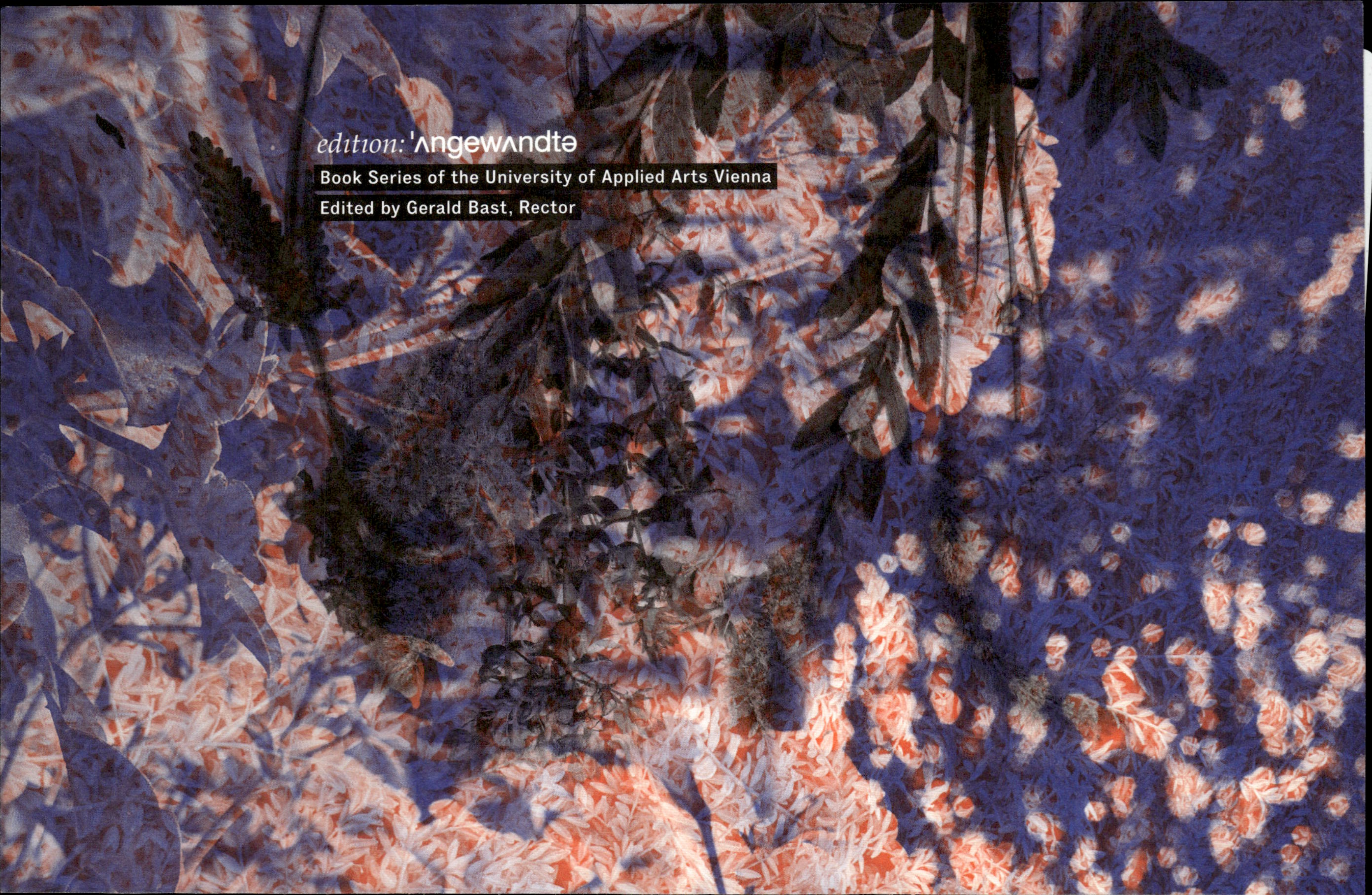
edition:'Angewandte
Book Series of the University of Applied Arts Vienna
Edited by Gerald Bast, Rector

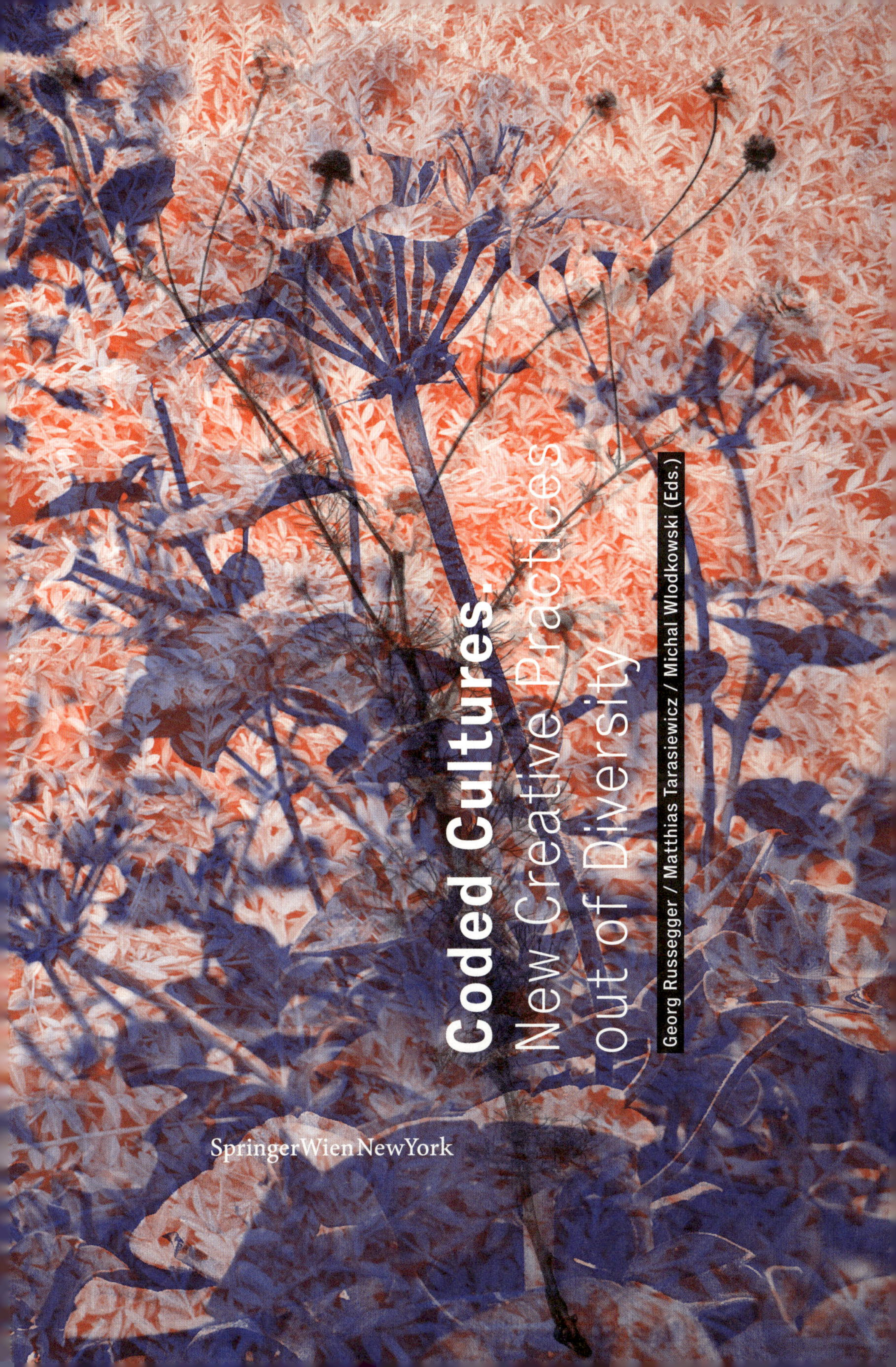

Coded Cultures.

New Creative Practices out of Diversity

Georg Russegger / Matthias Tarasiewicz / Michal Wlodkowski (Eds.)

SpringerWienNewYork

1

8 Georg Russegger

Coded Cultures.
New Creative Practices out of Diversity

In recent years global economies and city policies have set their sights on the codes of creative cultures. With questionable terms like creative class and cultural industries, this movement has not been able to grasp the complex state of the art in which new innovative operations are being pushed by creative and artistic modes of delineation. This essay will give an introduction to the book of coded cultures focusing on the deeper meaning of terms like creativity, codes, programs and how they are invented and applied in a complex set of diversities based on transdisciplinary and intercultural vectors of artistic project-dispositions.

Introduction

42 Christian Reder

Projects … Project Worlds … Project Cultures

Project Cultures: All the many-sided existing project worlds but also continuous structural false reactions show how necessary project cultures are for integrating diverse potential towards a »culture of participation« and »media-integrated cultures of knowledge«. Especially »a change in the way we change things« and »collective experimentation« become more and more necessary. Otherwise unforeseeable and unbelievable data and media based power games will influence our daily life, our political systems, all the efforts towards stable democracy.

Coded Cultures.
New Creative Practices out of Diversity

Georg Russegger

In recent years global economies and city policies have set their sights on the codes of creative cultures. With questionable terms like creative and cultural industries, this movement has not been able to grasp the complex state of the art in which new innovative operations are being pushed by creative and artistic modes of delineation. In fact the involved inventors are becoming »disoriented« within the parameters of these unstable policies. Being creative, flexible, mistake-friendly, open to life long learning, economically stable and socially networked are the abilities needed to earn a living in creative labor. The current situation calls for the development of a broader view of inflationary used terms like creativity, innovation or code. This introduction presents examples and sketches theoretical descriptions as pathways to a non-economical understanding of codes and programs that underlie creative cultures. From a business perspective, these terms are reduced to potential sources of profit and distort the general meaning and importance of these phenomena for our times. The introduction will also function to bridge the gaps between the different viewpoints of the authors and contributors on coded cultures and show how the contexts of their work have been developed out of a strong, transdisciplinary network of artists, writers, researchers, designers, producers and a variety of people with creative potential and skills, who do not even have a common sense description of their »profession« in a broader sense. Based on a two year journey between Europe and Asia that occurred in the course of producing the festival *CODED CULTURES* in Austria and Japan, this text should also give some impressions of a nomadic lifestyle and give insight into its ups and downs, which are becoming commonplace for a generation that is forced to be creative, with everything that implies, in a standardized and sometimes very exhausting way.

Strictly speaking, like Beuys once stated with regards to the artist, everybody is a creative in modernized and post-industrial societies. What once was a sign of uniqueness and something to strive for has become a standard, which forces us to design homes, friendship, products, communities and ourselves. This leads us to the problem that the term »to create« is not easy to define. »Creare« based on Latin seems to be the root, which has the basic meaning »to select« or »to elect«. Furthermore, the current meaning of »creativity« is closer to the French »création«, which was mainly used in the 20th century. There is a third, more hidden meaning of the term as well, which can be related to the Latin word »crescere«, which means »to emerge«, »to grow« or »to nurture«. This last semantic dimension, in combination with the meaning of creation or special touch, offers a perspective that I want to underline in the context of contemporary cultures: It has the strongest resonance with the definition of creativity we can observe in coded cultures. Creativity needs to grow in an environment, interdependent with social and cultural possibilities, codes and programs, which will be described in detail later on. Ideas and projects are always related to, and never isolated from, their surrounding situations. In short: No culture without cooperation, no cooperation without communication. Communicational cooperation is one of the great accomplishments of humankind. Within this recursiveness based on »indirect reciprocity«, to use the term of the evolutionary anthropologist Michael Tomasello, creative processes emerged and were synthesized primarily as a byproduct. The core development was human self organization of various kinds. From this perspective, interaction appears as the key ability in the individual's relation to human and non-human environments. Social interaction, which is much more than swarm-like forms of self organization, might be the kernel of cooperative patterns, encompassing a complex relationship between egoism and altruism. Herein we can see one of the stable lines, which still dominates human relations, exchange and imitation. Without the possibilities of doing things in a closer relation, where the exchange of things and non-things can take place, there would not be the possibility to compare, learn, project, synchronize or diversify and finally to invent and delineate. Within a hyper-mediated perspective surrounded by machines, automats and computers the situation grows enormously in complexity. There are more likely intelligent and smart combinations of symbols, forms, methods, selections and codes, which have been evolved in the later stage of mediated self empowerment of humankind. The history is rich in examples of how the rise of a new technology always changed society and the way humans organize, socialize, communicate, learn and produce.

Back in history, humans had to invent and self organize lifesaving programs, like hunting, collecting, preserving and so on, over thousands of years. I will not go into the details of these archaic modes of self organization. It is just important to name the difference to explain that our archaic ancestors didn't have much time or many resources to pursue activities outside of their every day survival routines. So to say: Higher cultural and artistic development would not be possible without abundance in general. Without a running operation system, which generates the fundamentals of life, there would not be the resources and the esprit for creative and artistic development. Even if these are helpful tools to understand the actual situation, these derivations are not generating a valuable difference to discuss the major changes in cultural backbones transformed by the introduction of the automation based on digital media and computer based communication. We have to be careful how we label the shifts since we have been overwhelmed by scientific, economic and political »turns«, prophesy the rise of all kinds of new forms, transforming our environment and us so tremendously.

Codes and Programs

It might seem needless to say that codes and programs have existed much longer than digital media, but it is often forgotten. I want to raise the question concerning the divergence of the technical terms and the philosophical ones. One can bypass this thought and enter the term »code« into a computer network based search engine: 1,420,000,000 results. That's still a low number compared to the quantity of codes existing. Even *Encyclopaedia Britannica* returns several pages of sub-categorization for »code«. One definition related to communications is: *»Code is an unvarying rule for replacing a piece of information such as a letter, word, or phrase with an arbitrarily selected equivalent«* [1]. Another association which might come to mind is: »Code is Law«, and it was, since the first known appearance of the Babylonian *Code of Hammurabi* (3770 years ago). But all these lines of thought are not very helpful when it comes to finding a precise description of why codes are so important to cooperative modes, social interactions, common backgrounds, shared activities and creative inter-relations among humans and artifacts. The major motives in this interdependence of »shared intentionality« (TOMASELLO, 2009) are »helping« and »sharing«. These altruistic practices are basic elements of cooperation. On the other hand history is, of

1 http://www.britannica.com/EBchecked/topic/123881/code [Accessed: Jul 13, 2010]

course, full of terrible acts of destruction and catastrophic events, in which humans showed no compassion. We should keep this in mind as we undertake the next step of abstraction.

Talking about today's population of artists and cultural developers, curators and researchers is a pretty risky task. Too many people are involved in work based on creative abstraction and artificiality. To narrow down the field, I want to talk about the experience and networks involved in the *CODED CULTURES* festival. The people involved in the festival have been mainly thinking about new forms of art and expression based on digitally networked media, at the intersection of different disciplines and cultures. This heterogeneous network led to the first »cultural code clashes«: Language, background, symbols and references differ greatly among the participating individuals and among people in general. If one thinks about the differences between Asian and European cultures, this is fairly obvious. In this situation technology and media became the main transponders, because they encompass globalized standards and exchange formats. The informative and communicative relations based on the infrastructure of networked computers and the *World Wide Web* were the core structure and the lowest common denominator. Technology in this context stands for more than an assembled thing that is made to organize or transform environments. First level technique was the ability of the participating entities to create their forms of art, second level was to make it connectable and transform it in a way to fit into the greater context of coded cultures. The second level technologies and techniques were open and short-term adaptations and attitudes in the framing of projects and populations that were developed from communication interfaces as an open and mistake-friendly process. Imagine several subdivisions of special interest communities involved in an exhibition. Fields like bio-hacking, Do-It-Yourself media, toy bending, cosmonautics, playful interfaces, game-like installations and so on, all have their own forms of codes, references, relations and communities. The (sub-) cultural program consisted of learned and agreed codes of abstraction and common sense patterns that were used in these framings to understand, exchange, share and expand existing ideas and projects. Transformations take place as an exchange between different fields of interest in such a setting in which people want to understand how materials and strategies relate to each other. The creation of a meta-project outline like a festival, which is still adaptable and therefore unstable, is a proto-typical effort. The shared background of all participants involved in the production cannot be taken as granted, so the communicative framings have to be translated in every specific field. Following the example of the festival we have arrived on the level of a proto-cultural program that agrees on loose codes, which include options and preferences, models of use-ful complexity for the differentiation, shaping and sharing of modes of inclusion and exclusion as well as an inherent openness for communicative fine tuning.

Complexity sensibility is an essential skill for the navigation and coordination of these fuzzy processes. Complexity is a subjective degree of interpretation. At the same time there is no dualistic approach for simplicity. Complexity cannot be reduced or simplified. Codes and programs are shared, functional and useful models that can be applied as complexity transformers and shapers. Or as Peter Wippermann puts it in the Ars Electronica catalogue titled *Simplicity*: *»It's about maximum choice with a minimal loss of orientation«.* We have been talking briefly about different options and levels, in which creativity is applied in the frameset of a project such as a festival. The first order of modeling complexity in this context is the ability of creators to generate their art and make it adaptable and connectable in their own field and communities. The second order is the transdisciplinary approach to exchange and communication with dissimilar disciplines and fields. This is one of the most fruitful activities, because in this mode trained and stabilized methods and operations have to be reconfigured and adapted for other contexts. The third order is a functional model, which has to be developed to display first and second order operations. Erwin Schrödinger coined the term »Negentropy«, which might be useful to evaluate the level of complexity by the measurement of the degree of organization internal to any system formed by interacting components. I am afraid, at this time there is no such science available which has developed the tools and methods to research these fields on a cultural level, but the contributions in this book will elaborate on this topic. Dominick Chen for example will think about the future of creative commodities in coded cultures. It includes an analysis of Gregory Bateson's idea of prochronism and homology, posting perspectives of a possible future in code-dependent cultures and how our definition of creativity can evolve by focusing on the idea of process and inheritance. Obviously this introduction can't go into details about basic theoretical elements of »code«, as Niklas Luhmann has proposed them in the context of social systems for example. Besides this there is the whole examination on cultural programs, which is missing. This would lead to examples proposed by S. J. Schmidt or references to Manuel Castells, connecting the rise of the networked society to mediated human self empowerment, which would be Manfred Faßler's terminology, based on *Co-Evolutionary Anthropology*. Furthermore, an entire range of theoretical reflection on cultural programs could be mobilized for our line of inquiry. Some explorations of these lines of thought can be found in the contributions of authors such as Manfred Faßler or Marina Gržinić in the theoretical section of this book.

Invention and Delineation

As a memento: The meaning of »crescere« is »to emerge«, »to grow« or »to nurture«. Based on this origin, there has to be something, which can emerge and grow. Invention does not need a cooperative act per se, it might take place as a mental process, but when someone is starting to design or to delineate, in most cases other people and materials are needed. Something to imitate would help as well, in contrast to designing from scratch. Talking about real/fake dualism is not helpful in understanding this process, rather it's

about pre-limitations that have to be expanded, or it's about developing methods to overcome standards. A bit oversimplified but catchy formula: »New« in this relation, is a smart recombination and reinvention of the »old«, in a new way.
It does not make sense to ask here how things started, because this would lead to the classic »chicken or egg« discussion. With reference to Boris Groys, who writes about the creative recycling of cultural waste and the profanity of the »new«, or Schumpeter, who speaks of »creative destruction«, we should dismiss the idea of newness that comes from »nothingness« and the concept of »godlike entry«. The new is generated by experimental co-creative processes, in cooperative interactions between humans, artifacts, ideas, codes, programs, systems and their environmental test drives. The playful and ludic method of circumventing limitations in an unpragmatic and non-result-oriented behavior underlies this open framework of delineation and is currently becoming more and more a central hub for the exploration of new creative possibilities, even when they have nothing to

do with what is classically thought of as digital games. We will find some examples in the articles of Mathias Fuchs and Margarete Jahrmann reporting on ludic artifacts and interfaces and their greater impact on artistic developments.

Invention on the other hand, often happens as controlled coincidence, intended or unintended accident, and as forced emergencies. The cooperative act stands for a co-creative interdependence of several heterogeneous players such as artifacts, concepts, people, codes, programs or media. The distinction between the objective and subjective organized in project realities appears obsolete and this leads us to Vilém Flusser, who coined the formula »from subject to project«. This insight also connects to theoretical outcomes that describe new sociocultural forms as » Smart Populations « (FASSLER, 2006) that consist of » Smartjects « (RUSSEGGER, 2007) and »Smartifacts« (IBID.) . Smartness, if undefined, is a controversial term, but as an articulation situated between creativity, intelligence and innovation, it helps to overcome the limitation of these descriptions. Smartness is not a stable value or solely an ability of human relations, it increasingly appears as clever, artful, sophisticated, and diplomatic behavior of people and artifacts, especially in the relation of egoistic-altruistic patterns of cooperative abilities and to display social functionality. This smartness is always an applied dynamic in relation to new forms of environments, technologies, techniques, projects and people. It is the ability to have fresh eyes that enable the discovery of new perspectives in existing landscapes, the ability to alienate the existing. Additionally, the term »smart« appears increasingly in material- and technology-based environments. Some »smart ups« can be observed: smart-phones, -houses, -buildings, -cities and so on. It is a monitor where we can see the key-aspects of a huge gap in the definition of innovation. It points as well to the stupidity of some of our socio-cultural systems, for example how thin and unsustainable bubbles in the business sector create fake innovation. The gap is also recognizable in fields of techno gadgets that represent the artform of »un-useless objects« or *Chindogus* (KAWAKAMI, 1995) . This controversy sheds light on the multisided discussion on art and innovation and feeds the easy-to-use and funny-to-have side of innovationalism based on technology driven gadget cultures. Within the essays section of the book there will be a closer look, describing the active fields of device art and do it yourself modding and hacking cultures and histories. By these means objects carry a symbolic and reputational multiverse of designed republics and aesthetical relations to underline the owner's affiliation, choice, taste, individuality, emotions or orientation. Based on the observation of long term innovation in the field of developmental biology and the co-evolutional interdependence of humans and environments, there is an exponential increase of innovative developments besides these market-driven short term inventions, especially since automation and computerization gives the possibility to compute biology, physics, mathematics, arts, etc. Managing these intense unstable and changing cultural drifts raises the question of sustainability with regards to human development as society, biology and technology in the future.

Together with Natascha Adamowsky's ludic media theory we can ask: »*Why did evolution give us the joy of gameplay?*« [2] (ADAMOWSKY, 2000). To motivate us to experiment, to get serious in unserious ways, to invent and delineate a free flow of creativity, to generate test cultures before they are converted into large-scale systematic and organizational approaches? More questions than answers can be developed from the perspective shift Adamowsky proposes. Tools, methods and models have to be observed in combination with their appliance and within the polylogical dispositions in which they appear. Space and environment move into the center of attention. Where do things and actions take place? And does »invention« have an action dimension or place of action of its own? This line of thought will fill much more than a chapter of this book, so we have to follow the dimension of abilities, delineations, things which can be observed and described even if an elementary morphology is missing. The phenomenon outlined within the festival *CODED CULTURES* points to the capacity of playfulness to become a powerful

2 — In German: *Warum hat uns die Evolution die Lust am Spiel beschert?* (translated by the author)

tool and mindset for individuals, to overcome existing patterns and standards of culture, art, science and technology. The ability to play can be applied by every person who derives joy from discovering ways to circumvent limitations. By these means »play« is very different from »entertainment«. As mentioned before, playful behavior is employed by people who are not very much involved in digital gaming, as it gives them a chance to experiment with the world in the mode of »as-if«. Play as a method of dealing with reality and developing new ways of looking at the world. »I am playing« means that I can do something that I don't usually do. The creation of playful experiences uses existing resources in new ways by operating on the intersections of different levels of »inventive smartness«. Play foments creative patterns because it »requires interpretation and resists operationalization« (CF. ADAMOWSKY, 2000) .

Communities and Cultures

We are still in the field of creative cultures and communities, even if we had to take some detours to narrow down the carrier units of what creative codes can stand for in artistic delineation cultures and in the interpretation of coded cultures. The technical and aesthetical dispositive used for applied abstraction and implementation is becoming a major marker of identification in »Communities of Projects« (FASSLER, 2006) . Cultures become Cults, and one of the most prominent ones under today's conditions is »The Cult of Information« (CF. ROSZAK, 1985) . This brings us closer to the relation of counter cultures and the » laws of cool « and how these cults foment mainstream community cultures. Alan Liu, with his excellent analyses of knowledge work and the culture of information (LIU, 2004) , shows a very deep understanding of how the tribes of cool and the implementation of large scale »coolness« via industrialization and knowledge work have been dominating the last century's development of labor and production. Here we need the critical understanding of how political representatives of cyber-economy and E-Industries create environments hostile to creativity through their tele-power and detached thin innovation hunger. Furthermore why free access of the internet is still a »dream term« and why free flow of information is regressive or not even applicable. Business models and transactions are limited to big players and monocultures. The early euphoria about the net and its opportunities seems to have been exchanged by large scale consumerism of digital bohemians, eager to start companies, feel independent by producing apps and games for smartphones and social networks. The message propagated by the corporate world is: find freedom in the individualistic, consumeristic and interfaced realm, give up your privacy and be afraid of piracy. Gentrification transforms creative destruction into » destructive creativity « (LIU, 2004) . Artistic communities, single protagonists, organizers, curators and producers should be aware of their dislocated area and create their critical potential inside of systematical approaches from countries, regions or cultural capitals. Coolness carries a different meaning than » cool hunting « or »being cool«. It is a mode of acting that strives to create connectable information and to stay oriented in a world of cold fascination, a mode for working in the mediacultural ice age.

Going where the action is would mean to participate in proto-cultural approaches, being part of artistic test drives, constantly reinventing and questioning things, actions, processes. It's not a bad learning paradigm, but the question is if humankind is capable of creating a livelong immune system against commodification and secure sustainability by choosing the life of conformity. It can work out if the modes of cooperation are providing such outlines, without working in precarious circumstances, supporting the generation of new configurations of self organizations. Besides there still will be the problem of grown institutional framesets, celebrating their geriatric value without getting the paradigmatic shift of mediamorph lifestyle and the *»hermeneutics of the digital everyday«* [3] done. It's not about digital natives, it has never been. The solution can't be about downgrading socio-cultural and evolutionary developments to the »medial« and its user culture. Understanding media is just the first step in mediated self empowerment. There are several steps more waiting to be

3 – Geert Lovink, Interview with Alan Liu, Institute of Network Cultures. http://networkcultures.org/wpmu/geert/interview-with-alan-liu [Accessed: Dec 01, 2010]

taken to understand coded cultures in the age of a globalized, multiethnic, transnational and diverse environment. Going over the notes from the conference of the *CODED CULTURES* festival, in which most of the authors of this book participated, I was confronted with a vast diversity in the approaches pursued to break down the dimensions of coded cultures. There was a high communal aspect between the participating entities that didn't show signs of becoming a closed or homogeneous community. The cultural transformations of backgrounds and knowledge exhaust the interpretational power, the language clash handicaps precise communication, the multisided approaches tire the senses. Because of this it was especially compelling that there was so much exchange, cooperation and motivation between the participants to create something from what on the first glance appears to be a huge limitation. It would be helpful to have more fundamental research, new methods and scientific research models to analyze these dynamics in embedded laboratories. There has to be more effort to bring these topics to attention, especially to funding and supporting entities when it comes to new scientific and artistic approaches between disciplines. The fear of doing something wrong, not fitting into a league or canon, of crippling one's own development and thoughts because of the predomination of discourse or fashion still hinders the invention of new paradigms in art and science. Transdisciplinary approaches have to be taken into account in the same way »hard sciences« are taken seriously when it comes to support and funding. With the conditions of »no direct outcome model behind«, »no time pressure« and »no result oriented programs«, projects could be established and implemented to invent theories, research tools, observation models and assessment criteria for coded cultures, and to explore the underlying ghost terms creative and cultural industries. This is still dreamwork for the science of mediacultures and an *Anthropology of the Medial* [4]. People are forced to create start up economies, dealing with clients, which don't even have the basic alphabet of the language of new media at hand.

4 – Originally German: *Anthropologie des Medialen.* (Manfred Faßler, FAMe Frankfurt: www. fame-frankfurt.de)

Description is fine and useful to expand information and knowledge, but if you feel like you are in the digital stone age, it is hard to do rocket science.

One important turn in the work of exhibitions and festivals is the change of view from display to interface. Interface cultures like festival communities and exhibition laboratories have been decoupled from the classical understanding of a technological or medial interface. They have become more like a cultural program, fomenting creative codes of delineation and prototypical experience development for participants and audiences; a field where ideas, things and projects can be seeded in cooperative modes of shared knowledge and intellectual support. As John Thackara says, *»Whatever you choose to do, don't try to do it alone. We are all designers now«* (THACKARA, 2006) . I want to add: Let's design smart and viable practices and apply them within creative project cooperations that are open to large groups of people. For the interface laboratory of a festival it would be important to function as an ensemble, to exhibit artists in combination with their (proto-, counter-, sub-) cultural codes. It is unproductive to post questions like: »What has happened to media art?«, because it is already clear that the distinction between contemporary art and media art was an artificial invention to position a systematic and community based interest against modern art and the art market. It shows quite well how paradoxical situations can get, if discussions are too media centered and disposition oriented.

Egoism and Altruism

In this section, I want to present some personal and emotive elements because they are often unpublished and buried deep under functional competence and professional liability. To co-organize two festivals, one in Austria and one in Japan in the same year, with limited resources, to work with a team of 60 people to talk to hundreds of people about the goals and strategies, while traveling between Japan and Austria nearly every second month, has been an unforgettable experience. Powered by an egoistic drive to give the best I have, to make everything happen in the best way I could, to show that I was able to do so, and on the other hand to realize a metanoia together with a good team, where things can be done together, even if it seems impossible sometimes, sounds like a sports philosophy but still provides a warm bellied feeling. During some sleepless nights where solutions had to be found for all kinds of problems that kept on appearing, it sometimes felt like a burden. Running around in Tokyo and Vienna selling ideas which have no need to be sold, having no distinct product or clear target group, was highly intriguing, especially since I came straight from finishing my Ph.D. and had minor understanding of creative markets and funding systems. In this situation, the only chance is to give everything you have, be happy listening to people and make them listen to you, and not to think too much about double bind interests you have to fulfill. Altruism and self affirmation are sometimes close friends, especially in the pursuit of shared operations with different goals.

The core ability needed for this kind of work is communication in all of its modes and styles. Especially Japan was a great challenge for these reasons. All the high context idiosyncrasies and hidden agendas in the communication let the fear grow that things would go wrong without understanding why. Without the institutional background as a Post Doc. at *Tokyo Geidai* (Graduate School for Film and New Media) and the support of Masaki Fujihata, this project would have been an impossible venture. The ability to use the research time at the institute to delineate and outline a research frameset for the festival was helpful beyond words. Additionally, the many people interested in developing new dynamics and ideas in the organization of something different have to be mentioned. The artists Shimura Bros. and the curator and co-producer of *CODED CULTURES* Takahiro Kaneshima have been very close friends, who have greatly helped the project to overcome kickbacks and keep the goals achievable. I received structural coaching, which is more than needed in Tokyo, from Yukiko Shikata and Shiho Fukuhara. It would be an endless task to list all the help received in Japan. The sharing of knowledge by friends and supporters upheld the flow in the project so that we never lost faith. The association *5uper.net*, which founded the *CODED CULTURES* festival in 2004, has been the home base and hub for the festival—with up to 10 people working in a small office space in the center of Vienna, managing several international projects at once, while retaining a student like collaborative environment. Of course there were some hard times and tensions concerning the distribution of tasks and positions as well as the success and failure of suggested ideas, methods and proceedings. It is difficult to have a handle on processes and tasks if things are being done for the first time, the complexity of the project is high, and the participants have limited experience. In short, I have to thank all the people who have been involved in this project. It was a great experience to be part of a team doing something new, learning so many things and implementing such an experience-based process. I hope that a reciprocal outcome was evident for everybody involved as well, even if the basic democratic mode of decision-making was not always applicable.

Conclusion

Within the framework of *CODED CULTURES* my focus lies on ability profiles, knowledge cultures and projects of artists, researchers and producers departed from the digital realm. Working at the intersection of disciplines such as art, science, technology and design, requires strong networks of cooperation between individuals, communities and projects. In addition to the cultural diversity, which was a central characteristic of the festival *CODED CULTURES* during the *Austria—Japan Year 2009* and which will be done again in 2011. Complementary issues were raised through the socio-technological tools and methods used. Based on the idea of intermediation between disciplines, cultures and entities, this book will give a look into new developments and practices that depart from digital media related art and cultures and which can be subsumed under the broad topic of coded cultures. The following pages present an outlook from different viewpoints, questioning how contemporary cultures are dealing with the conditions of complex media realities and polylogic artistic strategies on the intersection with other fields of activity. Researchers, artists and curators play a major role in the development of test environments for upcoming cultural emergences in a prototypical sense. It is important to reflect on creative practices to bridge the gap between expert knowledge and educational approaches within artistic production processes. The sharing of knowledge leads to a communicative challenge and art as an idiosyncratic idea which can transform highly accumulated topics from fields like biotechnology, game studies, informatics, anthropology, politics a.s.o. Since the artist or producer does not always have an interest in greater contextualization of their creation, the critic and the researcher can engross their thoughts on enhanced experiences and observations. Thus the structure of this publication involves theoretical articles from media anthropology, cultural studies, communication science, essays about art and knowledge transfer, creative commons, fashionable technologies and ludic interfaces combined with interviews and essays from participating artists from Japan and Europe. Emerging creative ideas from fields like device art, playful environments, sonic art, time based media, performative arts and media art are presented to make new forms of contemporary artistic cultures accessible.

References

Ars Electronica 2006: *Simplicity—The Art Of Complexity.*
Ostfildern: Hatje Cantz, 2006

Adamowsky, N.: *Spielfiguren in virtuellen Welten.*
Frankfurt a.M.: Campus Verlag, 2000

Castells, M.: *The Rise of the Network Society.*
New York: John Wiley & Sons, 2009

Groys, B.: *Über das Neue—Versuch einer Kulturökonomie.*
Frankfurt a.M.: Fischer Verlag, 1999

Liu, A.: *The Laws of Cool.*
Chicago: The University of Chicago Press, 2004

Luhmann, N.: *Soziale Systeme.*
Frankfurt a.M.: Suhrkamp, 1987

Faßler, M.: *Der Infogene Mensch.*
München: Wilhelm Fink Verlag, 2008

Faßler, M.: *Nach der Gesellschaft.*
München: Wilhelm Fink Verlag, 2009

Flusser, V.: *Vom Subjekt zum Projekt. Menschwerdung.*
Bensheim: Bollmann Verlag, 1994

Kawakama, K.: *101 Unuseless Japanese Inventions: The Art of Chindogu.*
New York: Norton & Company, 1995

Russegger, G., Tarasiewicz, M., Wlodkowski, M.:
CODED CULTURES—Exploring Creative Emergences (Catalogue). Wien: 5uper.net, 2009

Russegger, G.: *Vom Subjekt zum Smartject.*
Wien, Turia und Kant, 2009

Roszak, T.: *The Cult of Information.*
Berkeley: University of California Press, 1994

Schmidt, S. J.: *Kalte Faszination.*
Weilerswist: Velbrück Wissenschaft, 2000

Schrödinger, E.: *What is Life—the Physical Aspect of the Living Cell.*
Cambridge: University Press, 1944

Thackara, J.: *In the Bubble—Designing in a Complex World.*
Massachusetts: MIT Press, 2005

Tomasello, M.: *Die Ursprünge der menschlichen Kommunikation.*
Frankfurt a.M.: Suhrkamp, 2009

Projects ... Project Worlds ... Project Cultures Models of Intervention-, Cooperation-, Investigation-Based Approaches

Christian Reder

Revolutions

»Never before in the history of this planet«, we learn while reading Thomas L. Friedman's optimistic bestseller *The World is Flat. A Brief History of the Twenty-First Century* (FRIEDMAN, 2007) , on the dawn of the digital revolution *»could so many people find so much information on so many things and so many other persons without any outside help«*. Google had expressly set itself the radical goal of *»making the entire knowledge of the world easily accessible to everyone in every language«*, that is to say, to make it largely possible *»to create one's own individual chains of value creation«*. This would trigger unknown *»forces for leveling the world«* —a sort of removal of barriers. Through »globalization of the local« cultural differences could be expressed in a new way. *»Political activism and social entrepreneurialism«* would be activated. Ultimately, everything in digitalized

form—by whomever—could be »searched«. These new freedoms sprung up on their own, it seems, from an »accumulation of events« consisting of boundless possibilities. In reality, though, it were the countless parallel »projects« that ultimately fed into powerful entrepreneurial structures or became such themselves.

Apropos of such freedoms: when doing a Google search on the word »freedom« one is first directed to the Australian business chain *Freedom™ Furniture and Homeware* and then to the Wikipedia page »Freedom« with links leading to »free will«, »political freedom« (with the telling note: »may require cleanup«), to »economic freedom«. If one types in »liberty«, the first thing to appear is a page of the London company *Liberty. Gifts for Her and Gifts for Him*, the British *Liberty* NGO with the motto »*Protecting Civil Liberties. Promoting Human Rights*«, the *Fundamentalist Baptist Liberty University in Lynchburg, Virginia* and finally the Wikipedia page »Liberty«. On »freedom« one could find, at the time this text was written, 162 million, on »liberty« 93 million entries.

Yet in this confusion that evades all criticism, all semantic hierarchy and lexical certainty, one could even find a number of details regarding early revolutions, as, for instance, how aptly Manon Roland (who was to remain famous as *Madame Roland* for this very reason) had expressed the destructive potential lurking behind promises of freedom when in November 1793, aware of her own imminent end at the guillotine, she cried in exasperation: *»O Liberté, que de crimes on commet en ton nom!«* (Oh Liberty, what crimes are committed in your name!) But hadn't precisely she, at the age of only 39, supported the French Revolution from the very beginning, backing the many reforms it initiated, establishing important ties among the democratic powers from her salon at the Parisian *Hôtel Britannique*, denouncing the rampant discrimination against women and serving herself as parliamentarian? (Her husband Jean-Marie Roland had briefly been Minister of the Interior.)

Modernism? Modernity?

Remembering such a revolutionary »accumulation of events« in the early phases of modernity and the intentions the prevalent has the indirect result of bringing forth remarkable associations with the »unfinished project of modernity« (Jürgen Habermas), a »second modernity« (Ulrich Beck), »postmodernity« as a more or less accepted »end of the great narratives« (Jean-François Lyotard) and illusions—the social state is meanwhile also seen as such. It also has to do with how one now deals with basic concepts of the *condition humaine* coined at the time, such as freedom, equality, solidarity—as pragmatics of structural exercise of power, which at best plays a sporadic role for human rights and perspectives on how the world is to be developed and individual societies. In this unforeseeable course of events, »automized« as it were through supply and demand, gleams of hope or even premonitions of the future depend on fortunate constellations and the unflagging project work taking place outside of normal routine. Even circles associated with the

New York Times meanwhile welcome what their columnist Thomas L. Friedman—with symptomatic delay—appeals to in the book published after the one on digital revolution which I cited at the beginning: *Hot, Flat, and Crowded: Why We Need a Green Revolution—And How it Can Renew America* (FRIEDMAN, 2008) .

Extensive innovation emerging from the *Exploring Creative Emergences* projects in Yokohama and Vienna is also a subject of the *CODED CULTURES* initiative—an example of experimental design diversity based on affordable contributions to globalization. It becomes clear that »content« often arises at a remove from superficial commercialization, the former requiring free space.

Even if previous periphery-center divergences have been eliminated in real-time, what is really at stake is power and impotence, top and bottom, outside and inside. But there are also subversive initiatives demonstrating diversity, »multitude«, undertaken against the hegemonic *Empire* and its uniformity (HARDT, NEGRI, 2004) . Seen from the fringes of market economy and the perspective of those who are marginalized, some aspects of these developments become clearer—social visibility, groups that spontaneously endorse something, people who work on problems and innovations, which organizations are no longer capable of. Hackers who have become sought after experts have already set things in motion. As a result the structural characteristic (only variable in terms of method) of rulers to keep the masses somehow under control, to paralyze self initiative, to make everything and everyone consumable is subverted. Over and beyond lip service, even »liberal democracy« is not recognized by all as a model, otherwise one would have to keep working on it—according to its untiring defender Richard Rorty—so that it *»itself already contains the institutions for its improvement«* (RORTY, 1989) which, in turn, only stands a chance of being feasible with consistent, publicly debated projects.

There are striking counter-trends. An energetic civil society focusing on such initiatives and making people aware of these connections is feeling the pressure everywhere—at least in financial terms. Companies, politics, justice and authorities all act in ways that are often contradictory. The political insider Daniel Ellsberg, who has been ostracized for having betrayed strictly confidential Vietnam documents, has stated something to this effect on the model case of the USA notwithstanding all signs of liberalization under President Obama in the spring of 2010: *»Today in the United States we have the infrastructure of a police state. To be sure, it is not a police state yet but only because we have not switched it on yet. For this we are still lacking another 9/11. Credit card statements, E-Mails—the secret services today have completely legal access to all information. The material for bribery attempts keeps growing. These are possibilities of which people like Nixon could only dream«* (DER STANDARD. VIENNA, MAY 29, 2010).

Immanuel Wallerstein, by contrast, even sees it in his book *European Universalism. The Rhetoric of Power* (WALLERSTEIN, 2006) as being highly likely that the present phase of transformation—in spite of any rhetoric to the contrary—is moving into *»a newly hierarchical, unequal world«*

»which claims to be based on universal values in which, however, our behavior continues to be governed by racism and sexism, perhaps in an even more extreme way than this is the case in our present world system«. As simple as it may sound, one would have to seek to create constellations *»in which everyone would be giving and received«*. So-called freedom that cannot be influenced can also spawn fear, extending way beyond the failure of the financial markets and their administrators that is tangible everywhere.

Project Thinking

Such automatic responses and threats clearly illustrate that energy—be it positive or destructive—can mainly be channelized in projects, as an effort of strength of people working together for a limited time in the desire to achieve something—as diffuse as the goal may initially be. In cultural, artistic spheres »projects« and their implementation are the normal case and a pattern for self organization: films, exhibitions, performances, concerts, festivals, publications, competitions. Architecture evolves in the form of a project. The more dynamic part of the economy is geared to projects, to new products, new sites, re-organizations. On the political level, however, since economic power has long prevailed, one is often only able to respond to critical threats in a resolutely project oriented way, as most recently in connection with the bank bail out, the Greek financial crisis, efforts to back the Euro itself. Similar big initiatives relating to social concerns, education, research or ecology are hardly conceivable even if they are permanently discussed.

The European Union is a »project« that emerged from the preceding caesura of civilization and is far from being really consolidated. It also sees itself as a platform for intervening projects. Yet a defensive stance has been assumed everywhere through prevention, supervision, control—and by governments as such. Barack Obama's reform of the health care system, announced as a central project during his election campaign, illustrates how tough and controversial the phase of realization can be. The helplessness vis-à-vis the BP oil spill in the Gulf of Mexico demonstrated that even such powerful nations lack the project structures for intervening when corporations simply act without considering the risks. While such many-sided project worlds, continuous structural false reactions show how necessary projects cultures are for integrating diverse potential, the readiness of non-governmental organizations to deliver on humanitarian deficits shows clearly what is called for—a very unique form of »privatization« and internationalization. Without the refugee aid of the UNHCR, without the *Red Cross*, without *Amnesty International*, *Greenpeace*, and thousands of similar project oriented initiatives, the world would be a very different place.

This once again leads us back to the early phases of modernity, to Daniel Defoe's illuminating text *An Essay Upon Projects* (DEFOE, 1697) in which he propagated the notion of »project« for the first time, describing in highly pragmatic terms the »project worlds« to be aspired to: *»Projects of the nature I treat about are doubtless in general of public advantage, as they tend to improvement of trade, and employment of the poor, and the circulation and* *increase of the public stock of the kingdom; but this is supposed of such as are built on the honest basis of ingenuity and improvement, in which, though I will allow the author to aim primarily at his own advantage, yet with the circumstances of public benefit added«.*

The very reason that all talk of »public benefit« has been robbed of all meaning, thanks to its inflationary use and profit benchmarks, stock rates, election opportunities, market forces, efficiency and cost structures have come to govern our realm of action, as if there were hardly any more »deviating« freedoms. For this very reason, voluntary corporate government guidelines and non-profit projects are now more necessary than ever before—in Defoe's sense (1697!). How such voluntary action, unwritten rules, social behavior, cooperation actually plays out tells something crucial about the state of affairs and the necessity of a general parameter.

Artistic Research

Significant in this context is the extent to which even science and art—both governed by project worlds and project work in an exemplary sense—are dependent on operating systems, well-established settings and institutions. This is how, as Bruno Latour notes in *Pandora's Hope. An Essay on the Reality of Science Studies* (LATOUR, 1999) , a »no-man's land« emerged between cultures that have hardly any more contact, because the »hard« natural sciences and technology and the »soft« humanities/literary studies only sporadically embark upon interdisciplinary projects. But the main reason is that *»a completely cold and inhuman world of science completely left to its own devices«* hardly takes note of the *»rich life world of intentional positions« »which are completely limited to man and entirely cut off from actual things in and of themselves«*. Research thus had to be understood in a more »offensive« sense as » collective experimentation « —as »collective experimentation with what humans and non-humans can tolerate or renounce«. As Latour concludes in *We Have Never Been Modern* (LATOUR, 1993) it would be false to speak of a failure of modernity since *»modernism* *was not an illusion, but an active performing but if we do not change the common dwelling, we shall not absorb in it the other cultures that we can no longer dominate and we shall be forever incapable of accommodating in it the environment that we can no longer control. [...] Neither nature nor the others will become modern. It is up to us to change our ways of changing«.*

To develop pictorial languages and abstractions that could be understood the world over—already a dream of a meanwhile classical artistic modernism, as an attempt to find universal relations—»collective experimentation«, an awareness of »rich life world of intentional positions«, certainly requires »research-oriented modes of thinking«. In artistic work, in particular, this can be exemplified while keeping sight of the singularity that so often eludes science. This has been the focus of one of my own research projects on *Art and Knowledge Transfer* at the *University of Applied Arts Vienna*, which seeks to illustrate such processes and ways of open-minded research (REDER, 2004) . Here the explicit subject is »artistic research with artistic means« that is, an expressly »different research« as an alternative to any »officially approved« development oriented on financial interests, as philosopher Burghart Schmidt said in reference to these approaches in a programmatic essay when addressing the question: »What is the position of the arts on the essence of research?« in the literary journal *Wespennest* (SCHMIDT, 2010). Precisely the arts are—in his words—able to *»address issues the science system is unable to because of its methodologies that rely on accreditation and its generalization that has to prevail in the arts of the highest specification«*. It would be possible to continue by means of art *»where science and theory formation are their wits' end«*, where something is manifested *»in the individual by the highly singular«*, that *»something would not be if it could be expressed by means of scientific generalizations«*. No science succeeds in conveying the *»leap to man's qualitative pictorial worlds«*, *»in which we seek the foundations of our own being«*. Who is even capable of thinking without images, that is to say who can create sensible connections when limited to conventional languages? It is precisely with artistic means that suppressed questions can be articulated, as Schmidt notes, some of which were once certainly a part of theory and which today belong to the suppressed need for theory. And with them it would be possible to *»seek answers by means of pictures or to reduce answers ad absurdum with the same degree of involvement and interest«*. At issue are primarily *»continuations in the sense of an engagement for research-based art as a counterpart to science without the former dissolving in the functional circle of the latter«*. Science that has become complex *»can no longer take any step without crossing over to the arts in its aspiration to singularity«*.

The arts by contrast, in their aspiration to singularity, cannot get around the »generalization of the sciences« without lapsing into esoteric ignorance«, if they do not take literally *»the generalization of the sciences«* in their research and *»trying to demonstrate ad hominem the singular situation«*. *»Without this the world will have become blind and empty«*.

Pictorial Worlds, Coded Cultures

The systems of access and distribution of the »qualitative pictorial worlds of man« alluded to above—like the deluge of other incidentals—are presently undergoing radical change as a result of the digital revolution and the expansive network culture in which everything is electronically transformed, conveyed in zeros and ones. The resulting potential integration of man, an almost global availability, a possibility of self representation, formation of network groups, as universal availability and reproducibility of news, texts, data, images, photos, films, TV, music, is influencing, even if not yet so noticeably, behavior, sensations and thinking, steps in a completely new way. Everything is welcome, otherwise the internet would have remained *»an application for expert systems«*—as communication theorist Frank Hartmann succinctly stated in response to the question: *Who's afraid of the Network?* (HARTMANN, 2010) . The *»far reaching change of the cultural codes«* would increasingly, with respect to mass communication, already be a consequence of *»what we know about the world,* *in which we live, being conveyed by Google and Wikipedia«* [...] *»The moving image has become the greatest competition of the narrated world«*. It's long been evident *»that the book cannot remain the leading medium for knowledge society but as a cult object of small groups it should be able to survive«*. A »culture of gatekeepers« (publishers, editors, newspaper editors) can certainly become a »culture of participation«—also in the sense of project cooperations as many publishing houses *»have largely given up their function as quality control«* and often live *»completely without any marketing and taking printing cost grants and other funding as income«*. The »network culture« as Hartmann concludes optimistically: *»is less hierarchical and more relational, which entails an aesthetic of distribution whose form is long not defined any more.—In spite of rampant idiocy the development is governed by acceptance and the use that the masses make of it«*.

One trend looms large. Millions of messages, texts, images, archived information have given rise to enormous quantities of data, with possibilities of access and hidden ways of usage and surveillance—all of which have long escaped the control of any political order. Everything »that can become digital« is stored and soon any, even anonymous sender can be *»traced by means of writing and speaking style«*—as Manfred Faßler, most notably in his studies on media revolution and media-integrated cultures of knowledge, points out in a recent analysis of the resulting cultural ruptures (FASSLER, 2010) . »Information consumption« is always also a *»resource for invisible functions of observation and policing«* we then read and that »an individual« monopoly of access to the network is guaranteed, is simply »ridiculous«. *»The data masses are offered to the customers as a great promise. It is not always clear that not the masses but rather the selections are decisive, not the serial switchings (that is to say, also not the endless links) but the selective codes«.* Since these developments in their confusing, even ominous dynamic can hardly be explored in analytical terms, having occurred more or less unnoticed, which must be perceived as a profound caesura, since as he argues: *»The individual finds him/herself in an anthropo-technical threshold situation. In network dependencies, unprecedented connections, new ecologies, chains of added value, products and economies of human life emerge in the 21st century«*. For this reason we urgently need *»contextual sciences«*, as Faßler claims, for *»renewed attempts at interdisciplinary thinking have succeeded in applications but hardly in results. In terms of bio-technical and socio-technical changes (in a broad sense) productive interdisciplinarity has hardly succeeded«*. Research must confront this subject matter in a more offensive way. *»By rough count, there are three experimental scenarios that influence the 21st century, namely, molecularization (post-genomic biology); miniaturization (nano-technological and biotic material research) and micro-logization (data and information technological changes). Together these 3m-scenarios have become mankind's operating systems and are changing mankind. It is wrong to criticize these developments as being extreme manifestations* *of technological or mechanical development. Without the digital micro-technologies, the computer virtual rendering of bodies, places, evidence, without the concomitant life sciences, bio- and medical computer science, this would not be feasible. Everything begins on a small scale and ends there. An egotistic micrologic.«* Yet *»all these processes have yet to be translated into a non-localizing, individualizing, socializing conception of mankind«.*

Praxis

Following two generations confronted with DNA research, microbiology, micro chips, computers and enormous memory capacities, perception is increasingly influenced by world patterns and world models, as that, in Faßler's words, *»don't leave one cold but are based on the invisible being made visible and vice versa. At the same time they guarantee that no form is reliable since they follow the invisible streams of information«*. The related *»loss of possible self references«* is, however, hardly noticed. The *»›smartness‹ required for dealing with them,* *cooperative skill and openness«* would be hardly attained because of *»too much information, too much mini, too many forms that have disappeared«*.

Precisely because of such existential issues, Georg Russegger has taken on these issues, addressing them from various perspectives in his book *Vom Subjekt zum Smartject. Kreative Entwurfspraktiken menschlich-medialer Selbst-organisation* (RUSSEGGER, 2009). With creative optimism he develops his ideas on the transformations of the subject and its options for acting in the age of digitalization, making a provocative contribution to a necessary, as he explicitly notes, *»problem-oriented study of the fact that in a highly technological society, characterized by quantitative and accelerated oversaturation with products on the one hand and by a growing scarcity of resources on the other, not every-thing that is produced under the label of new, innovative or smart can actually fulfill this promise«*—development the consequences of which cannot be foreseen.

The project *CODED CULTURES* that he has co-coordinated deals with subjects such as *Designing Complexity*, *Assembling Things*, *Expanding Locality*, *Creating Proto-Culture* continues this study taking into account many different voices—as a further test case of how in a setting of high technology free spaces and freedoms can be used. To deal with the possibilities and threats elucidates what is actually taking place and how one can react to it. Alone the fact *»that the invisible brings forth the visible and vice versa«* (Faßler) requires *»a change in the way we change things«*—and »collective experimentation« geared to creating connections (Latour). As for global perspectives and the real space as a »ground of facts«, it could also, in contrast to all the fictive, be more present that—precisely depicted by means of codes thanks to GPS—Yokohama (35° 27' N) and Tokyo (35° 41' N) are situated on the geographical latitude of California and Cyprus, Vienna (48° 12' N) or Munich (48° 08' N) on that of Kazachstan, Chernivtsi/Czernovitz (48° 18' N), Newfoundland, Canada and the small uninhabited volcanic island of Matua belonging to the Kurile Islands (48° 05' N) in northern Japan. In the town Lagado on an imaginary island located near Japan, Jonathan Swift—both a contemporary and adversary of Defoe—had established his *Academy of Projectors*, described so polemically in *Gulliver's Travels*. Here the *»typical projects«*, for instance, *»the extraction of sunshine from cucumbers«* or *»a new method for building houses by beginning at the top and working downwards« were developed. In the School of Language ›projects‹ are established for the simplification of language ... «*

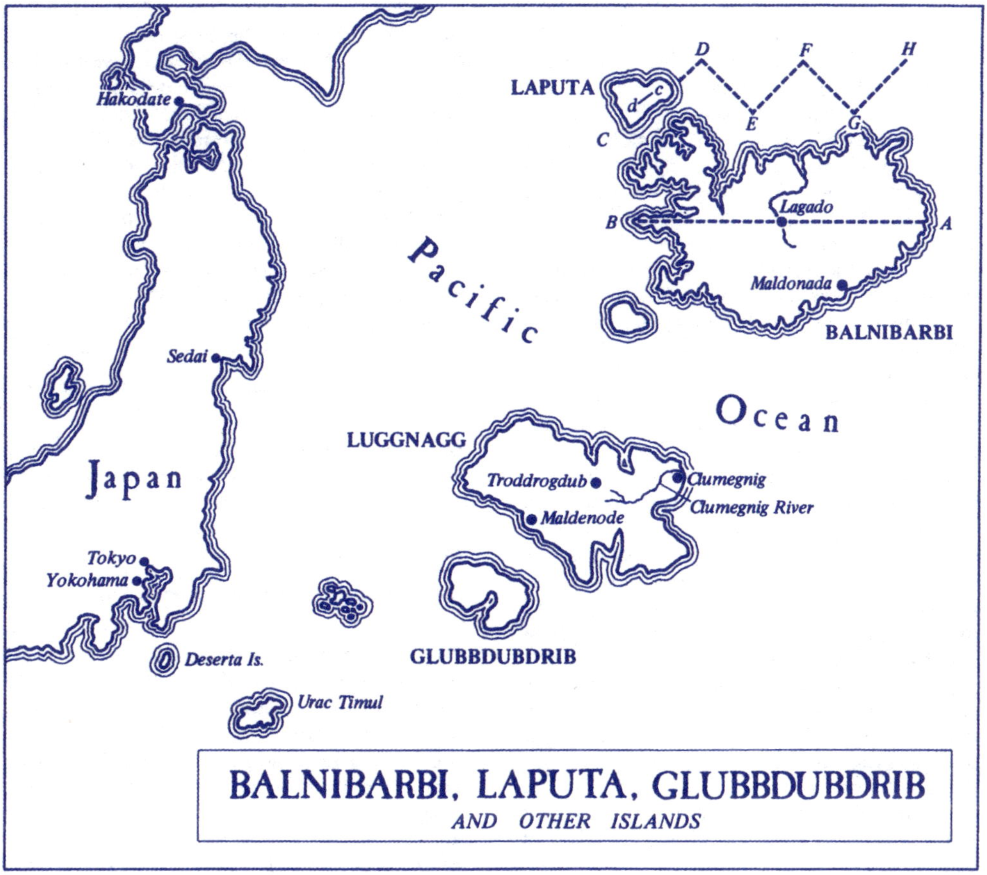

Fig. 1: Lagado with the Academy of Projectors.
Jonathan Swift: *Gulliver's Travels*, 1726. Drawing by James Cook.
In: Mangel, A., Guadalupi, G.: *The Dictionary of Imaginary Places*.
San Diego, 2000

References

Defoe, D.: *An Essay Upon Projects.*
London, 1697

Faßler, M.: »Kampfzone. Menschheit, bio-, neuro-, informatikökonomisch«.
In: *Recherche. Zeitung für Wissenschaft, No. 2/2010.* Vienna, 2010

Friedman, T. L.: *The World is Flat. A Brief History of the Twenty-First Century.*
New York: Farrar, Straus and Giroux, 2007

Friedman, T. L.: *Hot, Flat, and Crowded: Why We Need a Green Revolution—And How it Can Renew America.* New York: Farrar, Straus and Giroux, 1998

Hartmann, F.: »Wer hat Angst vor dem Netz?«, in: *Volltext. Zeitung für Literatur, No. 2/2010.*
Vienna, 2010

Hardt, M., Negri, A.: *Multitude: War and Democracy in the Age of Empire.*
New York: Penguin Press, 2004

Latour, B.: *Pandora's Hope. An Essay on the Reality of Science Studies.*
Cambridge, Mass.: Harvard University Press, 1999

Latour, B.: *We Have Never Been Modern.*
Cambridge, Mass.: Harvard University Press, 1993

Reder, C.: *Forschende Denkweisen. Essays zu künstlerischem Arbeiten.*
Vienna, New York: SpringerWienNewYork, 2004

Russegger, G.: *Vom Subjekt zum Smartject. Kreative Entwurfspraktiken menschlich-medialer Selbstorganisation.* Vienna: Turia und Kant, 2009

Schmidt, B.: »Wie stehen die Künste zum Wesen des Forschens?«.
In: *Wespennest, No. 158 (May 2010).* Vienna, 2010

Wallerstein, I.: *European Universalism. The Rhetoric of Power.*
New York: New Press, 2006

67

Christian Reder
Projects ...
Project Worlds ...
Project Cultures

2

From Albert Einstein the following sentence is conveyed: »*The hardest thing to understand is why we can understand anything at all*«. Knowing that each and every observation and reflection carries black spots and all our knowing is at anytime a sensory and cognitive reduced operation, understanding and knowing is world-spotting, selective, creative, interpretative. We code impressions, experiences and patterns to invent and communicate. Codes are the eyes of the needle, the eyes of human reality.

What does »the future« mean to art and technology? My argument in this essay is that we might be losing sight of the future in today's society. To recover it, I consider the culture of the post-war Japan, and attempt to position »art«, »geijutsu« (»fine art«), »media art«, and the problematic »media geijutsu« (the new legal concept including film, Manga, animation and digital artworks) in the historical context. Finally I suggest a wider perspective To grasp the true meaning of the future.

Digitalization has a double function. Predominantly in the First Capitalist World it presents itself being at disposal of biopolitics, according to which what matters is mode-of-life, good life and subjects as brands—on the other, in the Third and Second Worlds, digitalization being part of necropolitics reinforces structures of slavery, naked life and expropriations

Why Japanese media art is so often playful? Why artists turn their works into commercial products? In answering these frequently asked questions we need to understand both contemporary and historical aspects of Japanese visual culture. This essay provides with an alternative approach to art, including discussion on Device Art, which is a concept that attempts redefining relationship between art, design, entertainment and technology in digital era.

Today we live in cultures where our thoughts are instantaneously disseminated through countless web services and APIS. In such situation, the cost of self expression lower and the traditional delimitation of authorship creative of expression becomes outdated. This article aims at shedding light to the future state of such »creative commodities« in our increasingly code-dependent cultures; how our definition of creativity can evolve by focusing on the bionomical idea of process and inheritance.

The process *CODED CULTURES* started by *5uper.net* in 2004 intended to bridge the gap of current technological, sociological and artistic questions. In this text I want to focus on incidents based on a »synergetic potential«, »creative emergences« which can be brought up by inter-/trans-/meta-disciplinary and open cultures of production. Coded cultures describe a field that includes media arts as well as »expert cultures«. With a stronger amalgamation of these fields, coded cultures have the potential to not only bring media arts to another level, but also feed back to those production cultures, because they have to open up to a broader audience, to new publics and new discourses.

Theory

Manfred Faßler

Co-Evolutionary Anthropology of the Medial / CAM

»Creativity has always been fascinating. Cognitive psychologists generally agree that creativity happens when a new analogy is invented. When your mind connects two things that aren't usually connected [...] Most new analogies lead nowhere, but occasionally they reveal something important. Creativity doesn't operate when your focus is high; only when your thoughts have started to drift is creativity possible. We find creative solutions to a problem when it lingers at the back of our minds, not when it monopolizes attention by standing at the front [...] You can't make yourself fall asleep; nor can you make yourself have a creative inspiration (in the way you can make yourself solve an arithmetic problem) [...] Sleep and creativity happen only when your thoughts drift beyond your control [...] Which leads to a final observation. How do we invent new analogies? This is a major unsolved problem of cognitive science.« [1]

David Gelernter

[1] Gelernter, D.: *Dream-Logic, the Internet and Artificial Thought*. http://www.edge.org/ 3rd_culture/gelernter10.1/gelernter10.1_index.html [Accessed: Jul 08, 2010]

1 Code Time is Brain and Mind Time

»New forms of media have always caused moral panics«, Steven Pinker noticed in *Mind over Mass Media* [2]. I agree with his denial of panics. No culture, no cognition, no invention is an exclusive, static form which could be synthesized with dateless belief systems. For those who affirm culture as static, dateless and distinct, the ongoing transformations are bit-based display-tragedies, crisis inclusive. I choose a different approach. Every phenomenology—is it observed as semantic, thing, semiotic, or structure—is a conditioned product and a conditioned inter-actor. Condition refers to the cooperative dynamics of bodies and billions of arte-(f)-acts. Condition is no linear determination. The constitutional matrices for semantics, things, and others are emergence, complexity, codes, and conventions. In terms of bio-technological perspectives: it is the interactive, selective human body, who consumes his own inventions. For this body, panic is evolutionary coded, whereas »moral panics« are one of these strange co-evolutionary products. Moral panics are additional coded inventions, with which people argue a general clear view, far from any evidence and any necessity of learning adaption. We, the humans, have invented a lot of those normative counterfactual world gestures, be it moral, religion, juridical norms or economic laws. At this place I will not step into the code logics of religious or moral theme parks, or serious complexities of regulating code matrices.

[2] http://www.edge.org/3rd_culture/pinker10/pinker10_index.html [Accessed: Jun 15, 2010]

My questions are: How do codes come into life? How is the architecture of the relations between codes and the coded? How are the dramaturgies set on scene between body and any kind of contemporaries? These questions react to different basic problems, which I only can denote here. It is—for example—the vast field of interactivities between somatic and a-somatic processes, the neuro-physiological research on millisecond differences between brain and mind (B. Libet), or the universe of epigenetic rules C. Lumsden speaks about. Or: How do humans invent that cognitive slow food, called codes, to accelerate creativity and intelligence? And: What is the »time code« for this paradox? Looking for emergence of codes is looking for the relations between biology, codes, technology, media, and invention. Basically the sources of codes are both: passive and inter-active, non-intentional and intentional, they refer to biology of expression and to the invented artificial. Codes are passive in the sense that the brain reacts to specific sensual impressions with the abstract modulation of figure, status, form and rules of repetition. In those fields of inter-reactions markers are produced—

preferential emotional markers, as Antonio Damasio (Damasio, 1994; 2004) pointed out. They are the permanent richness of life and resource for the multiplicity of invented reality. An »artificial« coupling with things and situations emerges and builds the fundament for social markers, pro-active structures, or codes. This is the birth of mind, integrated in the »evolution of indirect reciprocity« (Nowak, Sigmund, 1998) . Code time is brain and mind time.

2 Deep Coding

Code highlights microdifferences. It marks no territories, no things, but the heterologics of self observing body facing situated contemporaries. The accent on codes moves or rather dislocates the limits of things, bodies, machines, or of social and cultural »figures«. Today it is not enough to observe the relations between forms and figures, hoping to detect reasons for those. It is no more a question of causality, of linear »foreign affairs« between inflexible things. To get closer to the different levels of self organising processes and their co-evolutional convergence, code mining is needed. Neither the social nor the cultural »figures« follow transcendental reduction—which usually end in the container of valence consciousness (for example in Edmund Husserl's *Phenomenology*). Thomas Luckmann invited sociologists and philosophers to integrate things, animals and humans into the causal transcendental reduction. That was an important step defining the social independent from an exclusive human centred idea. Bruno Latour and Michel Callon adopted this rejection of naïve belief offering the *Actor-Network-Theory*. But the answer is still not given to the question: What constitutes the obvious deep, but ubiquitous organisational relations between biological individuals, species, given environments, mechanical, medial, technological and scientific environments? And how do these life-relations emerge?

The step I offer is, to start with the selective and interactive convergence of body and codes. Code is the key invention. With this, individuals can express, describe, and organise their intention, targets and memory. It is the body that makes permanent thinking and the permanent revolution of thinking possible, not contrary. Or better said: the couplings between thought and things. The emergence of markers, the invention of codes and the pragmatics of arte-(f)-acts change the situation, the body and the physiological and semantic way of thinking. Codes are re-experience, re-entry, re-production. They are the invented »genesis machine« (Amos, 2006) for content and culture. The contemporary situation is that »mind children« (Moravec, 1998) live in » global brainscapes « (Philipps, 2005) and in global mindscapes. The inner life of codes is analogy, the invention of artificial relation. Analogy can be a dream world, emotion, calculation, virtuality, immersion, an equation, reasonable or unreasonable option, a format, hope, or adaption. From the point of view of aesthetic and intellectual elegance, analogies and co-evolution are un-comely, not fantastic. Maybe »most analogies lead nowhere« (D. Gelernter) . But without these »emotionally marked« inventions of analogies, without this basic creativeness, there will be no codes—and no culture as we know it. On the other hand: creativeness is that moment, when the end of coded information appears to us as the beginning of our own analogy and invention—participative singularity. It is the act of going beyond the code-conventions, ignoring reasons, causes, and centuries or years of »well done codes« proposing new deep cognition. The current major sorrows are focused on the apprehension: *»Do we lose the deep reading brain in digital culture?«* [3] . Do we lose the ability or the fun to invent analogies, to offer new pathways of coding, looking for new deep practice of transitions, transfers and transformations? We have to take the question seriously: How the evolution and co-evolution of coding, decoding, recoding brain takes place? How neuro-anatomy of the brain is transformed under the mixture of typographic and digital reading, seeing, thinking? Different material and medial generation of codes refer to different cognitive resources. And they entail different options for content and culture. M. Wolf's worry is that digital reading will create »short-circuited« reading, »confronted with a digital glut of immediate information that requires and receives less and less intellectual effort«. I agree with her that we know very little about the digital reading brain, or the digital coding brain. The asked ability, to pause and pull back from »speed reading« (or, as I would say: speed coding) shows into the direction of virtual plasticity, the asymmetric relations between brain and mind. The modes Homo Sapiens thinks are transformed again under the conditions of multi-sensual cognition and environments. The core generation principle still exists: invent analogies and transform them into code options. But the referential systems and programs of generating presence and awareness have been transformed. Certainly, we face multiple distractions for attention, compared to former typographic and slow-going, slowed times. But these »former times« have been accelerated times too—

[3] Wolf, M.: *Our »Deep Reading« Brain: Its Digital Evolution Poses Questions.* http://www.nieman.harvard.edu/reportsitem.aspx?id=102396 [Accessed: Jun 25, 2010]

compared to their »former times«. The plasticity of human brain managed that. Today's question is: How do we generate analogies, codes, inventions (= creativeness) under the conditions of co-evolving online-offline realities? This has nothing to do with »Quick and Dirty«, but with »Quick and Complex«. Unprepared, we step into global networked conditions of speed and deep coding.

3 Create, don't wait

Codes always refer to materiality, even though mind thinks it-/him-/herself being »immaterial«. Understanding codes is understanding the universe of marked but open differentiation of matter—here preferential understood as elective affinity— of multi-logics of codes and of an open end of analogy. The »reality of matter« I refer to, is bio-technological co-evolution. My observations use the reduction of code, but in the sense of plausible bridges between brain and mind (Lumsden, 1999) . I advert to the pragmatics of human life, which produces codes as additional cognitive and communicational reality, or as key virtual for combinatorial intelligence. Pragmatics is, on the first step, non-intentional. They follow the frequency and iteration of sensory impressions. Passive samples and patterns collect them and consign the inner world of clusters. Based on this passiveness of developing intelligence one could say: humans (as species and as biological individuals) became able to create models and codes, to invent artificial evidences as forced reaction to environments. Once started, codes afford codes. That is valid till today. Rules, regimes, and (cultural, emotional, economic, social, technological, medial) systems of standardised use imbedded codes. They conduct them in circulations of codes. But no circle is a closed system, neither from inside, nor from outside. Expanding complexities show the permanent recombination and finally the re-figuration of codes. All this is founded in the »Biology of Reality« (H. Maturana), in irreversible emergence of code-ability of mankind, and claims a sensible interactivity of intention, invention, institution and information.

»Panics« are insensitive, but have their reasons. The massive irritations that lead to the panics are based on multiple changing: the tight relations between typography and institutions are decoupled by post-typographic media, post-genomics and bio-synthetic engineering, and digital networks. And with these de-couplings the promised controllable homogeneity of culture is transformed into the heterogeneity of codes, into the heterogeneity of becoming. The panics do not react only to a shift of morality. They react to an epistemological earthquake, or let me say: a life quake. No longer forms-of-life stand for the integrity of life. Life became program, concept, option, strategy, in politics, medicine, therapy, economy, research, labs, and digital networks. The message is: Follow the flow (of information, data: of codes). Create, don't wait.

4 Understanding Codes = Understanding Generation

The launch of modernity was deeply rooted in the idea that the world could be described as a synthesis of form and natural law. This supported the faith in implicit, given order. This implicitness is—in the running 20th century—superposed by explicit codes of calculation (Cybernetic Turn and the start of Cyber-Modernity) (Faßler, 2001) . With this turn, the evolving and reproductive logics behind forms and laws conquered the attention of humans all over the world. The career of that specific group of calculation codes changed the architecture of epistemology: the career of codes triggered the career of micro dimensions / modules / logics / flexibility. Their message is: think smaller, act broader. Some kind of »post-thing« reality started and opened the universe of »weightless things«, which describe the net-status. But instead of pure calculation, instead of the aesthetics of algorithms or the axiomatics of »Laws of Form« (Spencer Brown), the usability of codes started a transcultural firework of cybernetic, virtual, artificial »generation«. Micrologics and selective, interactive generation are the fundaments of global case communities and case-cultures. This is the background for panics: the erosion of traditional belief systems of code- and communication-free orders. The »death of distance«, which F. Cairncross marked in 1997, is at the same time the birth of realtime networks of fluid differences. The distances between lifetime and realtime seem to disappear in the fusion of »physics of information« (Gershenfeld, 2006) and biology of information. The challenge is: How to make the difference between physical, biological and cultural micrologics observable, thinkable? H. Haken asked in 1986: *»How can we plant semantics into information?«* The question is still relevant, though the terms are different: *»How can we plant creativity into realtime communication?«* How to create new analogies between real- and lifetime? And that is where we are now: Understanding Codes = Understanding Generation. The thesis behind this formula is: culture is a product of codes. It is the niche of the artificial and abstract. This niche, populated with thoughts and things, emerges as back office for cognition and code. In this sense codes become products of culture, in the way culture cares for the all previous code families. The recursive dynamics of codes and culture is brilliantly described by Gregory Bateson: a difference that makes a difference. Currently these logics and realities of differences are accelerated by info-, neuro-, bio-, and nanotechnology. Within these processes, former »formal« code concepts lose their distinctiveness, their radical differences, and their regulative uniqueness. Today we face the complexity: Code = Generation. The promised lands of non-ambiguous different cooperation are undercut by scientific, technological and medial developments: by cooperative differences, cooperative codes. Their message is: go with the codes, go with the information. It is the demand to observe reality with micromonitors of codes. In fact, only a concept of micro options and fluid micro continuities makes it possible to observe, explain and understand the ongoing transformations of contemporary cognition and communication. But it is more than that: it enables us to analyse permanent bio-cultural co-creation.

5 Pre-Cultural Standards

Micro options and fluid micro continuities have been activated by research, engineering and techniques in the fields of digital calculations, cells, genomes, and neuro-logics the last 60 years. This started an irreversible shift from predominant ontology of forms to the universal principles of micro differences. No laws of nature have been changed but the neuro-anatomies of cognition. The universal principles of micro morphosis, which raise—as gene, for example—all kind of life, became the guiding line for bio-, media-, socio-, neuro-engineering. It took two decades, from 1990–2010, to get the idea, that this does not only challenge formative ideals of culture and society. The way to think about body, gender, things, and mind changed. Until today, the frames to think of reality in terms of multiple micro logics are not invented and conventionalised. With these changes the status of codes has been transformed: from catalytic assistance (for human behaviour) to constitutional dynamics. Step by step, code by code, scientist and artist uncover the pre-formative conditions of reality. The irritations are massive because this diffusion of the concept of unobservable but constitutional micro differences not only belongs to digital media, but to each and every status of biological, physical, technological, cultural reality. To get this into a concept of self inventing cultures, I will focus on the evolutionary scales of code inventions, on pro-active micro modules for contents, which are understood as resources for culture. Not the media as such, like press, newspapers, and television are suspected »threats to consumers' brain power«. The panic orchestra starts, because the—in former times—hidden cultural logics of biological, binary, neuro-physiological codes became an active powerful structure. The challenges are not the distinct forms, opinions, or media. The challenges are the logics and programs of codes. The old school visions of codes were: formal tools, maybe catalytic instruments. But now codes are producing products, are re-productors in sense of ongoing changing dynamics of world modelling.

6 Form of Water, Form of Life

Micro modules are re-productors, not replicators. They are fluid. That causes panics, because the answer to the question: »What is the form of life?« is as endless as the answer to the question: »What is the form of water?« (or: code). Not the changing generation of codes is the main cultural challenge. It is the uncontrollable use of networking, interactive selecting codes, which are highly productive and cannot be overruled by institutions, form-administrators, and system owners. The clashes do not take place between different habits of media-uses, but between the rules and regimes of observation and explanation. Cultural clashes have always been clashes of code-conventions and the freeware of analogy and creativeness.

Hence this text is part of the research and discussion about *CODED CULTURES* (Conference Title Vienna 2009). The title *CODED CULTURES* implies the thesis that culture is a product of codes. For many colleagues this pre-dating of culture is as difficult to accept as the thesis of culture as product. Especially modern sociology and cultural theory start from the assumption that culture (or society) is actor or producer, no matter how they are constituted. Asking how the complex architecture and dramaturgies of observable culture is generated, one steps into the fields of rules, conventions, abstractions, and the artificial. Asking how these bio-cultural co-constructions emerged, one opens the door into the universe of bio-technological codes. The accent of code/coding should not be simply equalized with proto-formats (such as »code as proto-culture«). Deriving from signals (first order) and signs (second order) codes do not determine action and form. They are invented and conventionalized assistants for selective interactions, principal supporters for the production of contents, which, may be, could be, hold as culture. But interaction, selection, variation and change elude codes from proto-formats. If I speak about coded cultures, I focus on the bio-cultural, co-evolutionary conditions of creating and abolishing codes. Though the genetic or genomic research on biochemical codes influences the actual discourses, I will keep the distance to and difference between somatic codes (genes) and exo-somatic codes (pre-cultural standards of cooperation, selective interaction, cognitive and innovative variations). Basically, invented code is cooperative difference. This difference includes selective interaction. Using codes is creating/producing presence, the presence of me as inter-actor, and of me as inter-action. If »presence« can be understood as one »form of water«, as artifact, idea, habit, organisation, we have to recognize at the same time: using codes changes the world of micro option and micro contents. Their selective network pragmatics create and reproduce the phenomenology of culture(s). These recursive dynamics are what I call cultural co-evolutions. It is bio-cultural co-construction (P. Baltes et.al.). Codes, in sense of modules for selective interaction and cooperative organization, are reproductors (not replicators) of content. As reproductors they are an integrated function of any culture, but at the same time more or less than this observed culture: more in the way that their selective use changes any status of a given culture; less in the way that they do not carry the complexity of a vital cooperation. But they don't have to: their constitutional power figures in the different scales of networking, the scales of co-evolution.

7 The Basic HCI: Human Code Interactivities

The approach of *Co-Evolutionary Anthropology of the Medial (CAM)*, which I offer, is based on the firm conviction that the open differences between genetic determination, morphogenesis, and neurophysiology are the nonintentional resources for cognitive differences, human intelligence, and human self organisation. All migrated and migrating groups of Homo Sapiens developed specific couplings between their biological determinations, found a-biotic conditions, invented biotic and a-biotic artifacts. These couplings are created or accidental, cooperative products or individually offered, linked to tacit, implicit knowledge or part of explicit, communicated knowledge. All formats of couplings are considered as conditionally determined and therefore strictly bound to selective interactivities, which happen between biotic and a-biotic terms and conditions. Even though today *Human Computer Interactivities* often are regarded as structurally new, one might say, that with the first signs, instruments, drawings or forms of numbers *Human Code Interactivities* started. 40,000 years ago this was the beginning of an unprecedented generation of abstract models, virtual realities of any kind (from cognitive programs as space, time, paradise, past, to function, division, organisation, body presence and disembodied presence, symbols, norms), imaginations, fictions, or the birth of »Second Worlds« starting with visualisations. The transformation from the direct, signal coupled *1st Human Life Mode* to the heterogeneous sign coupled *Human 2nd Life Mode* took time, but not as much as one might assume.

- First Second World (1st 2nd W) emerged through the abilities to produce explicit visualisations, as to say first drawings in caves on stonewalls all over the world (Palaeolithic);
- Second Second World (2nd 2nd W) emerged in the world of invented numbers, calculating machines (*abacus*) and rules to calculate, proliferated numerical addition, subtraction, division and learning curves in endless spaces of numbers; these inventions of numerosity are tightly woven with the so called Neolithic Revolution and early urbanisation about 12,000–9,000 years ago;
- Third Second World (3rd 2nd W) emerged in the formalized, imaginary, fictional spaces, of writing systems, which expanded about 5,000 years ago and ended in the so called »Gutenberg Galaxy« (M. McLuhan).
- The Fourth Second World (4th 2nd W) is where we are in. Four main transformations have taken place in the last fifty years: the career of molecules, genome and post-genomic research; the bio-technological miniatures, nano technologies, synthetic biology; digital micro logics and cultural micro modules; the neuro-science, neuro-economics, neuro-aesthetics.

All four brilliant abstractions, which took place in every group of Homo Sapiens—with a little timeshift—refer to a human speciality: the capacities to invent and to believe in the vividness of abstract models and bodyless/weightless immersive spaces of information. Since Palaeolithic times, religious and scientific systems, institutions, machines, technologies, and media widened and transformed cognitive spaces. We are used to call this culture (coupled with meaning) or society (coupled with instruments and methods). The basic processes are still the same: the pro-active using of cognitive capacities to invent and create non-natural systems of abstract self references. We still organise global life under the conditions of 2nd Life Modes; there is no other way. The bio-cultural reproductor for that is the basic *Human Code Interaction*, which I mentioned above. Unlike the first period—which was determined by the unquestionable status of form, macro diversities, territories, and identity racisms of any kind—the outlines of the present transformations are marked by explicit programs. They include generating data, information, micro diversities, global networking, dissipative dynamics, highly selective inter-activities, sunset culture = cultures with expiry dates, instantaneous information flows, »smartjects« (Russegger, 2009) —instead of subject-object divisions. We are not leaving the conditioned and co-evolutionary modes of virtuality but we are dedicated to learn the handling of the carnal dimensions of diversity, difference, data, and information. That is one of the central definitions of the »age of information«.

Reduced to a thesis: Between 40,000 and 5,000 before now, Homo Sapiens became the unique specialist in creating interfaces. And—under the conditions of media coupled reflexivity—he still tries to understand, what these capacities to create informational virtual realities are about.

For a long time these abstractions and their sources—information—have been forgotten, were suppressed under platonoid form ideals or fell silent under the conditions of renaissance and the noises of industrialisation. The Cybernetics 1st order of the 1940s, with Norbert Wiener, John v. Neumann, Alan Turing, Claude E. Shannon, and the Cybernetics 2nd order of the 1950s, combined with Heinz v. Foerster, Ernst v. Glasersfeld, Gregory Bateson opened the perspective to information in a radical new way. One can say that the formula, which they tried to explain and work with, was:

$$\text{Co-evolution} = \text{multisenses of abstraction} \times \text{Co}([-\text{operation}^n] + [-\text{construction}^n] + [-\text{reality}^n])^n \times \text{interactive selection}^n$$

8 Raw Material and Fine Culture?

Let me go a bit slower and back to these startups of 2nd world. Despite the massive differences between startups of visualisations, of numeric orders, and scriptographic/typographic systems, these sources of 2nd world had and still have epigenetic connections. And these can not be reduced to any cultural relativity, to some kind of closed shop of culture and identity, as cultural studies of any kind long for. I respect the important ethnographic or ethnological research on specific cultures. But, coming from a *Co-Evolutionary Anthropology*, the general, global and comparative aspects are more relevant for code research than isolated local identity studies. Based on the idea that information is raw material for (invented) forms, it is at the same time raw material for structure (structured processes). The status of collateral structures or of con-structures (associated, contingent, random structures) makes aware of the asymmetric relations. That concerns the relations of information to form, form to form, embedded usefulness to embedding structure etc.

These contingent/asymmetric relations accentuate the simultaneity of formal construction, which I use to call co-construction. With the inventions of explicit ways to design, create and functionalize »things«, Homo Sapiens started a learning curve, which has no specific direction and no finalized program. Why? Well, all formal or procedural inventions are beyond fundamental reproduction and therefore separated from any idea of linear evolution. Collateral structures and co-constructions develop massively contingent processes, which can be influenced via selective interactivity and selective intentions. But they are not strong enough to influence these processes constitutionally, because they do not command the information streams. The growing interdependency of information streams and selective constructive decisions (= the invention of difference and of form) and the growing capacity of informational reduction (as archives, storages, institutions, secret societies, secret cultures, or as collective neglect) ask for scientific concepts to observe these. The one I have chosen amongst others refers to C. Lumsden's term of »bio-cultural epigenesis«. Lumsden describes emerged and developed (artificial, a-biotic) epigenetic rules. They keep the asymmetric processes together, anyway. Based on collateral structures, co-construction, selective interactivities and intentions, and epigenetic rules, I propose co-evolution as the term to describe and observe the cognitive and communicational creativeness of Homo Sapiens wherever he lives and whatever he has to decide.

9 Co-Evolutionary Learning Curve

The co-evolutionary learning curve started about 100,000 years ago. The fundamental processes transformed the small wandering groups of 50–100 individuals (between 150,000 years and 40,000 years before now) into the learning and self referential groups, settled somewhere (12,000 years ago) and started to define territories, localities, trees, landscapes, ideas, symbols as their own property. That is what M. Kaku calls »the Great Diaspora«. A new using of brain by itself, a new synapto-genesis started, which finally transformed the Homo Sapiens (the observing and thinking human) into Homo Sapiens Sapiens (the self observing, self reflexive, but non the less: highly selective acting human). And with the self monitoring by signs, pictures, drawings, architecture, infrastructure, notation systems, archives etc. specific forms of self organisation emerged. Since the 19th century they are called culture and society, economy and technique. Johann Beckmann coined the term »technology« in 1776, John Stuart Mill, Adam Smith, David Ricardo spoke about »economy«, and George Spencer created »sociology« as partner of »biology«. That period of 40,000 years ago is what I subsume under started medial turn, which constitutes the Great Diaspora of settled human groups as cultural container. The word »medial« might sound a bit unfamiliar. It carries the difference to media, which I use as the material system of storing, reproducing, diffusing, setting, sending selected information as reality performance. With »medial« I combine the

· multisenses of cognition,
· and the emerging brain capacities to invent inconceivable and intangible realities and define these as preferential reality with
· the invention of archives,
· the proliferation of material artifacts as carrier current system of transmission and
· as carriers of meaning.

Medial turn is constitutional cognitive turn. It changed and changes the neuro-anatomy and neuro-functions. That is the starting point of *Co-Evolutionary Anthropology of the Medial (CAM)* [4]. Today we are used to overlay all themes and theories with the term »information«. Accepting the initial arguments, information becomes the highly productive interface for human life streams within biotic and a-biotic processes. On the level of informational materialism this is not new and performed life from the beginning,

[4] state of mission / of vision: www.fame-frankfurt.de

and human life streams since a very long time. Information is like a generating principle that couples all interactive agents, are they machines, media, humans, things that think, automatic agents. But what is interesting about these informational and medial couplings is the chance to combine available information in a way, new terms, concepts, and things come up. We are used to say: they are invented. Invention, as information, is a co-product in which specific interface programs do their job: is it archive, transfer, selective preparation, or is it combining, focussing, and deciding. Generation, couplings, inventions took place and take place in each and every *smart population* (Faßler, 2006/2008) all over the world. They can be used on one hand as categories of ethnography, like A. Appadurai spoke of global media-scapes in association with landscape arguments of former times. On the other hand those ethnological terms are helpless without referring to conditional determination of human life. Consequentially we are able to describe Homo Sapiens as a more or less intelligent performer of informational interfaces. This opens

· a global co-evolutionary perspective as well as
· a local co-evolutionary perspective.

Information is the (collateral or cooperative) interface of co-evolution. Found, invented, observed information is the key virtual of (human) life. It keeps the differences between unobservable data flows and observable formats and monitoring. The human use of this information interface is to organise the calculation between exploding differences and reducing decisions. Only the managed coupling of ongoing differences and decisions makes it possible to create distance (time-space-thing-body-distance), which gives space for new creative destruction and destructive new information.

10 Shifts and Learning Constructions

Three interwoven conditions build the focus of the Co-Evolutionary Anthropology of the Media:

· streams of matter,
· streams of energy (metabolism),
· streams of information.

Since Cybernetics 1st Order (N. Wiener, J. v. Neumann, A. Turing, C. E. Shannon, W. Weaver) information (or data) are the centre of computer science research. For the initial definition it was clear that information should be separated from matter and energy. Norbert Wiener wrote in *On Cybernetics* (Wiener, 1949) :

»Information, neither matter nor energy«.

Information was understood as the global principle for any process of difference and organisation, distinction and calculable collaboration. Each formula, format and form was reduced to the processing of information, to the logics of collateral combinations, instead of using any argument of essence or transcendental promise. The difference that N. Wiener opened with this sentence, was one between physics (as to say predominantly mechanics) and applied physics or applied mathematics. Application was understood as growing complexity of interrelated codes, networking systems, interfacial relation of humans and computers. Though this concept of complexity was addressed to the using of the physical systems of computers, it carried a new question: are information systems just catalytic or are they constitutional for cooperative populations, cultural organisation, or social contents? 70 years ago the question was not as clear as it is today. Under the influences of modern rationality which was bound to

· reason-causes-structure of processes,
· mono-linear dynamics (such as progress, future),
· single channel and one way communication,
· the separation of machine from human body and incompatibility of technology and subject, the idea of the catalytic functions of technology, matter and energy dominated the discourses and scientific positions.

In the 1950s–1980s for Social Sciences, Humanities and Arts, that new and expanding concept of Information was not as interesting as it should have been. Most of the science representatives were information averse and technology averse. They were not interested in or argued against the technological impacts on cultural self references, and organisations. Culture was and still is to them a singular product of mind ideals. Others concentrated on symbolic orders, communicational organisation or, under a growing technological interest in media (H. A. Innis, M. McLuhan). Looking back it seems that all of them tried to keep some kind of high culture formats, condensed in the idea of fulfilling communication (J. Habermas), symbolic orders (P. Bourdieu) and identity (E. Erikson). The consequences are formalized in that small hierarchy:

- The old-school winner was **COMMUNICATION** (the authentication of a closed, symbolic regulated order);
- This refers to typographic **MEDIA** (as storage, archive and referential system of truth, entertainment, education and science).
- Separated from that, in sense of faceless **DATA**, **INFORMATION** was accepted as a technologically helpful but for (symbolic) communication not important material dimension—as a slave to communication and media.

Meanwhile this hierarchy eroded. The plausibility of communication as a symbolic self referential process which takes place in social systems based on explicit topography, closed education system, monolingual distribution system, national economy (and so on) is repelled by networks, transsocial migrations of information and individuals, by calculable topologies, global Communities of Projects (Faßler, 2005/2006) , digital portals, internet next generation, or Second Life.

11 Pragmatism of Micro Diversities: Key Virtuals

My considerations are based in the conviction that all human poiesis creates a trend to the cooperation of micro diversities, or, as Norbert Elias would have said, a trend to abstraction. And it was Norbert Elias who noticed in his Essay *About Time* the missing of a theoretical concept of development of abstraction and micro synthesis. This could be understood as a comment to the fact that human populations have become cooperative experts in abstraction, signs, codes, and design and we still don't wonder why. The trend to a pragmatism of micro-diversities is nowadays observable as digital code, post-genomics, post-biology, neuro-logics—and this will not be the last step. It's like an actual showcase of global, dissipative co-evolution. This status includes three very different dynamics:

- First: the expansion of mathematical bijective distinctions as fundament of digital coding;
- Second: the growing implausibility of traditional social and cultural coherence, combined with the expansion of accidental networks, contingent Communities of Projects, and—for that moment—a radical re-figuration of net based interactions,
- Third: the combinatorial explosion of interactivly used codes and expanding complexities, in which the logics of contents are sought after, even though complexity is unobservable.

I will focus on some aspects of the second field, on reality fragments, which are code made. This refers on one hand to Marcel Duchamp's *Ready made*, and on the other to Thomas Feuerstein's *Media-Made* (Feuerstein, 2000) . The difference to that lies in my micro perspectives. The inventions of diversity, consolidated in the virtual family of codes, clusters, paradigms, models, stand at the border of elsewhere. But these more or less attentive and accurate inventions do not carry any specific or definite order—at least after humans left the ages of holy signs and hieroglyphics far behind. These key virtuals as codes, clusters and models, are no neutral programs. They define the options of using, but not the emergence of simple or complex dynamics. Therefore it is necessary to keep the conceptual distances between

- the sensation, experience, formalisation of differences,
- the invention of related codes,
- the practices of using codes,
- reinvent the coded options and

· create new ones—options and codes, and
· the incalculable dynamics of networked consuming.

For every spoken dimension it will be helpful to keep in mind not only the differences between experience, intention, option, invention, and intervention, but also network, non-biological infrastructure, technologies, programs, and the so called emergence of complexity. Art and science are well-advised to centre their capacities on the logics and richness of coded promises and options, not on basically unobservable macro logics of dynamic complexity. Theoretically I do not disagree with the statement of emerging complexity. My notion refers to the consensus that neither emergence nor complexity is an analytical or cognitive monitor. The evidence of this consensus derives from the resignation that we are not able to observe changes, co-evolution and multiple combined growing of structures. Complexity is like a temple of oppressive blindness. If we want to describe the becoming and even dimensions of emergence of structural continuity of change, often named culture, at any scale, we have to stay on the levels of coding. These are the »mille plateaux« Gilles Deleuze and Felix Guattari thought of, or the »infogenic fields« (Faßler, 2008; 2009) that I focus my research on. There we have a lot to do.

I am not fond of juggling with two black boxes: the unobservable emergence and complexity. Following some basic ideas of Robert Axelrod's *The Evolution of Cooperation*, I will encourage the world of micro diversities and the world of codes. The trend to cooperative micro abstracts ignores the idea of a collapse of differences, the regressive idea of a code death or collapse of information, as it was said in the narrative of entropy. Micro diversities and codes are like the abstract property of humans, shared by biological and non-biological systems. I explicitly do not speak about post-biological systems, as for example Hans Moravec did, not because he was fundamentally wrong. Since the first functional visual signs more than 40,000 years ago, humans lived together with their non-biological (or a-biotic) relatives, with the coherency of bio and non-bio. With codes of cooperation and codes of functional using of signs, our ancestors and we simulate content and stimulate content, creating our material, virtual, medial and technological niches.

12 Codes: Indirect Biology

This refers to the conference title *CODED CULTURES*, especially to the interesting passive construction of cultures, in which culture appears as a product of codes. All research should go back to this cognitive starting point: the priority of coding. Under this perspective the »thematising« (K. Kinder) of culture in a featured part is well chosen and could be understood—or I understand and use it that way —as an animadversion on estimated technological determination. All logical and technological devices, all semiotics and semantics are no self referential systems as such. They are no timeless structures, not even formalisms, but dynamic dimensions of co-evolutionary processes. No code, no formalism, no abstraction stands alone. They are produced under the laws of neocortical »infogenic fields« (M. Faßler), the conditions of cognition, and the conventions of observation. Their realities are the procedures of communication. There is no question that the neocortical processes are controlled by the genes and cells too, but not in the strict sense of direct control or linear determination. Since O. Wilson and C. Lumsden discovered indirect biological processes of life formation, which they called »epigenetic rules«, the research on epigenesis became important for biology and anthropology. And that is the portal to co-evolution and the exploration of information controlled couplings of biosphere, media, and the virtual spheres of cognitive abstraction.

This concept of co-evolutionary anthropology must not be mistaken as symbiosis. It is—or they are—processes of permanent differentiation, selection, learning. Bringing biology, physics, learning, selecting, and inventing together with natural evolution is not as new as it seems. That goes back to the 1950s. According to G. Bateson, individual development and natural evolution are processed by the same laws. His idea of an ecology of behaviour ignored the permanent invention and change of virtual models and formalised options. J. Piaget, offering a coupling of physiology, psychology and environment, did the same. He oversaw the creativeness of individual development. S. Moscovici favoured invention as the fundament of human viability. What's new with co-evolutionary anthropology is the coupling of differentiation, information, coding and culture. Consequently we have to think about the cooperation of simple differences, the iteration and transparency of billions of simple codings at the same networked moment. That takes us back to the cooperation of individuals and their invented, conventionalised, and used visual, numeric, acoustic, mechanic, organic technologies. Or, translated into my approach: we should take time to think about how we monitor the co-evolutionary dynamics of proto-coding and the difference between reproduction and replication in science and art.

The hypothesis is:
culture follows the codes—codes vary culture.

Culture administrates coding via normative meta codes. Today most of us are used to combine codes with digital soft- or hardware, with 2 billion daily users of networks, with more than 40,000 local area networks, with more than 80 billion websites and so on. That is not wrong, but not enough. The reality of big humanities is still that fantastic cognitive micro monitoring. Without micro any big is nothing. Without the neocortical ability to perceive iterations, creating clusters, models, codes, there is no way to process and produce intra information of brain; and there is no way to transform this into inter information of cooperative coding—or into mind. From this point of view, ***CODED CULTURES*** is another title for *Convergence Cultures*, regarding convergence as permanent recursive processes between biotic and a-biotic life conditions. Humans live in and with their codes. If they do not, technology will be scrap, and human beings will fall into the merely lucky status of pre-cognitive idiots. Supposing that no one really wants scrap and idiots as cultural relatives, we need artistic and scientific concepts which combine *Autopoiesis*, as Humberto Maturana and Francesco Varela evolved it, with *Geopoetics* and *Geopoietics*, as Kenneth White asked for.

13 Micro Logics of Codes versus Heroism of Forms

Across computer- and neuro sciences, the arts, theories of design, and techno- or media sciences a research of the becoming or emergence of form is springing up. Its central question is: How are forms related to the complexity of streams of matter, energy, and information? A special kind of common sense accompanies this question. It is summed up in the headline: information first. This widened the thesis of a trend to micro diversities. The fragile, exciting encounters of informational programs in form of avatars, biocasting, E-Card, RFID, ethnomorphing programs, serious games, things that think, show us: there is no digital form, but the status quo of informational poiesis and the ability of humans to share or produce the performance of in-formational coexistence between the multisensual body and the informational rest of the world. Today we deal much more with proto-forms, with form options, than with the spectacle of forms. Yet we lack a mutually informed crossdisciplinary inquiry into the infogenic fields of human cognition, expression, behaviour, and creativity. The traditional and heroic modern institutional orders were based on the definite priorities of forms. Starting with Plato or Pythagoras, the European history of the senses, cognition, and invention was strictly framed by pre-cultural forms that could no one leave behind. It was a set of reachable orders; and complexities of human adaption and differences were defined as strictly reduced variations of these ideals. This was the source of what we know as a canon of forms, colours, knowledge and behaviour. Forms have been the trans-religious master narratives for more than two and a half thousand years. Embedded in mathematics, the practices of calculation, and digital effectiveness of explicit programming these priorities of forms have survived until today. G. Spencer-Brown's *Laws of Form* are an example for formalized generic principles, in which the differences between form, standards, conventions, selection and decision are neutralized for the sake of calculation or computing. But even mathematics is one of these languages which humans invented and professionalized since more than three thousand years. As a language, this system of abstractions refers to the dynamics of ongoing co-evolutional changes of its rules and coded informational basis.

14 Signs, Translation, Transformation: No Transfer

The basis of all co-evolutional changes are interrelations between consumers of information, matter, energy—be they biotic or a-biotic systems. Therefore I use the difference between information as signal and information as sign. A signal corresponds with immediate non-reflexive reaction that might start an observing gesture, but must not work that way. Signals are first impressions, accidental gifts *»from the phenomenal world to the human brain-in-formation«* (B. M. Strafford). Over a long period, signs have been performative. But humans learned to differ between the accidental gifts and the self constructed option of line, circle, and sign. In the beginning of invention of signs they were, regarding the Hieroglyphs in Egypt, religious culture, strictly coupled with that immediate meaning of signals. In Uruk, northern Iraq, Palestine and Greece, the idea became reality to free signs from one unmoveable meaning and to use signs, their combination and linear writing for different meanings or interpretation. From that time on, about 5,000 years ago, the sign was combined with the options of interpretation, and, therefore, could be transformed into a re-combinative observing and expressive practice. Visible and readable signs opened the cognitive space for imaginative and fictional presence. Body, things and physiological encounters are transformed into an informational reality. With these artificial experiences new processes of inventions started. Even though signs today are combined with the promise of almost instantaneous reactions, these complex patterns of interactivity carry the optional structure of content (speed and deep coding). Meanwhile signs are the coded surfaces of information. They are invented, conventionalized, diffused and standardized. The »transfer« of signs between humans or in *Human-Media/Technology/File-Interfaces* is always translation and transforming the connected fields of signs. This field related existence of informational signs allows us to say that information is proto-culture and will be used as proto-culture. Information is neither behind the scene, nor behind the screen, it is the core of the non-formative monitoring of coding and coded processes. Cognitive meaning derives from the emerged linkages made among the highly parallel streams of information with others distributed throughout the cortical system in a vast associational network enriched by feedback and re-entry loops from the body, its surroundings and internal modelling.

15 From Large Scale Forms (Institutions) to Information Sensitive Situations

Forms are not the gatekeepers of culture no more, as promised in the hierarchical cultures. The empire of ideal platonoid forms or archetypes did not end in a Turing Machine, but in the transfer protocols of networks. There, in the inner life of collaborative informational clusters, territories and institutions, archaeology and self evident hierarchies are left behind. Instead of form, the open combination of codes became the presence of information. The celebration and liturgies of forms or form systems, with which over a long period cultural, political, economic and social systems were legitimated, have come to an end. It was Niklas Luhmann who analysed *Love*, *Knowledge*, *Power*, *Money*, *Science* and even *Society* as *Generalized Media* within the social system. With this argument, he promised a longer life for these inventions of macro formalisms. But what we do and see is different: it is the global career of micro diversity, of informational individualism and communities, which include collateral learning and design, not references to fixed norms, institutions and forms. In this sense I speak of infogenic fields. I understand this as a criticism to the non-legitimated forms and the endless descriptions of the estimated qualities of pre-informational heritages. But it is not a discoursive criticism alone. The critique comes from inside the forms, bodies, and the structure, it comes from the deep corporeal capacity for drawing a single or numerous distinctions, using them as data and information. The inside is information. It is the discovery and handling of relationship between the micro logics of differences, abstract structures and the real world of specific bodies, situations, events, cooperations, or collaborations. I will not derive some general claims out of this booming and buzzing universe of information. Thinking of coded cultures, coding cultures, coded codes, I will do some steps into the direction of living of complexities, like *Human Media Networks*, locative media, works of art. They are internally heterogeneous, composed of a number of different clusters and properties, of different time-space relations, or cybernetic localism and so on.

16 Informational Materialism—Informational Virtualism

We have limited and little control over the flitting set changes of informational emergences. Informational materialism, always on the run under conditions of changing complexities, is the inner life of cells and organs, dunes and machines, cognition and images, still and moving targets. Asymmetries of informational materialism lead to stability, to ephemeral making of a form, of a state of information, which is more a miracle of latent and selective continuity, than a gate-keeper of culture. We need to formulate infopoetics of human adaption and self-design, which integrates the three dimensions of matter, energy, and information streams. They should be combined with auto-poietic and geopoietic, as I mentioned before. With this hypothesis of uncalculable synergies between the status of matter, energy, and information I accept Norbert Wiener's definition of the cybernetic focus: Information, neither matter, nor energy.

Knowing that this difference cannot stand alone, information has to be re-defined for all biological, coding and aesthetic practices. Information should be understood as a source of energy and artificial nurture, as *Lebensmittel*. Long time ago, the human biological system randomly invented the power of the artificial by using empathy and prospective ideas as additives to signals, non-verbal gestures, trans-situational wishes, that the moment will last for ever or a group could meet together under the same conditions that exist now. For example:

The performance of passion and restraints was used as model for a coming situation. Within these processes of invention of time, space, different location, different time, same or different meanings—speaking only about a few aspects—the human biological system creates an internal reflexive monitor: it was and still is cognition, and, as a high end product, self reflexivity, consciousness and self evidence. Historically that was the transformational recoding of culture from Egypt to Greece, from the heavy weight of holy signs, to the self reflexive and permanent fighting Odysseus. Today we are in a comparable situation: the transformation of the controlling sets of identity, managed through media and communication, into user generated, created and processed content.

17 Informational Materialism, Programs, Art

With informational materialism I accept that no sign, no code, nor norm can leave the conditions of the matter behind. No one can ignore biology or the non-physical and non-biological status of the virtual. Streams of information happen as material transformations, no matter how abstract or transcendent they are presumed. It was Norbert Wiener who defined information in the short sentence: »Information, neither matter, nor energy«, knowing that these three concepts have different status in the same space of phase. For Cybernetic 1st order this definition was clear. On the level of Cybernetic 2nd order codes had to be imported to understand the different uses of the different transformational and communicational intensities. And within the last 40 years we learned that codes are no late invention of cultural or military classes, but the unconditional condition for any communicative practice. It was an important step, when *Ars Electronica 2003* titled: *Code: the Language of our Time*, because this detected codes as basic language. But »our time«, understood as presence, is not the home of codes as language, and codes, even though they are dominantly discussed as numeric codes, should not be reduced to numbers. Numbers as signs are aggregated differences. This aggregation prepares numbers and signs as tools for collaborative communication. In this sense codes can be understood as paradox mini programs, as formative sets. But they cannot stand alone, as single inventions they have no function, no life relation, are nothing without any reference. By the way, that was the trap Vilém Flusser stepped in, in the chapter *The Metaphysics of the Code* in his *Kommunikologie* (Flusser, 1998) . Saying code or codes, we say systemized relations, connections, potentials, and above all: programs. And system means: try to keep the paradox of never ending externalisation / internalization, of coding as decoding stable. J. Burnham wrote in his text for the outstanding *Software-Exhibition* 1970 in New York: at a time when knowledge options and aesthetic becomes a part of »technological decision making« the division between software and hardware, aesthetic and science makes no sense (Burnham, 1970) . And:

> *»In computer design we recognize no absolute distinction between machines and programs«.*

This concept of program, formulated almost 40 years ago, for me still is a pilot through the world of Neo-Platonism, religion, transcendence or the dreams of pure technology. It is so helpful because it combines cognition, design, concept, machine and matter, without making the constructed and constructive differences invisible. The step J. Burnham did, was one into the direction of software art. This step has not been forgotten, but for decades the hypothesis that art and software are both products of and actors in the same program, has not been as relevant for disputes as the question: »Is media art possible or not?« But there still was an ongoing critique against the post-platonian stereotypes of art, culture and tactics, and against the modern and post-modern heroisms. The need of software art on one and program sciences on the other hand became obvious. And in the spotlight of discussion code was set as *primus inter pares*. Let me please quote only the position, the one from F. Cramer and U. Gabriel from 2001. Under the title *Software Art* one can find the following position:

> *»Code can be diaries, poetic, obscure, ironic or disruptive, defunct or impossible, it can simulate and disguise, it has rhetoric and style, it can be an attitude. Such attributes might seem to contradict this fact that artistic control over generative iterations of machine code is limited, whether or not the code is self written ... Program code thus becomes a material with which artists work self consciously.«* [5]

[5] http://www.netzliteratur.net/cramer/software_art_-_transmediale.html [Accessed: Dec 07, 2010]

18 Interactive Performances, Formative Options, Formative Practices

Culture, therefore, is the storage of used options, performance of finished action, the *mise en scène* of the past as presence. The term proto-culture locates codes in the heterogeneous fields of formative dimensions. Formative dimensions or formative fields are non-intentional aggregations of coded and prefigured form options. They could be used or not, be forgotten or being present at the actual offers for formative practices. Proto-culture opens a temporal and creative difference between the ongoing inventions of imagination, fiction, sign and design on one hand and of institution, function, conventions and performative regimes on the other hand. This difference between formative fields and performative regimes is kept stable by institutions, or nowadays by couplings. Institutions set and kept order in the long periods of authoritarian, religious, and feudal systems; even in heroic modern societies, people believed in the archive and storages of accumulated knowledge, wisdom and legitimation. The frame for that all was defined by symbolic order, representation and object/subject hierarchies. After the crisis of representation, poststructural and postinstitutional discourses, different approaches of systems theory came up. I will not mark the differences between these approaches, but one astonishing topic, that all theorists worked on: it was and still is the idea that adaptive couplings keep the observed systems stable. Couplings do not refer to institutions, but to *non-jects* (or in german: *Un-jekt*) as Peter Fuchs says, or to *pro-jects*, as Vilém Flusser did, or *smart-jects*, as Georg Russegger pointed out the life of the biological individual: swinging between intelligence and function, creativeness and sediments. Smartness is the capacity to prepare culture with crosslinked analogies and codes, not being overwhelmed or suppressed by the classical steep order. Smartjects are the micro networks of human-nonhuman actors under post-classical, or let me say: post-social conditions (Faßler, 2009). They build together system dynamics, which I describe as co-evolution, as bio-cultural co-invention.

19 Art is Part

Let me finish: Maybe for some activists contemporary art in media or through media leads back to the collaborative universe of art, technology, machinery and mechanics of the 18th century, before the industrialisation of the 19th century separated them. And indeed, some aspects could be regarded as a revival of the art and apparatus relation, of art and mechanics or art and intelligent handcrafted works. But that's an illusion. No way leads back to the homeostasis of the 17th century and no way leads back to the 19th century, when artists described themselves as avant-garde, disconnected from presence and technology. The segregation from art and industry opened the way for the idea of avant-garde. But losing the avant-garde position, art was not weakened, because it became part of coded activities. It became part of the present again. Consequently the focus of any intellectual work, be it science, humanities or art, is to observe and explain the logics of global ***ICONOCRACY***. It is the informational high integrity of visualisations of an indiscernible micro reality, which became digitally plausible as geocultural resources for contingent (networked) communities. ***ICONOCRACY*** sets the standards for global instantaneous communication under the conditions of technological pervasiveness. It is the glow of understanding in a project, a community, a game or cooperation and a targeted collaboration. ***ICONOCRACY*** redefines the typographic traditions of democracy as global contingent visual trust. And that is where we should start:

Art is part.
Micro morphosis is evolving reality.
Culture is code made.

References

Amos, M.: *Genesis Machines. The New Science of Biocomputing.*
London: Atlantic Books, 2006

Axelrod, R.: *Die Evolution der Kooperation.*
München: Oldenbourg Wissenschaftsverlag, 1987

Barabási, A.-L.: *Linked. The New Science of Networks.*
Cambridge, Mass.: Perseus Books, 2002

Barabási, A.-L., Albert, R.: »Emergence of Scaling in Random Networks«.
In: *Science Magazine 286/1999, 509512.* 1999

Bateson, G.: *Ökologie des Geistes. Anthropologische, psychologische, biologische und epistemische Perspektiven.*
Frankfurt a. M.: Suhrkamp, 1985

Bateson, G.: *Geist und Natur. Eine notwendige Einheit.*
Frankfurt a. M.: Suhrkamp, 1995

Braitenberg, V.: *Vehikel. Experimente mit kybernetischen Wesen.*
Reinbek b. Hamburg: Lit-Verlag, 1993

Breidbach, O.: *Das Anschauliche oder über die Anschauung von Welt.*
Wien / New York: SpringerWienNewYork, 2000

Cairncross, F.: *The Death of Distance. How the Communications Revolution Will Change Our Lives.*
Boston: Harvard Business School Press, 1997

Chaitin, G. J.: »Algorithmic Information Theory«.
In: *IBM Journal of Research and Development, v.21, No. 4.* 1977

Damasio, A. R.: *Descartes' Irrtum.*
München: List Verlag, 1994

Damasio, A. R.: *Der Spinoza-Effekt. Wie Gefühle unser Leben bestimmen.*
München: List Verlag, 2003

Damasio, A. R.: *Ich fühle, also bin ich. Die Entschlüsselung des Bewusstseins.*
München: List Verlag, 2004

Deacon, T.: *The Symbolic Species. The Co-evolution of Language and the Brain.*
New York: W. W. Norton & Company, 1997

Dor, D., Jablonka, E.: »From Cultural Selection to Genetic Selection: a Framework for the Evolution of Language«.
In: *Selection 1.* 2001

Edelman, G. M.: *Neural Darwinism: The Theory of Neuronal Group Selection.*
New York: Basic Books, 1987

Faßler, M.: *Cyber-Moderne. Medienevolution, globale Netzwerke und die Künste der Kommunikation.*
Wien / New York: SpringerWienNewYork, 1999

Faßler, M.: »Communities of Projects«. In: Reder, C. (Ed.): *Lesebuch Projekte.*
Wien / New York: SpringerWienNewYork, 2006

Faßler, M.: *Der infogene Mensch: Entwurf einer Anthropologie.*
München: Wilhelm Fink Verlag, 2008

Faßler, M.: *Nach der Gesellschaft.*
München: Wilhelm Fink Verlag, 2009

Feynman, R. P.: »There's Plenty of Room at the Bottom«. In: *The Pleasure of Finding Things Out.* pp. 117–140.
Allen Lane: Perseus Books, 1999

Fidler, R.: *MediaMorphosis. Understanding New Media.*
Thousand Oaks / London / New Delhi: Pine Forge Press, 1997

Gershenfeld, N.: *The Physics of Information Technology.*
Cambridge: Cambridge University Press, 2000

Grotsky, S., Markus, M., Walle, Dieter v.d.: *The Evolution of Communication.*
http://library.thinkquest.org/26451. 2004

Guest, T.: *Second Lives. A Journey Through Virtual Worlds.*
London: Hutchinson, 2007

Haken, H.: »How we can Implant Semantics into Information Theory«. In: Folberth, O. G., Hackl, C. (Eds.):
Der Informationsbegriff in Technik und Wissenschaft. München: R. Oldenbourg, 1986

Huhtamo, E.: »From Cybernation to Interaction: A Contribution to an Archeology of Interactivity«.
In: Lunenfeld, P. (Ed.): *The Digital Dialectic: New Essays on New Media.* pp. 96–110. Cambridge, Mass.: MIT Press, 1999

Kinder, K.: *Ubiquitous Computing in Industrial Workplaces: Cultural Logics and Theming in Use Contextes.*
Thesis submitted for the degree of Doctor in Philosophy, Lancaster University Management School, 2009

Laughlin, R. L.: *Abschied von der Weltformel. Die Neuerfindung der Physik.*
München: Piper, 2007

Maturana, H., Varela, F.: *Autopoiesis and Cognition: the Realization of the Living.*
Dordrecht: Springer, 1980

Maturana, H., Varela, F.: *Der Baum der Erkenntnis – die biologischen Wurzeln des menschlichen Erkennens.*
Bern: Goldmann, 1987

Maturana, H.: »Biology of Cognition«. In: *Report 9.0.* Biological Computer Laboratory. pp.2–62.
Urbana, 1982

Moravec, H.: *Mind Children. The Future of Robot and Human Intelligence.*
Cambridge, Mass. / London: Harvard University Press, 1988

Moravec, H.: »Die Evolution postbiologischen Lebens«. In: *Telepolis. Magazin der Netzkultur.*
http://www.heise.de/tp/deutsch/special/vag/6055/1.html

Moscovici, S.: *Versuch über die menschliche Geschichte der Natur.*
Frankfurt a.M: Suhrkamp, 1982

Nettle, D.: *Linguistic Diversity.*
Oxford: Oxford University Press, 1999

Newberg, A., d'Aquili, E.: *Der gedachte Gott.*
München: Piper, 2003

Nowak, M. A., Sigmund, K.: »Evolution of Indirect Reciprocity by Image Scoring«.
In: *Nature 393.* pp. 573–577. 1998

Phillips, H.: »How Life Shapes the Brainscape«.
In: *New Scientist*, Nov. 26, 2005. pp. 12–13

Russegger, G.: *Vom Subjekt zum Smartjekt.*
Wien: Turia und Kant, 2009

Schooler, C.: »Environmental Complexity and the Flynn Effect«. In: U. Neisser (Ed.): *The Rising Curve.*
Washington, DC: American Psychological Association, 1999

Foerster, H. v.: *Observing Systems.*
Seaside, CA: Intersystems Publications, 1982

Weidlich, W.: *Sociodynamics. A Systematic Approach to Mathematical Modelling in the Social Science.*
London: Harwood Academic, 2002

Wheeler, A.: *At Home in the Universe.*
Woodbury, NY: American Institute of Physics Press, 1994

Hiroshi Yoshioka

Art is about the Future; Otherwise, Nothing

Art and Media in the Context of the Post-War Japan and Beyond

What I am going to focus on in this essay is the meaning of the future, in regard to questions of technology, media and arts, reconsidered in the social and political contexts of the post-war Japan. It is an attempt to show how the present Japanese culture, especially in relation to those issues of art, technology and the future, has been »coded« for the past sixty years. What I would like to suggest is that we might be made incapable to understand the proper meaning of the future today, in spite of the fact that our society of global capitalism is full of futuristic hyperbolae. We live in a society where a social hope for justice and democracy is systematically replaced by technological and industrial predictions. Our view over the future is miserably limited. In order to understand this limitation, it is inevitable to consider the historical context of at least sixty-five years since the end of WWII, which seems, in most cases, to have been plainly ignored in discussions about media arts. Reviving the actuality of the past like Hiroshima, however,

I believe my approach is not retrospective but prospective. I hope a refreshed look over the past will help clarify confusions we have about such concepts as »art«, » media art « and » media geijutsu « (a recently coined Japanese legal concept including film, comics, animation and digital artworks). However weird this concept may sound, I think it reflects a particular history for the country to have imported and assimilated the Western technology and arts, which is worth being seriously examined. Finally, I will suggest viewing on our present situation from a much longer, almost geological point of view, which I hope will enable us to retrieve a feeling of the future, at least in a meaning totally different from that as a mere extension of present technological innovations.

1 1945: Hiroshima as the Beginning

It is always important to look back once again on the past before we start thinking about the future. Otherwise, we will easily end up with a mere repetition of the past. The past, the present and the future—these are not simple marks for the separated areas which could neatly be arranged on the timeline. They mirror each other. They are intertwined, or mutually nested. A popular Confucius teaching *»wūn gù zhī xīn«* (»know the new by learning from the past«) is true to some extent, but sounds a little bit too broad when we address the issue of how the past, the present and the future are interrelated in regard to art, media and technology. In my general view, we have been stepping into a totally new era in the human civilization, with a progressing union of our body and mind with technology, at least since the latter half of the twentieth century. I think we should point a divide separating this new era from the old. I think it is important to be specific about a particular past we focus on, because referring a classical or ancient past would blur this divide. So I start with Hiroshima on August 6, 1945, as a divide marking the beginning of our age.

Of course Hiroshima has already been internationally known as one of the most important names to remind us of an atrocity done with highly developed technology. And for the post-war Japanese the name has strongly been associated with the national determination against war declared in Article 9 of the Constitution. In spite of this established image as a monument for peace, however, I have long felt that this is not the whole story. I have had a strong feeling that there is a clue in what Hiroshima represents to think of the future of mankind, but we still haven't found it. An obstacle blocking the way to address Hiroshima properly might be, at least for my generation, a deep rooted ambivalence in our mind about nuclear technology, or modern technology in general.

Let me refer to my personal memory, just to try explaining a little bit about this ambivalence. I was born in 1956, 11 years after the atomic bombing, but images about Hiroshima, in a way, always felt unconsciously behind many things I experienced even through childhood. Many of my favorite gigantic monsters (cultural descendants of *Godzilla*) in stories, Sci-Fi movies and animations had been born (or mutated) by the influence of a nuclear explosion, or the exposure to radiation. Imaginary weapons used to exterminate them were, again, supposed to be a highly developed application of nuclear energy. Robots and superhuman heroes who fought against these monsters (for justice, for the earth and humans) were also powered by nuclear energy (Tezuka Osamu's *Astro Boy—Atom* was the name of the hero in the original Japanese version—has a miniaturized reactor inside its mechanical body).

In the real world, the ambivalence was even deeper. Brought to the *Peace Memorial Museum* in Hiroshima as a school excursion, we got scared and almost traumatized by mannequins to represent the horrible spectacle after the bombing, real size figures dragging their burnt skins. They seemed for a boy at twelve to testify not only the cruelty of the »enemy« to use this weapon on our people, but a fundamental mistake of the humankind to invent such a weapon, and to have attained modern technology threatening ourselves with total extinction from the earth. In classrooms, on the contrary, we were supposed to learn how wonderful science is, and urged to dream the bright future through the development of modern technology. Many boys in the late 1950s and 1960s in Japan spent a more or less schizophrenic life, in which they were typically encouraged to become scientists, engineers or businessmen supporting the industrial development of the post-war Japan, while in the imaginary world inspired by Manga, animation and Sci-Fi stories, they firmly believed that the world would come to an end either by a total nuclear war between the USA and the USSR, or by destruction of the environment.

Except occasional official condolences, I have for years felt Hiroshima as an issue too far away—although the city is actually located so close from mine that I have visited it quite often—to address from my point of view as a theoretician, as one involved in cultural philosophy and aesthetics of media and technology. I have recognized the importance of constructing a cultural or art theory of peace, the subject once felt so keenly among many just after the end of WWII, in the context of our present society with advanced technology. I have thought Hiroshima should be one of the central topics in such a theory, but I have not been able to find the place of the topic in the whole question about culture and technology. I have to confess that it is quite recently that I started thinking seriously that there is a way, from my point of view, to recontextualize Hiroshima in art theory, encouraged by a couple of artworks.

One of them is the *Projection in Hiroshima* by Krzysztof Wodiczko, in August 1999 (Kishimoto, 2000) . It is a public projection of the hands of fourteen people on the riverbank, with the *Atomic Bomb Dome* behind them. The images of the hands show their emotions—fear, anger, hesitation, etc. as they try to remember what they experienced—and their voices are heard clearly. The interviewees include Japanese and Korean residents in Japan, survivors from the bombing as well as those in younger generation in the city. Their talk sometimes mentions the atomic bombing, but also other topics. I was especially moved by a confession given by a young speaker, who told about her unhappy childhood memories with her grandfather. Her grandfather experienced the war, but one day when she was a child she got shocked to hear him shouting *»Good! Keep it up! Hit'em again!«*, watching TV news reporting the Gulf war. She asked why he said things like these and he replied, *»Don't talk back to me! War is just ›kill‹ or ›be killed‹«*. She got a habit of lying, just to run away from this repressive family atmosphere, ending up with becoming a girl bullied by her class mates, being always told »You should die!«. What I found most impressive is the realization of an astonishing closeness of the public space and the private memories, the topic of war and the story of personal distress. This is a moment of encounter between history and emotions, enabled in a form of artistic practice. And it is important that this encounter was shared in front of the A-Bomb Dom in Hiroshima.

Another example of recent artistic approaches is the series of photographic works by Miyako Ishiuchi. In 2007, when she started photographing clothing and other personal items—things worn by victims of the bombing—preserved in the city's Peace Memorial Museum, I had an opportunity to have an open dialogue on photography at a panel in an academic conference. I was surprised to hear that she had been to Hiroshima for the first time in her life, seen the A-Bomb Dom and, unexpectedly, felt it »kawaii« (cute). I felt the use of this particular word seems to scrape off the layers of conventional images accumulated on Hiroshima as a monument of the nuclear attack that human beings experienced for the first time, and suddenly brought Hiroshima to the present moment through the time of more than sixty years. Her work *Hiroshima* [1] proved my impression. Ishiuchi photographed blouses, skirts and glasses which belonged to people in Hiroshima in 1945, as if they were items belonging to our parents, or even things we ourselves wore years ago, found in a forgotten corner of a closet. Though some of the items show the obvious damage caused by the bombing, there is an astonishing feeling of intimacy when we look at the photographs, and I thought this feeling of intimacy clearly distinguished the work of Ishiuchi from the former photographic attempts done on the theme of Hiroshima.

[1] Miyako Ishiuchi's photo collection *Hiroshima* was first shown in Hiroshima City Museum of Contemporary Art, Hiroshima, 2008, under the title *Hiroshima—Strings of Time*, and the photo book *Hiroshima* was also published: (Ishiuchi, 2008). There have been many exhibitions both inside and outside Japan.

I would like to point out that, both in the case of Wodiczko and Ishiuchi, the special feeling of immediacy or intimacy has been evoked through the use of media—projection of moving images, and high-resolution colored photography. In these works, media technology is used in a way to enable a fusion between the public and the private, the official history and the intimate sense of personal experience. Through this feeling of intimacy we are led to feel Hiroshima surprisingly close to ourselves. These works surely evoke emotions, but these emotions seem to have an intelligent quality, to contain a clue to look forward to the future. They enlarge our range of time, and provoke a still vague but sharable feeling that humanity is stepping into a new phase in its history. And it is exactly this feeling of the future that many of us today have been made insensitive to.

2 1960: The Future in a State of Detention

What happened to our sense of the future, and when? Today people seem to be more concerned with »sustainability«, the capacity of social, economical and environmental to endure with a certain degree of stability. In our view over what is to come, the idea of sustainability functions as a substitute for that of the future, but unlike the latter, the former does not encourage us to imagine and ally, but to urge us to calculate and compete. Below, I will give a rough sketch of what happened to our basic sense of the future, fifteen years after the end of WWII.

Recently I saw the documentary film ***ANPO*** directed by Linda Hoaglund (Hoaglund, 2010). ***ANPO*** is the Japanese acronym for *Treaty of Mutual Cooperation and Security between the United States and Japan* which was signed on January 19, 1960. The prime minister who agreed to sign this treaty is Shinsuke Kishi, who was arrested shortly after the end of the Pacific War and imprisoned in Sugamo as a »Class A« war crime suspect, until 1948. Unlike Hideki Tojo, a general in the Imperial Japanese Army who was sentenced to death by the International Military Tribunal for the Far East, Kishi was not indicted or tried by the Tribunal, but released (symbolically, on the next day of Tojo's execution), due to a change in the occupation policy by the US which felt the menace of the Cold War and planned to make Japan function as a breakwater against communism in the far East [2].

[2] Recently I wrote a short article about this film and this moment of history, quoting an episode told by an actress Keiko Hida, who was once nearly given to Kishi as a young mistress (but she escaped) by her own grandmother. (Yoshioka, 2010)

What I found most interesting in the film ***ANPO*** is that it is not a film directly dealing with the history and politics against the Treaty, but a film recording candid and straightforward voices of people—many of them are artists—about the time around 1960 when the Treaty was signed. Some of them remembered incidents of anti ***ANPO*** movements; others belong to the generation born years later. It is important that most of the speakers in the film are not experts of the history, nor activists deeply involved in the movements. The ways they tell their stories convey memories of emotions, not mere facts, shared by many Japanese at that time—disgust of war, fear of catastrophe created by modern weapons, split feelings about the US as the superpower, etc. Those who haven't experienced the time of ***ANPO*** themselves also express their feelings about the issue (some of them are from Okinawa). Watching the film, we learn it was the power of emotions, rather than rationally stated theories or politics that drove a large number of people to mass protest against the Treaty. The protest was finally defeated and the treaty was enacted. But there surely existed a moment when a large number of people could see a chance for democracy, a chance to develop radical discussions about the future of the nation: How they should develop the relation of Japan with other nations in the far East, and with the US, what role the country could play in the post WWII era, and what new culture they should develop as the only nation that suffered by the atomic bombings.

The Kishi cabinet resigned in September 1960, and was taken over by the new cabinet with Hayato Ikeda as the prime minister. Instead of showing any direct political direction, Ikeda introduced the long term *Income Doubling Plan* which boosted the country's miraculous economic recovery and industrial growth through the 1960s and 1970s. This big change of Japan's political history has had a decisive influence on culture as well as the society. It produced the general attitude valuing hard working, cooperative mentality and loyalty to one's organization (instead of loyalty to *The Empire of Japan* which had existed before and during WWII). The plan was welcomed by large parts of the nation. One easy way to understand the general atmosphere of people's life after the 1960s in Japan would be to pay attention to a typical characterization of a new generation male white-collar worker: *Salaryman*. The word itself had been coined earlier, but it is in this period of the post-war economic growth that it came to be known widely as referring to the average, hard-working man in suits and tine, commuting by jam-packed train, almost irrationally loyal to his company and working overtime, trapped in homosocial relations with colleagues and bosses, and often seeking diversion in getting drunk in a bar on the way home [3].

[3] Salaryman is sometimes called an »industrial warrior«. This is why I invited Slovenian artist group *IRWIN* for Kyoto Biennale 2003, and asked them to show a new version of their performance series *NSK GUARD*. In previous performances done in several European countries, they had four real soldiers of each country guard the flag of their virtual state (»State in Time«). In the Japanese version, four real Salarymen played it in front of Kyoto City Hall.

It is important to know what this particular character means in Japan after the 1960s, to understand Japanese films, TV dramas, Manga, animation and even some contemporary art works produced since then, because the life of Salaryman is so frequently depicted, treated as a necessary background of a story, and sometime bitterly caricatured. It became a popular cliché to say *»salaryman's life is hard«*, and it's true that some died from overwork, but in general, people seem to have accepted this lifestyle as a model of average happy life in post-war Japan. I have to add that the life of Salaryman has always been compensated with its opposite, that is, the life to quit a company and start one's own life—live in the countryside, run one's own shop, etc.—which is called by the special word *Datsu-Sala* (Post-Salaryman).

Whether one may stay in or escape Salaryman's life, it stays the same that all debates about life have been circled around the issue of—personal and national—economic welfare, and any political argument beyond this has been largely marginalized in the society in general. Of course, the habit of hard working itself is neither good nor bad, but we can say that devotion to work in the period of post-war economic growth in Japan tended to function as a collective and unconscious strategy to divert attention from important political issues. And this tendency reflects itself in culture, too. In many works of contemporary and media art works, political messages generally tend to be minimized, or made to be unintelligibly vague, and a work with any explicit political message is treated as a special kind. I have seen that in education at art schools and colleges, students are rarely encouraged to develop their political interest to an artistic expression, compared with the situation of their counterparts in other countries.

I am afraid my description might sound to suggest the existence of any exclusion or inner censorship being at work in the psychology of the post-war Japanese. On the contrary, there have always been a large number of criticisms to point out a »closed« character of Japanese mind, written by Japanese as well as non-Japanese authors, and they have been welcomed by general readers (typically by Salarymen reading such books in a commuter train). The genre of publication called *Nihonjinron* (arguments on the Japanese) has occupied one of the most popular shelves in a major bookstore. Some authors admire; others cynically or bluntly criticize Japanese culture and society. But both have equally been enjoyed by Japanese readers, because all these arguments have one point in common—that the Japanese is unique and peculiar in the world. I think this faith in uniqueness and peculiarity (either in a positive or negative context) of the nation has functioned as a kind of psychological buffer to cancel any movement of thought for the Japanese to go beyond the limitation of Japanese modernity, or at least beyond one settled around 1960. The celebration of cultural uniqueness has repeated in many different forms, and we can see its most recent fashion in the admiration of Japanese pop culture including Manga, animation or computer games, the phenomenon often referred as » Japan Cool «.

I hope the picture I described above will help understand the background to rethink the basic situation of artistic practices, and its relation to the future. Though I know I could be blamed for oversimplification, I dare to say that large part of artistic activities in Japan since around 1960 has moved around in the society assuming the economic recovery and industrial development as the supreme command of the nation, and putting aside real political issues as something of secondary importance. It is even more the case when art takes the critical or oppositional standpoint to the economic and industrial principle of the society—in fact it does in many cases—because it means that a compensatory role is prescribed to art and the theater as a whole is made even more stable by the presence of a clown. This basic situation has survived the time of the postmodern culture and bubble economy in 1980s and the time of their collapse in 1990s, when there was no reason to stick to the principle of economic growth anymore.

Since 1990s, in step with spreading of mobile phones, personal computers connected to the internet and other electronic devices, our life has become inseparable from machines. Communication has surely been accelerated, but at the same time, the act of communication has been replaced by the act of typing on the screen. With this change, there emerged a new habit that has proliferated society, which can be called a »habit of control«. Every sector of society—administration, business, research, education, and individual sphere—was exposed to the influence of globalization, and our world got suddenly full with a formidable amount of electronic gadgets and unfamiliar instructions to deal with them. Those who could not adapt themselves to this new environment—mainly those in older generations—were relegated to the *Madogiwa* (window-side desk meaning less important position), and they were persuaded to accept this because it was the result of rationalization and progress of industry. Neoliberalism was getting more and more power to decide the course of national politics. It culminated in the time of the Prime Minister Junichito Koizumi (2001–2006), who introduced radical reforms in large parts of the society.

I would like to argue that, through these decades, we have come to lose sight of the future, so to say, dazzled by a succession of technological innovations. New electronic products, in spite of being advertised as if they belonged to the future, actually all belong to the present, reinforcing the existing labor condition and the mode of production. Electronic gadgets, by being fetishized, dull our imagination about the future. Meanwhile, through general adaptation to the mechanized environment, the habit of control has come to form a » culture of control «, by which I mean a pattern of behavior to encourage people to think and act as if all human activities—not only economy and industry but science, education and even art—can be organized in terms of systematic planning and numerical evaluation, as if they were all production processes in factories. The essential meaning of the future—coming of the unpredictable, things beyond calculation, and room for hope however hopeless reality may look—has been undermined in this pseudo-futuristic society.

To conclude this section, I would like to say that the future as we know today, as something we can predict as a result of scientific calculation, is not a future at all, at least for those who attempt to think about how art and culture will turn out for coming centuries. We are losing sight of the future. The future is in a state of detention, deprived of its freedom in our contemporary world, just like Aung San Suu Kyi and Liu Xiaobo are in their own states. What I want to suggest by this is that what is called »global world« or »international community« can be totalitarian enough to suppress our imagination of the future. What we need to do is to look for a way to rescue our future in each cultural and historical context.

3 Decoding a Cryptogram of *Media Geijutsu*

I believe it is in this historical context that questions around media art in Japan have to be discussed. Otherwise, we would end up (as we often actually do) with hopelessly vague and abstract definitions of media art. But let's first see how such an abstract definition looks like. What is media art? Perhaps the simplest answer to the question would be: it is a new form of art employing (digital) media technology. Or, from a broader point of view, media art can include various artistic attempts not actually using technology, but in some way inspired by, or well aware of today's media society. Though the scope of media art may differ among people, the word »media« in this expression constantly seems to refer to something new, a future element, while »art« to an old, established value, which has been firmly coded for centuries through the development of the modern Western culture (and it has been adapted to Japanese culture very earnestly throughout the time of modernization since the Meiji restoration). Therefore, the expression »media art« is a combination of the old and the new. To define it in a more positive way, media art means a renewal, an upgrading of art through new media. It's *Art 2.0*.

The point I regard as hopelessly vague and abstract in such a definition of media art is that it takes for granted both »media« and »art« as two separate parts, one referring to technology and intended for the future, and the other grounded on the centuries old value system of Western culture. I think this kind of definition of media art will take us nowhere. I would insist that, if we are to take the question of media art seriously, we cannot avoid asking fundamental questions about »media« and »art« themselves. This is more the case with a country like Japan, where both ideas have originally been imported from the West, interpreted and assimilated to fit the indigenous cultural environment. It has surely made the culture so discouragingly complex to be analyzed, but I hope this process of translation and complexification might give us an advantage to consider »media« and »art« in a more fundamental way. Here I would just like to give an outline of such consideration.

One of the peculiar characters of the modern Japanese language is its easiness to accept a word of foreign origin and allow it to coexist with an older word having a similar or related meaning. This linguistic flexibility, however, has caused confusions as well as convenience, and it is very much the case with the word meaning »art«. In contemporary Japanese, there are two words referring to »art«, that is »geijutsu« and »aato«. »Geijutsu« is an older word used as a translation of English »art« or »fine art«, while »aato« is a word which has come to be used recently. »Geijutsu« is normally written in kanji (Chinese characters) which sounds relatively more significant, while »aato«, a phonetically borrowed word from English »art«, is written in katakana (the angular Japanese phonetic syllabary which shows it is a foreign word). The point is that the two words sometimes mean the same, sometimes totally different things. In the normal usage, »geijutsu« means »fine art«, or relatively conventional sense of art (traditional, modern and avant-garde art), while »aato« refers to a more recent (maybe after 1980s), wider range of artistic practices. »Geijutsu« sounds more official, focusing on the serious, individual and modernist side of art, while »aato« is generally used in a more friendly, fashionable and postmodern manner. »Aato« is relatively preferred by younger generations, or by producers and organizers who like to attract more people to their art shows, but the word is often disliked by those who want to take art more seriously. For a couple of decades, there has been a general tendency to prefer »aato« to »geijutsu«, because for more and more people »geijutsu« sounds too highbrow in the daily context, though the word has been preserved for names of art schools, academic writings, official documents and so on. Media art has always been called »media aato« in Japanese, perhaps because it is one of the latest developments of art, and it sounds more natural to keep its phonetic correspondence to its original English words.

In 2002, the enforcement of a new law called *Basic Act for the Promotion of Culture and the Arts* added a further confusion to this situation [4]. According to the Act, *Media Geijutsu* is defined as including film, Manga, animation and arts using the computer or other electronic devices (Article 9). There are at least two points in this text which directly conflict with natural terminology. First, taking film aside, *Manga* and *animation* have normally been regarded as subculture or popular culture. They are maybe fit for the concept of »aato«, but for many people it sounds uncomfortable to call them »geijutsu«, except with a sense of humor. Second, *»arts using the computer or other electronic devices«* seem to mean media art, which is already called as »media aato« in Japanese, but in the Act it is defined as a sub-species of the species »media geijutsu«, which itself is officially translated into media arts in English! At this point the correspondence between Japanese concepts and English (and other European) concepts finally comes to break up. Does the Japanese culture administration start promoting a new nationalistic concept of »geijutsu« that has finally freed itself from its Western origin?

[4] The whole text of the Act can be read at: http://law.e-gov.go.jp/htmldata/H13/H13HO148.html [Accessed: Nov 5, 2010]

I don't think so, though I know some may like to. As I understand, this enigmatic media geijutsu is a result of historical entanglement of cultural concepts in modern Japan. Though I have no quick solution to this confusion of categories, I can at least say that this reflects a basic attitude of modern Japanese culture to accept and assimilate the concepts from the West. Since intellectuals in the Meiji period introduced a new concept (like art) from the West, they have seldom attempted to positively develop the concept in their own cultural context, while there has been a spontaneous process of assimilating the concept into popular or mass culture. Instead of capturing this movement in theory, most intellectuals internalized the stronger Western self and played it in various different ways. (Some became a worshipper of the West and others converted to a nationalist, but they both shared this process of internalization. I once attempted to analyze this tendency as part of »internalized colonization« (Yoshioka, 1994) [5].) In a sense, a terminology like *media geijutsu* reflects a failure of modern Japanese aesthetics, art theory and criticism to theorize what is really happening in contemporary culture.

[5] The official website of Kyoto Biennale 2003 is archived at: http://www.bun.kyoto-u.ac.jp/~yoshioka/KB2003/original/ [Accessed: Nov 5, 2010]

So, what should we do with media geijutsu, and where could we find a hope in this conceptualization of culture? Conservative artists and academics seem just to ignore the term as another political mumbo-jumbo. Those involved in pop-culture welcome it because they can hope to get more chance and respect by it, but pay little attention to what it really means. I think there is no hope in this split, and it is crucially important to develop a theory of art and media which will be able to address fine arts, new media arts and popular arts including Manga and animation. For this purpose, I suppose Japanese experience of cultural development since the end of WWII, and recalling Hiroshima as the beginning of this cultural world will definitely contribute. I do believe that Hiroshima, not just as a historical memorial, still has a lot to tell us about the future, especially the future of art, media and technology.

4 The Future in Slowness

The following two episodes may sound a little unusual as an epilogue, but I cannot help adding them to conclude my essay by throwing light on the topic of the future from a certain distance.

In 2003, I directed the general art festival *Kyoto Biennale* under the theme of »Slowness«. For one of the symposiums held in the festival I invited Masako Nakamura, a biologist who has worked on the study of earthworms. She decided to choose this subject when she read Charles Darwin's famous study on the earthworm (Darwin, 1881) when she was a student. I had looked for interesting topics outside the field of art and related to my concept of »slowness«, a word often received with negative connotations especially in the society worshipping speed. I got totally impressed by her books on earthworms, and went to see her and asked to come to Kyoto to talk with me. When we think about nature, we are often influenced by TV programs showing scenes like whales spouting on the ocean, monkeys jumping between trees, or leopards chasing antelopes in the savanna. The images of these creatures are often used to emphasize the importance of preserving wild nature, for »the future of our beautiful earth«. However, the earth has actually been changed and taken care of not by these impressive animals, but by much humbler creatures like earthworms. Nakamura says:

»Normally people don't pay attention to earthworms. They never appear in the Bible, having no role in the Genesis. They are not depicted in the scene of Creation by Michelangelo. Earthworms have been ignored by God, so to say, but they have lived on this planet for more than 45 million years and we can count so many varieties. [...] Earthworms, having no eyes and no outstanding features, have lived for so many years and cultivated the earth. I think this is really a wonderful fact! This shows the true way to live in slowness« [6].

[6] An excerpt of a talk given by Masako Nakamura at *Art Complex 1928*, Kyoto, October 10, 2003. Included in: (Yoshioka, 2004)

I learned from her the important scientific fact that the fertile soil as we have now on the earth has been created by the work of earthworms, by their cultivation through eating soil with microorganisms (their food) and discharging undigested soil, for hundreds of millions of years. I really like this idea of creating the future in slowness, as I think we live in a society where we require immediate results from whatever we have done, almost in a neurotic way. But the story by Nakamura seems to point to a future self image of human civilization. I imagine that people in highly advanced technology and communication networks will come to understand their life in a way that might be much closer to that of earthworms than human beings as the lord of creation. I believe a real advance in ethics will take place through that change. But will such a new age be really coming? Can the future civilization be so different from what we have known so far?

Last year I was invited to stay in the city of Vienna for two weeks, giving lectures at the *Academy of Fine Arts* and at a symposium of the festival *CODED CULTURES*. During my stay I visited the *Museum of Natural History*, which I had wanted to visit. In the museum I found the exhibition about the *Ötzi the Iceman*, about which I had read in a book before. *Ötzi* is the nickname for a natural mummy found in 1991 on the Ötztal Alps, in an area close to the border of Italy with Austria (the mummy itself is now in the *South Tyrol Museum of Archaeology* in Bolzano). When it was first discovered, people thought it would be one of travellers who died in the mountain, maybe in the early twentieth century, the nineteenth, or the eighteenth century at oldest. They have sometimes found such old mummies. After the examination by experts, however, it turned out to be a body of a man from the Copper Age, around 5,300 years ago. This is the oldest natural mummy discovered in Europe. What I found most interesting is the fact that normal people watching at this mummy never imagined it could be a man from such an old age, though the body, the clothes, the shoes, tools and equipments were so well preserved. I think it is amazing at least for non-experts that there is no clue to distinguish a man who lived 5,300 years ago from a man of, say, a hundred years ago. People in modern times have emphasized the progress of civilization, but basic things don't seem to have changed so much for more than 5,000 years. It would be quite easy, however, to recognize a body of a traveler who died on a mountain at least after the second half of the twentieth century, because he or she must have a lot of things which had never existed before, such as clothes made of synthetic fiber, shoes of synthetic rubber, a lot of plastic materials, an electric flashlight, a transistor radio, a Walkman or even an iPhone! This thought leads me to imagine that, if observed by a Martian archeologist (or maybe an archeologist outside our solar system), the human civilization may look to some extent continuous from the late Stone Age through the nineteenth century, in its basic pattern of agriculture and cattle breeding, the mode of possession and exchange of goods, the formation of a community and a family, the use of wheels for transportation, and written symbols as an external memory to assist thinking.

But I suppose the alien archeologist will find several signs of change after the mid-twentieth century, signs showing that a great shift of human civilization has started to take place, in which the wide-spread use of digital computers, the emergence of the global network, and new forms of artistic activities responding to these new situations are just a few earliest obvious symptoms.

References

Darwin, C.: *The Formation of Vegetable Mould Through the Action of Worms, With Observations on Their Habits.*
London: John Murray, 1881

Hoaglund, L.: *ANPO: Art X War.*
USA / Japan, 2010

Ishiuchi, M.: *Hiroshima.*
Tokyo: Shueisha Publishers, 2008

Kishimoto, Y., Wodiczko, K.: *Projection in Hiroshima, 70m/color.*
Kyoto: Ufer! Art Documentary, 2000

Yoshioka, H. (Ed.): *Slowness at the Speed of Light.*
Kyoto: Kyoto Art Center, 2004

Yoshioka, H.: »Anpo to Aijin« (»The Anpo and a Mistress«). In: *Toxic Girls Review, Vol. 2.*
Kyoto: Voice Gallery psf/w, October 2010

Yoshioka, H.: »Samurai and Self-colonization in Japan«. In: Pieterse, J. N. (Ed.):
Decolonization of Imagination: Culture, Knowledge, Power. London: Zed Publishers, 1994.

Marina Gržinić

A Political Intervention in the Digital Realm

Capital produces and reproduces itself through economic, social and political disruptions and with the help of science and new media technology. As early as the end of the 1970s, it had already been claimed by Christopher Lasch that the notion of technological determinism, a kind of blind belief in technology, is at the base of all popular comprehensions of industrial and technological revolutions (cf. Lasch, 1979). Nevertheless, he argued, we have to be aware that new inventions, new processes and new applications of scientific discoveries do not put forward the changes in ameliorating production as well. Here, technology is used in the process of production to make it more efficient, rational, and to produce more surplus value, but not to improve our lives and labor conditions. And when these inventions are used in the process of reproduction, then it is for the sake of the new organization of labor processes (read: even bigger exploitation through rationalizations and efficiencies). In such a condition, technological changes are easily absorbed into the existing social capitalist structures. Therefore, according to Lasch, far from revolutionizing the society, technological inventions primarily reinforce the existing privileges and the appropriation of surplus value only by capital (cf. Gilly, 2009).

In order to understand the relation of new information technology and global capitalism I propose that the condition of digitalization is to be seen in a much broader sense as well. I suggest to think about a digital mode of production that codes, reproduces and forms the grammar and modes of exploitation and expropriation of the present financial capitalism, that is not limited to the realms of art and culture. I formulate such a proposition based on what Jonathan Beller named as *»the cinematic mode of production«* (cf. Beller, 2006) and it is a mode of esthetical production, characterized by the reliance on digital media and the visual labor of spectators as a value adding process.

Therefore the digital mode of production is analogous to the cinematic mode of production, but as well different to it, for it takes as its primal logic the calculation of the computer that is not at all an esthetical parameter but a form of social programming, a mode of constructing society and a mode of making profit that can not be divided from the financial capital logic. At the center of the digital mode of production stays knowledge as a knowledge production being elaborated through new media and digital technology into knowledge dissemination and storage systems. The digital mode of production is connected to knowledge production via *Information-Communication-Technology (ICT)*, forming as well what is known as *cognitive capitalism*. In the time of global capitalism the capacity of digital networks, platforms and circuits to unlimited exchange while producing and disseminating content through circulation of information is remarkable. In the background of such dissemination systems stays the ICT. ICT on one side provides the very condition for knowledge seen in relation to ICT as information, from ideas to images, from affects to effects. On the other side ICT, emerging from military sciences, allows for knowledge to merge with the capitalist market, corporations, (semi) public and private agencies. Dissemination knowledge systems in relation to and via ICT propose a new type of E-Learning that combines participatory educational institutions with participatory learning technologies. But behind the aura of participation and freedom, the corporate interests of the cultural industry are resurfacing. In fact, the E-Learning that is connected with the proliferation of knowledge dissemination systems is as well entangled with the E-Government measures that see in technology the salvation for the lack of content and alternatives.

On one side we have the hope of ICT for the future of unrestricted dissemination of knowledge, on the other a legislative criminalization of a large share of internet users is proposed. In contrast to the society of discipline, the society of control extends its control outside the structured sites of social institutions, merging itself with flexible and fluctuating networks. One such example is the case of Google intervention into mobile phones by offering an open-source operating system for VOIP phones that includes a GPS function alerting friends or signaling contacts that are in the immediate vicinity of the user. This presents a form of »playful« control. More, in the US, Google has already managed to appropriate entire cityscapes by photographing them systematically and pasting the results into 3-D rendered and geo-coordinated representations that are then used for environmental analysis and simulation, allowing business profit to radically change (read: to fully privatize) the urban environment. This is a new form of gentrification. It is a digitalized gentrification.

It is claimed that digital technologies are allowing for processes of networking and exchange that are being performed in the immaterial space of information and are virtually »free«. But if we think that ICT and their owners are monopolizing »the free world« of communication and making profit as owners of these protocols and networks, then we see that private property and profit are the major regulators of the supposedly digitally free world. The whole cultural industry today is not only about creation of products, markets, and consumers, but about revolutionizing the theater (in the »First World«) and the *necrospaces* (in the »Third World«) of capitalist production and reproduction. Knowledge as information presents itself as data and metadata conflated with (and as) knowledge that presents itself ultimately as a form of digitally processed and synthesized information. This implicates a repetition and circularity. Because of such conflation of knowledge and information the dissemination is done through the digitalized platforms that supports repeated usage and self circularity (as it is the case of the internet). For such storage and dissemination systems, as the internet, several »engines« work together, from search engines to government (or semi private) agencies.

I can immediately push the next thesis that not only knowledge is any information today, but that dissemination system of knowledge is at the same time its storage or vice versa, and that the new social relation is »access«. Digital coded cultures proclaim a twofold process, firstly, you access the network—else you are dead, and, secondly, what we get is an interminable process of self circularity, self reflectivity and repetition; dissemination presents an access to a storage of knowledge and the storage is nothing else than a dissemination.

In cognitive capitalism, as it is developed among others by Michael Hardt and Antonio Negri (cf. Hardt, 2000; 2004) , we see highly digitalized and virtualized »network societies«. The outcome of this networking is a »general intellect«, a collective intelligence so to say, that refers to a set of knowledge, competencies, linguistic uses, and ways-of-doing-things, more or less available to everybody. The way of capturing information goes through creating databases (in relation to hardware) and tools (in relation to software) for their usage. The general intellect or the collective intelligence is therefore a huge knowledge storage system. Cognitive capitalism, as elaborated by Yann M. Boutang, capitalizes, makes surplus value (profit) from controlling the development of collective intelligence in networks that interact using information (cf. Boutang, 2007) . The extraction of profit in cognitive capitalism takes place from embodied and intellectual social know-how services and knowledge sources in a mode of labor that is called *Post-Fordist* and presents a precarious mode of entanglement and networking that takes place »everywhere« and outside of what was known as the factory. Cognitive capitalism replaces the industrial capitalism and its Fordist mode of labor in the 20th century that made profit from the exploitation of workers labor-power in factories and from classical colonialism. Post-Fordist capitalism reproduces itself from what Paolo Virno (cf. Virno, 2004) defines as the »workers' virtuosity«, that goes beyond the once fixed hours of exploitation of labor power in the factory. But what is extremely important to emphasize is that it works through repetition of Post-Fordist labor amidst the Fordist labor modes that are today modes of clear slavery working conditions. Therefore Post-Fordist labor division presents a new division of labor between the First, Second and Third Worlds. This division is effective, but hidden under the veil of globalization. Therefore on one side it repeats the old hegemonic division on an international scale, hidden behind the Post-Fordist digital networking. On the other side, slavery labor is reproducing itself locally, captured in a matrix of capitalized vectors. Or to put it differently, resuming Beller, affective and cognitive-linguistic activities are little by little converted into worksites for capitalist not only extra value, i.e. profit, but also for what is termed simple capitalist use value.

The result of such an operation presents the core of the way coded and digitalized culture functions today. Referring to Beller I can state even more poignantly what it is about. It is as if global fetishism of the First Capitalist World, that is in a constant search for the spectacle of Third World poverty, and I will add, as well, in a constant search for the Second World (after the fall of the Berlin Wall) peculiarities, capitalizes on structures of desires that are in retrospect programmed, coded by the First World capital for the Third and Second World's labor. A good example is the film *Slumdog Millionaire* by the British director Danny Boyle that received an Oscar in 2009. It is a story of a young man from the slums of Mumbai who appears in the Indian version of the show *Who Wants to be a Millionaire* and exceeds all expectations. What calls our attention is precisely this double process of colonialism, exploitation and digitalization. The film is the hallmark of global fetishism in search of the spectacle of third world poverty. Or rather it is a process of capitalization of the structure of desire of a young man from the slums of Mumbai, that is already activated by the First World capital for the Third World labor.

The digitally coded images of the Third and Second Worlds become an essential mechanism in the continued occupation and exploitation of the Third and Second Worlds; in addition to the creation of surplus value, there is the creation of surplus pleasure, or surplus desire—again in such products we see how profit is being subsumed as ideological digital mode. This process is also effective in the First Capitalist World, just think of the erosion of the whole sector of critical thinking and the complete transformation of every image and network into a brand. The digital mode of production consists of computerization or digitalization of representational and interventional forms in culture and arts working in relation to television, cinema and computer screens, but as well with formats of imagination, the cognitive, the libidinal and the unconscious that are produced and reproduced by and through these formats.

The digital mode I state is not a symptom but is co-substantive, works hand in hand, with the process of calculation that is at the base of financial capital. Let me give an example, making a reference to Beller who states: *»A typical laptop computer running the calculations necessary to generate three minutes of industry standard CGI would have to run for 9 hours. If one thinks not just of the immense number of calculations that inform such cinematic images (with/of exaggeration, human lifetimes worth of math), not to mention the entire history of mathematics and computing that lead up to our current abilities (all* *that dead labor, and I will add the commons that we fight today for), then we begin to get a real sense of what we are looking at in the coded culture«*. As he argues further, everybody can attest that this calculation is predominantly financial.

I want to go on with an in-depth analysis of global capitalism. In order to do this, I will make a reference to Santiago López Petit's book *Global Mobilization. Brief Treatise for Attacking Reality* (cf. Petit, 2009) . Petit's book is a militant demand for further repoliticization of life. But contrary to numerous analyses of globalization seen as a process, Petit claims (through maybe Alain Badiou or even Gilles Deleuze) that contemporary global capitalism is an **EVENT**. Petit states that if we think of globalization as the result of a process, we imply a development and a progression (also temporarily a regression, a crisis), but definitely as something that is progressing—therefore we are not capable of understanding the way capitalism functions. In such a situation of global capitalism being a process, we therefore even imply capital emancipation (as it had been stated throughout the previous decade in numerous exhibitions, symposia, books throughout Europe and the US, that capital is social, etc.). We are ready to accept, almost naturally, I would say, fake discourses of morality with which capitalism tries to cover up the outcome of the crisis these days (financialization of capital) by stating that it was all just some sort of a mistake, as capital is noble and that financialization, making money from money without investing into production, is just a single perversion, an error. No! Capitalism is not an irreversible process, but, as stated by Petit, a reversible and conflictual event. Moreover, everything that is going on in the world today is brought back to one single event, and this is not the crisis, but what Petit calls the »unrestrainment of capital« (cf. Petit, 2009) . Neoliberal globalization, which is the synonym of the global era, is nothing more than the repetition of this event only: the unrestrainment of capital.

The unrestrainment of capital creates a paradoxical spatialization that requires two repetitions: on the one hand, Petit says: a founding repetition with which a system of hierarchy is re-established, leading to the constant reconstruction of a center and a periphery. On the other hand: a so-called de-foundational repetition that presents itself as the erosion of hierarchies, producing dispersion, multiplicity and multi-reality. The unrestrainment of capital, as argued by Petit, implicates both repetitions at once. Therefore, repetition not only produces the »jouissance« of minimal difference, it is also a mechanism of control, subjugation and repression. The repetition of the unrestrainment of capital, repeated vertically and horizontally, rearticulates a global space-time that repeatedly effectuates the co-propriety of capital and power. As argued by Petit, the unrestrainment of capital is the only event that—being repeated in any moment and any place—unifies the world and connects everything that is going on within it. Repetition is also de-foundational to the degree with which it exchanges differences for equality. I can therefore propose four major fields with which Petit tackles global capitalism and these are: reality, capital, power, and democracy. These segments are linked together through two almost old-fashioned mechanisms that are evidently still operative today: circularity in the way of self referentiality and empty formalism on the one side, tautology that produces obviousness on the other. Corporations make profit from appropriating the general intellect, presented always as collaboration and cooperation, as networking. Boutang says the source of wealth and making profit is no longer only labor-power, but rather the » intellectual capital « that is possessed less by individuals than by networks of individuals. That is expressed in things like capacity for innovation, institutional know-how, etc. Knowledge, language, verbal skills and networking, down to life itself and not only (we would say »less«) labor-power in the factories (mostly situated outside the First Western World) become sources of economic value. Though the general intellect is presented as the commons (according to Lawrence Lessing (cf. Lessing, 2004)) that should be a propriety of all, these commons are privatized and new formats of neocolonial knowledge systems, as elaborated by Walter Mignolo, are taking place (cf. Mignolo, 2003) . Such commons today are the huge storage systems known as the internet and its *www*.

To grasp precisely the changes of exposed cognitive capitalism connected to labor and the digital culture, it is of crucial importance to emphasize the function of new media and digital technologies (Hansen, 2006) . Mark B. N. Hansen stated that the knowledge storage systems (the modes of knowing) are today directly connected with digital technologies. It is not about our possibility to individually react to the knowledge storage/dissemination systems in the digital realm, as it is more about our capability to network, exchange and access. On one side the knowledge storage systems are based on freedom of circulation and virtual networking procedures and exchange, on the other we witness a commodification of knowledge in these storage systems. Through a reinforced legislative system of control, from patents to copyrights, we see privatization of almost every public goods or commons. Also digitalization of all kinds of knowledge(s) through the growing capacity of computing, copying and storage of information are removing the technical fences to property rights that used to help enforcement of intellectual property rights and the intensified privatization of the commons. Knowledge storage systems are not technical, but political tools allowing for new modes of capital accumulation. In the last instance, these systems redefine the context of whole nations, their capability for self definition and self determination.

Historically, the processes of gathering information/knowledge are known as standardization of knowledge. In the 19th century a shift in documentation occurred in order to regulate international trade, import and export of goods and people that resulted in the spread of illnesses. The regulations and standardization of data collections and information exchange, according to Geoffrey C. Bowker and Susan Leigh (cf. Bowker, 1999) , became an important system of measurements to ensure »strong international public health«. Standardization became the major way of constructing a rational world, of entering a world as a rational system. The introduction of scientific methods brought an objectivity that started to reinforce a positivist view of the society—precisely, these methods were at the core of the whole idea of preservation, conservation, documentation and archiving. Standardization was connected with a process of rationalization that was working and works today hand in hand with racialization. Anibal Quijano states that the characteristic of global, eurocentered, capitalist power today is organized around two axes: one is the coloniality of power and the other modernity (cf. Lugones, 2007) . The coloniality of power introduces the basic and universal social classification of populations on the idea of race, establishing domination as naturalized (racionalized) understandings of inferiority and superiority. To this, it is necessary to add a systemic understanding of gender and class divisions based on the colonial/modernity multiple relations of power. In such a situation the class division is not expired. It is actually intensified and, as said by Beller, blurred in the meanders of new language inventions and modernized grammars of exploitation, capital and profit relations. Through digitalization processes the coded culture prevents de-coloniality of labor and de-linking of life from capital, the latter being at the base of the *modus operandi* of digitalization. My thesis is that the digital, as the dominant mode of representation of financial capital, is not simply a mode of representation, but is as well the dominant mode of reproduction of capital today.

Digitalization has a double function. Predominantly in the First Capitalist World it presents itself being at disposal of biopolitics, according to which what matters is mode-of-life, good life and subjects as brands—on the other, in the Third and Second Worlds, digitalization being part of necropolitics reinforces structures of slavery, naked life and expropriations. Profit, as we can learn from financial capital, is not made only and solely through investments in the stock markets but is supported by a series of interventions and logics of exploitations that are produced through a process of a steady continuation of massive impoverishment and massive digitalized ideological subdivisions and submissions that change the »western« concept of governance over lives in the First world (known as biopolitics, still playing the card of modes of life) into necropolitics in the Second and Third Worlds. It changes biopolitics into necro (**DEATH**) politics. What is the difference between biopolitics and necropolitics? Biopolitics is a horizon of articulating contemporary capitalist societies from the so-called politics of life, where life (via Giorgio Agamben: it does not matter anymore, if it's bare/naked life or life-with-forms (Agamben, 2005)) is seen as the zero degree of intervention of each and every politics into contemporary societies. But today the surplus value of capital is based on the capitalization of death (*necro*) worlds. In his text *Necropolitics*, Achille Mbembe discusses this new logic of capital and its processes of geopolitical demarcation of world zones based on the mobilization of the war machine (Mbembe, 2003). Mbembe claims that the concept of biopolitics, due to the war machine and the state of exception being one of the major logics of contemporary societies, should be replaced with necropolitics. This means, making profit from a double death, from real massive impoverishment and from a symbolical death of the social and political intervention that instrumentalize digitalization and creativity. As argued by Aihwa Ong, management and administration are running our social lives through a system of calculations. Ong states that calculation is technology of optimization, from economics to politics, from nature to environment, and can be used by any political regime (with no changes needed in the system for improving the conditions of life whatsoever), in order to effectuate the calculation for profit. Marina Garcés, in her book *In the Prisons of the Possible* (Garcés, 2002), states that contemporary capitalism is not circumscribed within the articulation of a determined economic system and its production, but subsumes all spheres of life, thus coinciding with reality itself in the final analysis. The outcome is a political consensus called democracy, whose institutions do not carry any political status anymore, but are seen as an »environment« that can only be adjusted and improved but not subverted or ousted in any case. Garcés talks about the democracy-market in which anything can pass, or be taken for granted, and where the world is presented in its naked truth. Meaning: this is what it is! It is a terminal obviousness that presents a world not as open, but as closed and without a future, despite seeing such an intensified theoretical reworking of infinity.

In the First World the good life and creativity merge and as stated by Jaromil: »*Creativity must be rendered comprehensible, transparent and rational: there can be none of the destructive excesses evident in the lives of many of the greatest artists of European history. Creativity must circulate cleanly and quickly, and it should leave no dirty remainder. For what interests Hollywood and the market in general, is not creativity as a complex human process, but creativity as an abstraction, free of irrationality and pain, and light enough to hover like a great logo above the continents*« (cf. Jaromil, 2010) [1]. Financial capital is working hand in hand with, as stated by Beller, »*computer-generated imagery that depends upon the mathematical computational power, if not cognition, of a machine. The attack is launched and answered in a dramatic space entirely shot through with mathematicized vectors of not just computer graphics, but the industry that supports silicon mathematics as well as the film industry as a whole with its logics of genre, celebrity, distribution and the world market*«. So on the one hand we have, as argued by Beller, the hypersensitivity of the mind-body and on the other the off-screen universe of computerization, globalization and financialization scoring the action.

[1] Jaromil's answer to postings on *Nettime* on the topic of »Political Work in the Aftermath of the New Media Arts Crisis«.

In the background of the unrestrainment of capital, it is nevertheless necessary to think about the limits of capital. But to say that the unrestrainment of capital means going over the limit is, as Petit stated, not at all what this event is about. Because the only limit of capital is capital itself, so the unrestrainment of capital is not about something outside of it (as is said about the crisis, being something »abnormal«, and also something that will bring capitalism to its end); the unrestrainment of capital just means something more than capital. Petit links capital and power in the following ways:

· Capital is more (than) capital.
· Capital that is more than capital is power.

Such a relation presents a new situation between capital and power, which is named by Petit as *co-propriety of capital and power*.

Such co-propriety of capital and power needs a medium in order to take place. We have three fundamental medias today where capital and power own each other: innovation, public space and war. Innovation: new information and communication technologies, bio-technologies, the pharmaceutical industry and science are proposed as fields of innovation with which we will supposedly overcome the present crisis. Public space is increasingly privatized and depoliticized; instead of politics, we talk about catastrophes (ecological, educational). War allows for the management of life through the capitalization of death (Iraq, Pakistan and Afghanistan).

Petit states that such a situation of the changed relation between capital and power, which is the relation of the co-propriety today, asks for a different relation between globalization and the Nation State. The Nation State is not a victim of globalization, as is constantly argued; rather the Nation State successfully adapts itself to globalization. We see this in the intensified measures that are implemented by the Nation States in terms of privatization of all public sectors, from education to health and culture, and also in the way how class division and racism are managed in our capitalist contemporaneity. Intensified racism, if we just think about EU legislative policy, presents processes of class and institutional racializations that are supported by new, constantly reinvented neocolonial structures. For the unrestrainment of capital to handle conflicts, it needs a formal frame, and this is neoliberal capitalist democracy. Democracy articulates two modes of power: as argued by Petit, one is the *War State* (governance and violence with brutal exploitation, expropriation, discrimination, repression), and the other is *Postmodern Fascism*. They work as a grid of vertical and horizontal forces, and in order to escape Frederic Jameson's old cognitive mapping, we can think, I propose, of their working together as in the case of Computed Tomography. This also means, as I have already stated in the past, that it is not possible to understand global capitalism if we do not include new media technology, the digitalized mode of programming in its logic of functioning. Computed Tomography (CT) is a specialized X-Ray imaging technique. It may be performed, as it is stated in medical technical language, as »plain« or with the injection of a *Contrast Agent*. This makes a perfect metaphor for analysis, as we can say that it is used as »plain« in Africa, Kosovo, Chechnya, as well on the workers (without any rights and overexploited) from the former ex-Yugoslav republics in Slovenia, or when »just fixing« the situation with migrants (making them illegal, extrajudicial) in the EU through seclusions and deportations. *Plain* means with pure, naked, bare force. Or it can be used with the *Contrast Agent*, as in Iraq or Afghanistan or Pakistan. In these regions, major economic interests are at stake, such as petrol and heroin, vital for the US, EU, etc., and therefore, to cover this, it is necessary to have agents. CT creates an image by using an array of small individual X-Ray sensors and a computer. By spinning the X-Ray source, data is collected from multiple angles. A computer then processes information to create an image on the screen.

The War State is one face of democracy and serves for dominance. The other is Postmodern Fascism. It serves as the dissolution of the democratic state in a multi-reality of social technologies. Postmodern Fascism, as stated by Petit, is constructed on the autonomy of each individual. As such, it is a self governmentality that is based on the self management of a proper autonomy. The War State produces coherency. It homogenizes. Its action is propaganda. Think of the mobilization of the masses against terrorism, for example. Postmodern Fascism, on the other hand, is informal, non-coherent, as it is based on the autonomy of differences. It produces differences. Its action is communication. These differences are brilliantly described in Petit's book. I claim that the War State, in its verticality—functioning by way of force, violence, fear—is but a pure fascist state. However, it would be too simple if we used historical fascism for its naming, because we would fail to emphasize what the major logic of dominance in the world today is, and this is the logic of war. The War State definitely has elements of classical fascism: a sovereign leader, people, death as the management of life. While, on the other hand, there is also the neoliberal context of the autonomy of individuals, which is the neoliberal freedom of having rights to just be an individual brand. It is rightly so, as proposed by Petit, to name it Postmodern Fascism. As Petit says, Postmodern Fascism sterilizes the »Other«, evacuates the conflict from public space and neutralizes the political. It is not strange that we continuously repeat that global capitalism is about depoliticization. Postmodern Fascism works through a constant self mobilization.

The idea is to understand the size of the paradox—the War State is a pure fascist state, because it presents the unification of the national body, and therefore the migrants, people of color, etc., have to be expelled from the normalized fascist contemporary society. But it would be too easy today, at the time of global capitalism, to call this fascism, because we would be losing something very important, and this is the turbo technological and mediated war and its function today in transforming the Nation State into a War State. If we think about the Schengen Agreement—today the Schengen border is not inside the European Union, it's already outside of it. The Schengen border with its ICT police control and military forces is spreading into states that are not part of the EU. The border is not the old border of division but the border is in the center of the city in the form of huge Western Europe and US embassies like fortifications.

In the post Cold War era (that started with the fall of the Berlin Wall in 1989) the development of democratic structures and processes are tightly connected with new challenges of knowledge storage and dissemination. The arrival of the *Net* in the 1990s confirmed the US-led path of modernization for the world and as well for nations of former Eastern Europe. Controlling of geopolitical spaces by superpowers is connected with the dissemination of knowledge, it works hand in hand with privatization and deregulation. In the past it was a clear division within the realm of knowledge, the East-West and North-South divisions were clearly presented as ideological divisions; today the ideological is supposedly gone and knowledge is presented only as information flows. Those trapped in the past on both sides of the Iron Curtain can today disseminate their individual, liberal (capitalist) politics only through their profiles on Facebook. But Facebook's dissemination network documents not only friends' activities but as well our and of our friends the so-called secondary profile, these data are gathered without our knowledge. Privacy is at stake here. Personal life becomes a point across the IP network which is relaying on the SMTP message. As coined by *Critical Art Ensemble (CAE)*, most of the applications on the internet while being disseminated are being designed to capture as well our »data body« (cf. CAE, 1995) . CAE states that the data body is the total collection of files connected to an individual. The data body has two primary functions. The first purpose serves the repressive apparatus; the second serves the marketing apparatus. Everyone is under permanent surveillance by virtue of their necessary interaction with the marketplace. The second function of the data body as described by CAE is to give marketeers more accurate demographic information to design and create target populations. Since financial capitalism in the First Capitalist World has long left the problem of production behind, moving from an economy of need to an economy of desire, marketeers have developed better methods to artificially create desires for products that are not needed. The data body, according to CAE, gives them insights into consumption patterns, spending power, and »lifestyle choices« of those with surplus income.

The role of technology is of crucial importance. In this horizon it is possible to say that since technology is developed, distributed and democratized (made more and more accessible) in the West, the knowledge storage systems serve as West's (US and Western Europe) dominant epistemological, educational and power structures, which are instrumental in cementing systems of knowledge, practices and concepts distributed from the capitalist developed center to globally everywhere else. Dissemination is in tight relationship with technology development and forms of control of access and archiving of information. Belinda Kazeem, Nicola Lauré al-Samarai, and Peggy Piesche talk of the euro-centric system of meaning with a »highly civilized cultural heritage« that is conveyed and mediated by the West (cf. Kazeem, 2007). Therefore it is necessary to put under question as well the direct conflation in between dissemination and democracy, knowledge and colonialism, global capitalism and modernity. It is more accurate to state that behind the knowledge digital dissemination systems lays the myth of salvation from the crisis and bankruptcy produced by financial capital that started to be poignantly visible from 2008 on. The capitalist system sees its salvation in ICT and on a further capital accumulation based on digital dissemination systems.

The question that is posed is whether global dissemination knowledge systems are really possible as free systems of access and exchange. As dissemination systems initially promising freedom are more and more controlled and banned today. This is implemented on YouTube already. The knowledge dissemination systems are therefore substantially connected with their access through software and hardware and a broadband. Nicholas Negroponte in 2006, in order to really envision the possibility of global dissemination systems of knowledge, communication and exchange, proposed the project *One Laptop Per Child (OLPC)* or a *100 Dollar Laptop*. To build a knowledge dissemination system conceived on the web as Wiki pages in order to allow for uncovering hi/stories, means creating and designing knowledge dissemination systems that have at their center the notion of agency, but what matters is as well the access to any appropriate hardware in the end. Therefore, as Johannes Grenzfurthner/Frank Apunkt Schneider (*monochrom*), in their published manifesto with the title *Hacking the Spaces* claim, is that it is necessary to engage and enlarge the hacker community with those left outside from the white middle class nerds that lead and dominate it. It is true and we see clearly that this community is hostage to these white middle class nerds, but to change this and develop different politics for the future it is necessary to understand first and foremost how the digital mode of production works hand in hand with the logic of calculation inherent to financial capitalism.

In such a context it is important to also think in regard with the ICT knowledge dissemination systems about high-speed internet broadband infrastructure. This is as well the »ideal« (to have the access to it) for any country today in order to ensure its political future that is seen today as a full ICT future (therefore being technological but a-political at the same time). The so-called advanced capitalist societies are more and more reducing high-speed internet broadband access to special spaces of access, to mostly private spaces, as homes and offices. The future tendency in acquiring and implementing high-speed internet broadband infrastructure is contrary to the idea of thinking of a wireless unlimited connection in all public spaces. In Great Britain and the US in the future, the digital knowledge dissemination systems through high-speed internet broadband infrastructure won't be publicly fully accessible, which means accessible for all without payment. Instead, the trend today is going toward privatizing the high-speed internet broadband infrastructures so that in the hands of companies they will become a commodified and private property. We can then understand that global financial capitalism (re-)produces itself through dysfunctional logics, through economic, social and political disruptions, propped up by science and new media technology. Science and technology are being implemented for the figuration, representation, mediation and rationalization of the crisis, new forms of coloniality, deep processes of racism, discrimination and exploitation. What new media technologies put forward is in fact, as claimed by Sarah Kember, an »anti-politics«! Such technologies are seen as a »consensual hallucination«, the new »final frontier« of an out-of-control realm where only » post-humans « will be able to live. But what are the real humans doing in the meantime, those who sometimes are not even considered to be fully human? They are looking for discarded food in the immense garbage dumps on the outskirts of the big cities of Asia, Latin America, Africa, and Eastern Europe. This is becoming more and more visible, especially with the present crisis of the financial capitalism, across Europe and the US.

The digitalization of knowledge can be seen as the digitalization of information that has at its core also the storage as a possibility of access. The dynamic and static elements of the process of storing is then connected directly to formats of power, as they imply how and when the information will be retrieved, who will have access to it, what kind of users will have a chance to dynamically reuse the information. Such systems are developing models of documentation that have a lot to do with processes of structuring accessibility and visibility, defining what is important and formulating this importance through a system that hides primarily the Western knowledge system hegemony. Rather than to claim that contemporary knowledge storage systems confront us with an already functioning digital open source archive, that promises an ever-smoother connectivity, these systems should be renegotiated through historical and political contexts that will dismantle their inherent procedures of global business, colonial geopolitics and inequality.

If free access to knowledge means equal possibilities for free dissemination of knowledge from both sides of the colonial divide (from the side of those who have all the technologies at their disposal and from the side of those who have almost none), that is the only condition for equal development in the future, then the access to the internet and its www, as central infrastructures for contemporary dissemination, exchange and co-operation, should be seen as being part of the general intellect of contemporary societies and should be made available and accessible to all. Instead, more and more commodified internet infrastructures that privilege high income classes control the internet access. Such structures have a tendency to exclude lower income groups from their access to the internet, and cutting entire geopolitical zones in the present global world from having any (free is just a wish) access to digitalized knowledge storage and dissemination systems. Due to *Information-Communication-Technology (ICT)* a process of circularity is established in between storage and dissemination. It is important to know that despite the impression that new media technology stores data automatically, there are, on the contrary, sophisticated ways of capturing, defining, preserving and finally making the material accessible for usage. The web archive is connected with more and more power of the search engines that are mechanisms for organizing and accessing the web content. Today it is almost impossible to divide, due to new media technology, the way how knowledge is stored and how it is disseminated. Google is a database in a sense of a huge archive and at the same time a search engine giving more and more services in expanding large amounts of information that are then gathered, stored and used. Google is at the same time a universal knowledge dissemination system and the most used search engine in the world, therefore it is central for the organization and dissemination of knowledge. It takes us to the question of economic value in cognitive capitalism and collective intelligence through its power of dissemination. Matteo Pasquinelli states that the search engine is the interface that is at the core of cognitive capitalism; it works with the invisible algorithm that is the *PageRank* (cf. Pasquinelli, 2008) . The origin of Google's power and monopoly is to be traced precisely in this invisible algorithm. What it does? PageRank ranks results by counting how many times the search term appears on the page. PageRank determines relevance based on the number of pages that link back to the original site and their importance. Web developers are engaged in a constant cat and mouse game with Google, working hard to optimize their sites so they emerge on top in Google's search results. Another point in relation to web search engines, besides context and classification of information, is their digital reliable profile they are creating of each user by combining a history of internet searches linked to the user's IP address. Even more, as argued by Alessandro Ludovico, Google, so to say internally, within a commercial realm, allows for a certain freedom of sorting and free usage, but externally, looking from a critical distance, Google brands and products result in commodification of knowledge with aggressive neverending new possibilities for advertisement and commerce (cf. Ludovico, 2005) . Web search engines in terms of their dissemination logic urgently therefore need to be addressed in their social and political dimensions. On one side, knowledge must be differentiated from mere information and from its solely locally embedded nature—on the other it is not possible to do so.

It is clear that all the raised questions coincide with technological power, domination, control (ranking), therefore only a determined analysis can give us back the radical politics of intervention in the digital realm for the aim of a better life and a decent future for everybody.

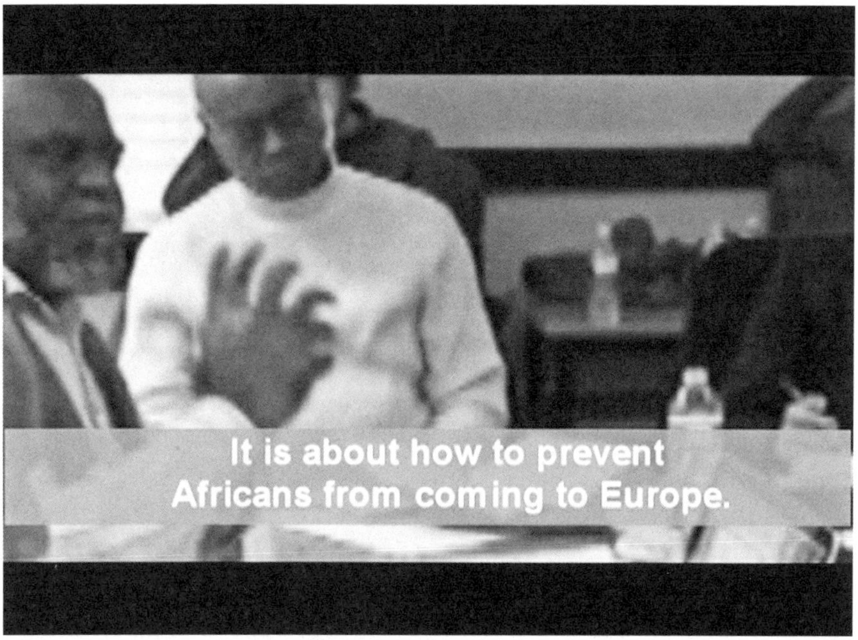

Fig. 1: Marina Gržinić, Aina Smid, *Naked Freedom*, Video, 2010. Courtesy of the artists.

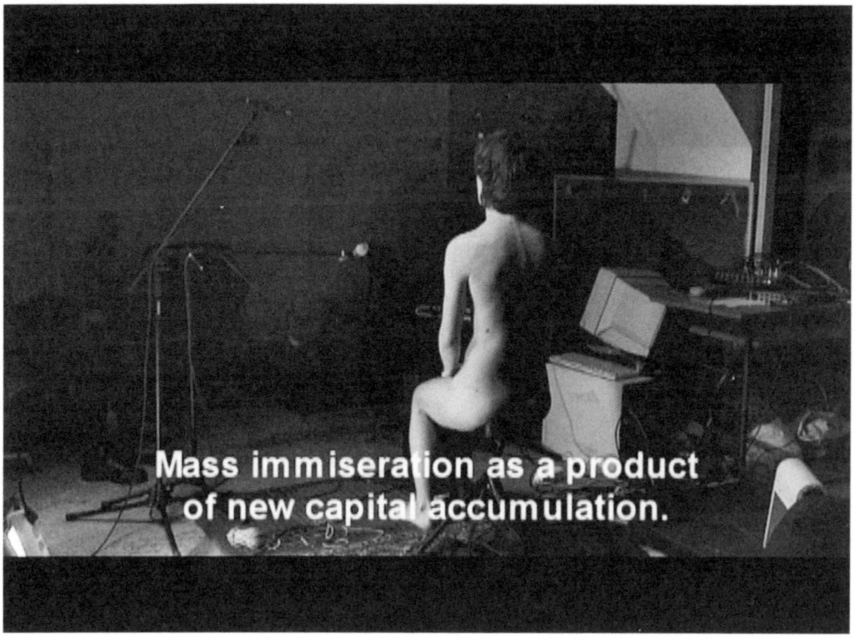

Fig. 2: Marina Gržinić, Aina Smid, *Naked Freedom*, Video, 2010. Courtesy of the artists.

References

Agamben, G.: *State of Exception*. Chicago: University of Chicago Press, 2005

Beller, J.: *The Cinematic Mode of Production: Attention Economy and the Society of the Spectacle* (Interfaces: Studies in Visual Culture). New York: Dartmouth College, 2006

Boutang, Y. M.: *Le capitalisme cognitif, La nouvelle Grande Transformation.* Paris: Editions Amsterdam, 2007

Bowker, G. C., Leigh, S.: *Sorting things out: Classification and its consequences.* Cambridge, Mass.: MIT Press, 1999

Critical Art Ensemble (CAE), »*The Mythology of Terrorism on the Net*«. USA, 1995 http://www.t0.or.at/cae/mnterror.htm [Accessed: Oct 28, 2010]

Garcés, M.: *En las prisiones de lo possible.* Barcelona: Bellaterra, 2002

Gilly, A., Roux, R.: »Capitales tecnologías y mundos de la vida. El despojo de los cuatro elementos«. In: *Revista Herramienta, No. 40.* Mexico City, 2009

Hansen, M.B.N.: *Bodies in code: Interfaces with Digital Media.* London: Routledge, 2006

Hardt, M., Negri, A.: *Empire.* Cambridge, Mass.: Harvard University Press, 2000

Hardt, M., Negri, A.: *Multitude: War and Democracy in the Age of Empire.* New York: Penguin, 2004

Jaromil on *Nettime*: http://www.mail-archive.com/nettime-l@kein.org/msg01643.html [Accessed: Oct 28, 2010]

Kazeem, B., Lauré al-Samarai, N., Piesche, P.: *Museum. Space. History: New Sites of Political Tectonics.* Austria, 2007. http://eipcp.net/transversal/0708/kazeemetal/en [Accessed: Oct 28, 2010]

Lasch, C.: *The Culture of Narcissism: American Life in an Age of Diminishing Expectations.* New York: Norton, 1979

Lessing, L.: Free Culture: *How Big Media Uses Technology and the Law to Lock Down Culture and Control Creativity.* New York: Penguin, 2004

Ludovico, A., in collaboration with UBERMORGEN.COM and Cirio, P.: *Project Google Will Eat Itself.* Italy / Austria,2005. https://www.tate.org.uk/tateetc/issue14/playingthesystem.htm [Accessed: Oct 28, 2010]

Lugones, M.: »Heterosexualism and the Colonial/Modern Gender System«. In: *Hypatia, Vol. 22, No. 1.* pp. 186–209. Bloomington, Indiana: Indiana University Press, 2007

Mbembe, A.: »Necropolitics«. In: *Public Culture, 15/1.* pp. 11–40. Durham, NC: Duke University Press, 2003

Mignolo, W.: »The Geopolitics of Knowledge and the Colonial Difference«. In: *SAQ, Vol. 101.* pp. 57–96. Durham, NC: Duke University Press, 2003

Pasquinelli, M.: *Animal Spirits: A Bestiary of the Commons.* Rotterdam: NAi Publishers / Institute of Network Cultures, 2008

Petit, S. L.: *La movilización global. Breve tratado para atacar la realidad.* Madrid: Traficantes de Sueños, 2009

Virno, P.: A *Grammar of the Multitude: For an Analysis of Contemporary Forms of Life.* New York: Semiotext[e], 2004

Machiko Kusahara

Assembling Art, Design, Technology and Media Culture: The Challenge of Japanese Device Art

Introduction

The relationship between art, science, technology and culture is a complex issue that consists of a network of influences and interactions. Today, media technology is shared as an everyday tool both for work and for fun, by practically everyone including artists, designers, engineers, scientists, businessmen, as well as amateur photographers who upload their works for public viewing and »consumers« who enjoy viewing artworks or buy designed furniture (or rather, much inexpensive gadgets) online. Works of media art integrate art and technology, often questioning what media technology means to us, but also showing how technology can push the border of art. Tools the artists use and venues where their works are shown—or experienced—are often very different from those in traditional art. Often it is not even clear if a work—a network project with public participation, for example—is to be considered art or not. Still, the definition of media art—although it can never be clear cut—seems to be bound by the traditional Western paradigm of art.

Device Art is a concept and a project that proposes an alternative viewpoint in media art (Kusahara, 2007) [1]. Launched in 2004 by a group of ten artists, engineers and scholars from Japan with internationally established careers in the field of art and technology, the project explores a new approach to bridge art and its related fields. While their artworks do not look particularly Japanese, their concepts and methods are often inspired by Japanese cultural traditions. Western art history was systematically introduced to the Japanese only in the late 19th century. Having a long history of visual culture that did not lay clear borders between art and its related fields, Japanese artists have a privilege, so to say, to lightheartedly step beyond the traditional paradigm of art [2]. This essay mostly explores the cultural background of Device Art and some of the issues it has brought up in questioning the role of art in the era of digital media technology. However, exaggerating the »Japan-ness« in Device Art or Japanese media art in general is not the aim of the essay. I believe in the importance of recognizing cultural diversities that are often invisible at the surface level. It helps maintaining the richness in art and creativity, and offers a wider possibility in their further development. By its nature, media art reflects people's understanding and use of media in each era and region. Device Art is an attempt to capture and analyze a here-and-now in Japanese media art, and to apply the findings to its further development.

[1] The *Device Art* Project is supported by CREST (Core Research of Evolutional Science & Technology), which is a basic research-funding program of JST (Japan Science and Technology Agency). For more details see: (Kusahara, 2007)

[2] In contemporary art, the artist Takashi Murakami has challenged the traditional Western paradigm of art with a strategic approach both in terms of themes he takes from popular culture and the production system that employs his factory and commercialization of works.

Art and Artists in the Age of Digital Reproduction

We live in the age of digital production/reproduction and communication technology. This brings today's media art an important characteristic that was not typical in traditional art. Tools and materials used by artists in traditional art were mostly those that were specifically meant for the purpose. Materials such as oil paint or bronze have little to do with our daily life. Marble would be used for columns and floors at mansions, but devices for handling them are not among tools that are familiar to us. There was a clear divide between the life of an artist and that of an ordinary person if we look at their studios and homes.

It started to change with the arrival of early media technology. Printing technology was shared by journalists, writers and advertisers, as well as by artists, while the process was still carried by professional printers. With photography scientists and hobbyists joining the list, developing photographs became part of the job for professionals, and a hobby for amateurs especially at its early stage [3]. At the same time the industrial revolution drastically changed the relationship between technology and human beings. Machines became part of urban life. Mass-produced inexpensive utensils were just one side of its major impacts. Under such circumstances, Duchamp's *Ready Made* brought everyday commodity into the arts, and artists such as Rauschenberg and César started using junk for their artworks. Still, despite what Benjamin had pointed out regarding the loss of the aura with mechanical reproduction technology, the art world coped with the situation by limiting the number of original prints (of lithographs, photographs, etc.), using special paper and numbering them (Benjamin, 1936). However, with the advent of digital technology, instantly reproducing and distributing infinite numbers of identical copies became possible. Traditional norms for art making, marketing and appreciating are challenged with the arrival of art in the age of digital reproduction. The aura of the original artwork is questioned once again.

Already at the early stage of media art, some artists using digital technology have responded to the issue in various forms, including web projects that consciously obscured the ownership of images [4]. One such example is a series of projects named *Renga* carried out by Toshihiro Anzai and Rieko Nakamura since 1992, which re-activated the old Japanese tradition of linked verse in online collaborative image production [5]. It is important to point out that Anzai discovered a positive link between the nature of digital technology and collaborative / collective creativity in Japanese tradition. Digital technology opened a wide possibility for ordinary people without an art education to be involved in creative activities. With digital photography and video, easily accessible editing software and services such as YouTube, instant and global publication of one's artwork is easier than ever without much cost. Amateurs are proud of showing off their works, happy to be able to connect to people through their photos and videos. For young artists, it is easier than ever to publish their works [6]. While the main trend of the art world still relies on the gallery system, enjoying art (or of its kind) has become much easier for anyone. Activities and activism support new forms of creativity. Creative Commons, the *Make* Community, Do-It-Yourself, low-tech, Circuit Bending, open source software such as Processing, for example, involve artists, engineers, scholars and hobbyists. Besides providing information on the Web, their typical activities include workshops. Here, the role of artists is in designing and offering an environment that people can enjoy with hands-on experience. In the end a participant would learn something about art

[3] Typewriter is another example of media technology that penetrated into society. F. Kittler analyzes how the technology affected people's way of thinking (Kittler, 1999).

[4] Still the majority was concerned by the immateriality and reproduction-friendly nature of digital technology. Protecting the artist's right and adding value to immaterial work had been an important issue already with video art. Creating video installations helped solving the problem.

[5] *Renga* started in April 1992 between Anzai and Nakamura, and sessions often inviting international artists took place between 1994 and 2002. *Renga* (linked image) is a word play of *renga*, which means linked verse created by multiple poets and is the origin of *haiku*. Anzai points out in the paper he presented at *IMAGINA '94* that »Digital media is beginning to divulge the invalidity of copyright system. At the same time it amplifies the pleasure of using each others works«. http://www.renga.com/archives/strings/note94/index.htm [Accessed: Aug 17, 2010] The project was also shown at *SIGGRAPH '94*, for which I coordinated the part of international session. It is important that already by then Anzai positively connects the absence of strong desire for monopoly of authorship in Japanese culture to what digital technology means to us today.

[6] It was only in the late 1990s that editing video and »bringing the computer image out of the computer« became possible with equipment for personal use.

and technology, but may not care whether the activity is called art or not. Actually, organizing a successful workshop requires much effort, ideas, and a certain charismatic aura as well as artistic direction. Eventually the workshop itself is often considered an art project today, and in fact there are artworks that need to be shown in the form of a workshop, if not demonstrated by the artist alone. It is an example of art to be integrated in our daily activities, in contrast to traditional forms of art, such as paintings hung on the wall of museums, galleries or in houses of rich collectors.

Bridging Art, Design, and Technology

Works of art can be integrated in our digital lifestyle, not as paintings or sculptures to be appreciated at museums or galleries, but as devices in our daily life. It can be seen as equivalent of what avant-garde artists did in response to media technology of the time, as in case of Duchamp's *Rotorelief* (1935) [7]. Duchamp's invention—he presented it at a fair—did not succeed at that time, only selling a few sets. Today, how would artists find their way to challenge the mass consumption society?

Art editions of cell phones by the avant-garde artist Yayoi Kusama are interesting cases [8]. In 2009, KDDI, one of the major cell phone network providers in Japan with its brand name *au*, collaborated with Kusama in launching *iida*, a new series of cell phones for design conscious high-end users. According to its website, *»iida and the avant-garde artist Yayoi Kusama have teamed up to transform the mobile phone into a ›work of art‹ that captures both the imagination of art and the wonder of life«* [9]. Featuring her well-known motif of polka dots, Kusama designed *Dots Obsession*, *Full Happiness with Dots*, and two other models [10]. The price of these models clearly indicates they are objects of art meant for Kusama appreciators, like the miniature versions of her *pumpkin* series that are available online from her official website. Still, these are functioning cell phones although there is a great doubt if those phones are really in use by those who bought them [11]. The idea behind could be as follows: Since the cell phone has become the most important personal item for Japanese people, buying a Kusama cell phone means that the user literally »lives« with art [12]. On her website Kusama writes: *»iida's cell phone and Kusama's avant-garde art has merged into one. Sensibility of our life corresponds to the mystery of the universe. [...] This magical moment of pleasure.*

[7] It is considered that Duchamp got the idea after creating his film *Anemic Cinema* in 1925. The discs are to be placed on a gramophone (which was a new medium) to bring mesmeric moving images to a user—a kind of home cinema on one's own, designed by the artist.

[8] http://iida.jp/english/products/yayoi-kusama/ [Accessed: Aug 19, 2010] Kusama is a painter, sculptor and novelist who was an active member of the avant-garde art movement in New York in the 1960s, who became famous for her happenings and works that are characterized by obsession for dots and organic shaped objects.

That's what I like so much. I love iida's cell phones with all my heart« [13]. It is an advertisement, of course, but there is a reality in it. The cell phone is a gateway to the world for its user [14]. What a pleasure for an artist to have one's work to penetrate so deeply in people's life.

Novmichi Tosa, who founded and leads an art unit named *Maywa Denki* (literally meaning *Maywa Electric Company*), has a long career in turning his inventions into commercial products. While some of his sophisticated robotic instruments he invented and uses at his performance are available at the price range similar to Kusama's art edition cell phones through its online shop by placing an order online, the major part of *Maywa Denki* commercial products are in the easily affordable range. By the way, *Maywa Denki*'s performance is called »product demonstration«, since he presents the art unit as a minor company producing electric/electronic devices that thrives to survive in the industry with the CEO's inventions. Tosa himself and all the »employees« are dressed in the »company uniform« at the performances [15]. The »company's« first commercial product was *Na-Cord* (1994). *Na-Cord* is a fish-bone shaped electric cable for home use. The spiky cable will hurt a user's foot if one steps on it barefoot by mistake (as shoes are not worn in Japanese houses), reminding of the nature of electricity that we tend to forget [16]. The gadget playfully reveals the nature of electricity—its danger, which is hidden behind the comfortable and convenient life we enjoy. Such nature of technology, or technology itself, will be even more invisible as the so-called ubiquitous environment is realized. While the goal for the industry and engineers is in providing a foolproof environment in which technologies become invisible in a black box or hidden behind walls, one goal of art is in visualizing technology itself at users' homes, outside museums and galleries. Making an artwork as a functioning commercial product is certainly an effective way to reach a wider public. »Mass producing« these gadgets is both a commentary to the capitalist society that is driven by mega companies, as well as to consumer society and the art world that continues to pay respects to »originals« [17]. Since affordability is an important part of the concept, its mini-size version is easily available as a cell phone strap in various colors at a modest price for those who could not afford *Na-Cord*. When attached to a cell phone, the strap will surely damage one's pocket with its spikes. Useful-useless, funny-ironical, pop and being a part of daily life yet artful, these products have appealed to those who are not necessarily regular museum-goers [18]. While his works have serious concepts such as the relationship between technology and culture, or the role of artists in society, the way works are

9 http://iida.jp/english/products/art-editions/yayoi-kusama/ [Accessed: Aug 19, 2010]

10 *My Doggie Ring-Ring* and *Dots Obsession*, which are both limited editions of 100 sets and 1,000,000 Yen each, and *Hand Bag for Space Travel*, which is of 1000 sets limited edition and 100,000 Yen each. On the *iida* website, the description on *Hand Bag for Space Travel* is replaced by a text about *My Dog Lin Lin* (sic.) apparently by mistake. Therefore whether the title in English for the second piece is *My Doggie Ring-Ring* or *My Dog Lin Lin* is not clear.

11 Interestingly, these models are sold without connectivity. One should get a contract with the provider after purchasing in order to use it as a cell phone. Obviously people would hesitate using these expensive cell phones daily, with a high risk of damaging or losing them.

12 While the *Dot Obsession* is a combination of a peep box with infinitive reflection of dots and a cell phone with a normal shape (which means that one keeps the box at home as an art object) the shapes and names of *My Doggie* and *Hand Bag* models suggest these are meant to accompany the user anywhere—even to space.

13 http://www.yayoi-kusama.jp/j/information/index.html [Accessed: Aug 19, 2010] (translated by M. Kusahara)

14 In countries like the USA such perception seems to have started with the iPhone in 2009. Japanese cell phones had the internet connectivity since the late 1990s, enabling young users to use it as their major E-Mail and information retrieval device.

presented is full of playfulness that fascinates the audience [19]. More recent invention by Tosa became a smash hit on Japanese gadget market. *Otamatone*, a musical instrument in a form of musical note that »anyone can play« by touching, was completely sold out from physical shops for gadgets or musical instruments, as well as online shops during the christmas season of 2009 immediately after its release on the market in late November. The instrument, which came in both white and black, has a face of a tadpole, or *otamajakushi*, which is a term that is colloquially used for musical note because of the association from its shape. Sliding one's finger on its tail while pushing its cheeks produces funny wah-wah effects that make anyone smile. After practicing for a while (with the accompanying practice sheet, for example) one can easily play—but still with a funny, slightly out-of-tune tone that reminds us of *Theremin*. *Otamatone* immediately appealed to the Japanese's love for »kawaii« (cute) gadgets as well as the need for party goods. The price was quite affordable as well. Although it looks simple and one can even see the structure when opening the tadpole's mouth, the mechanism is based on much larger robotic instruments Tosa has created after research and development. *Otamatone* is unique in the sense that no other musical instrument of the kind had existed. At the same time it is a continuation of a dream shared by many artists—including Duchamp—to make their ideas and creations available to a wider public, which, in this case, was realized with a great success. There is not enough space to introduce more of his intriguing, funny and ironical works for performances, art exhibitions, and commercial products—he has been just amazingly productive. Tosa is a member of the Device Art Project, and has made a major contribution in articulating the project's concept.

Physical, Material, Tangible

Besides Yayoi Kusama and other artists who contributed to the *iida* Design Project, the company invites designers to propose concept models for futuristic ideas. We could imagine these concept models are probably useful for publicity. Design is an extremely important issue for the Japanese cell phone market, especially for young customers. This is nothing strange if we think of the importance of design when buying a car, which has a much longer history. The cell phone represents one's taste, or even more. However, a serious goal of the *iida* Design Project seems to be in introducing new ideas that their own engineers would not have imagined. A case in point is the

[15] Besides the irony on the importance of company life as the nature of Japanese society, it is also the artist's commentary on Japanese *kosupure* (costume play) culture.

[16] A video of Tosa presenting *Na-Cord* is available from YouTube. As a policy, Tosa uploads many of his videos online.

[17] The scene of *Na-Cord* being »mass-produced« at *Maywa Denki*'s »factory« is shown in detail in one of the official videos. Actually it is an artwork itself. In the video, a dozen of men and women in their company uniforms assemble *Na-Cord* in a rather dark room of an old building, probably like the time Tosa's father ran a company named *Maywa Denki*. The original *Maywa Denki* filed bankruptcy as the result of the Oil Shock when Tosa was young, despite the hours of forced afterschool labors by Novmichi and his elder brother.

[18] In fact *Maywa Denki* was chosen the most popular media artist according to a web-based voting carried by *Japan Media Arts Festival* in 2006.

[19] His *Edelweiss* series represents more personal thoughts on sex, life and space, yet being represented by a rich series of illustrations, storyboard, diorama, animation, jewels, robotic devices and books that can be regarded as an artistic version of a role playing game—or something similar to *sekai-kan* (view of the world) of a role-playing game.

one developed by the design team of Yamaha in 2008 in collaboration with au engineers. It was named *Gakki-to-ketai* meaning »musical instrument and cell phone, but probably also »from musical instrument to cell phone«. A rather normal looking cell phone would turn into a musical instrument with a series of attachments. The series of attachments called *Band in My Pocket* included wind instruments. *Sticks in the Air* already functioned, as a pair of air drum. Different types of cell phones with unique shapes and functions were also proposed. For example *Box to Play* was a box-shaped cell phone that could be played by moving one's finger inside the box. *Key to Touch* was a folding type cell phone with two octaves of physical piano keys appearing when opened. Strong interest in simulating physical touch can be observed in these concept models [20]. *Gakki-to-ketai* was partly realized in early 2009 as *Touch Session* on *au*'s cell phone *CA001* [21]. The user can enjoy playing eleven different instruments on his/her cell phone. However, software and a screen, probably to a great disappointment for the Yamaha designers, replaced the physical interface.

While it could have been impractical to realize a physical touch on cell phones, attention for right material and tangible experience is widely seen in Japanese culture. In the case of *TENORI-ON*, designed by the media artist Toshio Iwai in collaboration with Yu Nishibori from Yamaha, development of the extremely refined and stylish instrument took eight years in search for the right material and the appropriate interface design. On the Yamaha website it is proudly announced: *»Media artist Toshio Iwai and Yamaha have collaborated to develop a new digital musical instrument for the 21st century, TENORI-ON. A 16×16 matrix of LED switches allows everyone to play music intuitively, creating a ›visual music‹ interface«* [22]. It is interesting to note that on its Japanese website the first sentence is written slightly differently, *»TENORI-ON is a musical interface for the 21st century being developed by the collaboration between the media artist Toshio Iwai and Yamaha. A 16×16 matrix of LED switches allows everyone to play music visually and intuitively without knowledge in music«* [23]. Here, »musical instrument« is replaced by »musical interface«, and mentioning on »visual music« is omitted, probably the term is unfamiliar in Japanese and sounds too professional. The difference in tones may be a trivial issue, but the Japanese version seems to aim at a wider public, who may not be professional in music but is interested in innovative interface. Part of the reason may be that *TENORI-ON* had been already widely known in Japan among those interested in VJ, DJ, contemporary music, and media art, because of

[20] An importance of the physical touch can also be seen in the *ply* concept model designed by another designer.

[21] The model was manufactured by Casio with Yamaha's AudioEngine, and was announced on January 2009. With the combination of a touch screen and a motion sensor, the cell phone allows a user to play virtual keyboards, strings, drums, gamelan, hand bells and maracas by touching or shaking the phone. http://k-tai.casio.jp/products/ca001/touch.html [Accessed: Aug 28, 2010]

[22] http://www.global.yamaha.com/design/tenori-on/swf/index.html [Accessed: Aug 30, 2010]

[23] http://www.yamaha.co.jp/design/tenori-on/swf/index.html [Accessed: Aug 30, 2010]

Iwai's long career in these fields [24]. Another reason seems to lie in the curiosity towards new technology in Japanese culture, which has a long tradition since the Edo era or even earlier (Screech, 1996) [25].

Such feature can be understood more deeply by visiting one of *Tokyu Hands* shops in Tokyo or other popular towns—Shinjuku, Shibuya, or by walking through the *Electric Town* in Akihabara on weekends: there will be no doubt that the tradition continues [26]. There are products and materials of all sorts and varieties—with detailed information [27]. Besides normal electric and electronic appliances for home use, many products such as compact digital cameras and cell phones have gadget-like elements [28]. One would encounter a wide variety of gadgets as well, from inexpensive humanoid hobby robots to sushi-shaped USB memory sticks and crazy earphones that allow a user to wear bolts, miniature swords, bananas or mushrooms sticking out from ears as while listening to music [29]. They are functional, but their fun elements allow higher pricing. People will pay extra money for fun, while its functions (memory stick, earphone set, etc.) give a psychological excuse to spend money. Gadgets, figures and flush toys from Manga, Anime and game characters are also popular, transforming Akihabara from Electric Town into *Anime Town*. While bigger versions of these gadgets and toys are without practical functions, smaller versions are often meant as *Ketai Strap*, to be attached to cell phones (*Ketai*) as decoration, identification, and for personalizing a mass-produced device. These toys and gadgets allow users to carry and enjoy virtual characters, bridging imaginary and real worlds. At the same time they function as interface for face-to-face communication with friends as a conversation piece [30]. Even popular characters presented in commercial films are immediately materialized into the real world as miniature figures and cell phone straps. The quest for material reality and physical interfaces is a feature that is observed in a wide range of digital technology application in Japan, from robotics to augmented reality and media art [31]. Game design is no exception. Designing a game by building a diorama to share *sekai-kan* (view of the world) is a common practice among game designers, which became known with the development of the game *Xevious*, which was published by Namco in 1982 [32]. Since then, exhibiting such diorama at a game show has become a part of publicity for Japanese game developers, because of its appeal to users. *Kosupure* (cosplay, costume play) by Anime, Manga and game fans is another example of materialization of virtual entities [33].

24 Iwai had continued developing the idea for many years in various formats, including his *Ars Electronica Golden Nica '97* award piece *MUSIC PLAYS IMAGES x IMAGES PLAY MUSIC (MPIxIPM)* in collaboration with Ryuichi Sakamoto.

25 European missionaries who arrived Japan in 16th and 17th centuries already noticed Japanese culture of curiosity.

26 *Tokyu Hands* is an extremely popular department store for tools and materials for all sorts of home improvement, crafts and design, do-it-yourself, as well as »designed« goods, gadgets, stationary, travel supply, bicycle, etc. Shops are in major cities in Japan. It has provided a great support for artists and art students with raw materials they could use.

27 When compared to large-scale shops such as *Best Buy* or *Home Depot* in US or *FNAC* in France, the variety of similar products and availability of materials for open use (such as metal tubes with different diameters, all sorts of electric bulbs, etc.) are outstanding in these Japanese shops.

28 Besides basic functions these products offer features to attract users. You can make your eyes larger to make you look more beautiful, or to share the image with friends for amusement,

However, these phenomena do not mean that people firmly believe in the existence of such virtual worlds or characters [34]. The dialogue between real and virtual, physical and immaterial, takes place with multiple layers, including those that the users/fans can create by themselves. The interplay and sense of playfulness in it should be understood in relation to a long cultural tradition of *mitate*, which will be discussed later in this text (Kusahara, 2009) [35].

Designers as Curators—The Case of *21_21 Design Sight*

Postmodern mass consumption society has changed the meaning of design. Designing useful objects that will bring money for the client (including the industry) is no longer the top priority for top designers. As the title of a book by Kenya Hara *Designing Design* suggests, their goal is beyond the traditional framework of »design«, or commitments to commissioned projects (Hara, 2003; 2007) [36]. They understand that designing means reconfiguring space, the environment, human interfaces, among many other things, and propose their concepts not only within the frameworks of commissioned projects but also through their own projects. Naturally their activities overlap with those of artists. The border between art and design is no longer clear cut. Convergence of design and art is an international phenomenon. In Japan the idea seems to have a wider support from both ends. *21_21 Design Sight* in Roppongi, Tokyo, which was founded and directed by top designers including Issey Miyake, showcases the rich possibility the interdisciplinary field opens up [37]. A case in point is a recent (July–November 2010) exhibition curated by graphic designer Masahiko Sato that aimed at our identity in the digital era. Many artists with engineering background, as well as engineers with artistic activities, were invited to create a volume of interactive works. Each piece visualized—with an artistic twist—how latest identification / surveillance technology accurately identifies individuals in various methods, often without being noticed. The overall exhibition was extremely convincing, critical, and still interesting, because it involved cutting edge technology without just being a tech demo. Artists without background in engineering would have difficulties in conveying their messages relying only on metaphors.

The exhibition titled *Bones* (curated by the industrial designer Shunji Yamanaka [38]) invited Artists, designers, engineers, researchers,

for example. Such functions are supposed to bring more fun to users and serve as conversation tool.

29 These products are available both online and from shops such as Tokyu Hands and major electric/electronic shops in Akihabara.

30 While the origin of »ketai strap« is not clear, connection to traditional *netsuke* has been pointed out. *Netsuke* served for both practical purposes and for showing one's taste.

31 For example, a survey on competition entries to the Prix Ars Electronica over the years, which was exhibited in 2009 during the festival, revealed that one third of works from Japan are in the interactive category, which is a clear tendency when compared to other countries. (Currently there are seven categories including U19, which is only for Austrians.) For example French entries are focused on animation and the UK is strong in music. Entries from Australia are distributed equally to all the categories.

32 Private conversations with game developers from Namco and other companies of the time. It is a well known fact in Japan.

33 *Kigurumi Dollar*, a costume with a mask worn by human beings like Mickeys and Donalds walking around in Disneyland, can be also used at events to entertain these fans, who are not necessarily children.

34 The artist Takashi Murakami has been known for sculptures and paintings depicting imaginary characters that reflect popular culture – both contemporary and ancient. There are many layers of contexts in his works.

and craftsmen to create new works that present structures and movements of various objects. In this context, Novmichi Tosa created a robot that laughs as a visitor cranks, based on the same concept he applied to earlier mentioned *Otamatone*. With a precise mechanism that simulates the function of a human voice chord, the robot named *Wahha GoGo* laughs, changing the pitch and volume of its voice as humans do. The mechanism is visible to visitors, and Tosa even uploaded a video explaining its mechanism to YouTube. It is a conscious act of the artist to make the technology transparent. As the exhibition was very popular and attracted many people, the robot laughed a lot, making people laugh, in turn.

Another major exhibition that took place at *21_21 Design Sight* was *SENSEWARE*, which was curated by aforementioned Kenya Hara. While Hara himself is a graphic designer, he negotiated with an association of the textile industry to offer their latest fabrics to selected artists, designers, and architects, to create works with innovative use of the new fabrics. Following the great success of its first version in 2007 (in Tokyo and in Paris), the second version was realized in 2009 as a part of *Triennal of Milan* and at *21_21 Design Sight*. 17 Japanese and international projects were realized by artists and designers including the architect Kengo Kuma [39].

Among the invited was Hiroo Iwata, who used *KURALON EC* developed by Kuraray Co. to update his *Robot Tile*, which was shown at *SIGGRAPH 2005*. *Robot Tile* consists of a computer and a set of several »tiles« with wheels and modular boards. The system detects the direction a user walks to, and delivers a tile in front of him/her while all the tiles move back, cancelling the movement he/she has made. It is a sort of 360-degree treadmill [40]. By using a new fabric to cover the surface of each tile, a simplified sensing mechanism became possible with an aesthetically more refined look. With the sensor built into the fiber itself, the cloth detects the user's position and sends the information to the computer.

35 The author has dealt with the role of *mitate* in Japanese media culture and Device Art in other essays and papers including: (Kusahara, 2009).

36 Hara is a board member and the leading figure of MUJI (originally and in Japan *Mujirushi*, a word for »generic« or »no brand« in Japanese), an internationally known Japanese brand, with a concept of offering simple but good quality products. MUJI was launched in 1980 by the businessman/poet/writer Seiji Tsutsumi and the graphic designer Ikko Tanaka as an opposition to contemporary consumer products. Hara refers to Japanese traditional aesthetics for simplicity. For the MUJI Award 03 that was held in 2008 Hara and four other jury members (which included the CEO of MUJI) gave the grand prize to *Straw Straw*, a product proposal to package real natural straw as »straw« for drinking. The decision reflects the basic idea behind MUJI to re-examine what design means. An ultimate example of »re-design« (a concept by Hara) in another direction can be found in one of Hussein Chalayan's *transforming dresses* from his 2007 Autumn show. The dress rolls up inside the hat the model wears, ultimately leaving the model nude except for the hat. Many of Philippe Starck's products are meant for enjoying

Device Art and Its Background

It is a fact that Japanese artists have a strong presence in media art, especially in interactive art that uses physical interfaces [41]. Many works share features such as playfulness, open interaction, and an interest in technology. Developing a specific and unexpected their playfulness, as in case of *Juicy Salif*, a well-known »designed« device to squeeze lemon (but not very practical).

37 Designers such as Tokujin Yoshioka and Kennya Hara are among its directors. http://www.2121designsight.jp/en/ [Accessed: Aug 30, 2010]

38 Yamanaka himself collaborated with a *karakuri* master besides showing a flower-like robot arms that gracefully moved, which he made with his students at Keio University.

39 http://www.tokyofiber.com/en/ [Accessed: Aug 20, 2010]

40 It was originally meant as a mechatronic interface for a virtual reality environment. However, as he observed people's reaction, Iwata realized that a system that enables a person to walk forever without getting anywhere means more than a technical invention. While being an engineer with a long career in virtual reality, he had already produced a few artworks that take »users« into an odd situation as in case of *Floating Eye* (1996).

41 See note 31. At SIGGRAPH's Emerging Technology competition (for which creative and original use of new technology is the key criterion) more than half of the works selected for are from Japan over years. Actually this was a main reason why Hiroo Iwata, the engineer/artist who has shown his works both at SIGGRAPH and at Ars Electronica, conceived the project.

42 http://deviceart.org. The definition was settled by project members including myself, based on the original proposal by Hiroo Iwata.

physical device as a user interface is a widely observed trend. Besides art works created by »professional artists«, there is a body of works created by those with (only) engineering background. An appreciation of artistic or entertaining contexts is widely shared among them. In recent years activities encompassing art and technology have produced an interesting body of works from Japan as well as from an international network of artists and engineers. The concept of Device Art came out of such background and provides an alternative viewpoint in understanding the relationship between art and its related fields in the age of digital media technology. The Device Art Project started in 2004 with a joint group of artists, engineers and researchers to investigate and further develop a »Japanese style« media art that employs technology with a sense of playfulness. The project was launched by Hiroo Iwata and was joined by aforementioned Novmichi Tosa (*Maywa Denki*), Kazuhiko Hachiya, Sachiko Kodama, Ryota Kuwakubo, and Masahiko Inami, among others. The author joined the project with an interest in theorizing its concept, which challenges the traditional paradigm of art by its convergence of technology, art and design. Device Art possesses three main characteristics:

- The device itself is content. The mechanism represents the theme of the piece. Content and tool are no longer separable.
- Artworks are often playful and can sometimes be commercialized into devices or gadgets for use in everyday life.
- Refined design and playful features are traced back to the Japanese tradition of appreciating tools and materials 42.

As can be seen from the above definition, Device Art is a form of art that is based on physical material. Although most of the works that fall into the category are interactive, interactivity is not a part of the concept, because a system or a device that supports the core function of an artwork can be used either for interaction or for a performance, or even for an autonomous installation, depending on what to choose as an input. In fact, a definition of interactive art has been a problematic task for years 43. While interactivity is an important issue in art, Device Art takes a different approach by focusing on the relationship between the tool (device) and its user(s), who could be either the artist, a performer, or the visitor(s). What makes Device Art different from a »traditional« definition of art is the recognition of technology (=device) as being inseparable from content. Instead of treating the hardware—such as a system, sensors, physical interface, material used, etc.—as a mere tool for realizing an expected experience, they are treated as an essential part of an artwork. And this approach is considered to inherit the Japanese cultural tradition of respecting the right tools and materials.

Choosing and appreciating refined design, right materials and tools have been a long tradition in Japan. As in case of the tea ceremony, flower arrangements, or cooking: a sophisticated use of refined tools and devices is essential. They are not something that temporarily serve for a certain purpose, they mean more than that. Based on such cultural background and an analysis on contemporary media art, Device Art as an art form realized as a physical system (or a device) in which the device is the content itself. As an artist designs a physical system to realize his/her concept, the content is no longer separable from the hardware that supports the artistic experience. Today we see many such examples in media art, with artworks that involve original interactive interfaces. However, such an artwork often confronts criticism such as it is »a tech demo«, or »too positive toward technology«, or »too playful«. With the aforementioned cultural background in Japan we would ask back: Isn't technology an important theme of art, when our life and society is so much dependent on it? Isn't it an artist who could reveal and visualize what technology really means to us? Should an artist be always negative to technology? Why shouldn't an artist show a new, more creative use of technology that the industry would not think of? And what is wrong with being playful, if an artwork still contains a serious theme?

As a discussion among the members took place it became clear that elements from traditional culture play an important role, although they are not necessarily visible when looking at the artworks themselves. Almost without exception, artworks themselves share international aesthetics without a »Japanese« look. These elements are related to the borders between art and its related fields, and to the nature of interplay between artists and appreciators. However, these are the issues that media artists face, especially with interactive art. This is why stating and understanding Device Art can be a contribution to the international media art scene. In fact, Device Art practice is widely seen and accepted in Japan, but not limited to Japanese artworks [44].

43 There was a heated argument at *Ars Electronica* 2009 when an interactive category jury Erkki Huhtamo raised an issue that many of the entered works to the category are not truly interactive.

44 In fact, the art initiative *Kontejner* in Zagreb, Croatia, has organized *Device Art* exhibitions in 2006 and 2009 as a parallel phenomenon. After noticing each other's activity, Japanese device artists were invited to the 2009 show. In February 2010 I co-curated two Device Art exhibitions at UCLA with Eric Siu, one focusing on Japanese device art and gadgets, the other featuring works by UCLA graduate students and alumni.

Interaction between Art, Science, Technology and Entertainment

There is little doubt that science and technology have major impacts on society and culture, while their course of development is heavily influenced by social and cultural elements. Similarly, art and its related fields such as design interact with society, as well as with science and technology [45]. Although it is generally believed that artists use tools and technology that had become available thanks to scientists and engineers, desire for achieving unprecedented expression have often driven artists to develop new technology or new application that engineers had not thought of or dared to realize. In fact, works by experimental artists focused on exploring what media technology may bring us, pushing the border of art, and sometimes even influencing the industry [46].

Popular culture has also played an important role in the history of media technology. A case in point is the invention of photography, which was carried by Louis-Jacques-Mandé Daguerre who, originally with Joseph Nicéphore Niépce, developed the Daguerreotype out of the necessity to perform realistic paintings in a large scale for his extremely successful diorama shows [47]. Since the quest for novelty is essential in the highly competitive visual entertainment business, some of the ambitious and creative showmen/businessmen became inventors as in case of Daguerre. At the same time, better parts of visual entertainment often involved artists for whom aesthetic quality had an importance. Historical examples include panorama painting, film, and animation that are both artistic and entertaining [48]. From another aspect, turning the scientific experiment itself into entertainment used to be a popular phenomenon. London's Royal Polytechnic was known for such »spectacles« developed by scientists, including the famous mid 19th century *Pepper's Ghost* invented and performed by John Henry Pepper. It became a standard public attraction of its own, but was also used for special effects at theatres. Popular electric spectacles were shown in many places in late 19th to early 20th century. In fact, a history of science and technology as entertainment can be traced back to the 17th century curiosity cabinet [49]. Sometimes inventions by serious scientists immediately turned into entertainment, as in case of Sir David Brewster's *Kaleidoscope* (1816) and improved *Stereoscope* (1849) or the Belgian physicist Joseph Plateau's *Phenakistiscope*—which prepared a basis for cinema—for which the scientist himself produced beautiful picture discs [50].

45 Walter Benjamin pointed the impact of media technologies to art in *The Work of Art in the Age of Mechanical Reproduction Technologies*.

46 Examples of such cases are known in avant-garde art and media art. A case in point is the real-time satellite programs produced by Nam June Paik in the 1980s. Another example is the world exposition in Osaka in 1970, for which major pavilions and spectacles were designed by avant-garde artists, including E.A.T. members led by the American Billy Kluver. The Osaka Expo '70 formed a basis for later development in display technology, interactive entertainment, among others.

47 More recently some of the major inventions in virtual reality were done by artists and those who worked with artists, such as Dan Sandin, Tom DeFanti, Myron Krueger, David Rokeby among others. While high-end computer graphics in the 1980s was never real-time, and real-time graphics used in military or industrial application did not require aesthetics, artists working with dance, music, or interactive representation needed to acquire real-time and artistically satisfying image. Artists such as Christa Sommerer and Laurent Mignonneau, Rafael Lozano-Hemmer, and Paul DeMarinis are well known for innovative user interfaces they develop.

48 For example, Oscar Fischinger's works include publicities for

As can be seen from these examples, art, science and technology were not necessarily divided. Just to add, the history of optics was woven through the network of influences among science, technology, art, and popular culture [51]. Attitude towards technology in a society is a historical and cultural issue. Appreciation of technology as hobbies and entertainment took place in Europe toward the end of the feudal era, in forms such as wonder cabinets, grottos and automata dolls. However, it remained mostly among the nobles and the intellectuals, and had little to do with people's life, or mass culture. The collapse of the feudal regime and the arrival of the Industrial Revolution put an end to such casual use of technology. Technology was no longer fun when human beings were required to work according to the pace of machines, being used by machines, instead of using them. Although it is not a main theme of this essay, the cultural histories of automata and robots in the West and in Japan offer an insight on human-machine relationship in a society.

Jacques de Vaucanson (1709–1782) is known for his *Duck* and other extremely sophisticated automata, which he demonstrated in major cities and for the nobles. He was also the inventor of an innovative mechanical loom that was later in 1801 modified by Joseph Marie Jacquard into perfection to play a crucial role in the formation of the Industrial Revolution [52]. It is said that Vaucanson had to leave the region he had brought the new looms to, because he caused the rage of local farmers. They used old style looms to earn small money, but eventually lost in competition against »capitalists« who had introduced Vaucanson's efficient looms. Japanese automata (*karakuri*) master Hisashige Tanaka (1799–1881) was a famous showman with his *Arrow-Shooting Boy* and *Calligraphy Writing Boy*, among others. He also made tea-carrying dolls, which had been made by others as well, and were used at teahouses to serve tea for guests, including normal people who were interested in the new service [53]. Eventually Tanaka took a major role in industrializing the country as he was commissioned by the new Meiji government and founded his engineering company, which later developed into *Toshiba*.

cigarettes. Today music videos and »cultural« games created by artists blur the border between art and commercial activities.

49 *International Electric Exhibition* in 1882 at Crystal Palace attracted visitors to experience the new technology. Electric illumination and other application of electricity were a »must« at world fairs. The *Pavilon de l'Electricité* at the 1937 Paris World Fair sort of summarized the cultural history of electricity with a huge mural painted by Raoul Dufy. The history of science turned into visual entertainment is described in detail in: (Stafford, 2001)

50 Another example is the invention of usable magic lantern, which, according to recent studies, is attributed to Christiaan Huygens. Huygens, possibly reluctantly, performed magic lantern performances with ghost apparition, when his diplomat father requested it for his guests.

51 For example, discoveries and inventions in optics directly influenced art through the establishment of realism, while scientific discoveries achieved by the use of lens including telescopes and microscopes changed people's vision of the world and eventually helped reforming the society.

52 Later a Japanese inventor, Sakichi Toyoda, made further development to achieve

more efficiency, and exported his looms abroad. An example is preserved at the British Science Museum in London. His company developed into *Toyota*, which is known for automobiles today. Vaucanson was listed among the »great inventors« for his mechanical loom in a series of illustrated texts used for elementary education in 19th century Japan, reflecting the government's policy to make the textile industry a major resource for trading. A color woodblock print of Vaucanson as a young boy is in the author's collection.

53 A book of *karakuri* published by Hanzo Hosokawa in 1796 sold many copies and had been a popular guide for manufacturing the automata.

54 There are ample examples in the author's collection. There were strict cultural codes concerning gender, age and season that applied to colors and patterns for outer *kimono*. As the contrast, innovative patterns could be used for underwear. The codes did not apply to children's *kimono*.

The parallel and the difference between the trajectories of Vaucanson and Tanaka illustrate the historical condition of Japan. Tanaka lived almost exactly a century later than Vaucanson, and he became involved in modern mechanical engineering business in the urge of rapid modernization of the country. The new government, which started in 1868, was determined to modernize and industrialize the country as fast as possible: China lost the First Opium War in 1842, and its consequence was seriously understood in Japan. Industrialization was a national demand. While there were cases that rapid industrialization brought serious problems to local communities or to workers, it did not change the positive attitude towards technology among the Japanese. Appreciating technology for fun, as in case of tea-carrying automata, was soon woven into daily life and industry. Entertainment technology such as cinema and gramophone were brought to Japan immediately after their inventions. In less than forty years after the collapse of the feudal society, people were familiar with devices such as magic lanterns and cameras, among other consumer gadgets. Mechanical toys became a successful export industry until the use of metal for entertainment was banned in 1937 because of the war. Intimate feeling for machines for entertainment is most typically seen with kimono textile patterns depicting cameras, projectors, and gramophones, which were mainly used for underwear or for children's kimono [54] . People wore machines next to their skin!

250 Years of Isolation

Japan is one of the countries that adopted the Western paradigm of art only relatively recently—with foundation of museums and art schools in the late 19th century. The reason is historical: The country closed its border to the rest of the world for about 250 years, from the beginning of the 17th century to the mid 19th century, except for limited trade relationship with China and Holland. Although the closure was not total, unique features in Japanese culture developed under such condition (Screech, 2002) . The Japanese word *bijutsu* first appeared as a translation of the term fine art when Japan was preparing to take part in the World Exposition in Vienna in 1873. Until the late 19th century, there was no concept such as fine art or art in Japan. As ironic as it seems, this is the very condition that brought about the current richness of media art in Japan. Absence of art as a paradigm does not mean that pursuit of beauty or the desire for expression did not exist. Rather, they were woven into the fabric of the culture in the form of a sense of beauty in daily life and the tools or methods to realize them, instead of being considered a special or privileged act. From things enjoyed by ordinary people, such as *bonsai*, *kabuki*, and *ukiyo-e* (woodblock print), to the higher-class pleasures of their gardens, folding screens, and *noh*, values that did not strictly distinguish among art, design, and entertainment had spread widely into every corner of society.

Why Japanese art was not represented by paintings framed and hung on walls, as in the West? A reason is an architectural issue. While walls are fundamental elements with houses and buildings in the West, Japanese houses are structurally different [55]. Columns support the structure to keep the space open, as sliding doors enabled flexible use of space and sufficient airflow, which was essential in hot and humid summer. There is usually a narrow wall called *tokonoma*, which serves for a piece of hanging scroll and a piece of flower arrangement. Both the picture and the flowers must be changed according to the season and occasions. They had a temporal nature. The amount of walls is minimized, and so is the number and variety of large furniture pieces. This also explains, at least partly, why artistic creativity in Japan was focused on mobile objects (such as sliding doors and screens, hanging scrolls, prints, textiles for kimonos) and for daily use, smaller objects and gadgets (such as boxes for stationary, bonsai, miniature garden, or *netsuke*), which is considered an ancestor of miniature figures on cell phone straps today. The historical background is even more important when we consider the Japanese attitude towards technology. Both the absence of serious warfare during this period and the late arrival of capitalism contributed to the Japanese approach towards technology. While some of the latest scientific and technological discoveries reached the country during the time of closure, they were mainly used for hobbies, entertainment and spectacles instead of developing weapons or factory machines. Japanese love for technology, which is a well-known phenomenon, could be traced back to such historic background. Already in the late 19th century, foreigners who started arriving in Japan were impressed by the curiosity towards new things among ordinary Japanese people they met, which made a sharp contrast to the Chinese attitude that they had been familiar with (Screech, 2002) [56]. Today, curiosity towards technical innovation, a positive attitude towards technology, and an appreciation of playfulness are often observed features in Japanese media art. Device Art discusses these issues.

[55] The use of space is extremely different when comparing a typical Japanese family house to its equivalent in a Victorian era European house. Europeans who arrived in Japan in the mid 19th century and had chances to visit castles of Shogun or feudal lords recorded that they were surprised to see no furniture in wide, open rooms. Some of them understood the difference in culture while others thought it was a sign of poverty, judging from their own standard.

[56] The sociologist Kazuko Tsurumi analyzes curiosity as an important element in Japanese culture in: (Tsurumi, 1972)

Mitate as an Effective Tool

In interactive art, artworks should invite viewers to interact. Because of such nature interactive artworks are often playful, at least on their surface. Unfortunately such playfulness is often misunderstood as lack of seriousness or criticism. Especially in Western art history there is a strong tradition in appreciating seriousness, which is often accompanied by a bias against the use of technology. The situation is different in Japan. An appreciation of playfulness is deeply embedded in the culture, often accompanied by *mitate*, which is a method to present and read hidden meanings behind what is shown or written. *Mitate* has a rich meaning, but it basically means »seeing beyond the actuality«. The word also implies that the vision is temporary rather than final. *Mitate* allows alternative ways of seeing. It plays a magic to turn an ordinary or even trivial object into something extraordinary and unexpected, as in case of rocks and pebbles in famous Japanese gardens. As the result, *mitate* allows an artist to set a multitude of layers in his/her work. The top layer may be playful and entertaining, but a serious theme may be read behind the playfulness. *Mitate* itself is an intellectual play between the artist, the artwork, and the viewers. Like unexpected objects used in the tea ceremony, *mitate* provides fun of discoveries and imagination to participants. An attitude that finds importance in the process, in the way time is structured, and in the atmosphere of a place, rather than in the result of a series of performances, is typically seen with the tea ceremony and is closely connected to the absence of the concept of art. A playful relationship based on a common understanding is set between an artist and the viewer with *mitate*, in this case an act of appropriating things originally used for a totally different purpose as tea utensils.

The explosion of visual entertainment—supported by inexpensive full-color printing technology and high literacy rate in urban areas—was behind the scene. Finding a hidden meaning from *ukiyo-e*, a *kabuki* plot, or a garden, became a cultural hobby. Inexpensive illustrated novels became best sellers, and making satirical short poems called *senryu* and *kyoka* became popular among common people [57]. These short poems are casual and often satirical versions of *haiku* and *waka*. The long history of short poems—the first existing official compilation of *waka* goes back to the 8th century—nursed aforementioned *mitate* as a cultural tradition. A short poem could convey a rich meaning only by triggering imagination and association in a reader's mind, by fully using shared knowledge, common understanding, citation, reference, as well as techniques such as double meanings

[57] Full color woodblock printing technology was developed in mid 18th century by Harunobu Suzuki, who was not only a major *ukiyo-e* artist but also a member of a cultural and casual community of *kyoka* poets that included those who had access to latest technologies brought by the Dutch. Scientific and technical objects and knowledge were often distributed through

and wordplay. Already by the 11th century, poem making and reading became an important mode of communication requiring certain knowledge to be shared. It became a cultural game, in a sense, with which intelligence and playfulness were contested. When the feudal Edo Shogunate prohibited use of contemporary issues as themes of *kabuki*, *ukiyo-e*, literature, etc., in order to prevent critical or political messages to appeal to the mass, *mitate* became a popular trick for writers and artists to play. A contemporary event such as a political scandal will be transformed into another time-space story, while maintaining clues for the viewers/readers to get the real meanings. Since expression of extravaganza or appreciation of pleasure culture was also often prohibited, the art of suggestive expression and embedding hidden meanings highly developed. Such needs for disguise had another feature as a cultural game between artists/ writers and viewers/readers.

such communities that loosely integrated cultural figures regardless of the classes they belonged to, from normal towns-people to feudal lords.

The Culture of *Asobi*

Even during such period of strict control, playfulness was highly appreciated. The gap between the real meaning and its representation creates an extra fun as long as the clues work. The viewers' / readers' knowledge level and ability of imagination were also contested. It is a unique form of user participation in a sense that a cultural interplay is expected in presenting and reading images and texts. It forms a part of » culture of play «, or culture of *asobi*. *Asobi* is the word for playing in Japanese, which is closer to »jeu« in French, rather than »play« in English that also means acting and performing. Similar to »jeu«, *asobi* implies »flexibility within a machinery« in a positive sense. For example, certain space would be needed between gears to avoid excessive friction [58]. The idea behind may be interpreted as such: a machinery or society would not function if it did not allow an extra space for its components or members. *Asobi* is an extra space for our mind that may not directly contribute to productive activities but is needed to live better, and to maintain the society with less friction. A positive attitude towards *asobi* in Japanese culture is already clearly seen by the 12th century. *Choju Giga*, or *Scrolls of Frolicking Animals*, is a collection of illustrations depicting various animals behaving as human beings including rabbits and frogs enjoying *sumo* (Japanese wrestling) [59]. The fact that the set of scrolls is attributed to a highest rank priest Toba Sojo and has been kept as a treasure for many centuries suggests the playful illustration

58 The importance of *asobi* in machinery was probably a practical knowledge in Japan, where most gears were made of wood (for agricultural and other machines and sophisticated automata)

until late 19th century. (Hisashige Tanaka's elaborated mechanical dolls were also composed of wooden gears.) Although hard wood such as chestnut was used for such purposes, a wooden gear changes its size according to the degree of humidity. Typically it shrinks during winter when the air is dry, and expands in summer. Not only gears but also parts of furniture such as sliding doors or drawers have to be made under such consideration.

59 The calligraphic drawings are dynamic and based on accurate observation of animal behavior. Because of its style and playful touch *Choju Giga* is often considered the ancestor of Japanese Manga.

60 There is no evidence that the scrolls (currently in four parts) were painted by Toba Sojo himself, although he was known for such style. The scrolls were kept at Kozanji Temple in Kyoto, and are now deposited to National Museums in Kyoto and Tokyo as a national treasure.

61 Translation by Mitsukuni Yoshida (Yoshida, 1987)

62 For an analysis of the culture of *asobi* in relation to contemporary gaming culture in Japan, see (Kusahara, 2004)

of the animals enjoying their life was highly appreciated, approved, and loved even by priests [60]. A lyric from the same era also confirms positive attitude toward play. It is included in *Ryojin Hisho*, an official compilation of popular songs edited by the Ex-emperor Goshirakawa in the 12th century.

»Are children born with the impulse to play?
Are children born seeking the delights of play?
Ah! The merry sounds of frolicking children
Bestir the urge to play in this old body and soul.« [61]

By the 18th century, the culture of play was widespread [62]. Besides aforementioned *mitate* and short poems with comical or satirical nature, there were many forms of *asobi* that normal people could afford. For example, a card game based on *hyakunin-isshu* (a collection of one hundred *waka* poems by one hundred poets from the medieval era), which had originally been a game for aristocrats, grew popular among ordinary people as the inexpensive woodblock printing technology was established. Selected medieval poems are printed with beautiful illustrations. Hokusai, whose woodblock prints of Mount Fuji are well known, illustrated for such cards as well. Incidentally Nintendo was founded 120 years ago originally as a publisher of *hyakunin-isshu* and other card games. Playfulness, entertaining inventions, commercially available products—these features often seen in media art today reflect a long Japanese cultural tradition. Use of latest technologies for entertaining purposes has a long history as well.

Could Anyone be Picasso?

The process of defining art took place in the late 19th century with such cultural background. The academic notion of art began to gain a foothold through teachers invited from the West and painters who returned from studying abroad, while Western art and Japanese art continued to exist as separate concepts. Modes of expression rooted in mass culture did not change immediately simply as a result of building museums and providing art education. An awareness that anyone could try their own expression, as well as the culture of *mitate*, survived and developed outside the world of academic art. In a society that has an implicit understanding that anyone could produce aesthetic creations (a message also stressed by the avant-garde artist Taro Okamoto, who had a great influence in the post-war era) and that any aspect of daily life could offer an opportunity to create beauty, the boundary between art and its related fields cannot be automatically settled. A popular TV program that lasted for 12 years until March 2009 titled *Takeshi-no Daredemo Picasso* (meaning *Takeshi Presents Anyone can be Picasso*), an »art program« broadcasted at the best time of the week (every Friday evening from 10 to 11pm), with the internationally recognized film director and former standup comedian Takeshi Kitano, is an interesting example of an outcome of such understanding. The program invited professional and amateur artists, presenting their works that included lunch box art or paper cup art, to name a few. The title sequence and the website were designed by aforementioned Takashi Murakami, a contemporary artist who is known for his intentional activities to mingle art and commercialism as an artistic statement. While there was a sense of irony in the way Kitano presented the guests, placing clear borders between art and non-art was carefully avoided. People are allowed to enjoy the feeling that anyone can be as creative as Picasso, or to embrace an idea that there is no border between works by professional artists and those by amateurs. Recent popularity of creative activities such as fan fiction, *kosupure* and music composition using *VOCALOID* such as HATSUNE Miku could be also seen from that point of view [63].

[63] Vocaloid is a »virtual singer« system developed by Yamaha. By inputting voice data, a user can have one's music »sang« by a virtual character. HATSUNE Miku is a virtual character in a form of a young girl in Anime style that Crypton Future Media Inc. released in August 2007 as a VOCALOID, which became a phenomenon immediately.

Device Art Works and their Features

In this essay I have introduced elements in Japanese traditional culture from both historical and contemporary contexts. Instead of presenting a conclusion—which should be already quite clear—I will introduce some of the works from Device Art Project members and analyze how they could be related to what I have discussed. Ryota Kuwakubo's *Nicodama* is an example of conscious use of *mitate* in art [64]. It is a pair of »eyeballs« that blinks together when they are attached to any objects from everyday life. Since we have a specific sensitivity to recognize things with eyes as faces, the two artificial eyeballs turn those inanimate objects into some kind of personalities. The idea comes from the artist's personal experience from his childhood, but it also refers to our perception mechanism, and to his long lasting theme to create simple interfaces to help people understand their relationship to the environment. *Nicodama* is a device of *mitate*, to guide the viewers' perception. By turning objects such as chairs, a pair of boots, a flower vase, etc., into something we

[64] The piece was titled *Nicodama* when shown at museums. The production model is named *Nikodama*.

somehow recognize as »personalities«, the artist suggests we could establish a more friendly relationship with these objects rather than seeing them as mass-produced objects without any character. The approach is playful, but a serious concern about environmental issues and consumption culture is behind the artwork. Another aspect of the work is the artist's consciousness on traditional belief and its contemporary meaning. *»We cannot go back to Animism, through which people maintained respects to nature. But we could revive the positive element in animism by the use of latest technology«*, Kuwakubo says. Interestingly enough, an online advertisement by one of the distributors claims: *»You can be a god with this, giving life to anything!«* Kuwakubo has created a series of interactive artworks including *LoopScape*, a game-like piece for two people with an ironical interaction. It is a battle between two players who would try to shoot the other person's spaceship. It sounds like a most traditional shooting game, except that the game screen is a cylinder hung from the ceiling. One easily shoots and explodes one's own spaceship by mistake (thus killing oneself in the game world) if the other person manages to avoid the missile. The only way to win is to run around the screen, following one's own spaceship. Simply by changing the form of the screen Kuwakubo turned a shooting game into a playful yet ironical artwork asking many questions on the nature of games and game playing.

Kazuhiko Hachiya has a long career in creating artworks and projects, as well as commercial products, dealing with our mode of communication. In his recent *Fairy Finder* series fairies are discovered under a tabletop at a café, as the table is assimilated to the roof of the fairyland. *ThanksTail* is a car accessory, which was commercialized by a subsidiary of Takara, a major toy manufacturer. Once attached at the rear end of the car's roof, the »doggy-tail« could be remotely wagged to thank other drivers when they yielded the way to the owner of the tail. Since the concept of *ThanksTail* is in providing a friendly communication tool to drivers—and a surprise and smile to passers-by—Hachiya had no intention to keep it in museums or galleries. After creating a prototype he uploaded a call for collaboration on his website. It was discovered by someone from the company who was looking for an interesting idea, and thus collaboration took place. The work has features that I have described in this essay, such as playfulness, commercializing, and *mitate*.

Some other works by Hachiya, such as *AirBoard*, *Open Sky*, and *PsychoCommunicator* (co-developed with Taro Maeda, another member of the project) have direct links to popular culture [65]. These

[65] Open Sky is not part of Device Art according to the artist's concept.

works enable experiencing inventions presented in the following films: *Back to the Future*, *Nausicaa Of The Valley Of The Wind*, and GUNDAM. The artist realized these inventions using latest technology such as the world smallest jet engine. Playfulness and sense of danger co-exist hand in hand—Hachiya has been test-piloting the personal jet glider himself. The concept behind *Open Sky* is an objection against monopoly. He hopes to open the sky to individuals, not only by flying himself but also by using open source software, publishing his design/development process, uploading document videos on YouTube, and making the project an arena for collaboration and discussion. The internationally exhibited *Inter Dis-Communication Machine* shares playfulness and irony of technology mediated communication. In these works *Mitate* is used in association to popular culture such as a Hollywood entertainment film or a popular animation that everyone knows, providing an easier access to those who are not necessarily familiar with art.

Elements of Japanese traditional culture such as *mitate*, an appreciation of playfulness, respect for tools, the culture of *kata* (form, or practice patterns) and the fusion of art and entertainment are fully analyzed and used in an original manner by Novmichi Tosa (*Maywa Denki*). He uses *mitate* to assimilate his art unit as a small-scale company led by a CEO (Tosa) who invents strange products one after another to survive. By doing so, his works and performances acquire multiple layers of meanings. Commercial products are »mass-produced« at a factory in China. It is another important layer when China supplies a great majority of inexpensive goods to be consumed. Playfulness contributes in bringing art outside museums and galleries, enabling even commercial production and distribution of artwork to reach a wider public. Some of them could be used as devices or gadgets in everyday life. By rejecting the traditional idea that draws a line between art and commercial products, artists uncover possibilities and problems media technology brings to us. They offer us an alternative point of view by using well-known technology in a clever and unexpected manner. Like avant-garde artists experimented with the latest technologies of their time, contemporary media artists try to understand what it means to live in a world full of new technology. Their goal is not in residing within the traditional norm of art but in discovering new meanings of art. As the Device Art Project has revealed, rediscovering an alternative viewpoint on the relationship between art, design, technology and entertainment will be a useful idea. I believe in the importance of digital biodiversity and the role of art in it.

References

Benjamin, W.: *The Work of Art in the Age of Mechanical Reproduction.*
Frankfurt a.M., 1936

Driesche, F.: *Gramophone, Film, Typewriter.*
Berlin: Brinkmann und Bose, 1986; Stanford: Stanford University Press, 1999

Hara, K.: *Designing Design*. 2nd Ed. Baden: Lars Müller Publishers, 2007
Original Japanese version: Tokyo: Iwamani Publishing, 2003.

Kusahara, M.: »They Are Born to Play: Japanese Visual Entertainment from Nintendo to Mobile Phones«.
In: Kluszczynski, R. W. (Ed.): *Art Inquiry, Vol. V(XIV): Cyberarts, Cybercultures, Cybersocieties*. pp. 111–154.
Warsaw: LODZ, 2004

Kusahara, M.: »Device Art: A New Approach in Understanding Japanese Contemporary Media Art«.
In: Grau, O.: *MediaArtHistories*. pp. 277-307. Cambridge, Mass.: MIT Press, 2007

Kusahara, M.: *Mitate: Realizing Playfulness, Multiple Viewpoints and Complexity in Device Art.*
Belfast: ISEA, 2009

Screech, T.: *The Lens Within Heart: The Western Scientific Gaze at Popular Imagery in Late Edo Japan.*
Richmond: Curzon, 1996; Honolulu: University of Hawai'i Press, 2002

Stafford, B.: *Devices of Wonder: From the World in a Box to Images on a Screen.*
Los Angeles: J. Paul Getty Museum, 2001

Tsurumi, K.: *Kokishin-to Nihonjin (Curiosity and the Japanese).*
Tokyo: Kodansha, 1972

Yoshida, M.: *ASOBI: The Sensibilities at Play.*
Hiroshima: Mazda Motor Corporation, 1987

Dominick Chen

The Future of Creative Commodities in the Coded Cultures

This text is an extension of an article originally submitted (as *Prochronist Manifestation*) to: (Lovink, 2008) Based on a Japanese text originally submitted to the quarterly *10+1*, Tokyo: INAX Publishing, 2007. Special thanks to Naoki Matsuyama for all of his helps on initial translation and suggestions.

Today we live in cultures where digital data and our own material bodies interact in a ever-increasing intensity, especially through the dissemination of mobile communication devices. Our thoughts are broadcasted through the micro blogs and its synchronized feeds, to instantaneously pervade our surrounding social graphs. In such a situation, the cost of self expression continues to lower and creativity tends to become commodity; consequently, the delimitation of authorship for certain forms of expression becomes almost nonsensical. This article aims at shedding light to the future of such creative commodities in our increasingly code dependent cultures; how our definition of creativity can evolve by focusing on the idea of process and inheritance; and initiating a discussion of how to build its corresponding referential system.

1.0 Prochronist Manifestation

1.1 The Discreteness of the Completed, and the Continuity of Process

We are not a completed form of existence. Our bodies constantly undergo metabolic regeneration and our thinking constantly acquires new information. However, in order to formulate one's intentions or directives, it is inevitable to express them in a limited time and space. What one in fact does, is to dissect an aspect of thinking that constantly and fluidly undergoes altered formation, and to solidify it so to enclose it as something that belongs to one's own domain and subsequently release it to the other. Even the individuality of the individual who enacts this enclosure itself cannot easily be discerned. For a specialist of a certain field, one's singularity is unproblematically generated by the rarity of the own research. For example, if one's research field is only engaging 100 people in the whole world, there would be no effort required in identifying one's own singularity within that community. If however one attempts to work on a subject that more than a billion people in the world may be pre-occupied with, singularity is instantly diluted. Moreover, there is the issue, which could be named the »inertia of materialized expression«. When deciphering an abstract thesis or a logical connection, it is difficult to sense the originality of the writer as much as when looking at a drawing by a child. Umberto Eco said that a work would never come to resemble a dictionary. According to him, whereas the dictionary is inherently open to redefinition, the work requires a »minimum level of closure« in order to retain a certain identity (Charles, 1978) . What then, can guarantee this »minimum level of closure«?

Generally speaking, in our contemporary society, the recognition that a certain representational object, whether it be a text or a piece of music, was produced by an individual does not arise autonomously from the object itself. We accept a work as produced by a certain personage after the domain he belongs to, his ability in that domain and the context in which he lived, have been attested. We project diverse ideas to the context itself and therefore supplement the object in a different sphere from the one of the object itself or attribute excessive (or insufficient) value to it. There is an undeniable inaccuracy in this. The author has to communicate the essence of his self-hood without the temporal process that led him from production to result being known. In fact, we can only know each other in a way that eliminates most of the process, or in other words: the path that one took that demonstrates the »minimum level of closure« that assures the identity of the work. This is however an inevitable phenomenon that originates, to put it succinctly, in the increasingly complex social structure and the (physical) limit of human awareness. Even within an everyday conversation, we supplement each other's incomplete information to assess each other and repeatedly associating and dissociating contexts at extraordinary speed. This is especially true for urban life and its increasing flow of time and information. This is because our cognitive ability is not capable of focusing on the process. Despite the fact that even in every action of a child, when he is drawing, we can observe a rich accumulation and layering, we have cultivated neither a culture nor a technology that concentrates upon the accumulation over time of information that we daily exchange. Instead, by eliminating process we have, at an extraordinary rate, classified the world in grid-like manner and acquired technology to associate the similar elements within this classification. But what was all this for? Was it for worshipping those things that refuse classification under the name of the genius or the mystical? By dichotomising the world into the understandable and non-understandable, we could never attain a fundamental understanding of our own surrounding environment.

This is exactly why we now have to construct a method for collectively sharing not only the result, but also the gradual process that leads from generation to the present. It entails the shifting of our frame of reference from form to time and also points to the necessary experimentation on the critical point for human beings to dynamically record and share the processes of all the activities that affect interpersonal structure, from conscious self-expression to unconscious bodily gestures in the everyday. In this sense, just like philosophy was constructed as »love of wisdom«, what we today should begin to consider is »love of process« of information. This article will explore the epistemological inversion that a viewpoint based on the »process of information« would conduce to, and its eventual impact to our information cultures in this age of crowd-sourcing/ cloud-computing network.

1.2 Bateson's Prochronism and Homology

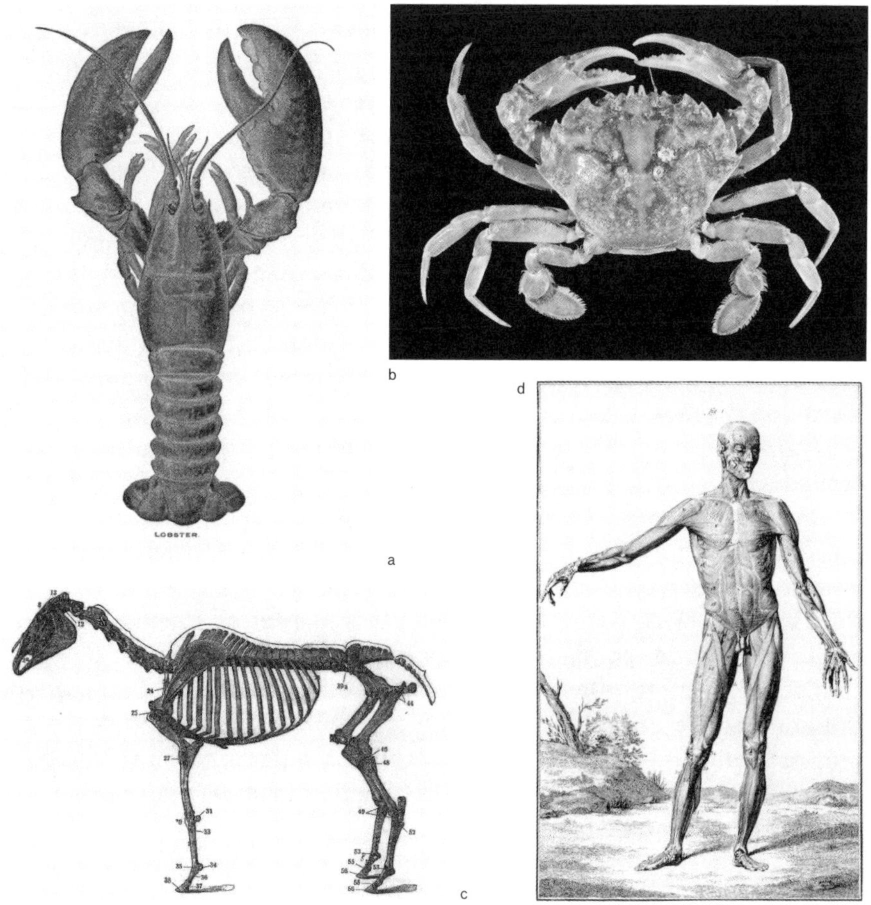

Fig. 1: Homologies of Crab and Lobster, Human and Horse.
a: Lobster Homarus americanus. Extracted from: Beach, C. B. (Ed.): *The New Student's Reference Work for Teachers, Students and Families*, 1914 / Wikimedia Commons
b: Excerpt from Crab Liocarcinus vernalis. Photograph by Hans Hillewaert from the Belgian coastal waters, 2005 / Wikimedia Commons
c: Bones of a horse (Equus caballus). Extracted from: *Nordisk familjebok* (1904–1926) / Wikimedia Commons
d: Human Anatomie. Extracted from: D'Alembert, Diderot: *Encyclopédie, ou Dictionnaire raisonné des sciences, des arts et des métiers*, 1751–1766 / Wikimedia Commons

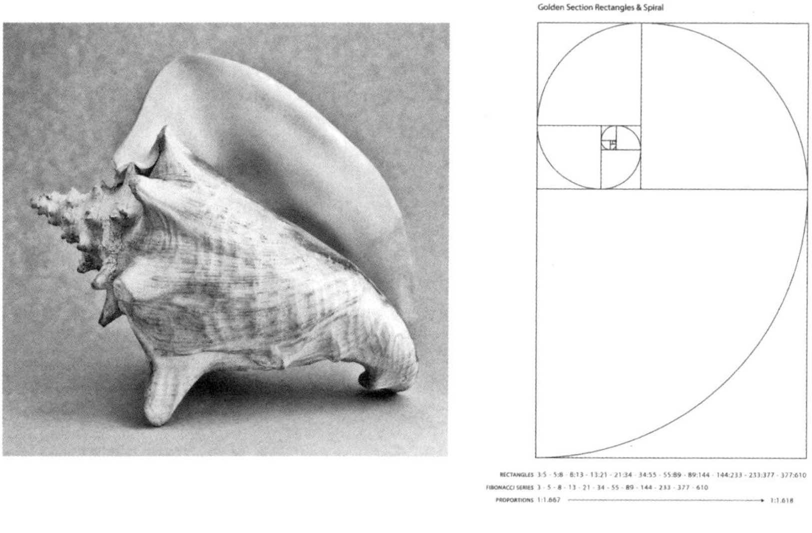

Fig. 2: Conch shell and the Fibonacci number. Excerpt from Conch Shell Photograph by windflower43.webshots.com / Fibonacci-number-Golden-Section.png, Wikimedia Commons.

The Biologist and cyberneticist Gregory Bateson asked the fundamental question »What is the pattern that connects all living organisms?« in his book *Mind and Nature* (Bateson, 2002) . He considered this questioning of the relationship between himself and a newly found entity, of the pattern that connects him with this entity as an »aesthetic problem«. There is a story about him from when he was a lecturer at the *San Francisco Art Institute* that is emblematic of this. One day as he entered the classroom, he abruptly placed a boiled crab that he had bought at the Fisherman's Wharf in front of the students. He then asked the students to assume that they did not know about an entity known as a »crab« and to prove that the object in front of them was the »remains of a living organism«. The bewildered students took some time to handle the crab to observe it, until one of them proposed an answer: *»This object is symmetrical. As all living organisms are symmetrical this object too is a living organism«*. To this Bateson replied, that »it (was) a good answer, but there (was) something more fundamental«, prompting a different answer from another student: *»the sizes of the right and left claws are different and therefore its morphology isn't symmetrical«*, however *»the two claws are made of the same pattern«*. Bateson appraised this answer as touching on the most fundamental point that can be the evidence of the crab being connected with other living organisms. In other words, he encouraged the students to draw their attention on the crab's embryological origin. By observing the morphology of each part of the crab and by speculating about the temporal transition that it underwent during its growth, it is possible to »understand« that the crab is a living organism just like the observer. In this case, the serial homology between the parts in the object's internal morphology forms first order connections, the phylogenetic homology between the crab and other similar living organism (e.g. lobster) forms second order connections and the homology between crabs and lobsters on one hand and human beings and other living organism (e.g. mammals) on the other form third order connections. This shows that the homological pattern is, unlike a simplistic analogy, a hierarchical connection. Bateson asked the students to carry out the same task with a conch shell. In this case the students could no longer rely neither on the similarities between different parts nor on the symmetrical property of the object.

What Bateson was here pointing to, was a law of a higher order: symmetry and segmentation are only the supervening outcome of the phenomenon of growth, and growth itself follows a morphological law. He described this as both the crab and the conch shell retaining the »prochronism« that presents the temporal transition that it underwent in its growth. In other words, all living organisms mark their own ecological process into their own body and exhibit this to the external world. It is because of this that living organism can, through the observation of each other's morphological layout, be homologous to each other. Bateson emphasizes that this hierarchical thinking owes itself to embryology. This means that the time that the living organism underwent from being an embryo to the present can be read at once, thus supplementing temporal observation on how the organism mutually interacts with the surrounding environment. This concept of prochronism is reminiscent of the concept of the invariant, a group of elements, which persists as invariable for a significant amount of time to the observing subject, coined by James Gibson in his theory of affordance. By perceiving the layout of invariants within an environment, living organisms understand what actions are possible, in relation with their own bodily specifications, within that environment (affordance). Similarly, by manifesting the trajectory of their lives through their own morphology, living organisms obtain a foothold for understanding the mutual association between each other. Moreover, an environment (a natural space that presents a certain amount of characteristics or an artificially enclosed architectural space) can be conceived as a living structure that also discloses a prochronism peculiar to itself when encountering another living organism. In this sense, we constantly afford each other, our prochronisms, in order to establish a mutual relationship. The manner of this affordance, as we shall see later, appears as »monstration« at the unconscious level and as »demonstration« at the conscious level, and we act and mutually interact on the basis of these different layers of information.

To directly read the subtle associations between an object that exists before our eyes and the surrounding environment including the observing self, not by compartmentalizing the world according to typological codes but by observing the internality of that object. The activities that a living organism has constantly carried out through its life are, in terms of a Uexküllian *Umwelt (environment world)*, identified differently according to the observer's mode of perception. We human beings have historically expanded our mode of perception by way of innovating and developing media technologies. What we should be drawing our attention to today however is the prochronism of the information that we daily produce, exchange, share and inherit through diverse media technologies. This will lead to the understanding of information as a living process and to the recognition of its embryology (Fig. 1 and 2).

1.3 Decoding Cultures: Observation Technology and its Epistemological Consequences

Today we live being surrounded by digital information. This domain, which has its foundation in the internet, forms for us a second nature (it could also be called »surrounding environment« or »environment world«). Before the permeation of the internet, our world-view was dominated by most information which was simply physically difficult to access. The mass of information that an individual can access today, however, exists there rawer than ever before. After the diffusion of the term web 2.0 and web-wares (general term indicating software that functions within the web browser or an operating system that functions within the server) the number of people actively transmitting information is steadily growing. Moreover, the rapid progress in information transmission and information sampling technology that is epitomized in the ever increasing weblogs, micro blogs and lifelogs, is now causing an exponential increase in the quantity of information around the world. These social as well as technological conditions are exerting a considerable influence on our cognitive awareness of the world. For example, when one wants to know, learn or remember something, the amount of information that can be literally accessed instantly is beginning to surpass our cognitive threshold for regarding the totality of information as a reliable resource. The digital data that constantly undergoes altered formation on the network, from software to contents, literally and not metaphorically, forms the environment in which our daily activities are performed. How do we interact with this environment?

In his book *Baroque of the Forest* (Nakazawa, 2006) , theologist Shinichi Nakazawa makes persistent reference to the epistemological inversion that occurred in the Western natural sciences in the 19th century, basing his analysis on Foucault's *Les Mots et les Choses (The Order of Things)* (Foucault, 1966) . Nakazawa draws our attention to the fact that the invention of the compound microscope at the beginning of the 19th century, caused the focus in the natural sciences to shift from phanerogamia to cryptogamia. Phanerogamia presents clear external characteristics that enabled, among other things, the development of Linnaean phylogenetic taxonomy. However, the dramatic improvement in resolution brought about by the compound microscope, enabled the observer to deal with cryptogamia that were invisible until then. Cryptogamia are a life form that function in a sphere that is imperceptible to the human naked eye (hence the name, crypt, something that exists as hidden) and it was the combined microscope that allowed scientists to discover them. Foucault states that the reason plant taxonomy flourished in the 17th and 18th century, was not because of an increased interest in plants, but simply because scientists only possessed a taxonomic space for the visible (»espace taxonomique de visibilité«) which was more adapted to plants than animals. The technological turning point caused by the combined microscope has, according to Foucault, led to the successes of Cuvier's anatomy and Bernard's physiology, which gave birth to a certain »vitalism«. This vitalism that focused on the invisible processes that internally drive living organisms, was later to be inherited by Darwin's theory of evolution and Mendel's genetics. Nakazawa asserts that *»although taxonomy may be one of the methods to approach the essential nature of life, it can never be the aim itself«*, illustrating the limitations of taxonomy by referring to the legendary scholar Kumagusu Minakata's research on mycetozoa which, because of their fluid alternation between animal-like and plant-like phases and the fact that each individual presents itself as a variant species, shook the very foundation of taxonomical natural sciences.

This 19th century vitalism later led to the observation of DNA at the molecular level due to the developments in scientific technology. Our society today is, at the most advanced level, able to observe up to the elementary particle level and is simultaneously beginning to equip the real world environment with nano-scale engineering technology such as M/NEMS (Micro/Nano Electro Mechanical System). This kind of technology however, is still out of reach for the general public to manipulate and in this sense the flexibility for its expansion only exists in limited form in the current situation. As mentioned before, our surrounding world is now replete with an enormous amount of information. In a paper entitled *Life (Vitalism)* (Lash, 2006) , Scott Lash elegantly unravels the genealogy of *Lebensphilosophie* (*philosophical speculation regarding life*). He distinguishes between the vitalists that focused on »perception« such as Jean-Gabriel Tarde, Bergson and later Deleuze, and those who focused on »power« such as Nietzsche, Georg Simmel and Foucault, and links these currents of thought to the contemporary endeavors of scholars such as Katherine Hayles and Donna Haraway to reconfigure our understanding of life within the totality of information (biomedia) in this information society.

> *»If classical vitalism conceives of life as a flow and in opposition onto the structure that would contain and stop it, then neo-vitalism would seem to have its roots in something like a media or information heuristic. Thus, there is talk today*

that ›information is alive‹ [...] The currency of vitalism has re-emerged in the context of (a) changes in the sciences, with the rise of ideas of uncertainty and complexity and (b) the rise of the global information society. This is because the notion of life has always favoured an idea of becoming over one of being, of movement over stasis, of action over structure, of flow and flux.« (Lash, 2006)

Surveying Lash's and Nakazawa's / Foucault's thoughts, one is left with the tangible impression that a vitalist thought process is a phenomenon that recursively emerges in the contemporary world. This is because of the correlation between the total amount of information that can be observed and manipulated and the limit of human cognitive ability. Here a possibility to explore the hypothesis emerges that—just as in the 19th century—the combined microscope increased the observational resolution of scientists, allowing them to access a sphere that was until then invisible. A similar change is occurring now at the beginning of the 21st century.

1.4 The Vitalist Interpretation of Information

Let us now look at the current conditions of the domain of media art. Here we will employ a broad definition for media art as all forms of representation that self-referentially utilize technology which is in each period advanced, encompassing the medieval visual apparatuses; the birth of reproduction technology such as the gramophone; the advent of electronic media such as the radio, television and video; and finally the dramatic developments in computing technology and the diffusion of the internet. Thus the historical view that is adopted is one, which sees the contents of the concept of media art being revised and redefined according to the alterations in media technology and society itself (cf. Huhtamo). The institutional space of media art, which is beginning to lose its radical quality within the context of art history after the 2000s due to the popularization of media technology as exemplified by the »cheap revolution« of the web, is currently facing problems regarding the multiplication/complexification of authorship, difficulties to establish a universally shared language, loss and recurrence of a comprehensive historicity. Despite these new developments the dominant methodology in media art research continues to be a taxonomical one. We are increasingly unable to critically discuss individual media art projects from the perspective of a sharable value system common to all. It is impossible to contribute to the construction of an evolutionary history by way of deducting the essence from an outcome. Archivists of media art are struggling in the confusion caused by post-modern rationale. It is in this kind of environment that we individually strive to connect philosophical thought, sociology, information sciences, aesthetics and poetics.

Wouldn't it be possible for us to begin to construct, just as baroque and romanticism prepared the ground for modernism, a new temporal axis which will succeed modernism and post-modernism? This is another objective of this present article. As a foothold for this, we have so far discussed the focus on process, the fact that such focus can be placed within the genealogy of vitalism, which then leads to the proposal of a value system based on such idea as prochronism and plasticity of information. Thus the present discussion will not take the position affirmed by bio-media, where life processes are reduced to the terms of information science. Rather, it understands information in a vitalist manner. What is the equivalent for the paradigm shift from phanerogamia to cryptogamia in the current mediascape that surrounds us? In order to answer this question, we must observe the formation and alteration of the different currents in software and contents development over the internet together with their groups of creators. Here, the environment formed by F/LOSS (*Free and Libre Open Source Software*) will be a crucial starting point. Black-box-like proprietary software can be regarded as phanerogamic software. What is now a synonym for proprietary software, namely the Windows OS of Microsoft, can only be assessed at its surface or functional level precisely because its source code is hidden. Contrastingly, the change that the birth of free software brought about was that anyone could access the internal algorithms that drive the operations at the surface level, because the code was now open source. We may regard this as the rise of cryptogamic software. Open source software and open contents are, due to the legal flexibility conferred upon them by digital copy-right licensing such as GNU GPL or Creative Commons, constantly open to the possibility of redefinition by individuals in different fields, or of inheritance and propagation to different aims and functions and contexts. Not only can we daily experience the manner in which information produced in different fields is automatically mashed up by several different algorithms to give birth to new information, but we can also observe such processes by utilizing log analysis technology.

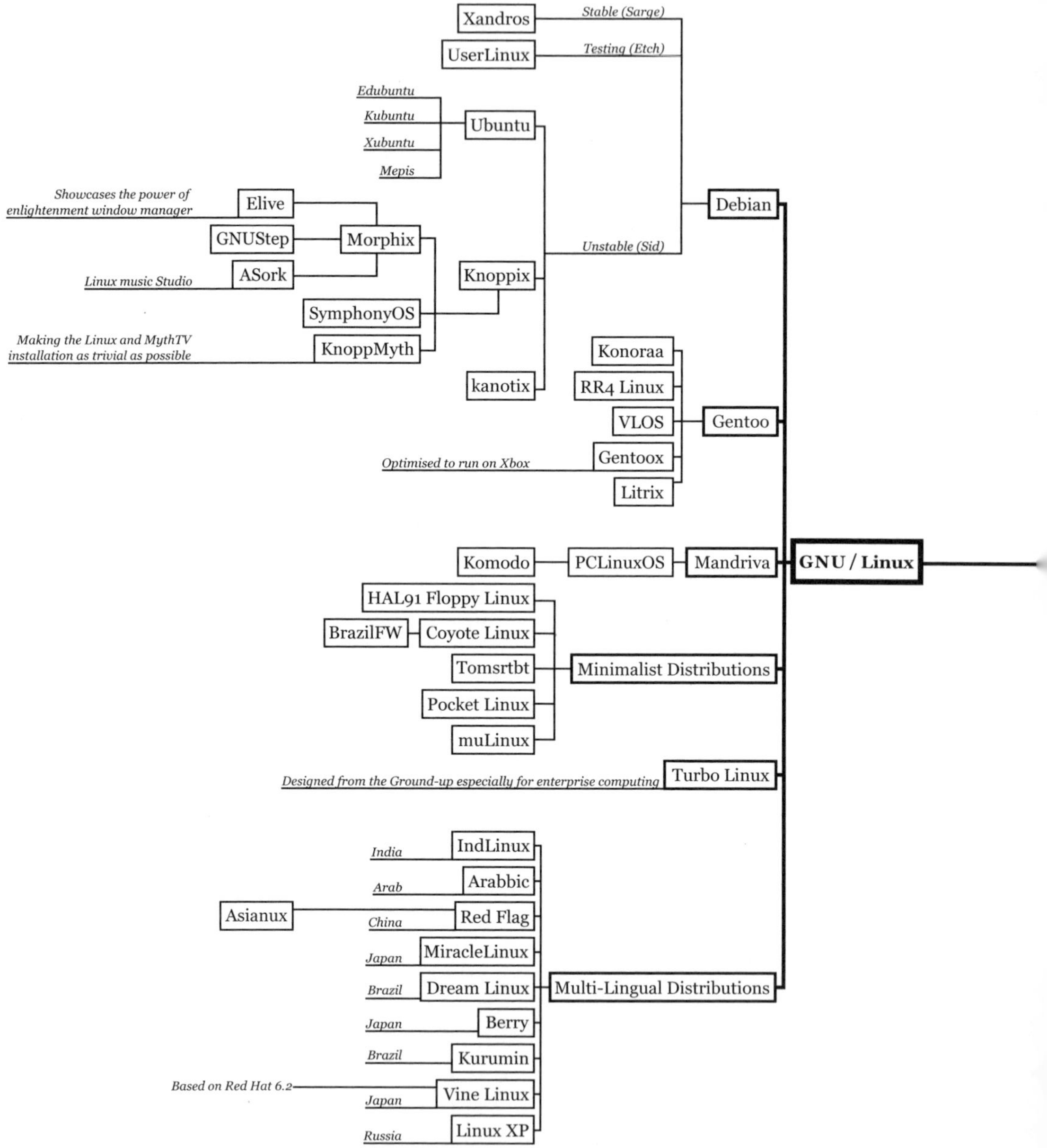
Xandros
Stable (Sarge)
UserLinux
Testing (Etch)
Edubuntu
Kubuntu
Xubuntu
Mepis
Ubuntu
Showcases the power of enlightenment window manager
Elive
GNUStep
Morphix
Debian
Unstable (Sid)
Linux music Studio
ASork
Knoppix
SymphonyOS
Making the Linux and MythTV installation as trivial as possible
KnoppMyth
kanotix
Konoraa
RR4 Linux
VLOS
Gentoo
Optimised to run on Xbox
Gentoox
Litrix
Komodo
PCLinuxOS
Mandriva
GNU / Linux
HAL91 Floppy Linux
BrazilFW
Coyote Linux
Tomsrtbt
Minimalist Distributions
Pocket Linux
muLinux
Designed from the Ground-up especially for enterprise computing
Turbo Linux
India
IndLinux
Arab
Arabbic
Asianux
China
Red Flag
Japan
MiracleLinux
Brazil
Dream Linux
Multi-Lingual Distributions
Japan
Berry
Brazil
Kurumin
Based on Red Hat 6.2
Japan
Vine Linux
Russia
Linux XP

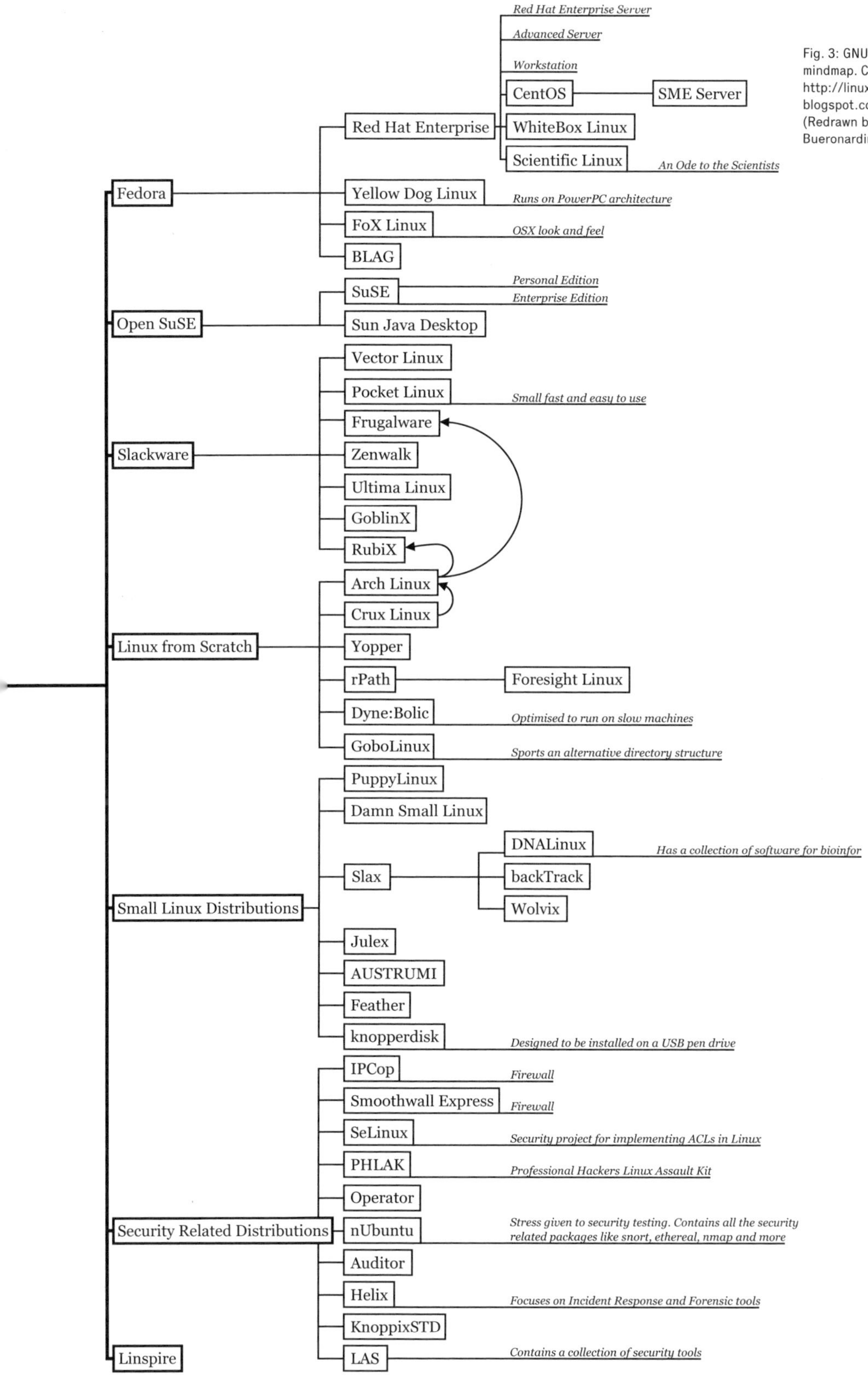

Fig. 3: GNU/Linux mindmap. Courtesy: http://linuxhelp.blogspot.com (Redrawn by Bueronardin)

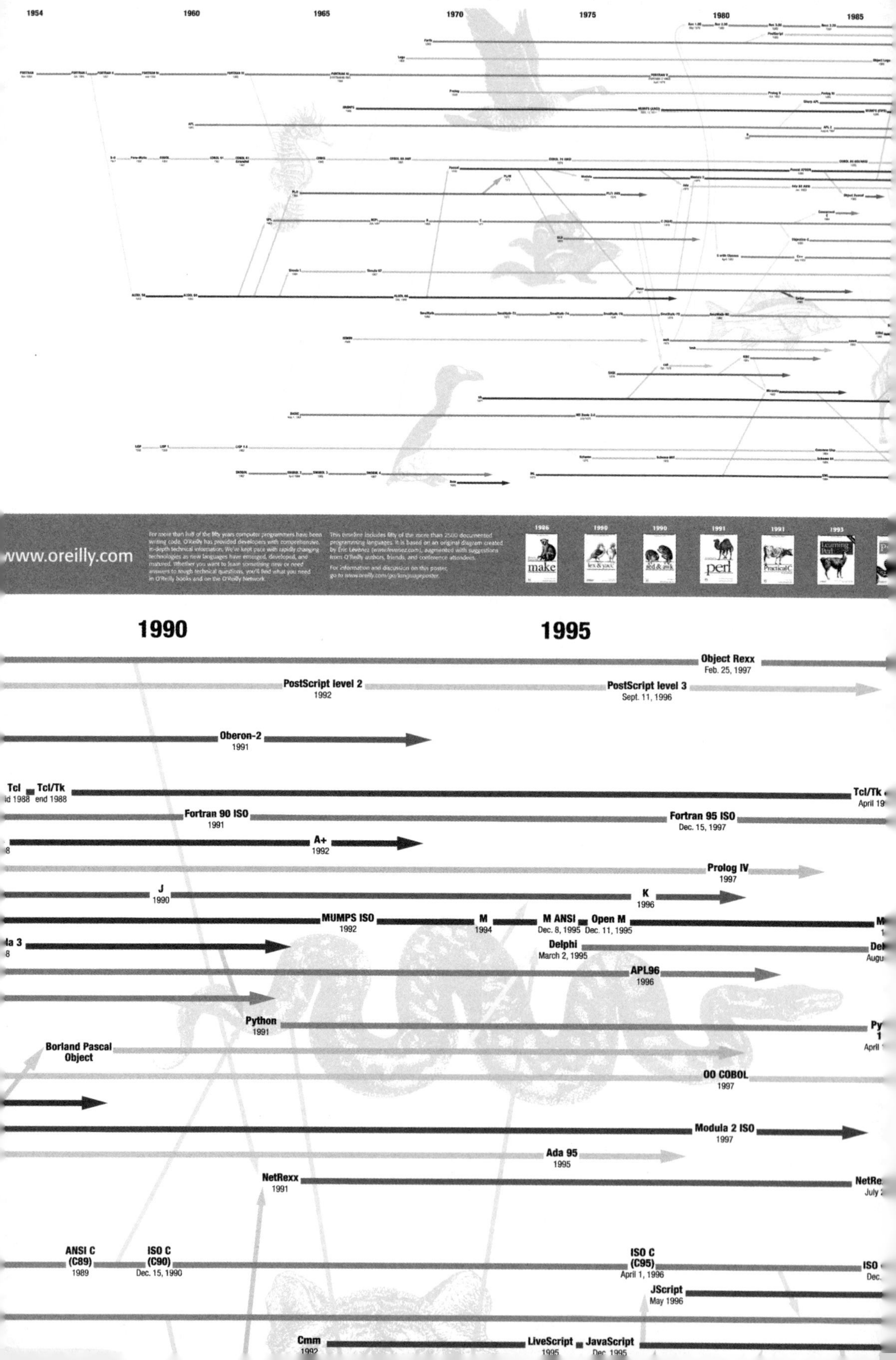
1954
1960
1965
1970
1975
1980
1985
www.oreilly.com
For more than half of the fifty years computer programmers have been writing code, O'Reilly has provided developers with comprehensive, in-depth technical information. We've kept pace with rapidly changing technologies as new languages have emerged, developed, and matured. Whether you want to learn something new or need answers to tough technical questions, you'll find what you need in O'Reilly books and on the O'Reilly Network.
This timeline includes fifty of the more than 2500 documented programming languages. It is based on an original diagram created by Éric Lévénez (www.levenez.com), augmented with suggestions from O'Reilly authors, friends, and conference attendees.
For information and discussion on this poster, go to www.oreilly.com/go/languageposter.
1986
1990
1990
1991
1991
1993
make
lex & yacc
sed & awk
perl
Practical C
Learning Perl
1990
1995
Object Rexx
Feb. 25, 1997
PostScript level 2
1992
PostScript level 3
Sept. 11, 1996
Oberon-2
1991
Tcl
id 1988
Tcl/Tk
end 1988
Tcl/Tk
April 19
Fortran 90 ISO
1991
Fortran 95 ISO
Dec. 15, 1997
A+
1992
Prolog IV
1997
J
1990
K
1996
MUMPS ISO
1992
M
1994
M ANSI
Dec. 8, 1995
Open M
Dec. 11, 1995
Delphi
March 2, 1995
APL96
1996
Python
1991
Borland Pascal
Object
OO COBOL
1997
Modula 2 ISO
1997
Ada 95
1995
NetRexx
1991
ANSI C
(C89)
1989
ISO C
(C90)
Dec. 15, 1990
ISO C
(C95)
April 1, 1996
JScript
May 1996
Cmm
1992
LiveScript
1995
JavaScript
Dec. 1995

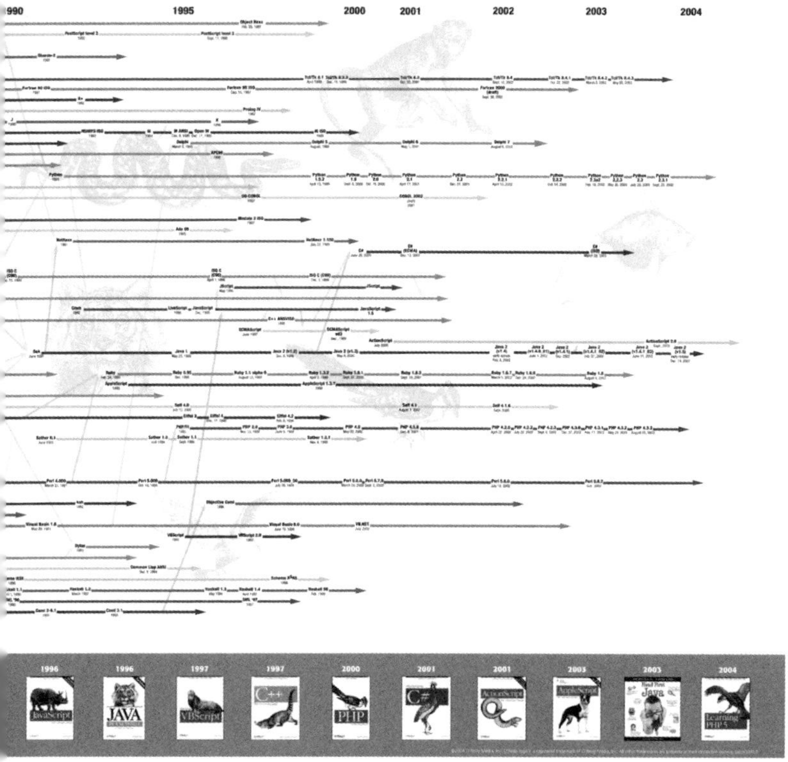

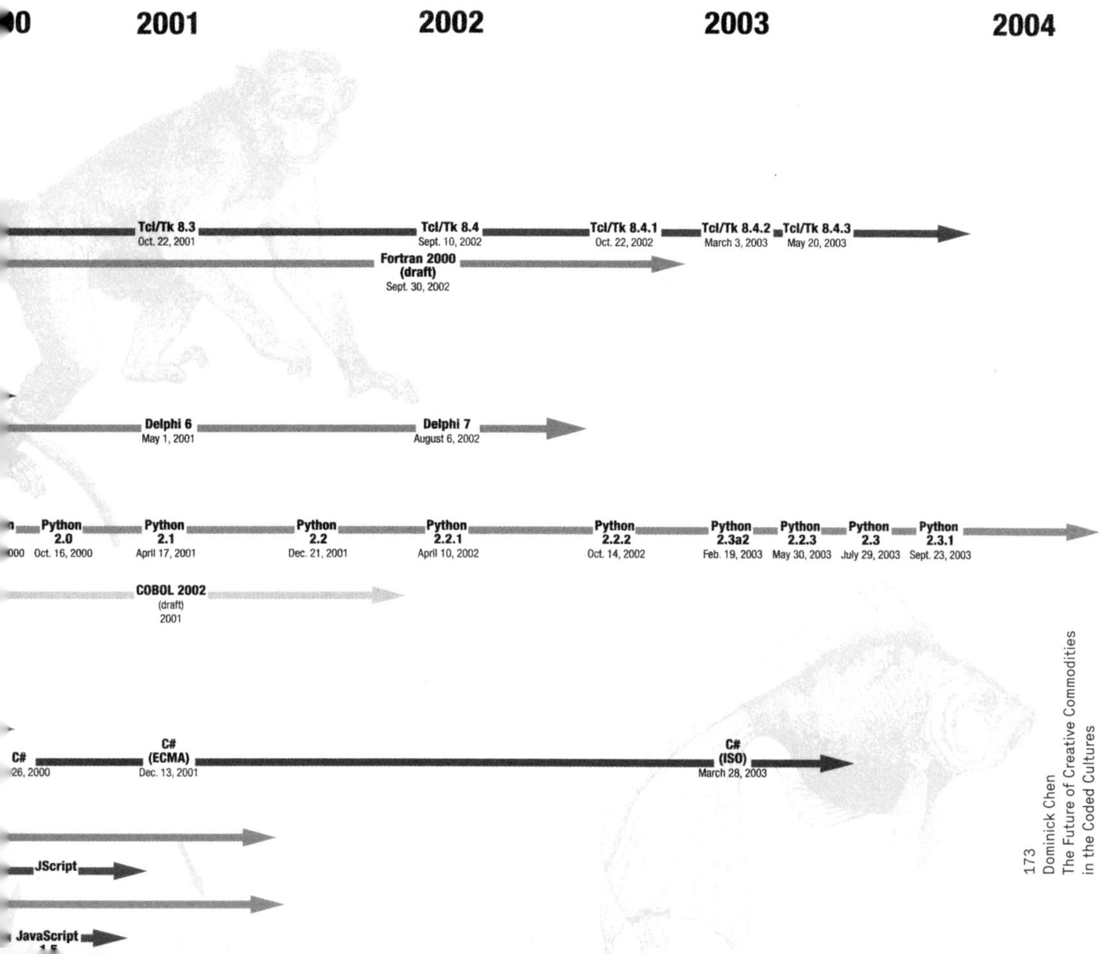

Fig. 4: The History of Programming Languages.
Excerpt from: http://www.oreilly.com/news/graphics/prog_lang_poster.pdf

Considering the fact that open source software has now established itself as the operating principle that leads the internet as an information infrastructure, we can consider the resolution for observing under what kind of logic information is produced and circulated (generally called media literacy) as increasing for everyone including the general user. In *The Wealth of Networks* legal scholar Yochai Benkler focuses, from a point of view of social justice, on the increased possibility for individuals in the 21st century network information society to know how the world functions, in comparison to the 20th century industrial information society (Benkler, 2006) . Insomuch as it is not only providing opportunities for wide-ranging communication between individuals but also the possibility to establish a deeper relationship with the »information« which we produce and share, the internet can be understood as a gigantic microscope. We are unconsciously acquiring the ability to break down information that surrounds us at an ever higher level of resolution. This viewpoint will aid in the reconstructive understanding of media art as an avant-garde form of representation in the contemporary world.

1.5 Transitions in the Modality of Cultural Production

It goes without saying that the current conditions of the network are engendering countless opportunities for creative expression that effortlessly surpasses the boundaries created by the privileged institutional space of art history. It is because of this however, that it is crucial to continue to strive to define art history, or more precisely the relationship between art and society. It is necessary to avoid relying on the term art as an easy excuse or to fall into a rose-colored appraisal of the network technology, and instead strive to establish an evolutionary viewpoint that encompasses network-based culture as a whole.

2.0 Territoriality of Expression, its Complementarity of Life and Death

»›Death is more precious than life.‹ For some time now these words have haunted me unceasingly. Yet at the present moment I am certainly living. I still do not break the bonds of this life, for I cannot, by my own efforts, cast off this habit which has been fixed since the days of my parents, my grand-parents and for yet longer: a hundred, two hundred, a thousand, ten thousand years.«

Inside my Glass Doors, Soseki Natsume (translated by Sammy Tsunematsu and Marvin Marcus) (Natsume, 2010)

»I need no gravestone, but
If you need one for me
I would like it to bear these words:
He made suggestions. We
Carried them out.
Such an inscription would
Honour us all.«

Bertolt Brecht (translated by Michael Hamburger)

»Besides, it's always the others who die.«

Epitaph on Marcel Duchamp's gravestone [1]

[1] »D'abord, c'est toujours les autres qui meurent.«

In the previous chapter it has been attempted to reconsider the referable recording of the embryological process of information from the point of view of prochronism, focusing on the current emergence of a vitalist interpretation of information. This prepared the ground for shifting our conception of creation from one based on a completed form of information where the process of development has been finalised to one where the process continues to progress at a higher level of resolution and for considering its function within society. This chapter will focus on the concept of » information prochronism « and on the question of how to make its application to information architecture possible. Let us first of all return to the notion of vitalism of information in order to reflect on the constructive consequences that it would entail. We can then move on to strip the veil of abstraction from the concept to lay the path for its substantive redefinition.

2.1 Process as a Closure

It has already been mentioned in the previous chapter that the standpoint of perceiving life as physical phenomena in terms of information theory (e.g. bio-media), such as is the case with media theories that arose from 20th century cybernetics, will be avoided. Instead, information will be re-conceptualized under the light of the fluid dynamics of the theories of life. In order to achieve this, it will be attempted to define information's emergence, operation, disappearance or inheritance, and reproduction by assuming the existence of information as a unit. Why do this? It is in pursuance of the autonomy of information as creative work that arises as a result of removing as much as possible, those factors that are external to the productive activity, that is to say factors such as subjective value judgement or the mysterious. Autonomy in this case, indicates the condition in which an object possesses a boundary that defines itself which imparts it with an identity. Francisco Varela named the modality of the autonomous generation of cells autopoiesis and in doing so, he defined the concept of autonomy of a higher level within this autopoiesis as »operational closure« (Varela, 1989) , or »organizational closure« (Varela, 1981) . In carefully pointing out that closure should be distinguished from enclosure, Varela is indicating the identity that arises as a consequence of enactment. It is therefore a concept that assumes some dynamism of the constituants of a system. In this sense Varela assumes the standpoint that regards identity as given or static as nonexistent. This is to extract the unit of information (representation) to define its operational closure just as Varela perceived the principles of autopoiesis in the organisms (cells) in physical space through the observation that information operates as a linkage of dynamic differences. Here, a question arises: how can this operational closure of information be defined?

As mentioned in the previous chapter, Bateson distinguished between evolution and learning in terms of phylogenesis and ontogenesis and described both processes as stochastic. This presents an ontology which is defined when a double-bind of two time axes, namely the macro and the micro, occurs. It should be noted however, that although in phylogenetic inheritance a process of natural selection as continuous change arises as the result of the interaction with the ever-changing environment, the results of learning of an individual organism of one generation is never itself inherited by the next generation. The conception of culture or communication in terms of the notion of memes, formulated by Neo-Darwinist Richard Dawkins, allows to imaginatively go beyond this limitation of organic individual inheritance, just like the invention of language itself is a pertinent example. This discussion has developed, as its background for selecting the prochronism of information as its subject, the idea that information goes through an original process of reproduction such as propagation, inheritance and alteration as memes. The sphere of learning was discussed by constructivists at length. The constructivist Piaget held that *»knowledge is not transmitted but actively constructed«*, a standpoint from which Papert's constructionism was derived from, while later social constructivist such as Vygotsky and Cole stated that *»knowledge is constructed socially«*. The radical constructivist as exemplified by Pask and v. Glasersfeld defined knowledge as an »adoptable function« emphasizing its fundamental interactivity (Scott, 2001) . According to them, knowledge is generated due to and within the learning activity thus repudiating transmission models of communication such as the one formulated by Shanon (more precisely, excessively stretched by researchers of different fields) (Jonassen, 1999) .

Reflecting on these developments in the conception of learning, aspects of the stochastic process that regulate the behavior of memes begin to emerge. In this respect, would it still be necessary to distinguish the trades between individual and environment from those between individuals? The chain reaction that provides feedback not after but concurrently to a self action is known as »reflection-in-action« (Nakakoji, 2006) in the field of cognitive psychology. Including external agents into this process can be understood as an action taken to promote the accidental in order to avoid the evolution/learning of memes to run into a dead end. Is it not possible to find in this the signs of a functional teleonomy in communication and in expressive activity? We can now think about the chain reaction between the eternally recurring externalization and re-subsumption of expression; the information that is here externalized, gains a certain closure (identity) inside the operation of the process, and taking on the characteristics of the orientation of the producer, travels within space and statements as a subject of predation for others. A cluster of information that roams about the network like mycetozoa, an entity which can not be clearly defined neither as animal nor as vegetal, or a living environment formed by them. This kind of information that exists externally to man but is designed so to be subsumed again, is not autonomous in any ordinary sense. If however, a functionality within the concatenated generative process of communication is to be recognized for the invitation character of intervention possessed by such information, it is possible to assert that the heteropoietic (external; consciously produced by man) aggregate of information exists as an environment for and influences the homopoietic (generated within a homogenous space) sphere, just like Varela affirms that life processes are realized due to the complementarity between autopoiesis (autonomous generation) and allopoiesis (heteronomous generation). At the core of the present discussion lies the contention that the manner of handling information at the everyday level is now developing into one which begins to recognize informational unit as a certain operational closure. This leads to elucidating the issue of the style of information production and sharing in the contemporary world, as well as the practices of law and economics and other norms that define our social dynamics, neither being adapted to the development of the autonomy of expression nor being orientated towards it. Some notes by contemporary composer and pianist Yuji Takahashi were quoted at the beginning of the last chapter. Let us now refer back to their main argument to revive it within the process of the current textual context.

> *»A work that presents not only the final outcome but simultaneously also the process leading to it. It would be performed together with notes written on dispersed scraps of paper and diagrams and equations projected onto the walls. Why should process be distinguished from outcome?«*
> (Takahashi, 2004)

It can be asserted that there is no sense in the distinction itself. The distinction is the result and re-enforcement of our limited rationality. We can only form a node for sharing the information in the form of a result stripped of the process leading to it, because of not only the sheer amount of information of process that includes temporal continuity, but also of our lack of a resolution capability for processing such an amount of information. All information that is regarded as reliable is then one that is fixed in which the process is halted and is marked with the seal of recognition and a specific time stamp. Mediation then necessarily contains the effects of arbitrariness such that restricts the time axes into a single one. If communication based on the derivation from a continuous process becomes possible, then expression will come to approximate immediacy closer.

> *»Collective creation can only be the integration, based on a concrete model, of the three different functions of composer, performer and audience. It should no longer rely on the privileged moment of temporary coexistence, but instead it*

should be understood as historical process. All works become works in progress.« (Takahashi, 2004)

Avoiding the discontinuity in the process of information, production entails no longer assuming the time of or the division involved in the fixing of a work. This will make the boundary between production and generation ambiguous to the utmost level. At the same time however, in order to define an identity without employing a fixed time, it will be necessary to have a standard for recognizing or identifying the information unit that continues to be becoming itself in dynamic time as a certain closure, for example a work. This standard may also be called intensity. When the definition of such standard is carried out in an open manner, the fairness of a fair assessment of public information itself would potentially be defined at the same time. This is because not only the »state (what)« of the final form or step, but also the »path (how)« and the »provenance (why)« will be fully disclosed. Regarding fairness there is, at the same time, a tendency towards imparting cooperative production with the element of social justice in terms of the transparency of the process (Benkler, 2006) .

»The application of an individual's intuitions without an established methodology: this is fatal. It is a process that is unrepeatable, difficult to apply to different situations, complicated, clumsy, unreliable, arbitrary and on top of all this, highly time consuming. It can never be detached from the ›genius‹ that has mastery over it. It is mystical. The operation becomes increasingly isolated, inactive, and dies off in the deepest angst.« (Takahashi, 2004)

It is not an overstatement to claim that, simply put, the value of engineering depends on the fact that the repeatability of a proposed technique is secured. This is only possible and the value is only generated because of the premise of objective factors such as function and aim, which is to say improvement and progress. Can expressive activity then be similarly debated on the same premises of improvement and progress? Considering the fact that Takahashi is referring to the act of composing music in this quotation, it is dangerous to straightforwardly expand its scope into other expressive territories. On this statement however, depends the very formation of the fundamental problem of the autonomy of expressive activity. This discussion, takes a position similar to Takahashi's, regarding a methodology (this must reflect, needless to say even in the details, the contexts peculiar to each expressive territory) as crucial for objectifying all expressive activities regardless of them being art or non-art. In this case, despite the expressive activity being *»unrepeatable, difficult to apply to different situations, complicated, clumsy, unreliable, arbitrary«*, or in other words being driven by a sterile intuition (that does not lead to a certain inheritance of its processes by another creative intention), it may be possible to draw out a method from the repetition of the intuition itself or on the other hand indicate such sterility in order to make a fair assessment if a certain generative process is included in the expressive activity. Let us now consider the methods for identifying the characteristics of creative processes that are widely sharable as value.

2.2 Territorialisation, Song/Singing, Shima (Island)

The concept of sterility is fundamental for any attempt at focusing on the process of formation. A certain communication (an expressive activity orientated towards a certain subject) breeding a different communication. The interruption of this process increases the temporal, physical and mental costs required for re-igniting such process. A process veiled in mystery complicates matters further. If however, an expression that is simultaneously mysterious and beautiful does most likely exist, it would signify that the disclosure of a process and the inheritance and the diffusion of the process amongst subjects do not per se engender beauty. If *»beauty is a result and it is impossible to create something out of a result«* (Takahashi, 2005) , then what exactly is beauty? Is there a beauty of sterility; what is the beauty of the mortal? Here we can imagine a living form that has removed itself from the infinite concatenation of generation and alteration. If there exist elements that make it possible to imagine the time axes of its past and possible futures (although this is something that the viewer should generate within his/her own contextual process), then the process may be both extended back and prolonged in the imagination of the viewer. One may ask however, what for?

Let us look at the example of architectural space. For example let us imagine two spaces; one that has been naturalized to its current state through the input of variables of diverse environments over the continuation of a long period of time, and one that has been designed as a severely hygienic new monument that does not allow interventions from the exterior. In the former the original purpose of creation is by now lost to sight, while the latter attempts to secure the permanence of an original signature. This situation can be understood employing Deleuze's / Guattari's dynamics of territoriality; the repetition of the cycle of territorialization, deterritorialization and reterritorialization. This cycle which is reminiscent of the metabolism of an organism, has been compared to singing by the two philosophers.

> *»This is where I think that me and Félix have done a good job together. If someone said to me, ›what philosophical concept have you made, because you talk about creating concepts?‹, we have created at least one concept that is very important; that of the ritornello [...] and what is a ritornello? it's a small air. Tralalala [...] And when do I say tralalalala ...? If I were to do philosophy, and I ask myself when do I hum tralalaala? I hum for three reasons. I hum when I go around my territory [...] that is to say when I am at home. I hum when I'm not at home and when I'm trying to get back to home when the night falls; a time of anxiety. I look for my way home and I give myself courage by humming. This is when I'm going towards my house, my territory. And then, I sing when bid farewell [...] when I go out of my house and go somewhere else. But where do I go? In other words, the ritornello is for me [...] absolutely connected with the animal [...] and also to the problem of territory, and the exiting or entering to territory, which is to say the problem of deterritorialisation. I go back into my territory, or I try, or I deterritorialise myself, thus I leave my territory. But what relationship does this have to music? [...] What is a lied? It is always voice as a song, voice that becomes song in relation to its position in regard with the territory, my territory, the territory that I've lost, the territory that I try to regain; that is a lied [...] I meant that I believe in the end that this is what affect is, when I said that music is the history of becoming (devenir) and its power (puissance) of becoming.«* (Deleuze, 1988) [2]

[2] Transcript by the author: *»C'est là qu'avec Félix je trouve qu'on avait fait du bon travail, parce que c'est une des choses qu'il me semble, eh, quand je disais, je pourrai dire à la rigueur si on me disait: mais quel concept philosophique tu as produit puisque tu parles de créer concepts, On a au moins produit un concept philosophique très important, celui de la ritournelle, et la ritournelle pour moi c'est ce point commun, c'est quoi une ritournelle? c'est un petit air. Tralalalala ... Quand est-ce que je dis tralalaala ...Je fais de la philosophie, et je me dis quand est-ce que je fais tralalala, je chantonne? Je chantonne à trois occasions. Je chantonne quand je fais le tour de mon territoire, et que je suis mes meubles, y a un fond radio, c'est-à-dire quand je suis chez moi. Je chantonne quand je ne suis pas chez moi, et que j'essaie de regagner le chez moi, quand la nuit tombe, l'heure de l'angoisse. Je cherche mon chemin et je me donne du courage en chantant tralalala ... Je vais vers mon chez moi. Et puis, je chantonne lorsque je dis adieu je pars, et dans mon coeur j'emporterai, ça aussi,*

Here Deleuze depicts the relationship between the cycle of territorialization and the music that remains as history (traces); a song/singing as the prochronism of the interaction between a territory and its occupant(s). One can recall that the previously cited Takahashi also refers to an idea of a *song to live (ikirutame no uta)*, that encompasses the meaning of such a recurrently *tout ça c'est la chanson populaire, lorsque je sors de chez moi pour aller ailleurs, mais pour aller où? En d'autre termes, la ritournelle pour moi est absolument liée à, ça nous remet à A, animal, au problème du territoire et de sortie ou d'entrée du territoire c'est à dire au problème de déterritorialisation. Je rentre dans mon territoire, où j'essaie, ou bien je me déterritorialise, je pars je pars je quitte mon territoire. Mais quel est le rapport avec la musique, ça? Alors Il faut progresser quand on crée un concept c'est pour ça j'invoque l'image du cerveau. Mon cerveau en ce moment, tout d'un coup je me dis bah le lied, qu'est-ce que c'est qu'un lied? Ça a toujours été la voix comme chant, qui élève son chant, en fonction de ses positions par rapport au territoire, mon territoire, le territoire que je n'ai plus, le territoire que je cherche a regagner, c'est ça un lied. Et que se soit Schumann ou Schubert, c'est fondamentalement ça, Et je crois que c'est ça l'affect finalement, lorsque je disais que la musique c'est l'histoire des devenirs et des puissances des devenirs. c'était quelque chose comme ça.«*

inherited process. It does not involve calculation or concepts but is transmitted, shared and altered as a sustainable record of affection and perception.

We can now, by reconceptualizing the externalized (aggregate of) information as an environment for the subject that is involved in an expressive activity as mentioned before, consider the territoriality of information. At the architectural level too, a space that has been artificially compartmentalized is imparted with an identity and structured as a closure detached from nature. It becomes possible to question, just as we aim to do with the problem of closure of information, whether it allows for the existence of a continuous process, whether there is a space for the song that should be sung to be engraved. How to objectify nature that arises as an external environment to the artificially constructed territory? The following statement by Chinese literature scholar Miyoko Nakano who compares Japanese and Chinese (as well as Western) gardens is highly suggestive for our purpose. *»In Chinese the term* 園林 *(yuan-lin) for garden includes the term* 園 *(yuan), which equally to* 苑 *(yuan), means enclosure [...] it is therefore a term that demonstrates the uncompromising artificiality of it, in other words the fact that it is a* 藝 *(yi = ars).«* However,

> *»despite the fact that it was artificially created in the track of the Chinese yuan-lin, the garden in ancient Japan was called ›shima‹ or island, thus alluding to something that is inherent to a coast line, something therefore natural that is surrounded by the ocean. The reason for this is nothing else than the deliberate attempt at removing its artificiality«* (Nakano) .

Here the question is how to artificially remove the artificiality, thus the arbitrariness, of something that has been artificially constructed. This kind of creativity characterized by this ambiguous intentionality, resonates with Daniel Charles' following statement made by extending Heidegger's mentioning of Nietzsche, to Duchamp and Cage: *»The one who desires in the purest manner indeed hopes that the desired object generates itself without any kind of intention nor intervention«* (Charles, 1978) . Charles carefully continues: *»The purity of such desire is always wily [...] because it simultaneously requires self-oblivion and the retention of the self that intends not to intervene to that desire«*. This duality between territoriality and deterritorialization cannot in any circumstance arise with the modern premise of the individual that can exist as independent from the environment. Only a poor form of expression such as, at most, *»an island of limited complexity«* can arise in such conditions (Kneer, 2000) . At the same time however, a complementarity between environment and subject that cannot be reduced to a dichotomy is here emerging. This *shima*/island-like naturalness (it may be appropriate to call it a programmed wilderness) appears to be impossible to both regulate and share in the context of the contemporary practice of the law. Art critic Noriaki Kitazawa describes as follows the incident in which the garden created by sculptor Isamu Wakabayashi was not granted moral rights and was relocated to give space for the construction of a waste treatment plant.

> *»Wakabayashi's garden was conceived of as one that would be gradually formed through a long period of time in which plants would flourish and stone would blend into the surroundings. That is to say, it existed as a process. The creator of the garden, in this case, is thus a collaborator to nature, and is not a strong subject that integratively creates a work, a certain world. The formation of the garden is carried out as collaboration between the creative subject and nature. This form of authorship is fundamentally different from the modern creative subject predicted by contemporary moral rights (of copyright law). It was here that the contemporariness of the garden lied.«* (Kitazawa, 2003)

It is widely known that, just like in Buddhist temple gardens, the authorship of the work of a gardener is usually recognized, but it seems as though this is only the case when the garden is created on request by those in power. The gardener always designs the interaction of the multi-layered time axes formed by the arbitrary sculptural decisions, the nature that is superimposed on it and the viewer that intervenes into the garden. A process that encompasses the conflicts between the creative intention and inevitability—the designing of an urban space, the governance of a nation, agriculture, farming, pasturage. Every activity in which an organization as a cluster of constitutive elements is managed. Is it not the case that it was due to the incessant revisions in recording media technology that we gained the ability to rapidly, on large scales and stochastically carry out such expressive activities that are based on the temporal premise of a long period? Duchamp spoke in a radio interview about the growth, development and alteration in the long time axis that are inherent to expressive activity.

George Charbonnier (interviewer): »*Marcel Duchamp, we all know or we think we all know what a work of art is. Then at which moment does it exist and who makes it?*«

Marcel Duchamp (interviewee): »*I don't know anything about what a work of art is [...] but I believe that first of all the artist who is doing the work doesn't know what he is doing. He knows what he is doing physically and his grey matter thinks normally. But he's not capable to assess the aesthetic result. And this aesthetic result is a phenomenon with two polarities. The first is the artist who produced it, and the second pole is the spectator. By spectator I mean not only the contemporary but also all the posterity and all the viewers of the work of art who by their vote decide that one thing should survive because there is something profound that the artist produced without knowing. And I insist on this because the artists extremely dislike such statements [...] the artist likes to think that he is completely conscious of what he's doing why he's doing it as he does it, and the intrinsic value of his work. But I don't believe it at all. I sincerely believe that the work (tableau) is done as much by the viewer as by the artist.*«
(Duchamp, 1960) [3]

[3] Transcript by the author:
GC: »*Marcel Duchamp, nous savons tous ou nous pensons tous savoir ce qu'est une oeuvre d'art. A quel moment existe-t-elle et qui l'a faite?*«

MD: »*Exactement, je n'en sais rien mais je crois que l'artiste d'abord qui fait cet oeuvre ne sait pas ce qu'il fait. Je veux dire par là il sait ce qu'il fait physiquement et même sa matière grise pense normalement. Mais que le résultat esthétique, lui n'est pas capable de l'estimer, le résultat. Et, ce résultat esthétique est un phénomène à deux pôles, le premier c'est l'artiste qui produit, et le second pôle c'est le spectateur. Par spectateur j'entends pas seulement le contemporain mais j'entends toute la postérité et tous les regardeurs d'oeuvre d'art qui par leurs votes décident qu'une chose doit rester ou doit survivre parce qu'il y a une chose profonde que l'artiste a produite sans le savoir et j'insiste là dessus parce que les artistes n'aiment pas qu'on leur dise ça l'artiste aime bien croire qu'il est complètement conscient de ce qu'il fait pourquoi il le fait comment il le fait et la valeur intrinsèque de son oeuvre, ça je ne crois pas du tout. Je crois sincèrement que le tableau est autant fait par le regardeur que par l'artiste.*«

What is discussed here is different from the notion that the value of any expression is only born in posterity. It is just that something of value is created and the other who inherits it carries on the process. As a result, the ground for the emergence of the time axis for the next production is prepared. Would it not be possible to design this multi-layeredness of time? In any case, there is no reason why the modality employed by those who inherit a work must be language. To respond to algorithm with natural language, to music with images, to moving image with sculpture. If criticism or critique is to be understood as a synonym for the continuation of the creative process, then what is discussed here can be conceived of as the multi-modalization of critique. At any rate, contemporary phenomena that, like the aforementioned garden designed by Wakabayashi, go beyond the situations predicted by existing law are surfacing all over the place. At the heart of the conflicts between those who champion new free, libre and open source web technologies and those with vested interests who claim that they will suffer losses because of them, often lie such discrepancies between old and new epistemologies. Open source and open contents arose within the landscape formed by computing machinery connected to global networks, have generated friction with the existing social structure and today continue to exert pressure for change. In the following and final chapter, let us observe the life cycles of units of expression and the ecological behavior of expressive aggregates through an analysis of the software culture that naturalizes thinking and expression in the environment.

3.0 Information Bionomy

»What is a self, and how can a self come out of stuff that is as selfless as a stone or a puddle? What is an ›I‹ [...] ?«

Douglas R. Hofstadter, Preface for the 20th anniversary edition of *Gödel, Escher, Bach: an Eternal Golden Braid*

The underlining thesis of this article that has persisted throughout previous chapters can be summarized thus: how can we, within the generation of communication amongst ourselves, continue to expand our recognition of the identities of »I« and »information« while accurately perceiving the collective capability of the information generation network? How can we design, as a methodology for achieving this, the process of information generation without lapsing into some mystic vitalism (Driesch, 2010) [4], a form of a negative theology. To put it differently, this is also an attempt to answer the question of how the increase in the resolution capability of the operation may be preferred to the lowering of the resolution of observation to deal with the physical constraint of the limits of cognition in the communicative act. In this chapter, the act of critique as an extension of the generative process and the designing of the prochronism as its history will be considered from the level of the minimum unit of information generation within the network, referring once again to the notion of autonomy in life system theory.

[4] The intentionality of Driesch who summons Aristotle's entelechy to set it as an ordering power has a deep relation with our concerns; however we are not satisfied with the »unmaterializable«, »unquantifiable« character of entelechy as he describes.

3.1 Towards the Definition of the Operational Closure of Information

The viewpoint of Francisco Varela, who systematized the autonomy of cells into the model of autopoiesis, was one which explored the minimum unit of an autonomous identity. The employment of *Autopoiesis* (hereinafter referred to as AP) in social systems theory as exemplified by Niklas Luhmann's attempts, can only eventually lead to a posterior macroscopic sociological debate. Varela himself was contrary to such dilations of the concept of AP, and defined AP as the minimum unit model of an autonomy that possesses a physical substance. His attitude can be described as one that consistently attempts to concretely and stringently answer the question on how homology arises and how it is dynamically retained. At the same time, he classified the structure of self production of a higher order as »operational closure« (Varela, 1979) . According to him, this does not designate *»only about the living beings, but about all the aggregations like the ecological niches, accounting systems, conversations, the animal societies, that appear everywhere emerges a feeling of a distinct being, detaching from a certain background and gifted with the ability of cognitively interacting with it«* (Varela, 1989) [5] . These kinds of statements highlight Varela's contention that since all behavior of a higher order stems from the autonomy of cells that are the minimum unit of life, this behavior should itself have a similar structure if observed from a macro point of view. This ascertains the validity of designing the systematization of information employing vitalism as a point of reference instead of reducing life phenomena to the sphere of information in pursuing the autonomous operation of information.

Varela's definition of operational closure, which he used to support his assertion (the thesis of closure), that *»all autonomous systems are operationally closed«* is as follows:

> *»We consider a system operationally closed if its organization is characterized by the processes that are: recursively depending to each other for the generation and realization of the processes themselves, and constituting the system as a recognizing unit in the space (domain) where the processes exist.«* (Varela, 1989) [6]

There is a text written by Varela that is acutely conscious of Douglas Hofstadter's magnum opus *Gödel, Escher, Bach* (hereinafter referred to as GEB) (Hofstadter, 1999) in which life phenomena and the emergence of homology as the extension of operational closure to higher orders are eloquently discussed. In the essay/paper, entitled

[5] This book was written 9 years after the original English book, but chapters other than II, III and IV were written after the original book's publication. Varela considers this book to be a continuation of the original (p. 16). The citation is an English translation by the author, from the original French text: *»Je ne parle pas seulement des êtres vivants, mais de tous les agrégats comme les niches écologiques, les systèmes de gestion, les conversations, les sociétés animales, qui se présentent partout où émerge le sentiment d'un être distinct, se détachant d'un certain fond, et doté de capacités d'interactions cognitives avec lui«.*

[6] Translated by the author from the original French text: *»Nous dirons d'un système autonome qu'il est opérationnellement clos si son organisation est caractérisée par des processus : a) dépendant récursivement les uns des autres pour la génération et la réalisation des processus eux-mêmes, et b) constituant le*

Sketches on the Natural History of Circularity (Varela, 1988) , Varela refers to Gödel, Escher and Mandelbrot (and not Bach) to expound his thesis that cells, language and nervous system are driven by fractal recursive structures on differing levels of hierarchy. Furthermore, he positions operational closure within the sciences as the definition of system equilibrium in cybernetics, and cites Eigen and Schuster's hypercycle model (Fig.6) as sharing the essential principles (Varela, 1988) [7] . What should be noted here is that the impossibility of cognitively tracing back to the origins of this operational closure that dynamically constitutes homology is repeatedly mentioned.

système comme une unité reconnaissable dans l'espace (le domaine) où les processus existent.«

Citing Escher's famous *Drawing Hands* lithograph print and Mandelbrot's fractal images (Fig. 7), and evaluating the undecidability of Quaine's version of the Epimenides paradox (Hofstadter, 1999) and Gödel's incompleteness theorem as a manifestation of autonomy rather than a limitation in logical language, Varela characterizes the structure of operational closure as an unknowable (mythique)

[7] *»En un sens, l'idée de clôture opérationnelle généralise la notion classique de stabilité d'un système, proposée par Androsov et Pontriagyn en 1930, et que la cybernétique a héritée de la mécanique classique... plusieur modèles de ce genre existent dans la littérature scientifique, y compris l'hypercycle étudié par Eigen et Schuster (1978).«* La clôture opérationnelle est aussi un proche parent du feed-back, mais elle en est distincte dans la mesure où le feed-back suppose et implique une source de référence externe : cette extériorité est tout à fait absente de la clôture opérationnelle.

Fig. 6: Hypercycle structure. Ii = RNA matrices, Ei = replication enzymes (i = 1,2,...,n). (2)

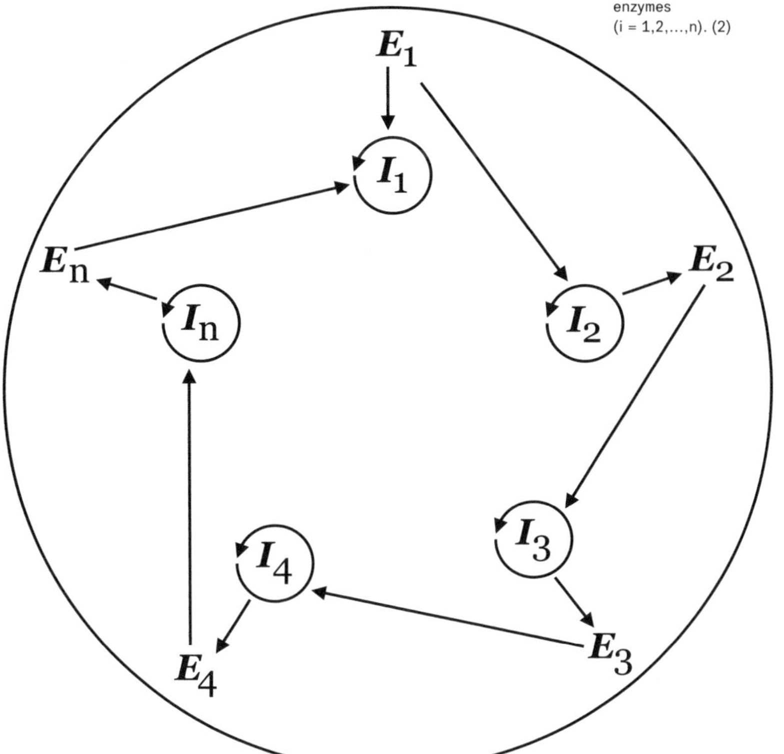

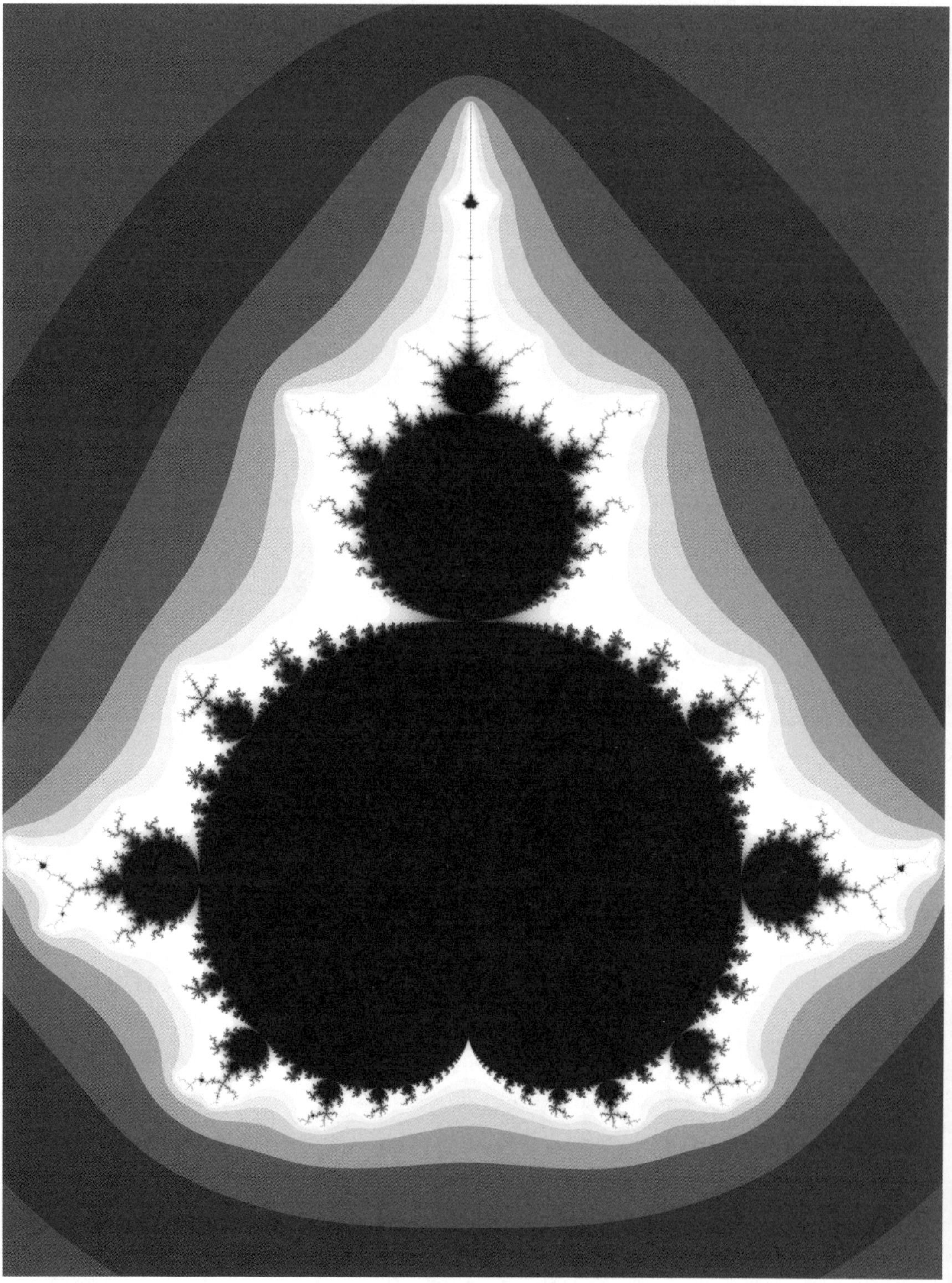

Fig. 7: Mandelbrot set
with (originally colored)
environment.
Wikimedia Commons

phenomenon in the sense that it can never be intellectually known in its totality despite the fact that it may be intuitively understandable. This fundamental impossibility to trace back can be partly understood as a cognitive limitation originating from man's short and long term memory capacity. This cognitive limitation still places diverse restrictions to man. In particular for us, the following issue becomes central: A limitation for perceiving the complex authorship relationship inherent to the generation of operational identity—it may also be called information or territory from here onwards—in other words a quantitative limitation of responsibility and inequality of results in the communicative activity arises, constraining results to a singular one and concentrating resources in power-law manner to a short-head. On the other hand, the backward traceability is oriented towards not only making a more accurate and fair assessment made possible by salvaging the eliminated process and ratio of loss of the participants at the present time, but more importantly, towards gradually linking the relationship of concatenation and derivation between processes on the temporal axis by causing a structural coupling between production and observation. This engenders the necessity to increase the subject's resolution capacity in order to accurately perceive complex phenomena, without solely depending on the lowering of resolution. It is possible to develop this argument to an ethical one or one pertaining to social justice, but we will limit ourselves to presenting a model for the gradual advancement of derivations from diverse processes [8].

Let us now consider the problem of the impossibility of tracing back in the autonomous process by once again recalling the concept of prochronism into the context of the internet as the basis for social activity, in order to give shape to the operational closure of information. The term information as employed here, refers to the acts of expressive production that are manifested as digital data, in other words to communication in general. We will here adopt the viewpoint of describing the environment world from within digital data, as a so to speak internal observation. The model of thinking that has the environment world of digital contents as defined by Lessig's four-quadrant (Lessig, 2006), is defined by architecture (code), law, market and regulations, does supplement the understanding or the conditions, but cannot be a methodology for information design. Let us instead, deal with the question of what an information bionomy of digital contents may be in bottom-up manner from the level of the metadata of information.

[8] In other words, this article aims at finding paths to build an informational relation with the information. To capture the fundamental value of information besides its economical values, we might refer to Gottfried Semper's *Materialgerechtigkeit* movement that strived to affirm the primary value of material. For a detailed history from Semper to Duchamp and later Gutai group, refer to (Wolff, 2007).

3.2 Information Prochronism

Prochronism refers to the history and the manifestation of the morphological alterations that a certain organism has underwent in the past. It is well known that Bateson, who focused on the homology between individual organisms and genealogies mediated by prochronism, defined information as »difference which makes a difference«, concordant with Varela's definition of operational closure, *»The result of the operation of the system is the operation of the system«* (Varela, 1988; 1985) . By combining the two, the generation of prochronism can be understood as the history of the operation of an operational closure. In this sense, prochronism can be illustrated with the model of understanding the object simultaneously through a perception of the optical structure without having to go through posterior linguistic processing [9] . Prochronism is also a framework for grasping the orientation that drives the subject internally and its connectability with the external without the need to separate them.

[9] The author made a similar statement in (Chen, 2007). Varela and Thompson study the invariables in the affordance theory, and criticize its fixity in (Varela, 1991). In order to fill this gap, we might say that the affordance is (originating from) the prochronism of an environment.

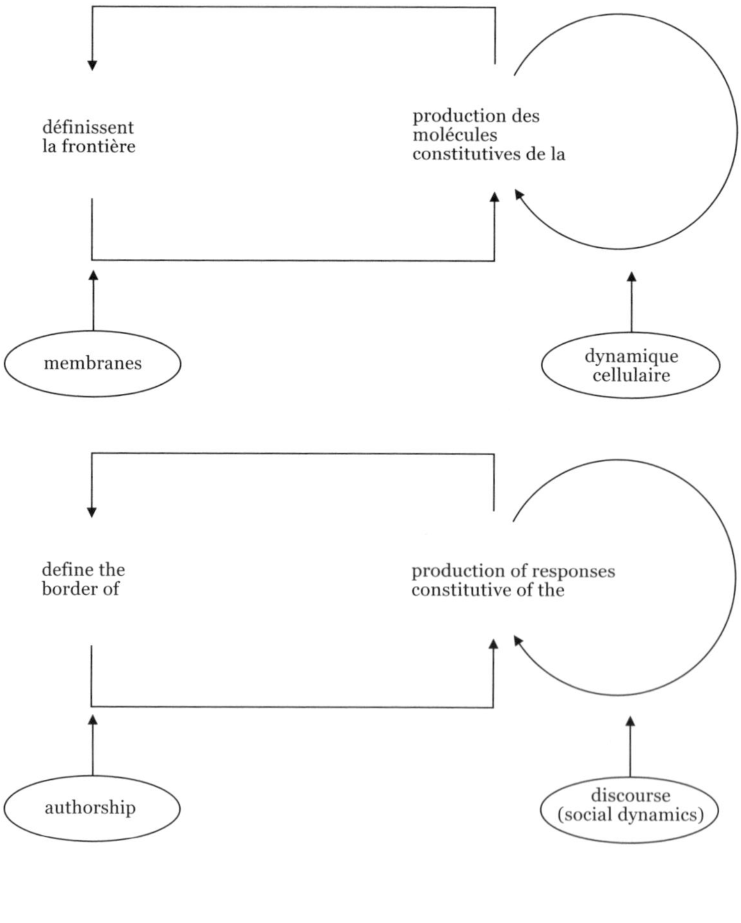

Fig. 8: Varela's model of operational closure to information generation: *Autopoietic Structure of Cell and Information*

Let us now apply Varela's model of operational closure to information generation (Fig. 8). The level of contents is here envisaged as the minimum unit of identity, but its boundary may hierarchically extend to authorship and commons (shared territory). The circularity, which structurally couples with this ontogenetic circularity presents itself as social forces. This indicates the degree of intervention that can be separated into different levels of hierarchy, of which constituents can be roughly divided into alteration and participation. This structural coupling is the epitome of the operational closure of information. With Varela's model, neither the depths of the layers of the recursively layered identities (contents, authorship, commons) nor the structural coupling with other identities at a higher order can be expressed. Let us here expand the aforementioned hypercycle model to the description of operational closure (Fig. 9).

Fig. 9: Hypercyclic operational closure of digital contents.
Vi = »Works«,
Di = Derivative Works
(i = 1, 2, ..., n)

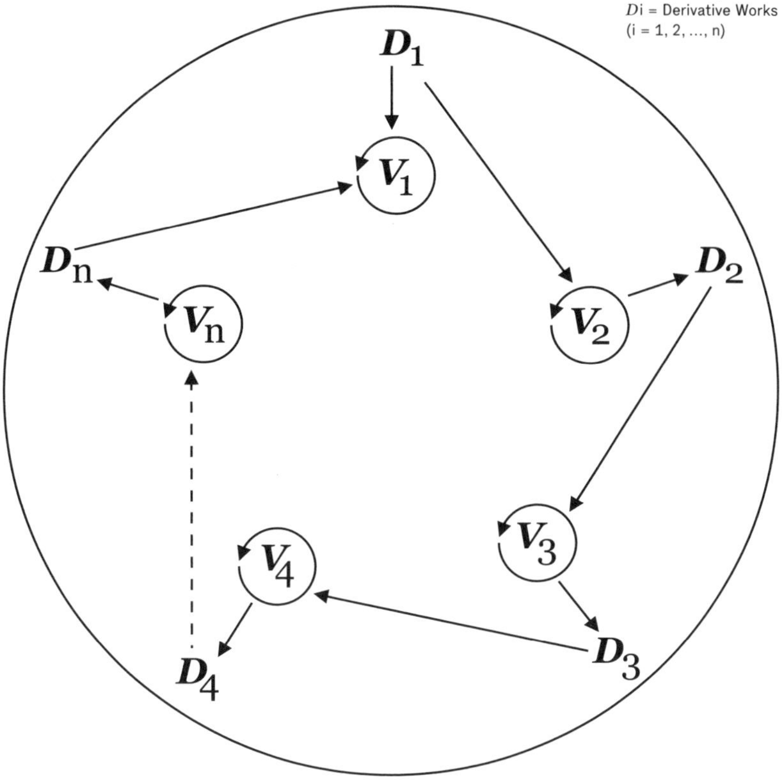

First of all, the authorship *Aa* is dynamically composed of the copulative production structure of contents *Ci* and intervention (derivation) *Di (i=1,2,n)*. It can be here assumed to be temporal transition. In other words, the structure that is generated by the structural coupling of *Ci* and *Di* is *Ci+1* and *Di+1* (the result of a derivation of a system is a derivation of a system). A production structure of a higher order is formed when a structural coupling occurs between this territory and an authorship *Ab* which differs in terms of intervention (derivation). The three different layers of content (data), authorship (individuality) and commons (society) are gently combined in this recursive nested structure. Hence commons is positioned outside the framework of this diagram as an operational closure of a higher order constituted by the structural coupling between different individualities. Let us now move down to the level of data that is even more minute instead of making a transition to a higher level. Fig. 10 is an articulation of the data structure of *Di* in Fig. 9, while Fig. 11 brings together, at an even higher level of resolution, examples of constituents of prochronism. For information to operate within multiple coupling, the plasticity of the content that shows what kind of yield property it has against the external operating pressure must function as the boundary (membrane) of identity, incorporating within it prochronism as the totality of the generative record (history). The content itself lies in a deeper layer.

Plasticity, as employed here, is regulated by such factors as licensing as the forging of a legal agreement regarding alterations (GPL, GFDL, CCPL, etc.) and the degree of the measures taken to technologically restrict access and operation (*Technological Protection Measure*, notion that includes *Digital Rights Management*) within the context of rules within society (law, technology) [10]. Prochronism is, as mentioned before, governed by the two vectors of phylogenetic homology and ontogenetic homology. Fig. 11 shows a magnified view of this part. At the level of individual homology, the phased recording and continuous process of the generative record of generative subject becomes crucial in addition to metadata that purely explicates content [11]. This indicates, when the information is observed internally and analytically, what degree of consistency and noise the information has in comparison to the logic of its emergence and by what kind of spontaneous rate of change it has been driven. At the same time, the data for the genealogical homology is constituted by the information about how much external pressure—citation, alteration, assessment and connection—the content has been subjected to. It is therefore dynamically and unceasingly

10 The author studies the similar problem in (Chen, 2007a).

11 The retention, manifestation and intervention of this time process can be defined as an informational structuralization of an enactive cognition. The author has studied this issue through the TypeTrace project. http://typetrace.jp [Accessed: Oct 25, 2010]

generated as metadata showing the heteronomous rate of change within the relationship of the structural coupling between identity and the external (network as a whole). It should be noted that the group of basic constituents that have been mentioned here is not the content itself but it stays at the level of metadata (that is to say text won't be involved with semantic interpretation). Thus in order to implement trades mediated by prochronism, the maximum versatility at data design must be secured and the shareability must be maximized [12]. If the sharing of prochronisms permeates, its power of historicity is expected to be manifested in many layers. Let us look at the level of data to begin with. A situation in which the homology of the users' generative information is semi-automatically mutually assessed, connected and altered by algorithms beyond the intention of the users, and in which such histories of concatenate alterations continue to generate prochronism of identity of a high order is to be expected. A technological debate on more concrete algorithms is sought at this level.

[12] The author presented an example of a prochronic metadata that englobes the modulation of physical environment's variables and computer operation history (Chen, 2007).

Let us now move to the level of individuals. In a situation where the continuous recording of prochronism for long periods of time is secured, an amplification of the minute behaviors (incomparably smaller than what has until now been known as representation = representative creativity) is expected at the layer in between the unconscious and the conscious, between the synchronous and the asynchronous (the presence of absence). It is a modality of perception in which the lifelog of the expressive result itself is autonomously constructed. It is therefore a model that differs from the existing one based on the conscious production by a creative subject. This will make the utilization of a database of representational objects which operates symmetrically to human existence (i.e. avatarization) possible and will contribute to the creation of a culture of assessing the creative process itself. This is where the potential lies for sustaining the monstration rather than the demonstration of existence in digital media. Fig. 12 shows the relative position of webware in regard to this debate.

The large-scale opening of digital contents makes the trans-clusion of the productive subject or domain, and is now beginning to ignite a chain reaction of creative processes. The $\sqrt{n}$ rule (a heuristic law stating that in a system formed by n molecules, $\sqrt{n}$ molecules present indeterminate behavior) mentioned by physicist Schrödinger in the debate on the origin of life [13], indicates the necessity for a vast amount of molecules to aggregate in order for an autonomous

[13] Erwin Schrödinger, *What is Life?*, Chapter 1: *»The Classical Physicist's Approach to the Subject, The $\sqrt{n}$ Rule«: The Particularly Exigent Demand is the 1,000 is Not Over-whelmingly Good, If a Thing Claims the Dignity of Being a ›Law of Nature‹.«*

Fig. 10: Minimum Unit of prochronological Data.

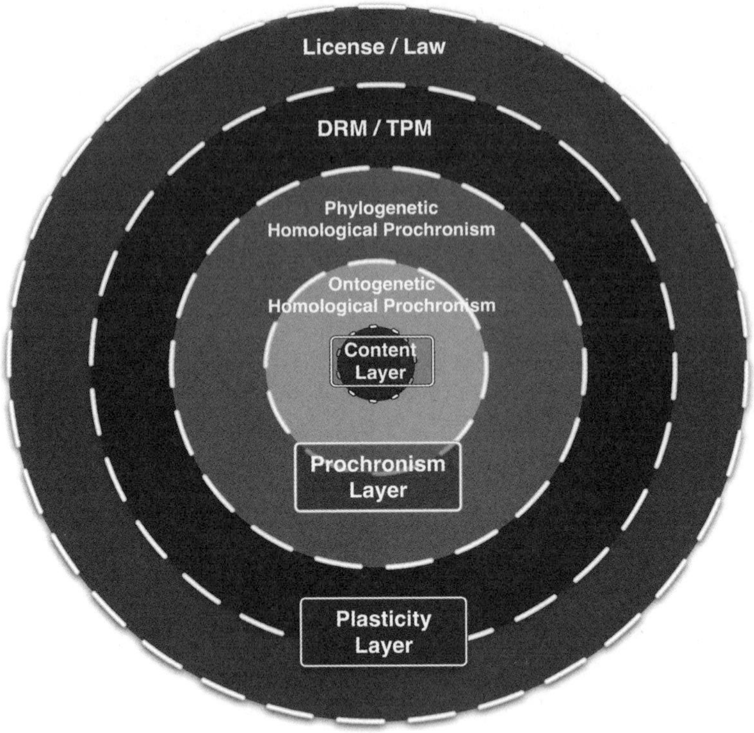

Fig. 11: Data Prochronism: Phylogenetic Homological Data and Ontogenetic Homological Data.

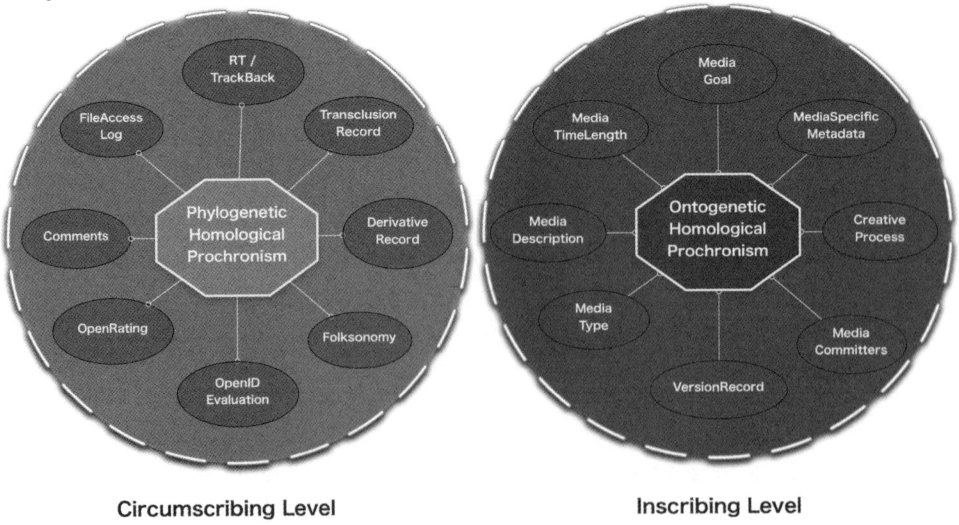

identity characterized by operational closure to arise (about one trillion molecules for an unicellular organism). Within the current explosive increase in the amount of information on the network that continues at a degree that surpasses our cognitive limitations, the ground is being prepared for the automatic repetition of processing, conversion and generation through the increase in open API and the higher level of programming language (abstraction) that connects such information, and the diffusion of licenses of a high plasticity. As a result, and as the »excessive inertia« of older industries that cannot adapt to the de-centralization of information is revealed, the critical point for archaic UGC (User Generated Contents) can be glimpsed beyond the multi-layering of web platforms as exemplified by large social networking services. Moreover, the superimposition of information layers will be a crucial issue for architecture and urban planning too, as platforms that combine portable information terminals with the global web begin to emerge. If we are to refer back to the debate in the first chapter now, we can ascertain that there is now, in this transitional period, an opportunity for a vitalist perception.

At the basis for the current commons however, lies an economic view that presupposes a strong subject, namely the individual. There is a need for creating an economy and creativity pertaining to it that is more Asian, more anonymously collective presupposing a soft subject. It must be designed in such a way that environment and subject are not severed, and above all it must gently expand our cognitive modality. Only after contents mutually interfere and a boundary emerges in the operation, can we reformulate our questions. Can digital contents as a form of human expression lead an autonomous process on the network, leaving the intentionalities and arbitrariness of man? Thinking about digital commons entails not only consideration for the cooperative body, but also for the evolution of autonomy in the information layer.

3.3 Media for Asymptotically Approaching Our Cognitive Limit

Below is a list of hypotheses regarding the information's bionomical ecology constituted by the totality of aggregates of information as operational closure:

- the intrinsic teleology of information: information solely aims to expand its identity through unceasing generative activity.
- All critical activities (intervention, alteration, derivation, remix) are an extension of the initial productive process of the object.
- The extension of the process is multi-modal.

By accurately perceiving the minimum unit of information that encompasses vitalist behavior, we, the human subjects responsible for the information, can gain a cognitive and bionomical feedback. This will not only allow the histories of each individual to be constructed as a consecution of a long-term process with the aid of information technology, but will allow us to be aware of the homology between the information for which we are responsible for the generation and our own existence. The author has been researching on data prochronism in a theory-into-practice manner starting from the project *TypeTrace* (Fig. 13) and through other web service's governance.

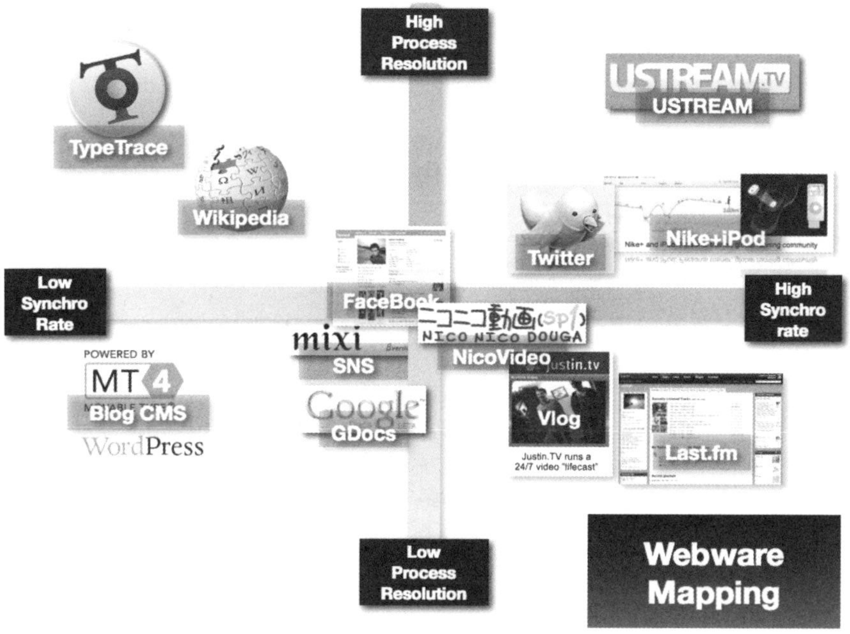

Fig. 12: Webware mapping based on synchronization rate and the resolution of recorded process matrixes.

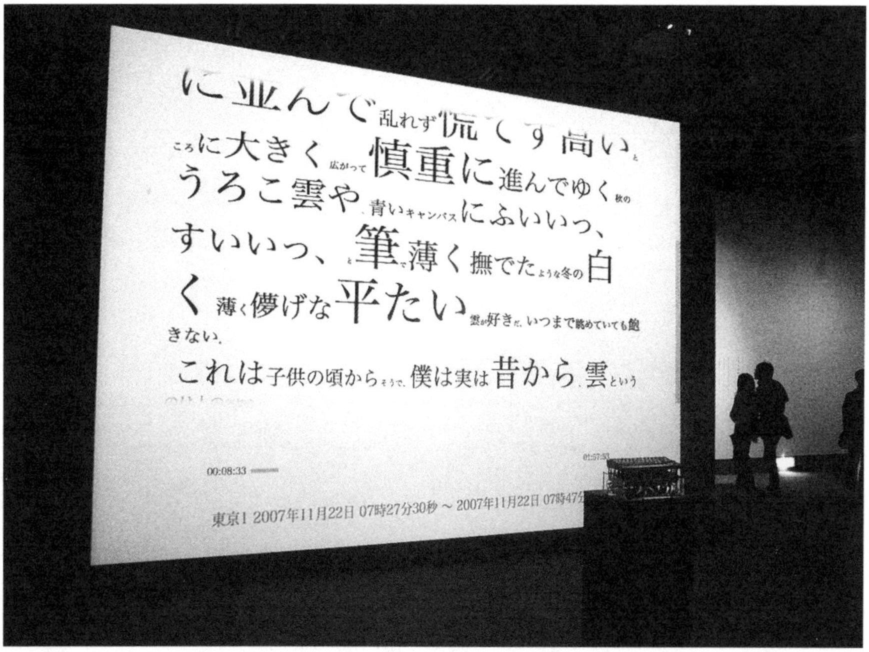

Fig. 13: Maijoh Ohtaro, dividual (Takumi Endo, Dominick Chen, Shinya Matsuyama), Norihisa Nagano (IAMAS): *The Way of TypeTrace*, Maijo Otaro Edition *Haptic Literature* Exhibition, Tokyo Metropolitan Museum of Photography. Dec 15, 2007–Feb. 2, 2008 http://typetrace.jp Photo by Takumi Endo

References

Bateson, G.: *Mind and Nature: A Necessary Unity (Advances in Systems Theory, Complexity (Advances in Systems Theory, Complexity, and the Human Sciences)*. Cresskill: Hampton Press, 2002

Benkler, Y.: *The Wealth of Networks: How Social Production Transforms Markets and Freedom.* London: Yale University Press, 2006

Benkler, Y.: »Commons-based Peer Production and Virtue«. In: *The Journal of Political Philosophy, Vol. 14, No. 4.* pp. 394–441. New York, 2006

Charles, D.: »Cage et Duchamp«. In: *Gloses sur John Cage.* Chapter 17. Paris: Union Général d'Éditions à Paris, 1978

Chen, D.: »Prochronism and its application to urban environment«. In: *10+1, No. 47.* Tokyo: INAX Publishing, 2007

Chen, D.:»On Plasticity, Criticism, Symmetry: an essay toward the correspondence between the network and real-world«. In: *Quarterly InterCommunication, No. 59.* Tokyo: NTT Publishing, 2007a

Deleuze, G., Parnet, C.: »O comme Opéra (La Ritournelle)«. In: *ABCDaire de Gilles Deleuze.* French TV Program, 1988–1989

Duchamp, M. in an Interview with Charbonnier, G.; Dec. 27, 1960. http://ubu.artmob.ca/sound/duchamp/Memorables/Duchamp-Marcel_Les-Memorables_04.mp3 [Accessed: Oct 25, 2010]

Driesch, H.: *The History and Theory of Vitalism.* Reprint. Forgotten Books (www.forgottenbooks.org), 2010

Foucault, M.: *Les Mots et les Choses: Une archéologie des sciences humaines.* Paris: Éditions Gallimard, 1966

Hofstadter, D. R.: *Gödel, Escher, Bach: An Eternal Golden Braid.* New York: Basic Books, 1999

Jimusyo, K.H.: *Perspective that creates the garden —from Kochuten to Sashikei.* (not translated)

Jonassen, D. H., Peck, K. L., Wilson, B. G. : *Learning with Technology: A Constructivist Perspective.* Upper Saddle River, NJ: Merrill, 1999

Kitazawa, N.: »Art and Craft after the Avant Garde«. In: *Situation—the End of Modernism, Dadaism of Bureaucratie.* pp. 162–166. Tokyo: Bigaku Shuppan, 2003

Kneer, G., Nassehi, A.: *Niklas Luhmanns Theorie sozialer Systeme.* 4. unveränderte Auflage. Stuttgart: Utb, 2000

Lash, S.: »Life(Vitalism)«. In: *Theory, Culture & Society, Vol. 23, No. 2–3.* Nottingham: Theory, Culture & Society Ltd., 2006

Lessig, L.: *Code: Version 2.0.* New York: Basic Books, 2006

Lovink, G., Niederer, S. (Eds.): *INC READER #4. Video Vortex Reader: Responses To Youtube.* Amsterdam: Institute of Network Cultures, 2008.

Nakano, M.: *Kikei no Zuzougaku (»Iconography of Strange Landscapes«, untranslated).*

Nakakoji, K., Yamamoto, Y.: »Software for Emergence«. In: Suzuki, H., The Japanese Society for Artificial Intelligence (Eds.): *Emergence and Origin of Intelligence*, Scottsdale, Maricopa: Ohm Publishing, 2006

Nakazawa, S.: *Baroque of the Forest.* Tokyo: Kodansha Academic Library, 2006

Natsume, S.: *Inside My Glass Doors.* In: Ohno, S. (Ed.), Shibata, T. (Input): Aozora Bunko Card No. 760. http://www.aozora.gr.jp/cards/000148/card760.html [Accessed: Oct 25, 2010]

Scott, B.: »Gordon Pask's Conversation Theory: A Domain Independent Constructivist Model of Human Knowing«. In: Riegler, A. (Ed.): *Foundations of Science, Vol. 6, No. 4* –special issue on »The Impact of Radical Constructivism on Science«. pp. 343–360. 2001

Takahashi, Y.: »Getting Around the Knotted Loop of Time-Space«. In: *Collection—1970s.* Tokyo: Heibonsha Library, 2004

Takahashi, Y. and Mogi, K.: *Open Discussion, Dec 17, 2005, 19:00–20:00.* Tokyo: NTT InterCommunication Center, 2005 http://hive.nticc.or.jp/contents/artist_talk/20051217/ [Accessed: Oct 25, 2010]

Varela, F.: *Principles of Biological Autonomy*. Chapter VII.
New York: North Holland, 1979

Varela, F.: »Describing the Logic of the Living—the Adequacy and Limitations of the Idea of Autopoiesis«. In: Zeleny, M.: *Autopoiesis: A Theory of Living Organization*. New York: North Holland, 1981. Vol. 3 in the North Holland Series in General Systems Research).

Varela, F.: *Complexity of the Brain and Autonomy of the Living*. Conference, Feb 1, 1985. Milan, Casa della Cultura, 1985. Published in: Bocchiet, G., Ceruti, M. (Eds.): *La Sfidadella Complessità*. Milan: Feltrinelli, 1985

Varela, F.: »The Creative Circle: Sketches on the Natural of Circularity«. In: Watzlawick, P.: *L'invention de la Réalité*. Paris: Les Éditions du Seuil, 1988

Varela, F.: *Autonomie et connaissance – Essai sur le vivant*. Paris: Les Éditions du Seuil, 1989 (originally written in French, based on Varela, F. J.: *Principles of Biological Autonomy*. pp. 306 ff. New York: North Holland, 1979)

Varela, F., Thompson, E., Rosch, E.: *The Embodied Mind: Cognitive Science and Human Experience*. Cambridge, Mass.: MIT Press, 1991

Wolff, V.: »Justice to the Materials or Revenge of the Materials: A Material Aesthetics for Modernity«. In: *Living in the Material World: »Things« in Art of the 20th Century and Beyond*. Exhibition Catalogue. Tokyo: National Art Center, 2007

Matthias Tarasiewicz

Coded Cultures Between New Media Arts and Production Cultures

Outlooks and Positions besides Creative Commonplaces

CODED CULTURES is a process we as *5uper.net* started in 2004, initially to address our self defined aim to display media cultures that work in the context of art. Apart from the necessarily apparent mediacy (which we thought is important in regard to those interested in contemporary art) we also wanted to bridge the gap of current technological, sociological and artistic questions by mapping subcultures of »art with media« as well as »art that reflects on media« (Reck, 2002) . Especially since the term media art had (and still has) a quite broad context of works and processes, we did not want to narrow it, but even enlarge it with the term *coded cultures* in order to also include cultures, that would not put their work in the context of art. This melange of works with technological, media related structures of (self) organization were brought together at a single place where a mixture of exhibition and symposia, workshops and concerts took place in an experimental setting. The approach was (and still is) to display »actants« (Latour, 1987/2005) and not objects: since works in the fields of new media arts are intertwined with the creator(s) and their cultural background, the whole context has to be made an issue.

In 2009, 5 years later, we performed the experiment *CODED CULTURES* again in Vienna (Austria) and in Yokohama (Japan), with a strong focus on exchange, not only of artists, theoreticians and thinkers between those two countries, but also of the general aims and cultural backgrounds. *CODED CULTURES—Exploring Creative Emergences* brought up lots of new food for thought in regard to coding and codification. Cultural accomplishments of individuals or differently organized forms of human beings in context with an ever-changing (transforming) environment bring manifold products and processes to surface: cultural artifacts, »distributed agencies«, »framed interactivity« (Rammert, 2008), collective ideas. My primary concern is neither popular culture nor technological inventions, I want to focus on incidents based on a »synergetic potential« (Fuller, 1969), »creative emergencies« [1] which can be brought up by inter-/trans-/meta-disciplinary and open cultures of production. We need to understand the correlations between culture, technology, codes, art and media to systemically comprehend what coded cultures do today to contextualize and state their ideas and concepts. For instance at the progress of an idea, which has different manifestations according to its location in the system of art, in the system of science, or in the system of economy.

Coded cultures [2] don't necessarily work in the realms of art—the term (as I see it) describes a field that includes media arts as well as »expert cultures«. With a stronger amalgamation of these fields, coded cultures have the potential to not only bring media arts to another level, but also feed back to those *production cultures* [3], because they have to open up to a broader audience, to new publics and new discourses. I want to include some of the questions which have arisen in our discourses since its very beginnings: What are the motivations of creatives/artists beyond the industries—are there (successful) role models or positions that are neither located in fine arts nor in creative industries? Where can these positions be found? What are systems in-between (art and science, etc.) and where is critical capability inherent in those systems? How can »new media art« (which is said to be cool, obscure and in a crisis (Lovink, 2003), allegedly) use the fragmentation of digital media—where is »really new media art« happening today? How can programmers/coders or technical production cultures position themselves in (or with) the fields of media arts? For the group 5uper.net, the term media arts still is understood not reduced to a forced practice with audiovisual machines, but with a self understanding of connecting arts reflexively with actual developments of technology and society (Rakuschan, 2004).

[1] CODED CULTURES 2009 had the subtitle »Exploring Creative Emergences«; the term »emergences« describes why things »emerge«.

[2] CODED CULTURES includes coders, hackers, media artists as well as »digital bricoleurs« (production cultures and expert cultures).

[3] I understand the term »production cultures« not necessarily related to creative industries, since they produce not mainly out of a capitalistic and economic reason, but out of other motivational backgrounds. The surplus of such non-economic production cultures is »cultural capital« (Bourdieu, 1983) and »symbolic

capital« (Bourdieu, 1982), but also a cultural surplus which can not be transformed to economic capital so easily, since it depends on social credence for a specific expertise.

The aim of this essay is, besides presenting approaches to the term coded cultures in regard to the discourse of this topic, to demand (and emphasize) a critical potential of media arts and production cultures in new amalgamations. Media art, as a *»cloud of micro-practices«* (Lovink, 2008) , is in its current situation (and with this I don't mean its crisis) because of its self-referentiality. While Lovink sees this as a negative development, I cannot fully share his pessimistic view, since lots of works are not only located in the field of art. Of course there is the common accusation of »selling out« when terms such as creative industries and prototyping appear. While media art still has *»no market, no galleries, few curators and critics«* (Lovink, 2008) —at least from a global perspective—the question arises if it should have a market in this sense. Isn't it true that because there is no traditional art market, media art forces much more creative approaches on where and how to position someone's work? I don't want to propagate leaving the art market, but from a perspective that it was never actually there (except in some rare cases) isn't it strange that some of the best works of media art are not positioned in the »traditional« art market at all? A possible answer is, to create new markets (not creative industries), as done by the art group *Minus Delta t* (Minus Delta t, 1982) for example, selling »shares« of their project, to let people take part in the project by financially supporting it. In the current precarious situation of projects as well as individual artists, it might be a no-brainer to understand why new media arts were very active in the time when the web arose: Coding and computer work were mostly seen as »magic« and therefore enough financial background was given especially to young media artists, to fund their own projects [4] . In this understanding, *»Dotcom culture has been ›anti-art‹ in a rather openly fashion«* (Lovink, 2008) but that did not matter—there are lots of examples of still active media artists that would work in the Dotcom field and still fund their own artwork (as an example, ***UBERMORGEN.COM*** and many others did).

[4] The projects Orf.at, 5uper. net and also CODED CULTURES (2004) were mainly funded by private money from people of the groups.

To my mind we have to make a distinction between autonomy and isolation (Blais, 2009) , media arts are much more isolated today, since—at least the young new media arts—were autonomous in times of the Dotcom era. In times of the wide popularity of the web and »creativity« becoming even a replacement for the term »art« (Raunig, 2007) we have to rethink what we call »new media arts«. I want to stress the roles of producers, coders and artists all together to create something beyond the usual artistic practice. It is true that discourses in media arts (and production cultures as well) are either self referential or reduced to a small part of experts, and opening up to a broader audience could force those fields to mature (art as a form of critique, intervention culture). In my understanding, coded cultures were much more present than traditional media arts all the time, because of their public which was not primarily galleries—and because of their self understanding of not being art in the first place.

While there are lots of different creative outputs, most of them are hidden (coded) for specific expert cultures and not intended for different audiences. Still, sometimes parts appear in other contexts, such as in media arts, showing the potential of the injection of production cultures in another context. Due to the transformation of goals, ideas and approaches from those production cultures for the media arts-context, new »proto-cultures« emerge (not in the sense of »art for technology's sake«! (Albert, 2001)). With ***CODED CULTURES*** (and in a sense also with this publication) we aim to observe this actual transformation from a technological, competitive or playful background to »artistic issues« or »interventional issues«.

Forms of Code

Codes in coded cultures can be seen as form building elements in regard to the systems theory of Luhmann, borders emerge through self referred operations which connect with each other (will of cooperation, same codex, same language, same aims, etc.) and are in this sense highly identity establishing for such socio technical systems. I also want to focus on the difference that emerges even within such systems (e.g. »forks« of software projects or group splits in art groups) and constantly produces new subsystems (components). Obviously it doesn't make sense to observe such heterogenous systems as if they were static and homogeneous, since they are in a constant process of re-structuring and re-formatting, always in resonance to each other. This is just one of the reasons why coded cultures don't have to appear only in the field of arts (and why they don't necessarily stay there, once they came up). The system »art« offers a higher connectivity (»self-referential« and »other-referential«) in contrast to economy or science. The term »contact« is very interesting with regard to Luhmann's systems theory, when we think of it as a place between the systems arts / media / technology / science / economy / etc. These contacts are what ***CODED CULTURES*** aims to discover, they are the subjects of coded cultures. Obvious terms of these contacts are Creative Industries (art / economy), Artistic Research (art/science) or Device Art (art/design/technology), but in my understanding of coded cultures they are relevant only to a limited extent, because they are mainly one thing: commonplaces. It is more interesting to focus on the subsystems, which are persistently altering—despite, or because of their possibility to vanish quickly.

Coding Cultures

CODED CULTURES explicitly was not meant to only deal with projects and groups in the art-context, but primarily aimed to bring together »cultures of production«, which work with new media on a daily basis. The *Vienna Perl Mongers* [5] were invited for software-talks and workshops (2004). Coders naturally have a (wide) creative potential, in this sense the *Perl*-community's motto is »There's more than one way to do it« (TIMTOWTDI). Coding cultures develop their own formats and contests to display new (creative) ways of problem solving—and to articulate problems. The often very specific problems can emerge in the following disciplines (specific, but not only applicable to the *Perl* community): *Golf* (the shortest possible code in ASCII characters addressing a specific problem), *poetry* (poems that are produced by the *Perl* interpreter without errors; also: *Perl-Haiku*), *Obfuscation* (»hiding« of the program code in various ways or making it extremely difficult to read), etc. In this context it is interesting to observe the ACME [6] name-space in the structured CPAN (*comprehensive perl archive network* [7]) directory: code modules that are fun in nature (see Chindogu) or highly experimental (not for production use and sometimes not even for productive use). Examples are *Acme::Bleach*—a module which renders the whole source code to tab and space characters, producing empty (blank) pages—with the code still working. Also, ASCII-art and »funware« is created in a playful sense to address the *Perl* community (or at maximum the programming communities) only.

Apart from *Perl* there is another computer language culture I observed: *Ruby*, which originated in Japan, and which also has a widespread creative approach [8] —even if only a few pop stars rose apart from commercial entrepreneurship: a positive example is *Why the Lucky Stiff* who created the meanwhile legendary *Why's (Poignant) Guide to Ruby* [9] (a comic-cutup teaching the computer language *Ruby*), and developed plenty of modules and approaches for today's *Ruby Culture* [10] and beyond. On August 19, 2009, *_why* deleted

[5] Community of the programming language *Perl*, http://vienna.pm

[6] Wiley E. Coyote often obtains complex and ludicrous devices from a mail-order company, the fictitious *Acme Corporation*, which he hopes will help him catch the Road Runner. Maybe chosen for its irony (Acme means the highest point, as of achievement or development)—ACME also is said to stand for »A Company Manufacturing Everything«.

[7] http://search.cpan.org/search?m=all&q=acme [Accessed: Dec 09, 2010]

[8] *Ruby*, in its beginning, was seen as exotic and only a few programmers were using it to create a distinction to programmers of other languages for web-systems. Lots of people adore it because of its »readable« code

his whole online presence—pieces of his work were archived and put together by people of the *Ruby* community. Very interesting about the coder/artist personality *_why* is—apart from his total anonymity (nobody knew his real name, although he performed as a musician and also gave talks at programming conferences)—his particular way of combining coding and art. While there is lots of speculation on why he has left the scene, I am most in favor of the thesis that he was disappointed on how the *Ruby* community evolved and how his work was misunderstood. I assume that a general disappointment about the hype that was produced around him was just one point (he wanted others not to admire him but to follow in his footsteps, as can be seen from his tutorials for kids). The main problem of your work being seen as funware and not as something between arts, coding and serious entertainment can be frustrating. Furthermore it is quite hard to take a position outside of the utilization machinery in an extremely meritocratic community of »liberal communist wannabes«—especially if you are being praised as one of the front faces for something that you don't want to stand for (in this case, the web 2.0 popularity of *Ruby* and the »Software-As-A-Service« rush that killed the spirit of the hacking scene [11], as some argue). In this sense, I understand his project *camping* as a criticism to *Ruby on Rails*—the whole code of this micro-framework fits on a single (printed) A4 paper page.

Coding cultures were close to media arts from the beginning of the popularity of the internet in the 1990s (and in other forms before, as the next chapter *Codex Cultures* points out). A well known example is the art persona *Netochka Nezvanova (NN)*, a pseudonym used by the authors of *nato.0+55+3d*, a real-time, modular, video and multi-media processing environment (mostly used by post-video-artists back then). Besides being *»a software programmer, radical artist and online troublemaker«* (salon.com, Mar 01, 2002) Netochka Nezvanova was famous for flaming (spamming) various lists such as nettime, 7-11, spectre, rhizome etc. in a rather creative way [12]. NN is a positive example for a successful amalgamation in the sense it was described before: by enlarging the audience, issues of programmers, media artists and software users were brought to surface (in a rather radical, spamming sense). By choosing to act with a »phantom«, the people behind NN created a pop figure that was recognized beyond the fields of new media discourse.

and its »sweet« syntax and semantics. 2005 it became popular because of *Ruby On Rails*, a Framework for web applications (Cf. Twitter, github, etc.).

9 http://www.ember.co.nz/resources/whys-poignant-guide-to-ruby/ [Accessed: Dec 09, 2010]

10 Cf. *Hackety Hack* (programming-environment and tutorials for children) and a clone of Amazon's web-service S3. *Shoes*, a User-Interface-Toolkit, was the first precursor of »desktop revolution«, which lead to the death of the web (Anderson, 2010).

11 David H. Hansson, creator of *Ruby on Rails* was awarded *Hacker of the Year* by O'Reilly and Google in 2005. The term »hacker« is used differently—also inside »hacking communities« (coding communities) there are different approaches on how to use that term. Especially the ideas of ethics and the position to popular culture, economy and publics is very different in this heterogenous field Cf. (Levy, 1984). Hacker in this sense is somebody of the programmer subculture(s).

12 See http://www.nettime.org/Lists-Archives/nettime-bold-0101/msg00011.html [Accessed: Nov 18, 2010] as an example.

Codex Cultures

Another culture we invited to *CODED CULTURES* 2004, is the so-called *Demoscene* (respectively protagonists of miscellaneous groups: Scoopex, Speckdrumm, etc.). Formed in the 1980s, this production culture developed computer demos, real time animations accompanied by music, similar to music video clips. These applications were mainly distributed by *Cracker* groups, which spread bootlegs of computer games (as well as other applications). The popularity of the demos can be seen as a result of floppy disks being the main media of the pre-harddisk era (and pre-CD era) when the animations had to be viewed during the loading process of an application. Even if the Demoscene later dissociated from the cracking scene, its golden age happened in the context of the *Cracks*: a (Europewide) contest took place to determine who bypasses copy protection first, and to celebrate technical superiority by means of an adequate *Tech-Demo*. The success of both the IBM-PC and the internet severely decreased the popularity of the *Demoscene*, nonetheless events such as contests, viewings, etc. have been and still are taking place.

In relation to coded cultures it is highly interesting that the demos are often produced with a very high technical excellence, often far beyond industry standards. Very strong and mandatory »codexes« evolved, and if someone did not respect those, other groups would criticize that matter in their demos [13]. One of the codexes was that the animations needed to be in real-time (in difference to pre-produced material, algorithms and often particular engines were developed). This culture, which is highly regimented through codexes, also used dissing (similar to the Hip-Hop culture) to prize someone's own work above the work of others. When I interviewed *Paralax* (a member of the demo-group *Speckdrumm*), I apprehended the self-conception of performing more than required: He understood his endeavors in the sense of the *Held der Arbeit* (»hero of work«—a honorific title of the German Democratic Republic and other communist countries) [14]. Codexes are also present in other groups and formations, as well as myth-building and branding, which have a very important position in the Demoscene. Beside those obvious facts, amusingly, the Demoscene found a way to bring their own discourse (flaming and dissing, as well as the demos themselves) to an audience, which could not fully understand the references and the contexts presented. Lots of people would not even know, these demos were in realtime [15]. This is a funny parallel to new media art, where self referentiality and isolation often led to confused viewers. New media art can learn from the Demoscene: in creating your own audience, autonomy is possible again. In this

[13] Cf. http://www.youtube.com/watch?v=xjFMoVyoCX0 [Accessed: Nov 18, 2010] In the year 2007, music producer Timbaland used the C64 sound of a demoscene artist in his song *Do It* without permission for doing so and therefore got dissed by the demoscene.

[14] Interview with Paralax (Speckdrumm) 2004, following interviews 2005 and 2010.

[15] In contrast to pre-developed audiovisual content, the demos were »coded«. In this sense, the audio and video is generated by the machine while being watched.

sense, even self referentiality is not a big problem. But since the media landscape pretty much changed since then, new ways of finding audiences need to be discovered—the Demoscene also did not accomplish this yet (although they are trying to position themselves in the media arts context).

Playful Cultures, Device Cultures, Modding Cultures.

I understand the term playful cultures in the context of the term » playfulness « which was the title of a symposium organized by 5uper.net and the Digital Arts and Architecture Lab (DAAL) in 2008. Playfulness describes the fundamental motivation of producers, which can be basically found in the DIY culture and in game culture (as well as in various fields of contemporary arts). The Do-It-Yourself movement emerged in the public sense of the 1950s in the context of »handymen« as a »culture of amateurs«; besides the Punk movement in the 1970s it is mainly located in arts and in activism nowadays. Modding culture in the sense of re-interpretation and re-configuration of (electronic) popular technology can be found in subcultures and youth movements since there are (technical) machines. Even the *Mods* can be seen as early playful tweakers—not only because of their name, but also because of the indeed impressive (although functionally dispensable) constructions of mirrors and »style-tweaks« on their *Vespas*. These constructions can be compared to the modification of computer cases of the case-modding and case-conning scene (the *Lego Mac*, The *Gingerbread PC*, *Steampunk Mods*). Modding culture also has its roots in music culture: Circuit Bending, the experimental manipulation of (audio-)circuits, has been existing since the 1960s and today it gains relevance from Open Source Hardware—such as the ×*0*×*b0*× (a clone of the Roland *TB-303*) or the *Audora 224* (a 2-Channel DJ Mixer). Beside the audio sector, with the *Arduino*, a programmable board, which is a very popular open device, many projects were carried out in the field of physical computing (hardware and software communicating with the analogue world). New possibilities of interaction with computers have always brought about a small revolution for users (computer mouse 1981/83, MIDI 1983, Nintendo Wiimote 2006, Apple iPhone 2007). I distinguish between two layers of playful devices:

- intended playful devices
- modded playful devices

»Intended playful devices« describes the intention of the industry to capitalize on »playful interfaces« (or ludic interfaces) and to use the playful approach to reach early adopters with its inventions. Often, ideas and concepts from prototypes in the media art context are taken and transformed into industrial interfaces. Making an intended playful device a »modded playful device« is possible, though Apple, Microsoft and other big players in the gaming and »ludic industry« are restricting the playful use to their own applications. Modded playful devices, obviously, don't necessarily intend modifications—they get different functions and uses (see Mathias Fuchs' »serious interfaces« and »ludic interfaces« in this book). The keyboard and the computer mouse can be defined as serious interface, compared to the Wii-remote, which is a (intended) playful interface (and the best example for a device that got modded from amateurs and experts worldwide with various functions; not because modding was intended by the manufacturer, but because of common technological standards and wide global distribution). An extreme example would be the aforementioned Arduino Board, which is an »intended modding device« (intended for being modded-playful). In the definition of intended playful devices, it is essential to consider time as a component: newly introduced devices are considered to be more playful than well-known common components (or implicate more playful potential, since they often include »intended playfulness« or trigger the techno-fetish of early adopters). Of course the interaction between hardware, software and wetware also matters: in the end, long-term playfulness is defined by the players—as any playful devices can lose their thrill. The cultural practices subsumed by Device Art and modding culture (re-interpretation and re- configuration) often occur out of ludic motivations: competition (to gain reputation in a certain field as can be noticed by reading the various blog-entries on the many Nintendo Wii mods), hacking (showing, that it can be done) or playfulness itself. Playfulness occurs between Lo-Fi and High-Tech: »Toy benders« (sound- bricoleurs converting sounding toys) as well as artists, who assign ludic features to non-ludic environments, are included in the term playfulness as are the gamers and bobos out there, using their playful devices as intended fetish objects (see Smartphones as the perfect intended playful devices, since their lifespan is quite short and their feature-count rises every year). While this is a very contemporary approach to the term, Machiko Kusahara shows how the idea of playfulness goes back to 12th century in Japanese culture (c.f. »Assembling Art, Design, Technology and Media Culture: The Challenge of Japanese Device Art« in this book).

The described areas bare a huge potential for new media arts, since the mobile-revolution brought lots of new audiences with intended playful devices into play. Still, in distinction from the game industry or the intended playful developers (because of the »mobile revolution« companies like Apple and Google press developers to push out new apps and »become rich quickly«), I have to demand a critical approach to designing applications for the newly appearing fragmentations of a new web. Possible approaches for artists and tweakers are either using the hardware, the software, or to combine both in a new way. While this is not different to previous uses of new media arts, the audience for such works dramatically increased in the last years. Apart from young people playing games, the Nintendo Wii and the iPhone triggered a »casual revolution« (Juul, 2009), so users of all age groups are eager to find new uses, abuses and applications for their devices [16]. I want to describe those phenomena in fields of intervention, where media art works are positioned in the context of playful/device/modding cultures. I don't want to narrow down the possibilities of intervention, so that the following structuring would only represent a snapshot and is by no means complete.

16 As can be seen by the popularity of blogs such as *gizmodo*, *engadget*, *crunchgear*, etc.

Radical Hardware

This term designates works such as *Device Art*-pieces as well as works from the modding cultures, extended with a critical component and transformed into media arts. Examples are works such as the *Insert Coin* arcade machines by *zugzwangzukunft* [17], the project *Constraint City* by Gordan Savicic [18], the *Painstation* by *//////////fur////*art entertainment interfaces [19] and *FuckU-FuckMe* by Alexey Shulgin [20]. Modding and the invention of new devices is enriched by a persiflage of prototyping: the possibility of those devices to be produced in masses is quite low; they are sometimes even »useless« (see Chindogu) as can be seen by the works of *Maywa Denki* (described by Machiko Kusahara in this book). Radical hardware describes a quite popular situation, since lots of people in the whole world are currently thinking about creative (ab)use of their devices and machines. I don't see much of the projects currently visible in the web as radical enough to fit into the category radical hardware, since they only criticize the industry's technical excellence and represent more of a tweaking-approach (for example, the *iPhone DSLR* [21] or the above mentioned *Gingerbread PC*). Saul Albert is right, when he writes: »*There is a common misconception in art and technology crossovers that any*

17 Media-art-pieces packed in (classic) arcade machines; visitors can only watch, when they pay 1 Euro. www.insertcoin.biz [Accessed: Nov 18, 2010]

18 »If electromagnetic waves are the new medium of city's communication system, then our everyday life is unavoidable entwined by an invisible

information cloud, built upon wireless interconnected networks. […] The project *Constrain City Walks* lets you literally feel this pain, by tightening a worn chest strap which is embedded in an ordinary jacket. The stronger the signal of perceived restriction, the harder your breath! Alternative routes through the city are the only constrained conclusion.« http://www.yugo.at/equilibre [Accessed: Nov 18, 2010]

19 Art object and arcade game based on *Pong* with pain feedback. http://www.painstation.de [Accessed: Nov 18, 2010]

20 http://www.welookdoyou.com/fufme/ [Accessed: Nov 18, 2010]

21 http://www.engadget.com/2010/07/17/iphone-dslr-the-next-generation-video/ [Accessed: Nov 18, 2010]

22 http://stelarc.org [Accessed: Nov 18, 2010]

23 Two casual *Nintendo DS* games, that track user behavior in the background. »[part of the] play is the creation and dissemination of an urban myth through spreading modified game cartridges back into the economic system.« The games deal with topics such as Terrorism and Nudity. http://www.yugo.at/processing/index.php?what=playsureveillance [Accessed: Nov 18, 2010]

24 »In 1996, ®TMark channeled $5000 from a New York shopkeeper as a reward to a Silicon Valley programmer for substituting hundreds of near-naked kissing boys for buxom babes, tuba players, and other computer game staples.« http://www.rtmark.com/simcopter.

cultural product can become art if it is robbed of its utility, that the product of a scientific or technological process is art if it has been done simply because it can be done. This misunderstanding replaces ›art for art's sake‹ with ›anything for it's own sake‹.« (Albert, 2001) . Radical hardware is not only approaching new media arts alone—of course *Tweakers* sometimes also have intentions to democratize technology or visualize social issues of new media. When prototyping gets enriched in a noncommercial, media based arts sense, I call it radical hardware. Radical does not mean radically new, but radical in terms of media-artistic utilization of the right hardware for the right job. STELARC [22] is a good example for somebody using radical hardware (in fact, he is the incarnation of radical human hardware).

Radical Software

Of course, there should be the term radical software as well, in order to describe game interventions and application art. For example works such as *PlaySurVeillance* [23] by Gordan Savicic, the *sim copter hack* [24] by *RTmark* and, to a certain extent, also the *I am Rich* [25] iPhone application. It can obviously appear together with radical hardware, but I have to draw a line by stating what is not radical software: everything that usually falls into the genre of software art, as well as educational games. I have to point on the term radical—and highlight it as a positive attribute of new media arts (in terms of quality, not in terms of conformity). While it is highly important to support open source, making it the sole message of a piece of work is problematic. To quote Dirk Baecker: *»the less talented lawyer attacks the objection to invalidate it, the gifted one develops his own argument and lets the objection dispose of itself«* (Baecker, 2007) .
I am stating this to make clear why I don't see software such as *proce55ing*, *vvvv* or *pure data* as »radical« enough to be called radical software. One can argue that *nato.0+55+3d* can be seen as radical software, because of its message and background. Radical software describes an interventional approach to applications and the usage of (software) systems. I do not want to point at interface design, but a synergetic (ab)use of software to address issues between technology and mankind, but also between economy and public, since the software industry (including also the game industry) is one of the biggest industries. I chose the term radical software to make a distinction to game art, since the term is used in an inflationary manner these days. People understand character design and good gameplay as game art,

while I want to distinguish between »moderate software« and »radical software«. In this sense, the game *Grand Theft Auto* is radical, but not radical software. I have to make this distinction to, again, stress a finer definition of new media arts as can be accomplished through a transformation process, which I understand as the artistic value, (radical) media artists add to a (pop)cultural commonplace such as game art and similar. Critical interventions with radical hardware, radical software and in coded cultures are always low-level: intended playful devices don't let you dig deep enough, as won't creative commonplaces such as creative industries. A good transformation process is multi-layered, in terms of being low-level (expert-discourse) as well as »easy to grasp« for the audience (public discourse/accessibility).

html [Accessed: Nov 18, 2010]

25 Application written for the Apple iPhone and sold for $999 a piece. The screen only contains a glowing red gem, and an icon, that reveals *»I am rich, I deserv (sic!) it, I am good, healthy & successful«* when pressed.

Critical Cultures

It is my self defined aim to outline and to claim critical potential within coded cultures. This aim is rather achievable using discourse theories than systems theory—although (or maybe because) both theoretical approaches have critical potential in terms of each other: *»One could argue that understanding, in the sense of Habermas, cannot come to an understanding with itself about itself in the same way, observation in the sense of Luhmann, cannot observate itself«* (translated from Füllsack, 1998) . I want to address the popular discussion between Luhmann and Habermas especially because of its basic questions: if sociology should describe society only in an objective sense, or if sociologists are forced to be critical within their scientific field (because sociologists are part of the society as well) (Habermas to Luhmann). Luhmann accused the critical-participative approach of the social, *»in its subjectivism unavoidably suggest the viability of conceptions of happiness and reconciliation, what lead to the fatal attempt of realization of a sociopolitical utopia, for instance as Marxism«* (translated from Füllsack, 1998) .

One can observe a similar debate in media art, where one question repeatedly occurs: »Sorry, but how exactly is your work critical?« Besides the fact that there are indeed many uncritical works in the field of media art (which is primarily because some parts of media art are interconnected with prototyping labs and departments of innovation in economic entities), sometimes the missing of a critical component can be linked to the problem of *pre-understanding*.

Today there is a generation gap already within media arts—using the example of digital natives and digital immigrants (since media arts is a commonplace of misunderstandings). Besides that, the media art scene as an heterogeneous system is surrounded by various different approaches and references, so that it is often impossible to pursue a discourse of experts (by that I do not mean art experts, but experts of production, as I described previously). The question arises whether art is being produced for the spectator or for a community of experts. This is a fundamental problem of coding as a process of pre-understanding. Lovink characterizes this state of media art by referring to the problem of self-reference. This reproach may apply to many works—but there are alternatives: Examples for accessible works are those of ***UBERMORGEN.COM***, *the yes men*, *moddr_* or ***BCL***.

In the panel ***CODED CULTURES***—*Exchange Emergences* at the *International Symposium for Electronic Arts 2010* [26], my attempt to explain the motivation of contemporary (Japanese) media artists using playfulness was criticized by a participant who said that *»playfulness as an approach lacked critical potential«*. Opposed to a game, the act of playing (play) contains—apart from its freedom potential—critical potential as well. Playing itself is a resistant contrafactum, which contains freedom potentials; but it is the intention of the player that adds the critical layer of meaning (see also the texts of Mathias Fuchs and Verena Kuni in this book). The term playfulness is often misunderstood: It is not about justifying the uncritical approach of prototyping labs and fun oriented artists. It is possible to create works that are playfully fine and critical as well, the artist does not have to suffer to be critical (although certainly a bigger part of media arts and creative scenes live in precarious conditions).

26 http://j.mp/ccisea2010 [Accessed: Dec 09, 2010]

In order to claim critical potential it is necessary to stress the term criticism. Besides the actual subject matter of critique, there is a need to use the term »critic« (the person who criticizes); mainly because of the fact that in today's technology centered society and within the »economy of attention« (Franck, 1998) critical positions can only reach the public and the mass media through »extreme interventions« (hacks, fakes) or »extreme excellence« (genius). But even then the interpretation of the media and the impacts of media coverage cannot be entirely predicted in advance—a point that adds a playful component to the »arts of intervention« (see Yukiko Shikata's essay on ***UBERMORGEN.COM*** in this book). In Foucault's lecture *What is Critique* (held at the end of May 1978), he points out that critique does not only contain art and virtue but also technique [27]. Foucault

27 *»Here, the term ›art‹ is closely related to the greek term techne, therefore in his lecture Foucault states*

mentions the term »*parrhesia*« (which can be loosely translated as »freedom of speech«) to describe the concept of discourse, which is very interesting in terms of the radical media artist. Firstly, *parrhesia* itself is a game [28] , and secondly the *Parrhesiastes* always has to take a risk. This means to jeopardize the status, or in the worst case even to gamble with the own life to tell the truth. The *Parrhesiastes* has to be courageous to take those risks—which is from my point of view essential to the radical media artist. (See in this context again ***UBERMORGEN.COM***, which had to face tons of lawsuits because of their project *Vote-Auction*).

criticism not only as ›art‹ and ›virtue‹, but also as ›technique‹. This is not Foucault's quirk, in fact it is a tradition going back to the original uses of the term critique. In Platon's Politikos, the term at first appears as the combination kritiké techne, which means the art, the crafts of distinguishing (translated as »ars iudicandi« in Latin). The label critique as ›technique‹ and as ›art‹ can be observed in the course of the centuries and of the different European languages.« (translated from Raunig, 2004)

28 *»Parrhesia is always a Game [or: Play] between the one who speaks the truth and his collocutor.«* (translated from Foucault, 1983)

In my opinion, the domain of (new) media art is, where fusions of technology-discourse and society-discourse meet: the dealings with new media, machines, effects and capabilities for cultural and artistic production. Apart from the question whether art is critical or not, the question also arises whether the public is included in this discourse. In my understanding, media art should illustrate *Lebenswelten* (lifeworlds), which improve current social situations. But media art is only able to do so, if it is critically self-reflexive and if it is in stronger regard to the forms of critique of the past. In the best case, media art can meet economic requirements of the creative industries when it is reduced to a form and object discourse.

Highscore Cultures

In the 21st century, the geek culture became pop: internet affinity, online identity and game culture are no longer going hand in hand with social incompetence. While it was »magic« back in 1999 when people had their own online-presence, tweeting, blogging (at least micro-blogging) and facebook-profiles are not separable anymore from our media usage. In the current global networks, new forms of lifeworlds are illustrated: the *Viewser* [29] should have lots of digital friends (rendering the term friend inflationary) and participate in the sense of the »interactive« web 2.0 to feed the global networks and receive a score (reputation or a real quantification of participation, such as »badges« or participation-levels). Users driven by *Statusangst* (»status anxiety«) (de Botton, 2004) are trying to be as creative as possible and innovate as much as they can, to stand out of the masses by their creativity, to get better jobs and better digital profiles (see systems such as LinkedIn, Xing, Stack Overflow). The digital profile, the digital fingerprint becomes a form

29 Jargon: *»viewer and user of digital or online media that combine interactivity with traditional broadcast entertainment«*

to quantify abilities, innovativeness, flexibility, adaptability, and self representation to make them comparable and measurable. With the current situation of intended creativity and creative commonplaces, we have to take a step back and think what the position of new media art should be. Claude Lévi-Strauss coins the term of the »bricoleur« (the »savage thinker«) and puts him into contrast with the engineer (the modern scientist). The main difference between them is the approach (the concept) of creating a whole out of pieces (modules) [30]. The »tinkerer« as opposed to the engineer can also be found in the argumentation of Nicholas Carr (Carr, 2005), who questions the positivity of the term »amateurism« in context with web 2.0. Because I look at the current global media situation using Lévi-Strauss' terms, I can relate to a position, where we are all professional amateurs, bricoleurs of our digital self. We are digital savages, being conquered by the global networks that we feed. In this sense, the web revolutions increased the computational power by the global networks with human resources, as outlined by terms such as »crowd sourcing« or »human computation« [31]. I want to coin this form of »distributed slavery« with the term » human computing « adding to the discourse of »social computing« (cf. Surowiecki, 2006). While obvious distributed data mining is taking place almost everywhere these days, still people don't even know they are being part of a global collection movement (see the distributed data collection from Apple and iPhone users around the globe [32] in contrast to the discussion of the permission of Google Street View cars in certain European countries).

Our interaction with reality and our understanding of the world has been radically changed by the infosphere, while the basic situation of power structures and world order stayed the same (see also Marina Gržinić in this book). 2006, Alex Soojung-Kim Pang and David Pescovitz posted their interviews with William Gibson, Vint Cerf and Neil Gershenfeld (and others) in *Wired Magazine* (Pang, 2006), asking for a new definition of the term cyberspace, since the web feels like »just another layer of life«. Terms such as »ubiquitous computing«, »augmented reality« and »global brain« (among others) came up. I understand the progress of the last years as follows: the infosphere becomes a »redundancy sphere« because of recent web 2.0 developments [33]. A critical and agile »Noosphere« [34] should be still be our main aim—which is only possible to reach with extreme measures. We have to reclaim the webs, after all the intended revolutions have only introduced more markets and are in this sense only micro revolutions of the hyper capital. While an artistic askesis may not be possible, at least the capital market is not as

30 *»Jedes Element stellt eine Gesamtheit von konkreten und zugleich möglichen Beziehungen dar; sie sind Werkzeuge, aber verwendbar für beliebige Arbeiten innerhalb eines Typus.«* (Lévi-Strauss, 1968)

31 See the *Google Image Labeler* and *re:captcha* (Luis v. Ahn) as examples.

32 Cf. http://www.spiegel.de/netzwelt/web/0,1518,70417,00.html [Accessed: Nov 18, 2010]

33 Cf. *re-tweeting*, *re-blogging* and the *capitalization of content* because of *Google AdSense* and the similar (*content-spamming, context-marketing*, etc.)

34 I don't mean the *Noosphere* as described by Marshall McLuhan (which can be roughly translated as a prophecy of the world wide web) but as denoted by Vladimir Vernadsky and Teilhard de Chardin: »sphere of human thought«.

untouchable after all (for example see *the yes men* and their BBC media fake [35]).

Possible countermeasures should be the goal of radical media arts in coded cultures: to illustrate another *Lebenswelt* that brings us closer to a sane Noosphere—that outlines the problematic over-fetishization of new technology and a critical position to data collections (and the power gained through possession of data). The digital bricoleurs—the savages—are the ones who can make a change. Neither the *microserfs* (Coupland, 1995) nor the »liberal communists« (Žižek, 1997) change the world (in a good way). Slacktivism is omnipresent, as can be seen in *causeclicks.org*: *»Thank You! Your click just generated a donation to build a school in Ethiopia«* [36]. It's so chic to be a slack-tivistic nerd [37] (bobo) nowadays—the main goals came out of focus: the web revolution was thought as revolution of the bricoleurs, becoming more open, not hypercentralized (nourishing the real divide [38] while fighting the digital divide) as we have it today.As Buckminster Fuller was right when he wrote *»specialization is in fact only a fancy form of slavery«* (Fuller, 1969), but more than that, even non-specialists become enslaved today. I see the radical media artist as the »grand pirate«, the Parrhesiastes who has to stand up and speak the truth, although it can hurt (literally).

35 *The Yes Men Fix The World*. 2009. http://theyesmenfixtheworld.com/

36 While *causeclicks.org* is offline now, I am not sure if it was not a (quite cynical) media intervention.

37 Cf. http://nerdboyfriend.com/ or *the big bang theory* (U.S. TV series) and others.

38 *»Here's a hot stock tip: Buy Facebook. [...] If you buy a chunk of Facebook and flip your shares in a few years, you could make millions. Oh, but wait: You can't. Facebook isn't a public company. The only people who can invest in it already are millionaires.«* (Boutin, 2010)

References

Albert, S.: *Useless Utilities*. 2001.
http://twenteenthcentury.com/saul/useless.htm [Accessed: Nov 18, 2010]

Anderson, C., Wolff, M.: »The Web is Dead. Long Live the Internet«.
In: *Wired Magazine*. August 2010

Baecker, D.: »Einleitung in Niklas Luhmanns Soziale Systeme«. In: Baecker, D.: *Nie wieder Vernunft: Kleinere Beiträge zur Sozialkunde*. pp. 456–466. Heidelberg: Carl-Auer-Systeme, 2007

Blais, J., Ippolito, J. in »Discussing the Crisis in New Media Art«, 2009 http://networkcultures.org/wpmu/geert/2009/02/ [Accessed: Nov 18, 2010]

Bourdieu, P.: »Ökonomisches Kapital, kulturelles Kapital, soziales Kapital«. In: Kreckel, R. (Ed.) *Soziale Ungleichheit*. Göttingen: Schwartz 1983

Bourdieu, P.: Die feinen Unterschiede. Kritik der gesellschaftlichen Urteilskraft.
Frankfurt a.M.: Suhrkamp, 1982

Boutin, P.: »Let the Little Guys Get in on Pre-IPO«.
In: *Wired Magazine*. August 2010

Carr, N.: »The Amorality of Web 2.0«. 2005
http://www.roughtype.com/archives/2005/10/the_amorality_o.php [Accessed: Nov 18, 2010]

Coupland, D.: *Microserfs*.
New York: HarperCollins, 1995

DeBotton, A.: *StatusAngst*.
Frankfurt a.M.: Fischer, 2004

Foucault, M.: *Diskurs und Wahrheit*.
Berlin: Merve, 1983

Franck, G.: *Ökonomie der Aufmerksamkeit: Ein Entwurf*.
München: Carl Hanser, 1998

Fuller, B.: *Operating Manual For Spaceship Earth*.
New York: Simon & Schuster, 1969

Füllsack, M. in: *Soziale Systeme. Zeitschrift für soziologische Theorie*. pp. 185–198. Jg. 4, H. 1/1998, 1998

Juul, J.: *A Casual Revolution: Reinventing Video Games and Their Players*.
Cambridge, Mass.: MIT Press, 2009

Latour, B.: *Science in Action: How to Follow Scientists and Engineers Through Society*
Berkshire: Open University Press, 1987

Latour, B.: *Reassembling the Social: An Introduction to Actor-Network-Theory*.
Oxford: Oxford University Press, 2005

Levit, Georgy S.: *Biogeochemistry, Biosphere, Noosphere: The Growth of the Theoretical System of Vladimir Ivanovich Vernadsky* (1863–1945)

Levit, Georgy S.: *The Biosphere and the Noosphere Theories of V. I. Vernadsky and P. Teilhard de Chardin: A Methodological Essay.* International Archives on the History of Science. New York: Fordham University Press, 2000

Levy, S.: »Ten Years After«. In: *Hackers: Heroes of the Computer Revolution*. Garden City,
New York: Anchor Press/Doubleday, 1984 (New additions in the 2010 Edition, Sebastopol: O'Reilly, 2010)

Lévi-Strauss, C.: *Das wilde Denken*. p. 30.
Frankfurt a. M.: Suhrkamp, 1968

Lovink, G.: *Zero Comments*.
London: Routledge, 2003

Minus Delta t: *The Bangkok Project*, 1982 See Minus Delta t plus.
Berlin: Merve, 1982

Pang, A. S.-K., Pescovitz, D.: »Cyberspace is Dead«.
In: *Wired Magazine*. February 2006

Rakuschan, F. E., 5uper.net: *Coded Cultures—Decoding Digital Culture*. 2004
http://j.mp/codedcultures2004 [Accessed: Nov 18, 2010]

Rammert, W.: *Where the Action is: Distributed Agency Between Humans, Machines, and Programs.*
Berlin: Technical University Technology Studies Working Papers, 2008

Raunig, G.: »Aussetzung und Neuzusammensetzung in textuellen und sozialen Maschinen«.
In: Mennel, B., Nowotny, S., Raunig., G. (Eds.): *Kunst der Kritik.* Republicart 10. Wien / Berlin: Turia+Kant, 2004

Raunig, G., Wuggenig, U.: »Kritik der Kreativität. Vorbemerkungen zur erfolgreichen Wiederaufnahme des Stücks Kreativität«. In: Raunig, G., Wuggenig, U. (Eds.): *Kritik der Kreativität.* Wien / Berlin: Turia+Kant, 2007

Reck, H.U.: *Mythos Medienkunst.*
Köln: Kunstwissenschaftliche Bibliothek, 2002

Russegger, G., Wlodkowski, M., Tarasiewicz, M.: *Coded Cultures—Exploring Creative Emergences.*
Wien: 5uper.net, 2009

Surowiecki, J.: *The Wisdom of Crowds.*
New York: Random House, 2005

Tarasiewicz, M.: »playfulness«.
In: *thegap.* 09/2008

Why the lucky Stiff: *Why's (poignant) Guide to Ruby.*
Milwaukee: Sam Warmuth, 2009

Žižek, S.: *Der liberale Kommunist.* 2000
http://www.cicero.de/97.php?ress_id=6&item=1215 [Accessed: Nov 18, 2010]

3

Essays

MARGARETE JAHRMANN / LUDIC CHINDOGUS AS EROTIC TOYS

280

This paper introduces a number of conceptual key terms around the art and politics of play, as Jouissance, Playsure Politics, Ludic Chindogu Interfaces and Ludics. Seminal practices of arts for the development of a critical consciousness through play are introduced, in order to emphasise the quality of enjoyment and erotic attraction in the agency dimension of play with an object. The contemporary slave and master relation of players in everyday life to their technological objects is identified throughout the argument as driving force for social agency in everyday life that really matters!

VERENA KUNI / URBAN PLAY-GROUNDS, ALTERNATE GAMES

304

Departing from a brief introduction into the field in focus—urban playgrounds—and into possible approaches to it offered by different games played in this field, the following essay will take a closer look at Alternate Reality Games. However, rather than giving a survey of what has been so far developed and released within this (sub-)genre of contemporary gaming, the aim is to dig deeper into ARGS from a methodological point of view—and to propose some thoughts on the potentials (and problems) of ARGS and ARG-related features as a tools for collective/networked research and action in urban environments.

YUKIKO SHIKATA / UBERMORGEN.COM / FROM SOMEBODY'S DESIRE TO EVERYONE'S RESPONSIBILITY

334

UBERMORGEN.COM is an artist duo created in Vienna, Austria, by lizvlx and Hans Bernhard. Behind UBERMORGEN.COM we can find one of the most unmatchable identities—controversial and iconoclastic—of the contemporary European techno-fine-art avant-garde. Their open circuit of conceptual art, drawing, software art, pixel painting, computer installations, net.art, sculpture and digital activism (media hacking) transforms their brand into a hybrid Gesamtkunstwerk. The computer and the network are (ab)used to create art and combine its multiple forms. the permanent amalgamation of fact and fiction points toward an extremely expanded concept of one's working materials that for UBERMORGEN.COM also include (international) rights, democracy and global communication (input-feedback loops). »Übermorgen« is the German word both for »the day after tomorrow« and »super-tomorrow«. WWW.UBERMORGEN.COM

»The Balance of my Wildness and my Intelligence was Way Off«

UJINO ON UJINO, A PORTRAIT BY DAVID D'HEILLY

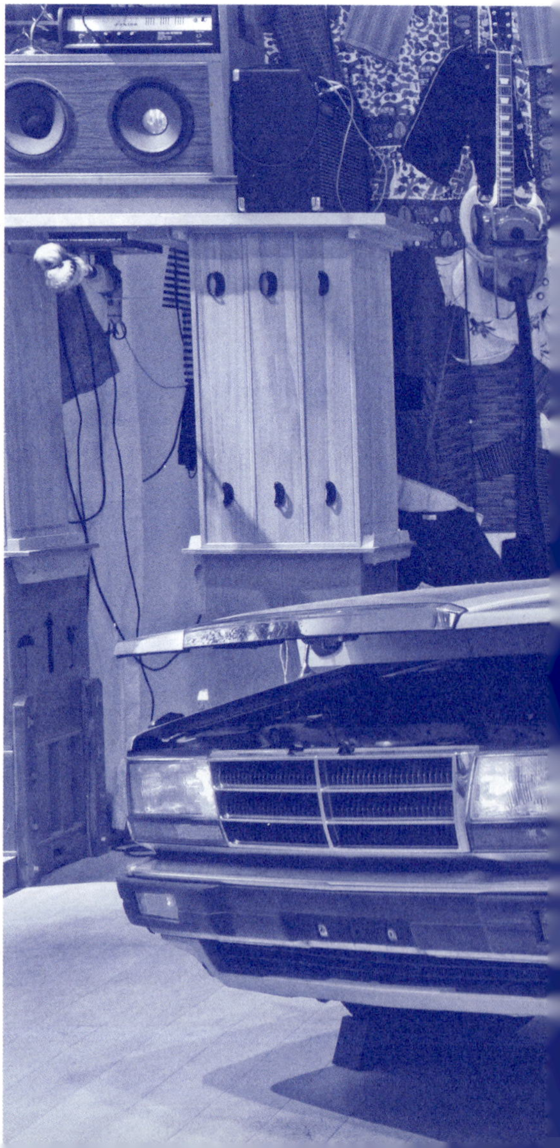

Fig. 1: Ujino: Ballad of Extended Back Yard, Pt. 1*, 2010. Detail.*
Nissan Cedric van, wood furniture, household electrical appliances and mixed media

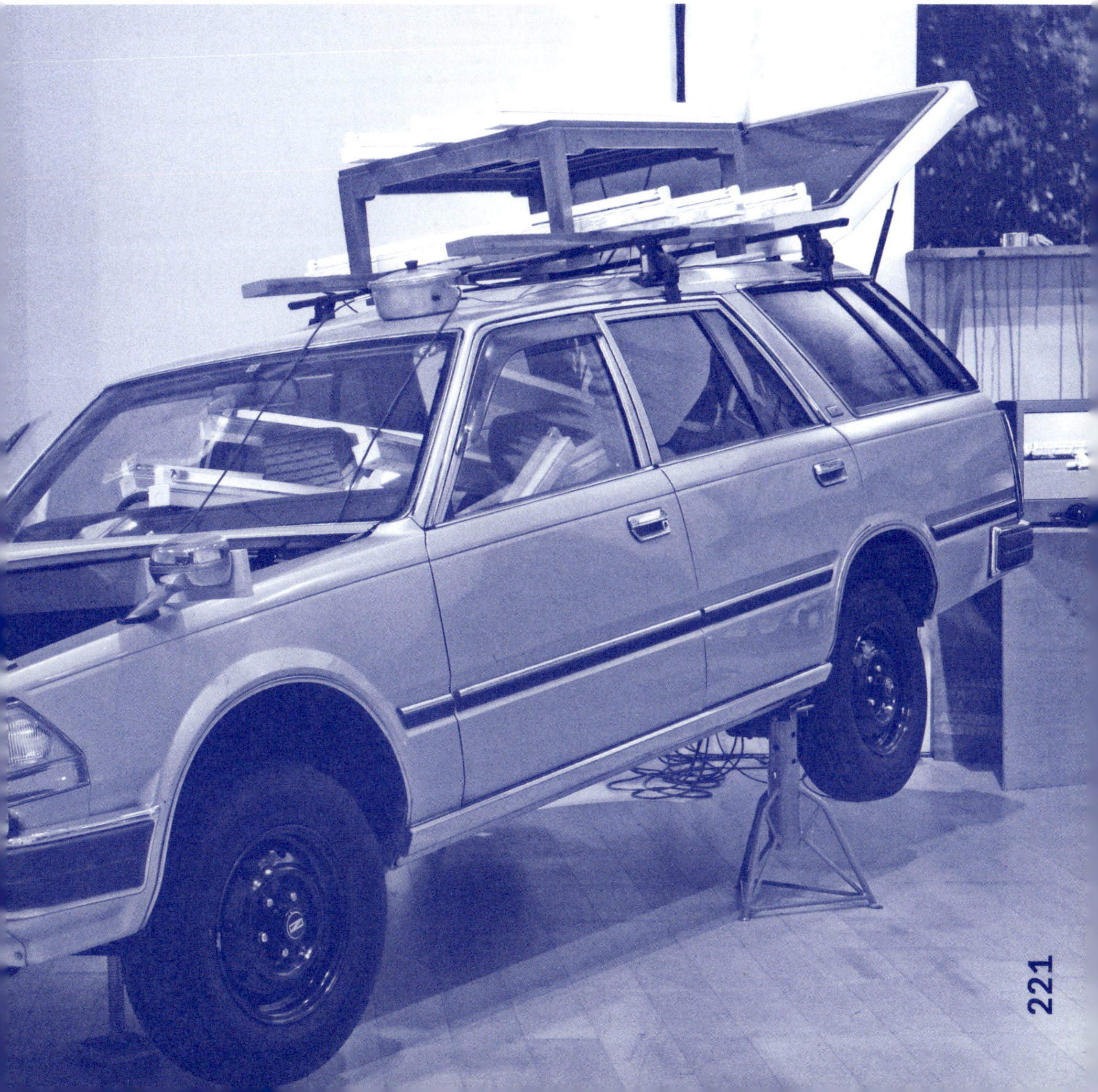

»I Always Knew that No Matter how Many Years I Aged, No Matter how Mature I Might Become, I would Never Become Him«

I was born, raised, and still reside in Nerima City, in NW Tokyo. Nerima was the last of the special wards incorporated after the War. It is in the center of a large plain directly inward from Tokyo Bay. It has the largest area of agricultural land, providing 40% of the cabbage grown in Tokyo. It has the longest life expectancy in the 23 Wards. When I was a child, the plots surrounding us were vast lawns and cabbage patches. I used to romanticize that it was like what Alaska is to the US 1 .

1 Pre-modern Tokyo, or Edo (1603–1868), was traditionally populated east of the imperial palace. The west was garden and farm lands. Japanese architecture then and now was ephemeral: major fires and floods were a regular feature of urban life. Buildings lasted a few decades. The turn-of-the-century industrialization of early Tokyo led to a run of land speculation, which was capped by Tokyo's first residential zoning laws in 1919. Four years later, the Great Kanto Earthquake struck and the city was once again decimated. This time though, rather than rebuild where the population had traditionally lived, downwind, in the east, everyone moved west, populating what used to be estates and farmland. Incorporation as a Special Ward is a designation as part of the old city, distinguishing a city from the massive prefectural conurbations that exploded outwards from the 1920s.

I was born into a prosperous family, in a prosperous time. It was 1964, the year of the Tokyo Olympics. Tokyo had nearly quadrupled its GDP in the previous decade, was now a member of most multinational trade organizations and was the star of its own Economic Miracle: very much like China today. My father was 50 and my mother 40 when I was born, I was their only child. My mother's parents were from Kyushu, but had joined the mass emigrations to Manchukuo (Japanese occupied Manchuria) and ran a shipping company there, where my mother was born. My father was in the army, assigned to Manchukuo. They met, fell in love and married there. After the war, my parents returned to Japan and my father resumed his post at a mining company. By the time I was born he was an executive there. My father passed away when I was 27.

Today my wife and I live in that same traditional Japanese house which is, by and large, exactly as my father designed it. He collected antiques. My childhood memories are of him, after work, sitting quietly in his indigo kimono—indistinguishable from a character in a Yasujiro Ozu film—wordlessly polishing a sword, or pot, or some small artifact. I remember that when drinking with colleagues he was sociable, affable—but at home, he was quiet. His musical tastes ran to classical epics and naniwabushi shamisen minstrel narratives. In western music, he'd listen to Sarasate's Zigeunerweisen, for example. His sport was golf. I used to watch him and I always knew that no matter how many years I aged, no matter how mature I might become, I would never become him. My mother is 86 now. She's still well, and enjoying life. My mother is the polar opposite of my father. She loves the trends of the moment. 40 years ago it was Tupperware. Today it's the latest home electronics, but she's dead serious about it. I think she's always been a bit susceptible to the frivolities of capitalism.

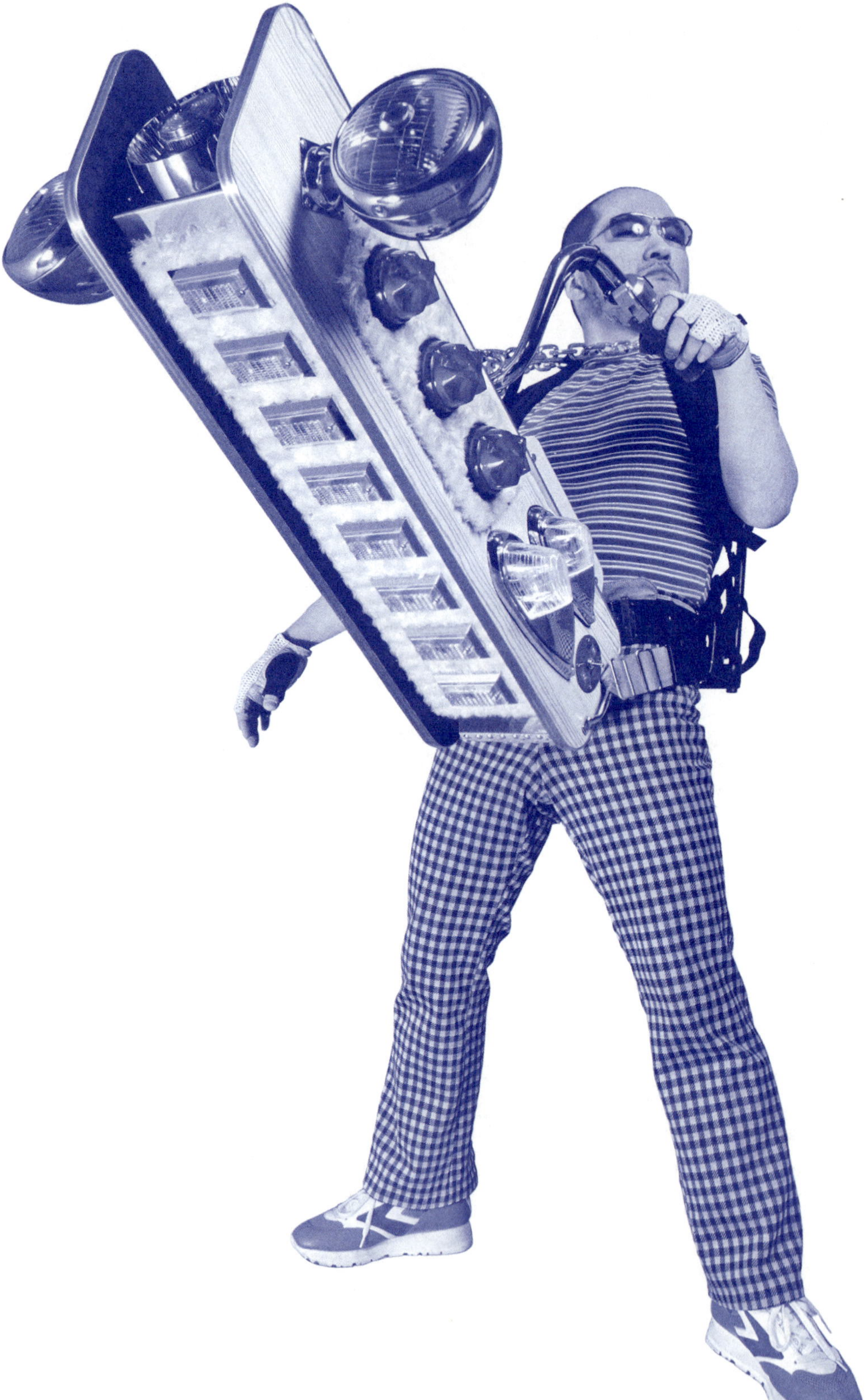

Fig. 2: Ujino: Love Arm 2pro *(American Standard)*

»Completely Brutal in a Very Positive Way«

I'm a first generation otaku [2] *.*

[2] A quick history of otaku. *Otaku subculture originally meant urbanites (typically males) with a strong commitment to one particular hobby. The cultural genesis of this »otaku« commitment is often described by decade of birth.*

1950s: Pre-Otaku. *Science fiction fans who came to respect* gekiga Manga, *with their more realistic graphic and narrative depictions, especially of science fiction themes, though they were still raised in an environment which considered Manga a child's medium. This generation, while too young to participate, watched the student revolts at universities in Japan (nominally against the American violation of its security treaties with Japan in prosecuting the Vietnam War but essentially the same kind of anti-bourgeoisie revolt seen throughout the developed world in the late 1960s) and became known for being apolitical later as a result. A pivotal old guard of many later otaku institutions.*

1960s: 1st Generation Otaku. *The fan base that made a phenomenon out of* Space Battleship Yamato *and established institutions like the comic markets, which continue to this day. Raised on »transformation type« TV shows featuring protagonists who are temporarily upgraded to defeat overwhelming, grotesque and belligerent creatures, they include both* tokusatsu *(special effect driven live action works) such as* Ultraman *and* Kamen Rider, *and Anime such as* Mazinger Z. *First generation otaku were known for carefully constructing their subculture, and are known as the »jargonists« for their use of code words to obfuscate their world from dominant culture and the cold war political polemic still prevalent at that time. A prime example of this is the word »otaku« which is about as vague an expression for »you« (in remote connotation with one's affiliation) as the Japanese language will allow.*

1970s: 2nd Generation Otaku, *the* Ganota. *These were the children of post war baby boomers. Their otaku awakening came through the* Gundam series *(*Gundam Otaku = Gan-Ota*). They connected with the Anime/Manga otaku canon and electronic media as aspects of the same subcultural phenomenon. Plastic models and figurine culture (such as promoted by the Gundam series, which is, in effect, a series of promotions for toys) became much more important.*

1980s: 3rd Generation Otaku. Neon Genesis Evangelion *is the pivotal series of this generation. Computers/technology are no longer special. The »subcultural« aspects of much previous otaku culture become irrelevant; the internet is just another entertainment like the TV. Women play an increasing role in »otaku« subcultures from this generation to the present. From the third generation on, otaku culture is more spatial than temporal. Fans are attracted more by the premise (worldview) of a story than its narrative. The idea of subcultural generations is less important than, for example, the ways in which urban subcultures organize themselves within the city, or develop alliances with rural subcultures.*

Like many other Japanese of my generation, I was heavily influenced by Manga, but I stopped living the otaku lifestyle when I was a junior high school student. I can still watch tokusatsu *film marathons—*Ultra Seven, Kamen Rider, *or* kaijyu monster films *(the most famous of which is* Godzilla*) —film after film without getting bored. The most important works for me were:* War of the Gargantuas, Kamen Rider, Android Kikaider *or in Manga: Tatsuhiko Yamagami's* Gaki Deka *or anything by Fujiko Fujio A. After that I started* *listening to American and British music on the radio and reading magazines like* Music Life *which taught me all about* KISS, QUEEN *and whatnot … This was just after progressive rock had peaked, but still before punk or new wave. For me,* KISS *was a crucial bridge between Japanese* tokusatsu *films and American pop music (I still listen to* KISS *even now. I saw them on their last tour).* KISS *were an ambitious attempt to represent a common urban culture, devoid of any ethnic or traditional elements. I was totally inspired by this.*

I entered junior high school just as punk rock came out. Regrettably, in Japan, punk rock was all about the fashion, so as an angry young man I had to rebel. (laughs) Later, I learned more about the New Wave *movement and the musical* DIY *spirit behind punk through bands like* DEVO *and the* Talking Heads. *In 1980, when I was sixteen, I went to see* DEVO *live at* Shibuya Public Hall. *The violence of their performance electrified me. From media I had understood that they were going to be cool and ironic. But their live show, while highly conceptual, was at the same time completely brutal in a very positive way. This was rock and roll! And I was thrilled to experience it in the flesh.*

So when I entered high school my dream was to start a band, but my high school was a kind of elite school where half of the kids go to Tokyo University. *I was a really inarticulate kid and I was quickly at the bottom of the class. All my classmates were devoted to becoming bureaucrats; which is to say that everyone I knew was terrified of making any kind of mistake. That's all that mattered to them.* Tokyo University *has the most competitive entrance exams in the country, so everyone basically operated under the principle that someone else's loss—someone else's mistake—was their gain. So I attended school, quiet as ever, during the day, and played bass in a band at night that performed* top of the pops *numbers at school festivals and parties. I started to hang out with girls, and go to discos. When I think back about it now, I didn't really have any musical talent. I used to accessorize my bass; painting it, or pasting mirrors on it. I was just up on stage, strapped to this amazing object, making it perform. It was pretty tricked out. I wonder who's playing it now?*

»It's Useless Telling You Anything«

I decided to go to art school on a whim. One day our teacher was asking everybody what their plans were. I had to say something, so I replied »Tokyo University ... of Fine Arts«*. It was just me being competitive.* Tokyo University *and* Tokyo University of Fine Arts *are the former Imperial Universities. They are sister schools, but academic examinations aren't as important to being accepted at the* Tokyo University of Fine Arts. *But they are both the very top universities in Japan. Anyway, I could draw Manga. I was knowledgeable about* tokusatsu. *I was good at making things and I was pretty familiar with my father's many not necessarily valuable Asian antiques—but I had zero knowledge of Western art.*

I failed my first examinations to enter the design department. Then I spent another year for preparation, going to cram schools. I'd heard of people who spend years to get accepted by Tokyo University of Fine Arts, *like four or five years just preparing, but that didn't prepare me for the very real cultural shock of actually finding myself in there with them. I was desperate to get out and worked really hard to master a certain set of basic techniques; »plaster drawings« of Greek and Roman sculptures, or »flat construction« to construct Western paintings. I learned about* Bauhaus *and three-dimensional design in clay.*

Originally I was aiming to become a designer, but somehow, vaguely, intuitively, I started to think that the core of creation lied somehow within the making. These days I've learned to articulate how Asian art is rooted in the handcraft, but back then, it was all vague intuition. What I did know was that I wanted to experience the journey of building up these, I don't know, somewhat animistic Japanese aesthetic worlds. I wanted that experience. So I tried for the craft department, and I got accepted. I was expecting university to be a cerebral, intellectual experience, but it was more like a guild of master and disciple. For the first two years we were expected to learn the basic techniques of traditional crafts; working with metals, ceramics, lacquers, dyes etc. Typical conversation: Me, asking one of my professors, »Listen, I'm having trouble understanding this exercise, why we're doing it, or what we're trying to achieve. I'm not asking about how to get good marks, I just want to know where I should set my objectives for this exercise … «

Professor, to me: »It's useless telling you anything. You signed up for this. Do as you're told«. *My classmates, most of whom were born into traditional craft families, were so cool about all of this —everything they did they did smoothly. But I was out of my depth, and deeply disappointed. In the end I chose textile dyeing because it had the fewest traditions and was more—how should I say—vivid, so I escaped into that. But university was horrible, still. All of that time and energy, all about endurance rather than edification. I guess it did teach me something about what animism is, in craft, though.*

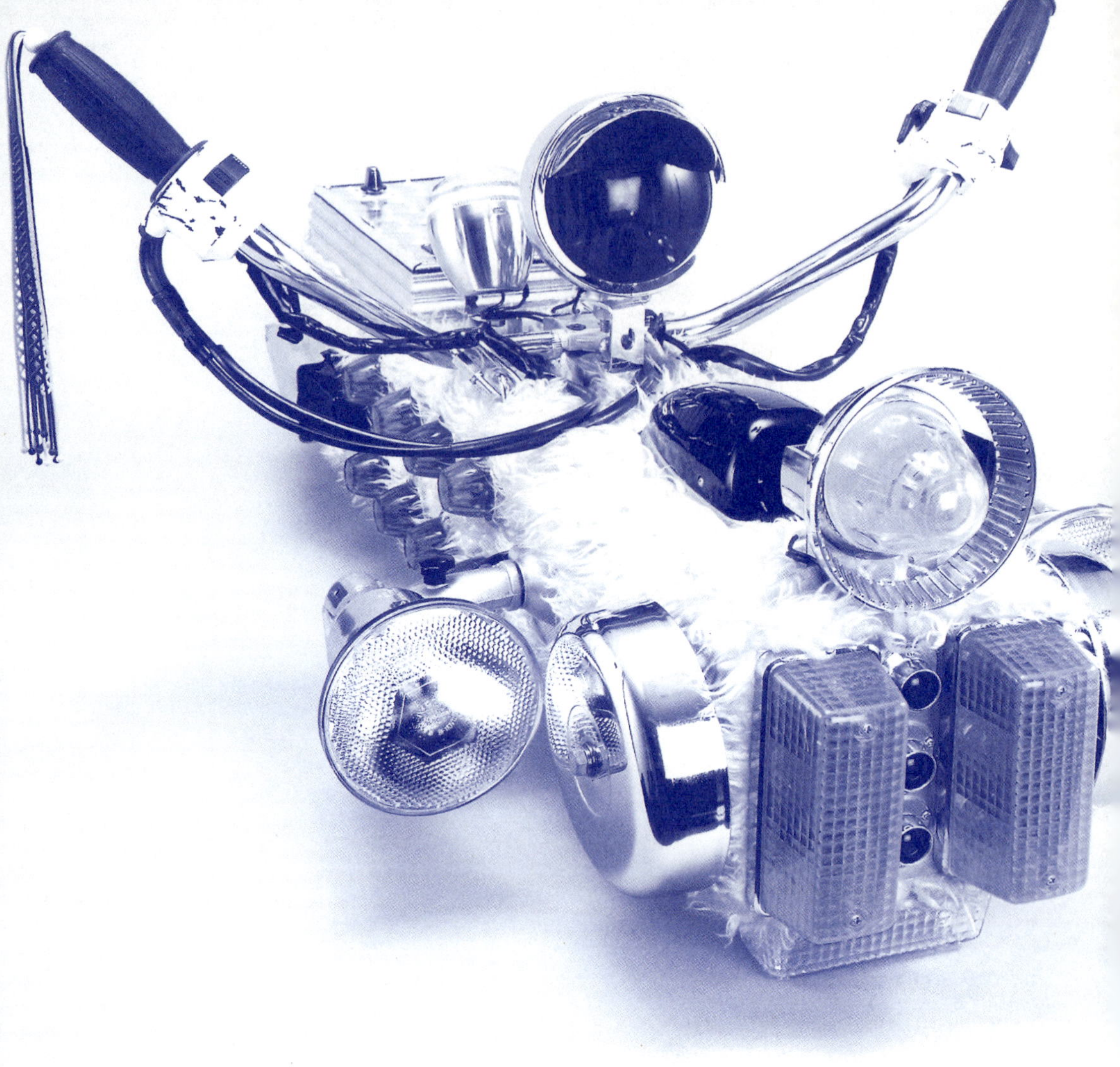

Fig. 3: Ujino: Love Arm 2, *1995. Mixed media, 83 × 73 × 100 cm*

»I Wanted to Create Something Weighty, Something Definite«

In the end, I did graduate. It was the end of 80s, in the middle of the Japanese asset price bubble. Personally I was alternately angry and melancholic, but in a super optimistic world. No one was anxious or serious like we are now. I sort of vaguely imagined that I could put off entering the workforce a few years longer by going to graduate school, but they didn't accept me. I mean, of course they didn't ... and by then my classmates had filled all of the really good employment opportunities, so I continued working part time at the cram school, the job I'd held while at university.

After a year of living like this, an old friend, the son of a tea ceremony and flower arrangement teacher, introduced me to a master gardener. Gardeners participate in tea ceremonies as they create tea gardens. I was still interested in that kind of mystical Japanese traditional world, so I spoke with the master, who accepted me, and I started to work in Japanese gardens. Of course, I again encountered the same problems as in the crafts world—while my body got tougher and healthier, my spirit and intelligence started to desiccate. Every morning I'd wake up super early, work until evening, then go out to drink with girls at night. The balance of my intelligence and wildness was way off. Around that time a really pivotal thing happened.

I got my own car, and for the first time I started to listen to music with a proper stereo system. Part of it is because I never went with the whole Walkman thing, but I think it's true that until that time, home stereos in Japan mostly didn't have the kind of deep bass we're used to these days. Simply, that sound didn't exist for us till then. So with my car and its stereo came the crucial third ingredient which is the majesty that is Nile Rodgers and CHIC. I used to listen to it all the time. It's hard to say how deeply the Rotators references CHIC and Prince's drum sounds. I got sick at some point and quit gardening. A graphic designer I knew was introducing Macintosh into his operations, and he hired me to do projects in Illustrator. I dug it, and soon I was taking on graphic design jobs. I got pretty good at it, with basic skills I learnt at art school and my powers of observation and my curiosity. It's still one of the ways I support myself. But I'm selfish, and while I was totally into it, at the same time, the computer world had no »weight«. I wanted to create something weighty, something definite, and so I made the first Love Arm in 1993.

I made the Love Arm *as a rock and roll tool and started performing with it. But the reaction was not good. People from the Japanese art world would tell me »it's not arty enough«, and people from the Japanese design world would tell me »it's not design«.*

As always, I wasn't articulate enough to present what I was doing, so it went nowhere. After a while I formed the performance unit Gorgerous *with my friend, the art director and performer Hiroyuki Matsukage. But I don't think that many people actually »got« what I was trying to do, including Matsukage. Everybody thought that we were trying to be conceptual, or just trying to get laughs. To me, it was a completely normal contemporary expression that fit perfectly well within the history of rock and roll. The Rolling Stones caricatured Black American culture; we were caricaturizing Arena rock culture. We were taking all of that bombast and elegance to the next level. Or at least that was my intention. The only people who seemed to »get« it, however, were westerners. Since leaving university I had essentially considered myself a »freeter«, someone with a series of part time jobs. That meant that I could go whenever and wherever I wanted.*

So for the next several years, through having some opportunities to present in different exhibitions and art scenes around the world, I learned that oh, ok, so the only place that this experience is going to work is the western art world. So that's why, in 2001, I gave up »freeting« and debuted as an »artist« at the Mizuma Gallery *with the* Ujino's Love Arm *exhibition.*

»I'm Epicurean but at the Same Time I'm a Total Vulgarian«

After the Love Arm *exhibition, I was invited to participate in two projects in Britain: one was to join an exhibition traveling British universities, and the other was the* JAM *exhibition, presented at the Barbican, and then the* Tokyo Opera City Art Gallery. JAM *gave me an opportunity to think about making pieces to hang on walls, which resulted in the* Nippon Series *(2002), a drawing series of Japlish (mistaken English) words in onomatopoetic katakana characters like one finds in comic books. Europe is generally very good at accepting and perceiving my works, very naturally, the way I am. In America, I've only been to New York and Miami, once to each location, but America hasn't been easy for me. I think I'm a* VERY *Japanese creator with a* VERY *Japanese background, but somehow I feel like I'm missing some kind of key to the Japanese code ... Japan is the most uncomfortable place for me. Honestly, I must do something about it. It's almost like I can't have conversations in Japan. I'm an outsider. I think people think I'm an outsider. In fact I know it. Actually I'm just a weird middle-aged guy in this society. Today people need strategies; they need good packages. They need good labels and brands. I'm critical but optimistic. I'm epicurean but at the same time I'm a total vulgarian.*

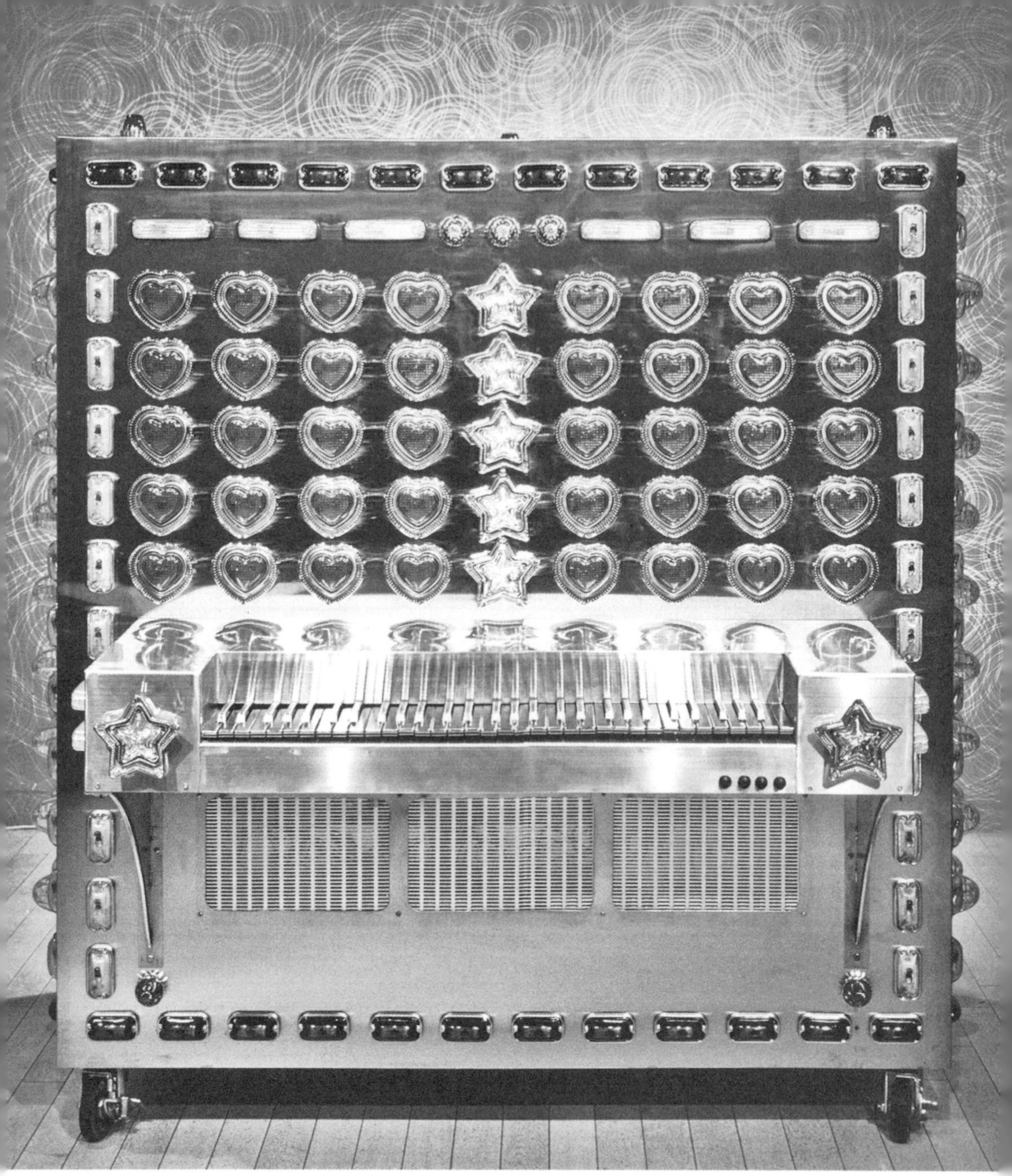

Fig. 4: Ujino: Decoratone, *1994. Stainless steel and mixed media, 74 × 43 × 120 cm*

From 2003 I made a series of sound sculptures such as the Decoratone, *which looked like an upright piano, decorated with lights like a tricked out freight rig (there is a really particular, and interesting, culture of freight truck decoration in Japan!). The half steps, (the black keys) were goldplated, and the white keys (the whole steps) were plated with silver. The keyboard was hooked up to samples of applause and young women screaming, while the lights flashed on and off.*

Pianos came into Japanese life from the very first generation of private homes in the 1920s. People didn't really »get« what a home was supposed to function as, or maybe they actually did see it for what it was—a mechanism for dividing society into Western style family units, which hadn't existed in Japan until then—so living rooms were not so much for living as they were for presentation. Early modern Japanese bourgeoisie would have things like pianos in their front rooms, whether they could play them or not. The truck lights were added to give a primal sense of pride and celebration. I liked the juxtaposition.

Another work in the sound series was the Hyung-Nim Ride, *which I produced in Korea. It was a bicycle, the sort of most typical type used for carrying things in the marketplace, carrying a payload of enormous Marshall speaker cabinets, the amp overdriven, blasting the noises that the bike makes when you ride it. The younger generation In Korea and China are growing so much. They are definitely my audience. They are dead serious about what they do. I think most Japanese artists are seen as being more flippant. They motivate me though. I want to challenge them, and it makes my work stronger.*

»This Paradox of Optimism and Regret is Something That has been Really Useful to Me«

After that, I started working on some ideas which evolved into the Rotators series, *which I first exhibited as part of the* Tokyo Style in Stockholm *exhibition on urban globalization (as the first ever art project in the former vault of the Kreditbanken at Norrmalmstorg, the site of the »Stockholm Syndrome« hostage paradox). I was thinking about Japan's DIY culture, whether or not it was disappearing in global monoculture, and I came up with this idea for a human scale drum machine, a kind of sound sculpture/performance project which I could create out of locally sourced second hand parts. Since then I've had opportunities to build them in many locations throughout the world, as a sort of cross cultural project.*

Its genesis is the mass consumerism, the disposable culture I was raised within, up until 1989, with the end of the Showa period, and the end of a Japan that was constantly growing materially richer. Looking back, I especially remember the bubble period at the end of Showa era. I remember how much we wasted, and consumed, without anybody imagining that one day the financial system could collapse. It breaks my heart. I feel terrible. I fully regret that time. I regret that I too was driven by magazines and advertisements. But I also remember the optimism it nurtured. This paradox of optimism and regret is something that has been really useful to me. You know, the recycling industry is not just cans and bottles any more.

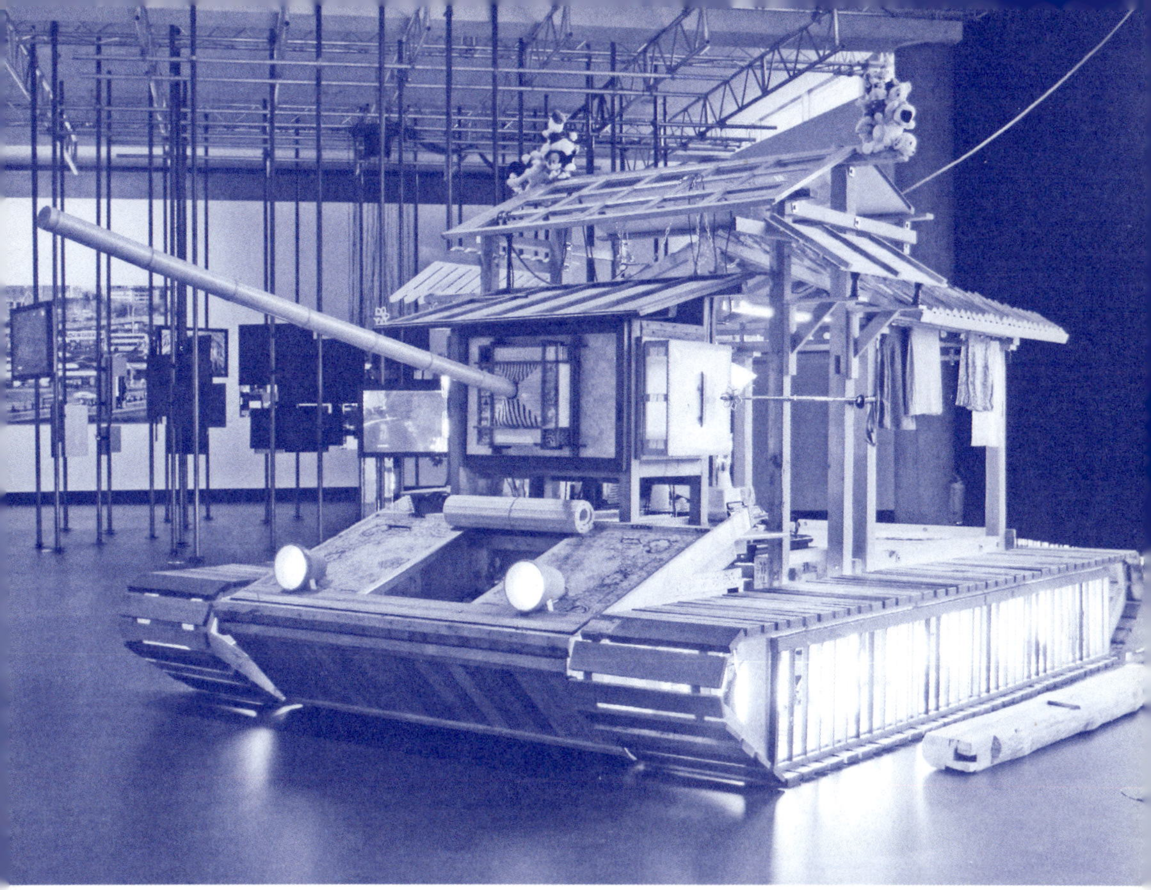

Fig. 5: Ujino: Ozone-So, *2004. Wood and mixed media, 300 × 580 × 260 cm*

Today people love Showa retro goods—but it's actually historically right thing to do, to love things correctly made in human sizes. For me, the Heisei era (from 1990) started with the Macintosh. Everything shifted scale. Everything became smaller, and more information dependent. Everything went digital, and became immaterial. Since then digital archives have become the public's common sense. DJing became a cerebral job—they're helpless without their databases. I've never actually taken an explicit position, but unconsciously I think I'm rebelling against it. Junk is no longer junk. Our brand new future may already have been our past ...

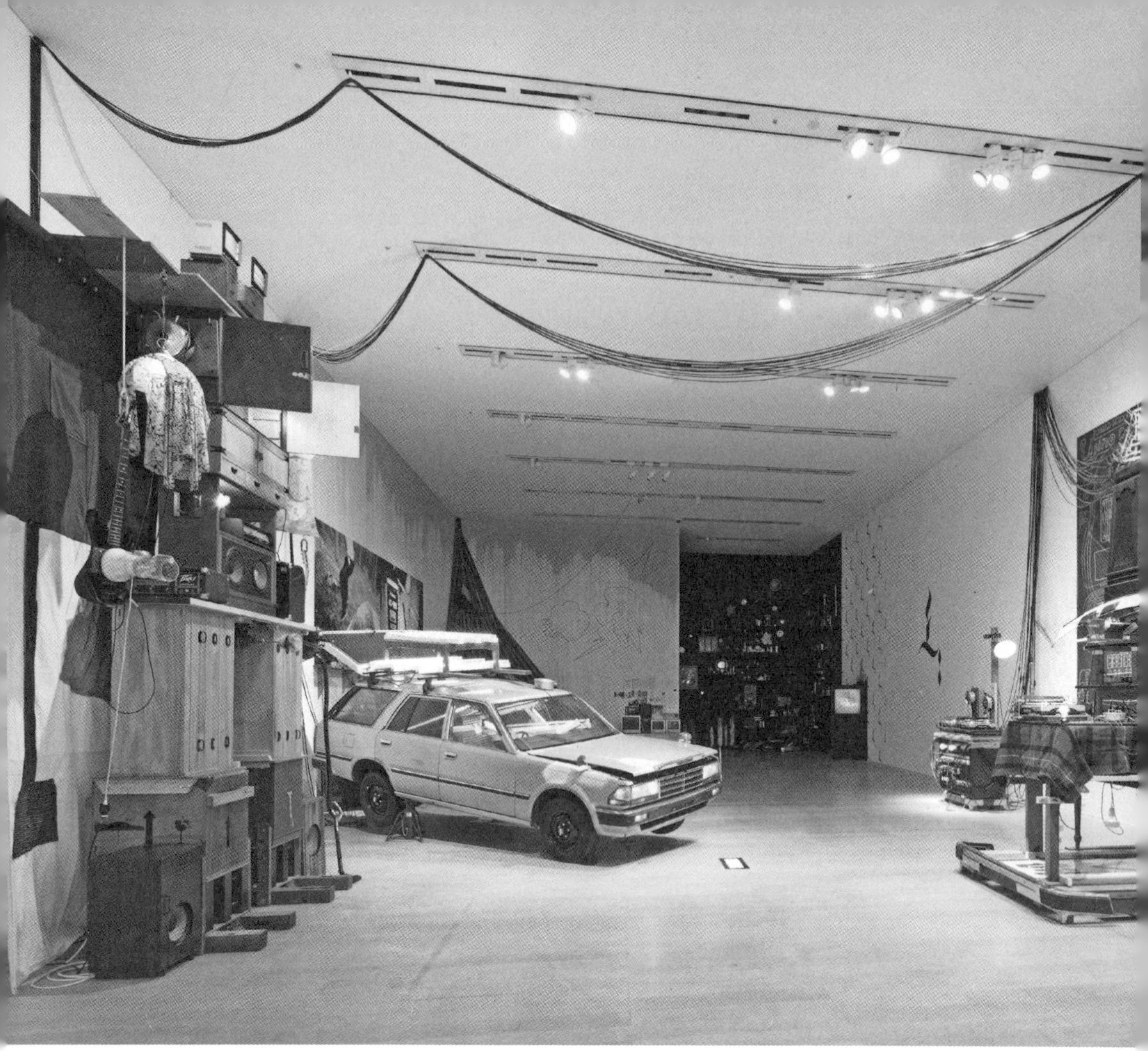

Fig. 6: Ujino: Ballad Of Extended Back Yard, Pt. 1, *2010. Nissan Cedric van, wood furniture, household electrical appliances and mixed media*

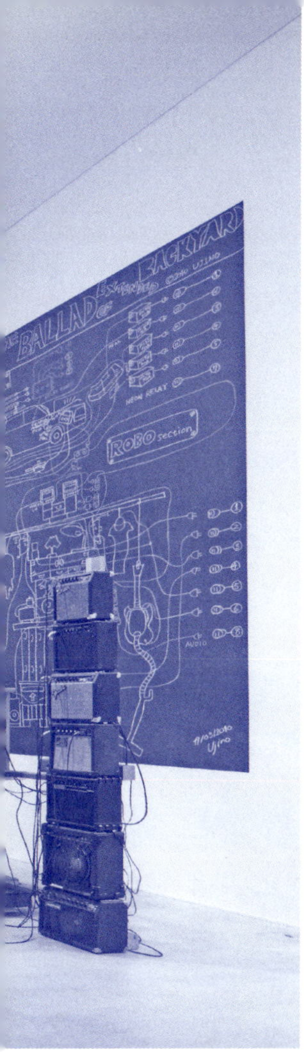

»Modern Art Began when Individuals Started Questioning how they Faced Modernity«

In 2004, I produced Ozone-So, *a sculptural piece composed of familiar residential waste, such as electric appliances, household junk, building materials and books. I collected the parts from all over Tokyo. First I cleaned and polished each to reveal its own intrinsic beauty. Then I assembled all of these very recognizable elements, with great care and delicacy, into a tank: an armored fighting vehicle. I built it to scale, so that both its form as a tank and its function as architecture would be unmistakable. Tanks are made of iron. They're definitively masculine. Japanese homes are made out of wood, and paper, and clay. The modern Japanese home is where women are meant to spend their lives. I named the exhibition* Karma Of Suburban Villa.

But around the time of the exhibition, the constitutionally mandated Japan Self-Defense Forces were dispatched to Iraq as part of a »peacekeeping« mission, which was actually a political test to see if public opinion would accept a remilitarized Japan. The work got lost in the context. Being an artist makes you think about your attitude towards modernization, which in Japan's case means reconciling modernity with such things as animism.

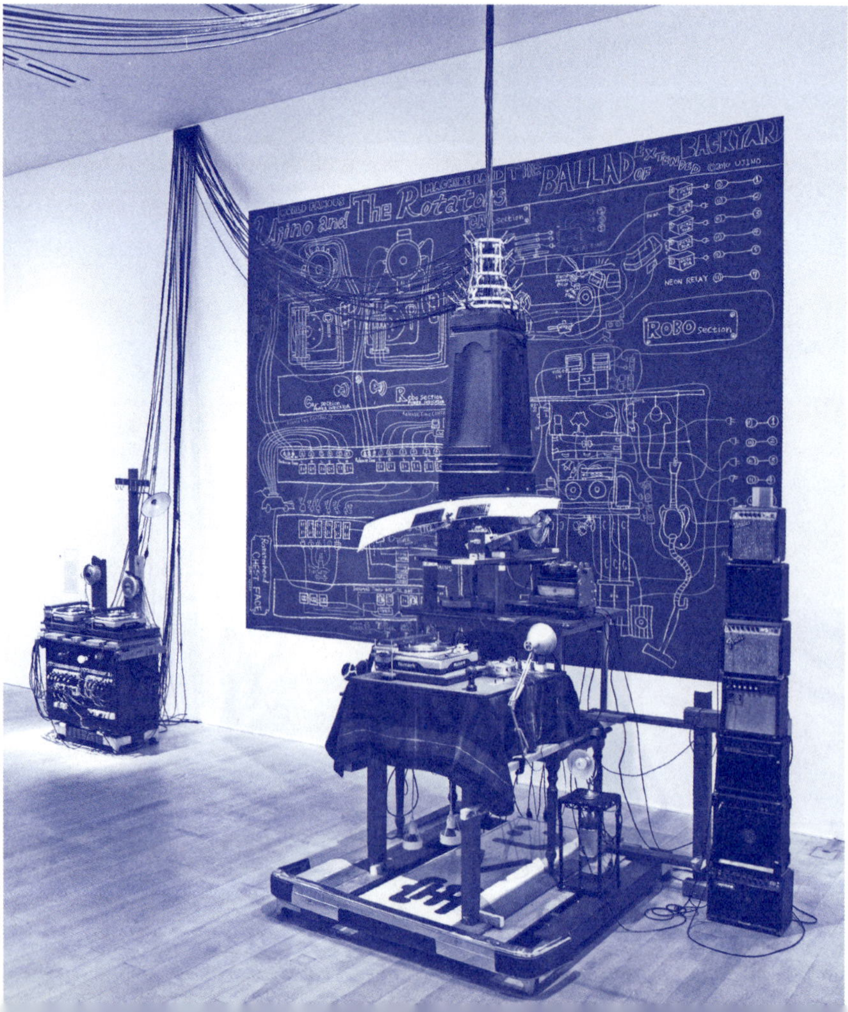

Fig. 6: Ujino: Ballad Of Extended Back Yard, Pt. 1, *2010.*
Detail. Nissan Cedric van, wood furniture, household electrical appliances and mixed media

Art didn't originally exist in Japan, it came with modernization, so art is essentially a reflection of that process. Wasn't it Duchamp who said something to the effect that modern art began when individuals started questioning how they faced modernity?

So since then, I've been continuing my research on the 20th century materialism (the increasing monoculture of a rapidly urbanizing world), and the unlikely future, which arrived here via America. I'm interested in the possibilities for ecological movements and recycling in many senses in the 21st century. I'm also interested in Japanese figurative expression, this character culture of automatons, which is certainly rooted in animism. Even in the tea ceremony and Noh dancing, the postures are like a robot's movements. I wanted to know why or try to discover potentials within that. My thinking is still blurry, but I want to organize myself, and put it out there. But I think that's how I arrived at Ballad of Extended Back Yard, Pt. 1, *the piece in the* Roppongi Crossing 2010 *exhibition at the* Mori Museum. *I was picturing a 1980s Japanese drum machine, in a culture where everywhere in the world we're dancing to the same club beats, and so I created a dancing drum machine sculpture with domestic detritus from the Showa era. And strangely enough, people seem to think it's a cousin to Nam-June Paik's robot family! Hah. So that's kind of where I'm at right now.*

Mouseology—Ludic Interfaces—Zero Interfaces

MATHIAS FUCHS

»When destroying the mouse, Trembling cursor represents last statement of the mouse. Motion of the mouse and the cursor are recorded simultaneously. They will be replayed in parallel on your desktop.«

exonemo

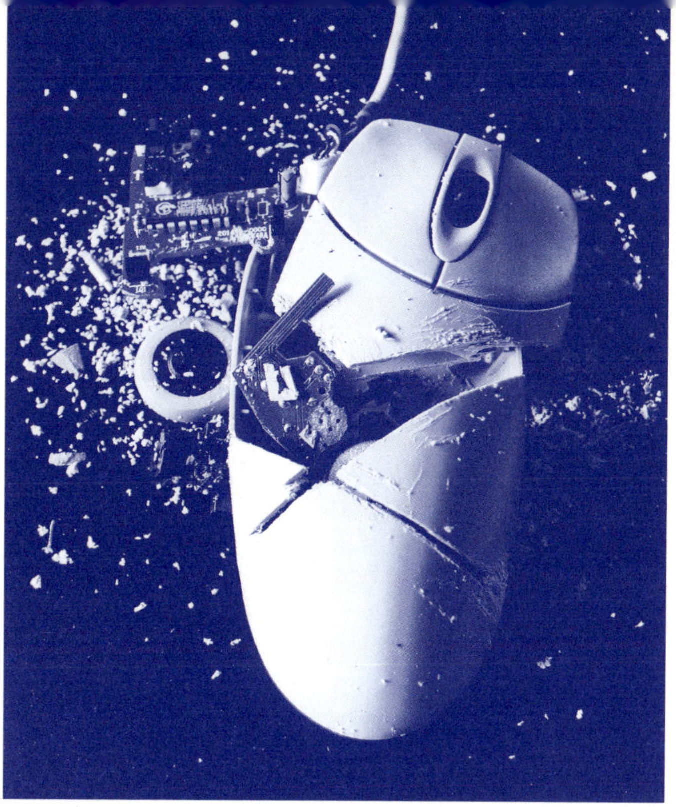

Fig. 1: exonemo: Danmatsu Mouse, *2007*

The destruction of a mouse is certainly a most radical act of interface modification. exonemo, the Japanese duo made up of Sembo Kensuke and Yae Akaiwa, have developed a series of execution rituals for computer mice that presents the harmless little electronic device as a victim of some weird kind of »Techno-Aktionismus«. The shamanistic ritual of torturing electronic devices with hammers, drills and feet or drowning them in pools is reminiscent of voodoo practice, where the lifeless needs to be killed in order to prove that it always was alive. exonemo kill mice on stage as if they would want to suggest to the audience that there is some life in the wires, the capacitors and the printed circuits. Several experimental works ranging from sound and video processing, software programming, hardware circuit bending and live performance have been developed by the artist bricoleur couple from Japan. In a performance that took place during the festival CODED CULTURES *in Yokohama on 18th of October 2009, one could spot post-animistic belief in the life of mice. Artists and audience did their best to destroy computer mice in various ways, some of them reminiscent of exorcism and pest related hysteria. The artists who label themselves* Mouse Art *pioneers, misinterpret on purpose what media art is about and what it is not about. To paraphrase Hans Ulrich Reck in a statement on the myth of media art* (Reck, 2002) *, we mistake Joseph Beuys by calling him a felt and grease artist, but we also mistake exonemo by calling them mouse artists. exonemo are quite aware of that and their attempt to mislead us into some mouse centered analysis should be defended through a mouseology that looks at mice from a mouseological (rather than a museological) viewpoint.*

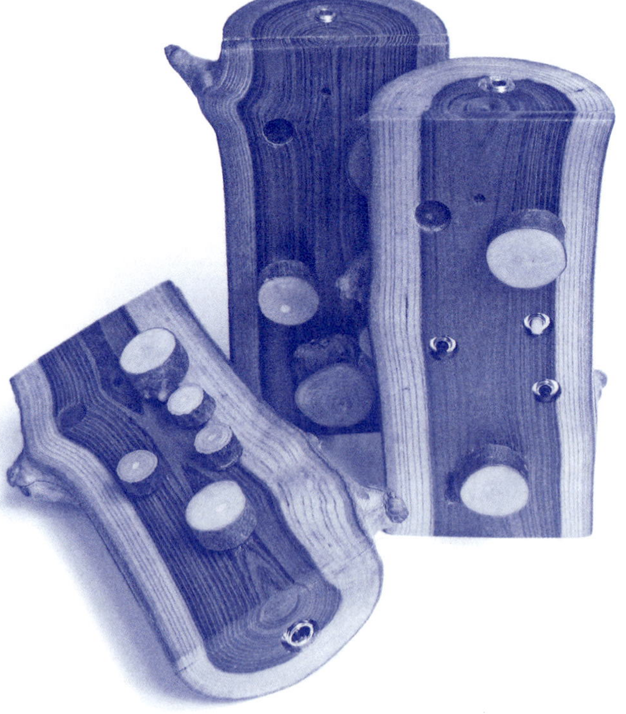

Fig. 2: Owl Project (Simon Blackmore, Antony Hall, Steve Symons), Manchester: iLog Rustle, *2006*

We need to understand exonemo's work as a rebellious attack on hardware and software technology and their work as a lasting commentary on our evolving relationship with technology—whether that be a sense of alienation or reconnection. The »concept driven circuit tweakers«, a label for exonemo invented by Vicente Gutierrez (Gutierrez, 2010) , have reanalyzed the contexts of computers and Human Computer Interfaces *and investigate a new potential of computer technology.*

exonemo's inviting DIY style and rising popularity have led these two rebel programmers to be often considered the new face of Japan's media art scene. The style and attitude exonemo cultivate so well is an international one, that a network of friends share, who are connected in an effort of »people doing strange things with electricity«. More than 100 groups in cities like Tokyo, New York, Manchester, Linz and elsewhere form a network of Dorkbot *electroshamans and produce such wonderful devices like the* Danmatsu Mouse *or the* iLog *by Owl Project, founders of the Mancunian* Dorkbot. *As you might have guessed an* iLog *is an iPod made from wood. Or to be more precise the* iLog Rustle *that you see on the image is of wood from the species Laburnum, a small poisonous tree with yellow flowers. The* iLog *reintroduces nature to electronics and even if the wood of the device only covers the electronics inside, it reunites forests with the urban contemporary jungle with a similar tongue-in-cheek attitude that make the* danmatsu mouse *a post-natural, digital device with an animal spirit.*

Owl Project paraphrases the tacky advertisement talk of Apple, when they announce the little wooden tool on their webpage: »Call it astonishing. Unbelievable. Impossible, even. Then pick it up and hold it in your hand. Take in the brilliant splinter-less wooden display. Run your thumb around the rose wood wheel. Your ears begin to perk up. That's when everything becomes clear: It's an iLog«.

Ludic Interfaces *versus* **Straight Interfaces**

Many years before the Wii remote controller made the gaming audience refocus from content to interface, artists explored new forms of Man-Machine, Machine-Machine, and Machine-Woman Interface configurations. Pieces like Jeffrey Shaw's The Legible City *(1988), Mary Flanagan's* Giant Joystick *(2006), Leif Rumbke's* Wargame *(2005) or Jess Kilby's* Center of the Universe *(2007) are art games with unconventional interface concepts based on playfulness as the main design objective. We will call these interfaces* Ludic Interfaces *to distinguish them from technically engineered interfaces like the ASCII keyboard or the mouse. The installations, tools and concepts differ from traditionally engineered systems as they are often*

- *playful,*
- *rich in connotative power and surprise,*
- *custom-built, aware of regional and historic context,*
- *critical, and*
- *inviting co-creativity, user-generated or user-driven content (or radically opposing those possibilities).*

Traditional interfaces of a type that is technically motivated and developed in a straightforward manner are often

- *effective,*
- *universally applicable,*
- *predictable,*
- *globally available, and*
- *unaffected by regional or historic context.*

I will call technically engineered interfaces »straight interfaces«, to differentiate between ludic and straight as two fundamentally different approaches towards Human Computer Interaction.

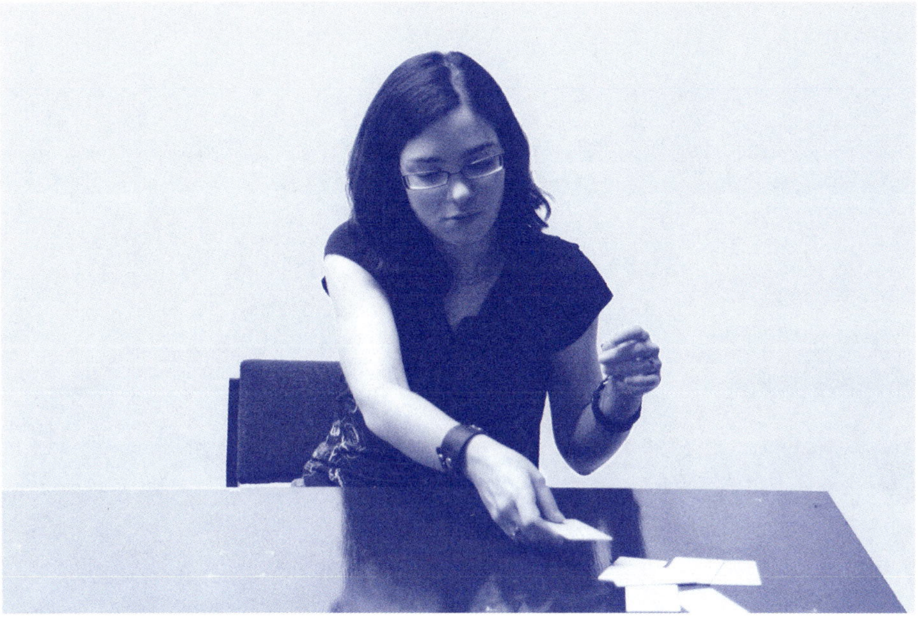

Fig. 3: Jess Kilby: Center of the Universe, *2007 (Ludic Interface)*

Ludic interfaces appropriate what they find in computer games, artistic experiment, interactive media, media conversion, social networks and modding cultures to offer tools which are adaptive to cultural specifics and cultural change and are sensitive to gender related, age related and ethnic specificities.

Jess Kilby's RFID Tarot Table *consists of a hand painted black table with letters and signs drawn upon it, and a white set of cards containing radio frequency tags. The installation is an example for a ludic setup where the interface contributes significantly to the magic of the game. Hidden information within in the blank cards allows the* RFID *reader, a digital tarot reader automaton, to interpret information hidden from the human eye. Kilby's system interprets the information contained within the cards and displays videos of a frightening future. The game could certainly be implemented as a Flash simulation or be built for a 2-D monitor display system, but without the materiality of the ludic interface, without the special lighting and without the artist dressed in a fortune teller's dress, the game would not work at all.*

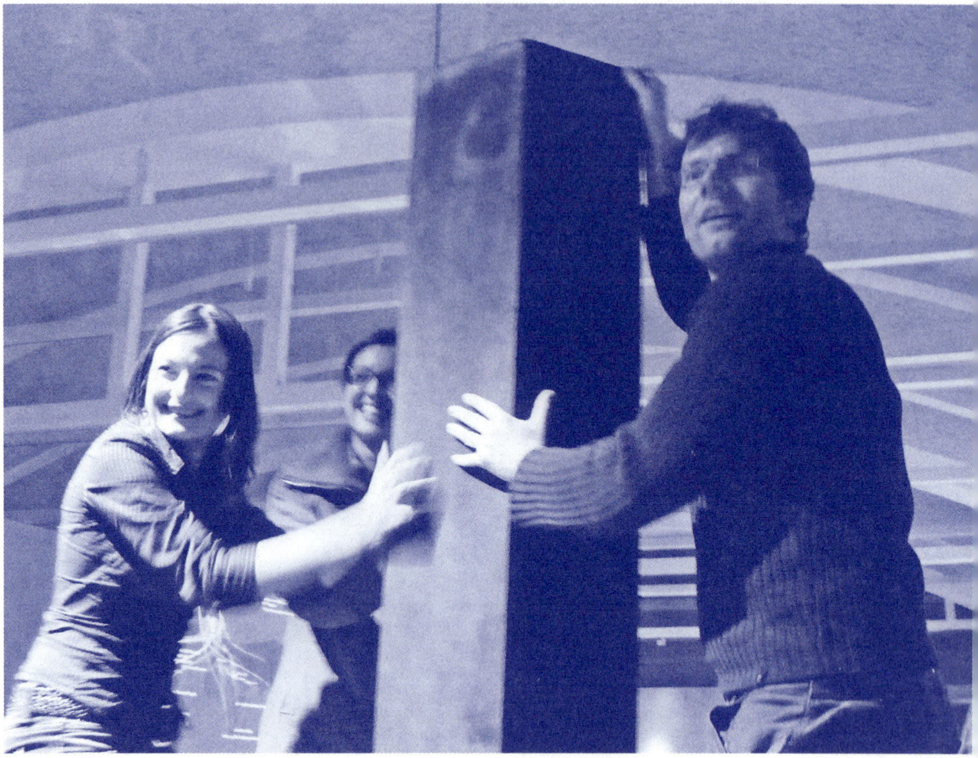

Fig. 4: Mary Flanagan: Giant Joystick, *2006 (Ludic Interface)*

The same holds true for Mary Flanagan's Giant Joystick. *It is the interface with all its materiality, erotic connotations and haptic features which makes the ludic installation work so well.*

Ludic Potential versus Lusory Attitude

At first glance it seems that objects do not hold a potential for playful application per se. A wooden stick can be a toy. A stone can be a toy. A cunningly designed toy can be a toy—or it can not be a toy. It depends on whether the object is used playfully—or not. It is not a property of a stone or stick to be a toy, as anything can be played with. It seems to be rather the application context that makes an object a toy in a given situation and at a given moment. Take a handful of LEGO bricks as an example and drop them in a 1970ies European child's bedroom. Then take the same bricks and place them in an Egyptian temple in 2000 B.C. Finally try placing the LEGO bricks in front of a curator of a contemporary design museum in downtown Tokyo. What you will find is that the bricks will be used as a toy in one of the cases and as a sacred object or a piece of design history in the other cases. It seems therefore reasonable to locate the ludicity not in the object itself, but in a potential user at a given time and space instead. It has been suggested by Salen and Zimmerman and others to assume that a »lusory attitude« (Salen and Zimmermann, 2004) is the main driver for playfulness vis-à-vis a toy or an object of any kind. But this approach is problematic. What is a toy, if objects are assigned ludic potential by the users? If a toy is an object that can be played, a stone is a toy as well. Taking a user centered approach in the style of Salen and Zimmerman and extending their notion in the direction of intentionality one would have to say that an object becomes a toy, when users decide to play with it. Does this imply that objects that are not played with are disqualified from being called toys? That would indeed make the LEGO bricks in the design museum non-toys. A consequence of such an approach would be a split in the world of LEGO bricks, some of them being toys at a given time and others being non-toys.

We seem to be caught in a dilemma! If we suggest that playfulness is owned by the object, we cannot explain how stones and sticks can become toys at times. If we suggest on the other hand that playfulness is constituted by the player's attitude, we declare everything on this planet as a potential toy. There seems to be a way out however. What keeps us from saying that ludicity is constituted by a socio-historic setting, in other words that culture owns the property of playfulness, or that play is constituted within culture. That sounds like a resurrection of Huizinga's (Huizinga, 1955) point.

We would however understand culture in a much smaller sense than Huizinga did. Not as an anthropologic constant, but as an instance of a set of cultures, that are coded and recoded at any time. Playfulness would from this point of view be an asset in a dynamic field of coded cultures. Playfulness would—as a consequence of that—also have different shapes and flavours according to the cultural codes it is embedded in. We would possibly have to sacrifice a notion of historically stable playfulness and have to replace it with a multitude of »playfulnesses«: Spartan playfulness, Roman or Carthagian playfulness, medieval playfulness, modern or postmodern playfulness, and the ludic attitude of our days.

To investigate more specifically about how play happens at any of the mentioned historical conditions, it seems worthwhile to look at the hardware and software connecting humans to a device or a built environment. These interfaces can be computer keyboards or skateboards—and sometimes both of them.

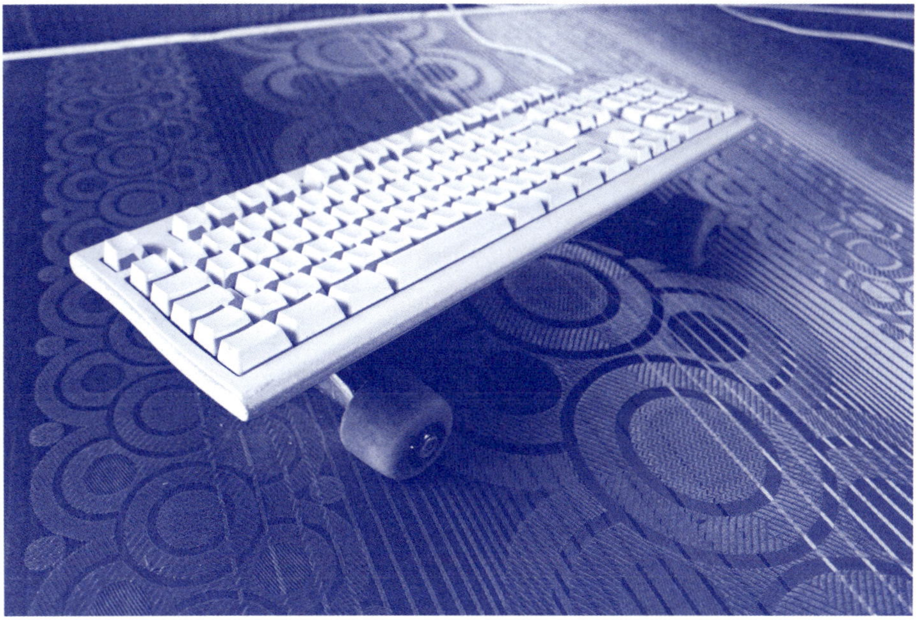

Fig. 5: Tobias Leingruber: Skatekeyboard, *2010 (Ludic Interface)*

The Interface is the Message

In order to understand the potential of interfaces for any human-machine interaction, it makes sense to look at games as a rich field of interaction setups and concepts. We conceive a game as a system of rules, a player, physical or virtual objects to play with and a regional and historical context to be played in. When we try to find out what a game is about, we might look for meaning on different levels of the game. We could find meaning in the rules and the development of moves within the rule system. We could alternatively search for meaning in the role the player adopts in the game. In particular the player's position in a socio-historical context could be interpreted as the meaning of the game. Another approach is however to interpret the interface between man and machine, machine and machine, or woman and machine as the crucial element in the production of ludic experience and ludic meaning. I want to call these approaches

- *ludo-centric,*
- *role-based,*
- *socio-historic and*
- *interface-led.*

Ludic interfaces lend themselves to shift focus from rules and roles to processes of deconstruction of rules, roles and socio-historic settings. For this reason, game art often focuses on the interface—or, as I will demonstrate later, on an apparent lack of interactivity within the interface provided. Both approaches, i.e. the deconstruction of interfaces or the destruction of meaningful interface functionality, are artistic strategies to criticize commercial interface design and to suggest provocative alternatives to »middle of the road« interface standards. Ludic interfaces and zero interfaces contain artistic statements intended to oppose ideological concepts in human computer interaction (HCI) and to set free playfulness in the process of (wo)man-machine communication.

Leaving the Magic Circle?

The level of »lusory attitude« (Salen and Zimmermann, 2004) that a game can provide seems to be enhanced by the interface used to play the game. A joystick glues the gamer's hand to any space fighter action game, a steering wheel feels good in the hands of someone playing a car racing game. On the other hand a fire button might alienate a gamer from conducting eco friendly simulations and a rocket launcher device seems to be of little help for Mattel's Barbie goes Shopping game (except in the case of extremely cynical gamers).

The interface also sets up a tacit agreement on how to play and how not to play. A steering wheel device with a gas pedal imposes constraints upon the player's actions. It clearly suggests to go right or left and to accelerate or decelerate. The setup does not encourage us to go up and down, because steering wheels are not designed to control z-axis moves. The interface is therefore as much of an inhibiting device as it is an enabling one. We are controlled by the interface's constraints when we think that we are in control. Straight interfaces are ideological in this regard, as they contain implicit rules, where we least expect them. Ludic interfaces and game art pieces like the ones mentioned above point our attention towards the potentially wide range of interaction patterns that we are usually not invited to take part in. Ludic interfaces oppose the ideological aspect of straight interfaces by ridiculing their functionality or by opening up the field of possible interaction. In many cases ludic interfaces are built on the attitude of the trickster, the spoilsport or of the jester.

Interpassivity

Interactivity is at the core of gameplay in any conceivable computer game. It seems impossible to imagine how gameplay would work, if there was no interactivity between human and computer involved. But what happens if a gamer writes a script to enable his or her avatar to perform certain actions in the absence of the player? The game artist, who lets the game engine go on its own, rejects his responsibility to control the avatars—he does not get entangled into the quest of loss or win and he rejects the basic rule of any game, which is: You have to play! The spoilsport does however not leave the arena completely. He remains a voyeur, a spectator of an action he enjoys passively. In this regard the introduction of auto-executables, i.e. software agents physically detached from the players, and other modes of delegated play can be righteously called interpassive gaming. Pfaller and Žižek point out that the psychological aspect of interpassivity is grounded in our subjectivity. Pfaller and Žižek convincingly demonstrate how certain works of art seem to provide for their own reception (Pfaller, 2000) .

One cannot help feeling that these artworks enjoy themselves or that we enjoy through them (Van Oenen, 2008) .

The mechanism described by Pfaller and Žižek can again be found in games and their modes of performance. It is not only Game Art, but everyday gamers' practice where interpassive phenomena can be observed. Delegated enjoyment and delegated fear are possible forms of letting go in First Person Shooters. We know that it can be fun to just camp in an MMORPG and watch others play through the eyes of an avatar. We have experienced delegated death fears when about to be shot and we know peer players who take some masochistic interpassive delight in being fragged.

But even less martial areas of disguise and simulation like the SecondLife environment will disclose interpassive delegation of love, lust and longing (Fuchs, 2008) .

Fig. 8: Leif Rumbke: Wargame, *2005*

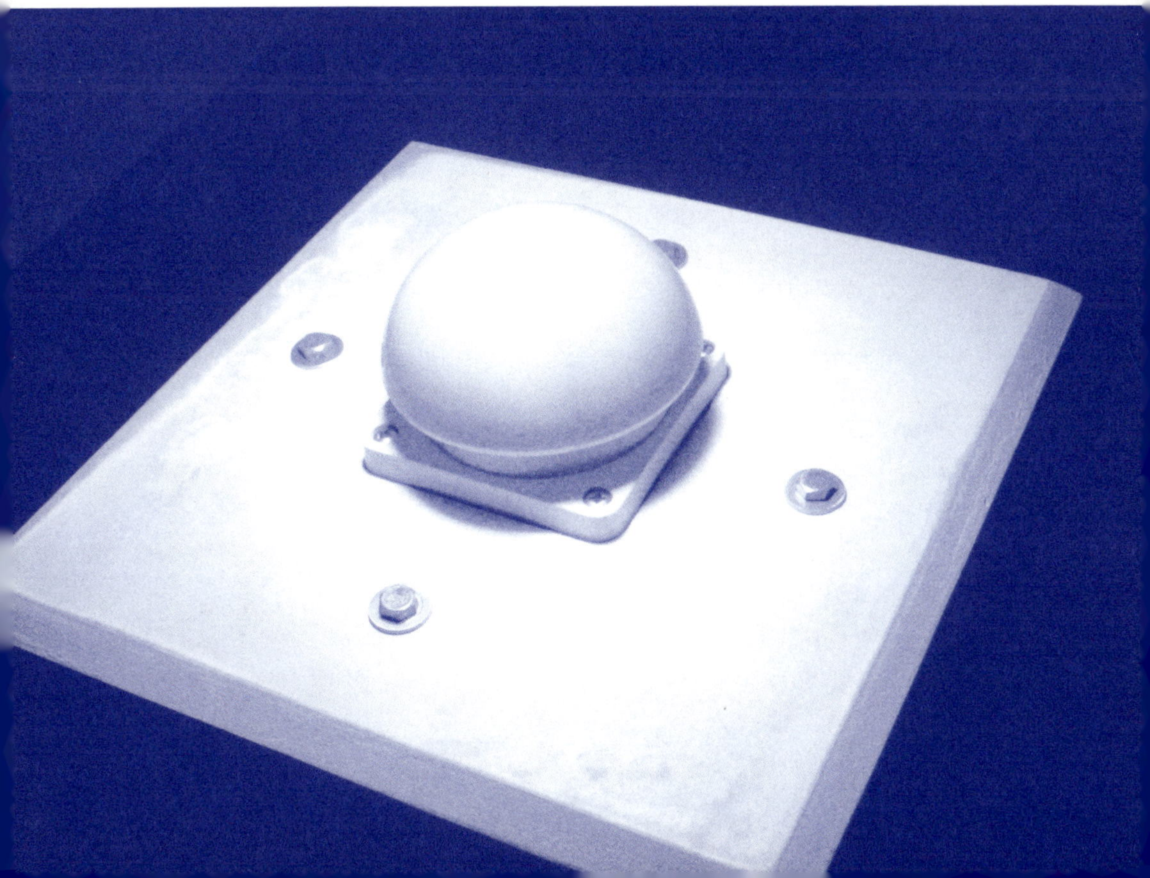

Artistic Interpassivity:* *Zero Interfaces

Leif Rumbke's Wargame *restricts interface action to a »Stop the Game« command only— implemented as a nuclear fire button's binary single function. The interface in striking red and its impressive size limit the player's interactivity to one single non-reversible command.*

Conceptually related but functionally inverse is game art like Corrado Morgana's CarnageHug. *The game runs in auto execution mode and does not allow for interactivity except for the minimal »Start« command.* CarnageHug *uses the* Unreal Tournament 2004 *game engine to set up and run a bizarre, self playing spectacle. Morgana removed the weapons from the level and has the player pawns attack each other in a ridiculous massacre without player based gameplay objectives or other constructive teleological human-player commitment. The game runs in a disinterested manner as far as winning and losing the game is concerned. If we are prepared to follow Kant's suggestion that disinterest will open the door to understanding the faculties of the observed object, interpassive works like Morgana's* CarnageHug *therefore qualify as a works of art or at least focus our attention upon something outside the magic circle of normal gameplay. Morgana is a spoilsport in the traditional sense of the word, because he denies us the simple pleasure of man-machine interaction and intentionally shrinks the potential of the interface usability down to degree zero.*

The interface is a Zero Interface *that mocks interactivity. Interfaces like those throw us back to a degree zero of playing* (Barthes, 1953) *. The installation however does not make us completely leave the magic circle of the game. We take part in a reinterpretation of boundaries of the magic circle.*

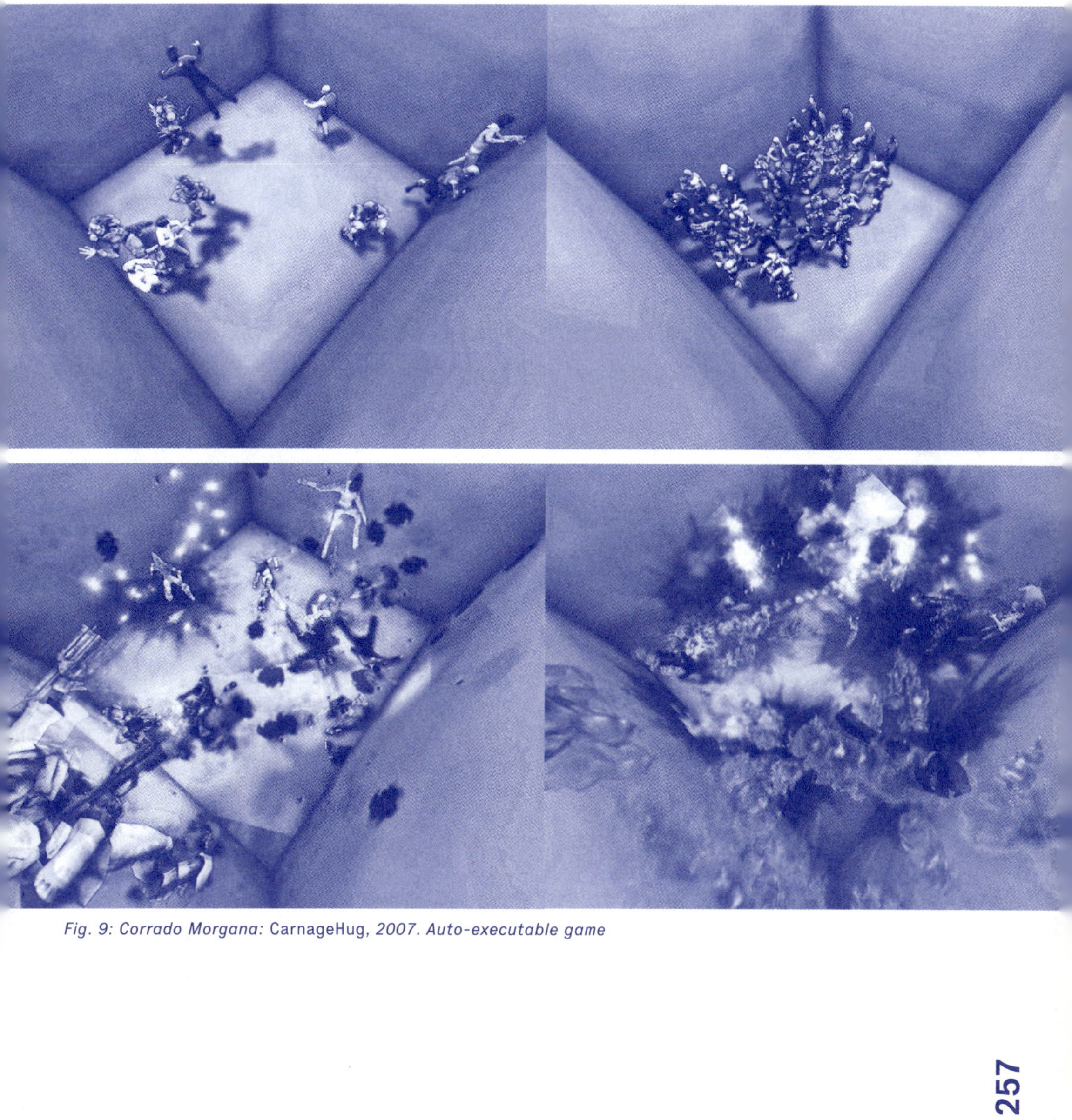

Fig. 9: Corrado Morgana: CarnageHug, *2007. Auto-executable game*

The tournament action as we know it is reterritorialized into the artistic arena. And almost at the same moment that we think of having left the magic circle of Unreal Tournament, *we find ourselves caught in the magic circle of the game called art. We keep watching and we keep being caught. In cinema this phenomenon is best represented in* machinima, *the theatre of machinic artifacts.*

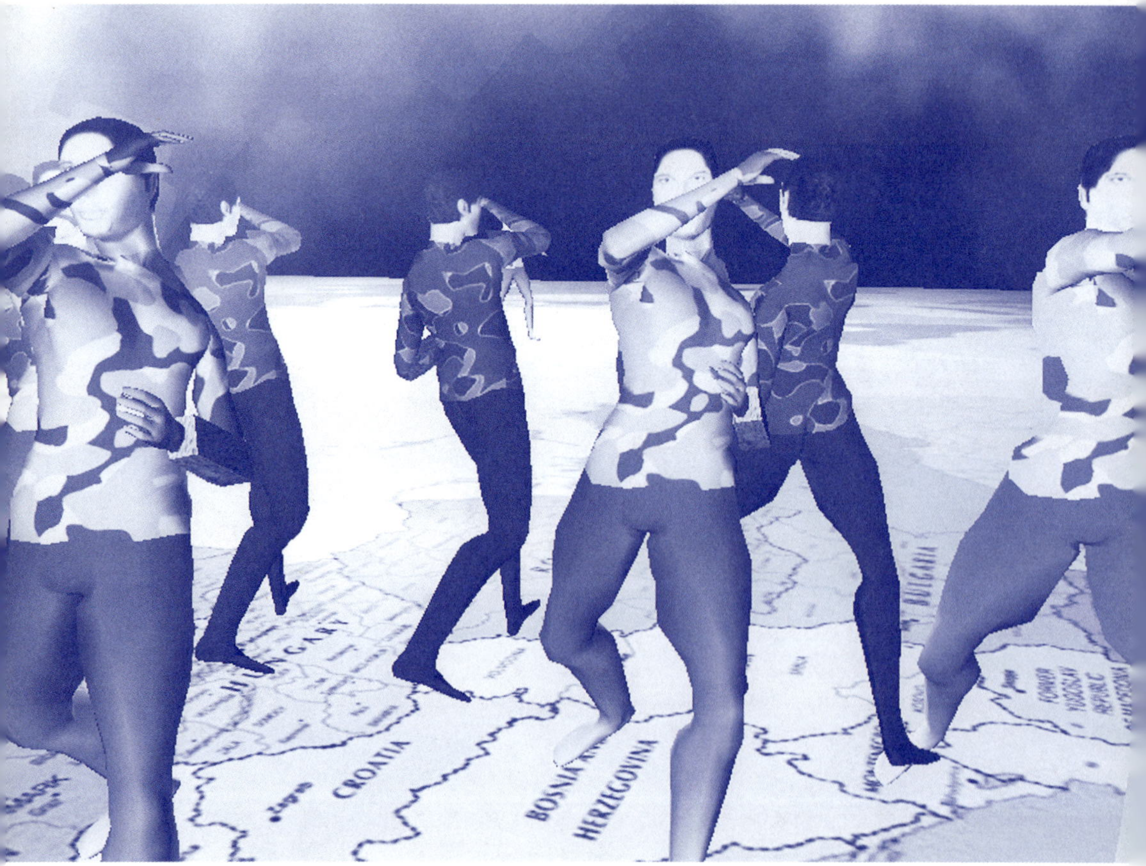

Fig. 10: Mathias Fuchs: Borderline. Machinima. *2009*

Machinima *as the paradoxical attempt to watch gameplay without playing is another popular non-sport where the spectator becomes spoilsport and traitor on the game's premises.* Machinima *puts the recipient into the voyeur's seat and keeps oscillating between cinema and game experience without fully committing to any of them. It is »meditative inaction«—as Christiane Paul rightly calls it—that ridicules interaction in games* *(Paul, 2006)* *.*

If we can enjoy the outsourcing of enjoyment, we have to either declare this as a perverse, a hysteric and a neurotic attitude in a Lacanian perspective *(Trevor, 2010; Van Oenen, 2008)* *, or analyse it as a sophisticated spoilsport attitude of staying in the magic circle when pretending to leave it.*

Conclusion

Ludic Interfaces, Interface Destruction and Zero Interfaces are artistic strategies to play the spoilsport in an environment where »fair play« means nothing else than playing it straight. The ideological design philosophy of interface designers whose interfaces are

· effective,
· universally applicable,
· predictable,
· globally available and
· unaffected by regional or historic context,

challenged by Ludic Interfaces characterized of being

· playful,
· application specific
· rich in connotative power and surprise,
· custom-built, aware of regional and historic context,
· critical and
· inviting co-creativity, user generated or user driven content (or radically opposing those possibilities).

References

Barthes, R.: Le Degré Zéro de l'Écriture.
Paris: Les Éditions du Seuil, 1953

Fuchs, M.: Ilonpilaajia ja pelihaita—Spoilsports and Cardsharps.
Tampere, Finland: Playfulness Conference, April 2–4, 2009

Fuchs, M.: »Cyberprovincialism«. In: Russegger, G., Tarasiewicz, M., Wlodkowski, M. (Eds.):
Coded Cultures. Exploring Creative Emergences. *Vienna, Yokohama: 5uper.net, 2009*

Fuchs, M.: »Interpassive Persona«. *Unpublished conference paper for* amber08.
Interpassive Persona Conference. *Istanbul: amber festival, 2008*

Gutierrez, V.: TABlog 2010. *http://www.tokyoartbeat.com/*
tablog/entries.en/author/vicente_gutierrez

Huizinga, J.: Homo ludens. A study of the play element in culture.
Boston: Beacon Press, 1955 (= 1938)

Juul, J.: Half-Real. Video Games between Real Rules and Fictional Worlds.
Cambridge, Mass.: MIT Press, 2005

Paul, C.: Catalogue for the Zero Gamer exhibition *at* London Games Festival.
London, Oct 22–26, 2006. http://www.http.uk.net/zerogamer/exhibition.shtml

Pfaller, R.: Interpassivität. Studien über delegiertes Genießen.
Vienna, New York: SpringerWienNewYork, 2000

Reck, H.: Mythos Medienkunst.
Köln: Verlag der Buchhandlung Walter König, 2002

Salen, K. and Zimmermann, E.: Rules of Play. Game Design Fundamentals.
Cambridge, Mass.: MIT Press, 2004

Trevor, T.: Robot-Me. Affective Machines and Object Relations, *2010.*
http://www.supertoy.org/cgi-bin/wiki/read.cgi?section=Supertoys&page=robotme

Van Oenen, G.: »Interpassivity revisited: A critical and historical reappraisal of interpassive phenomena«. In: International Journal of Žižek Studies. *Rotterdam, 2008*

Imaginary Agents— Flowers and the Common

VERINA GFADER

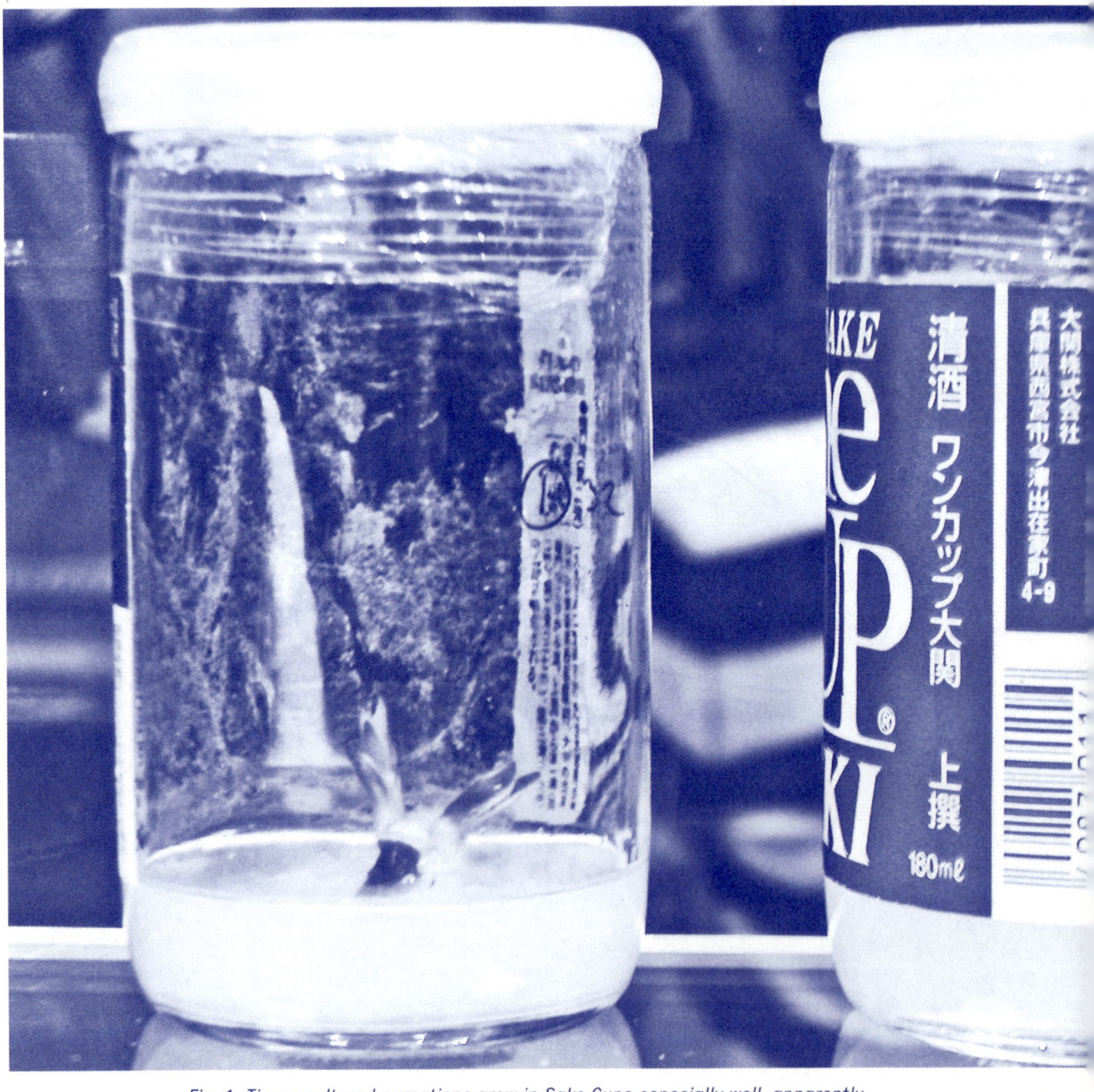

Fig. 1: Tissue cultured carnations grow in Sake Cups especially well, apparently because the insides of the labels depict nature scenes

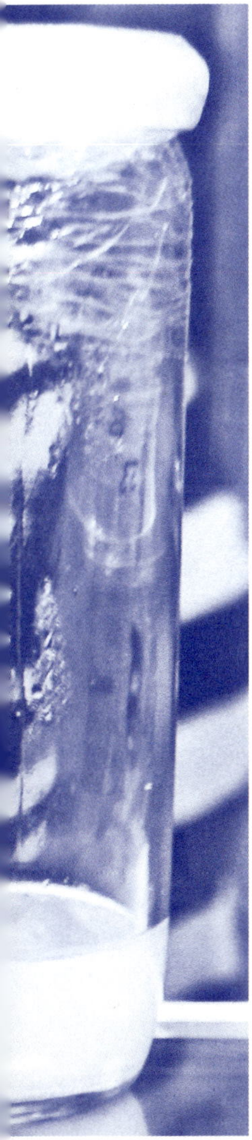

At First Sight, *in a glimpse, the blue flowers that are the result, the objects of* Common Flowers / Flower Commons [1] *, present an absence. They seem to manifest the missing, a ghostly presence, a substitute or placeholder. They provide a reservoir, field, root (or riot) of the imaginary. Blue flowers, more specifically blue roses and carnations exceed the familiar, the normative, the natural, the being there, while simultaneously they are already too removed from our understanding of these definitions or forces. In the immediate sensation there are elements of something parasitic, sublime, hybrid, multiple, rhizomatic, heterogenous, distributed, and non-systemic, if you like. There is movement—something alien, foreign, some* thing *has taken over a plant, has potentially penetrated the genomes of the flower petals. There are thoughts around notions of completion (for example towards a full colour spectrum: white, pink, red, green, black, orange, cream, purple, blue) and a desire for realising*

1 http://www.common-flowers.org/ [Accessed: Jun 8, 2010]

a totality. Underlying are economies of modelling, classifying, dis/ordering, dissecting, arranging [2]*. Ir/rational taxonomies. Science. Fiction. Pre-determined systems and de-re-coding. Consequently politics. In* Notes for a Liberated Computer Language, *the appendix to* The Exploit, A Theory of Networks, *Alexander R. Galloway and Eugene Thacker list the normative as an »operator«:* »normative—attaches a political evaluation to a type or code block« [3]*. Endowed with questions of the normative, the delicate, pretty blue flowers then might be charged with this weight of formulating political processes shot through with coding issues. But to declare the delightful flowers as a kind of model, possibly exceptional or expressing the qualitative as such sounds too imposed, too heavy, too much.*

[2] *One might be reminded of Bas Jan Ader's film and series of photographs titled* Untitled (Flower Work), *1974. The work presents the artist arranging and reorganising flowers in a vase according to segregating them into the three primary colours red, blue, and yellow. The seemingly random composing undermines rational classification. It has been noted that this work was also a reference to Mondrian and Rietveld. As an artwork* Common Flowers / Flower Commons *seems to be far more detached from references to art history, but can a work that is based on colour escape this dynamic or systems of referring?*

[3] *Galloway, A. R., Thacker, E.:* The Exploit, A Theory of Networks. *p. 162. Minneapolis/ London: University of Minnesota Press, 2007*

More like representing a writable, re-writable and readable entity they are capable of interrupting, of turning the flow of information into a still image. You can ***DIY*** *these flowers.*

Agency in the Form *of a corruptible science and distributed ownership is employed in the project* Common Flowers / Flower Commons. Common Flowers / Flower Commons, *2008—, is an artwork by* BCL [4]*, Tokyo-based artists Shiho Fukuhara and Georg Tremmel, which uses strategies of* bio-hacking *and* bio-sharing *to suggest formulas for the people—the common* [5] *—to appropriate genetic modifying techniques for their own purposes. Investigating the relation between emerging bioscience,* societal plants *and the public, the artists have reclaimed ownership of a GM blue flower developed and circulated by Suntory Flowers, a subsidiary of the Japanese beer brewing*

[4] *http://bcl.biopresence.com/ [Accessed: Jun 30, 2010]*

[5] *Throughout my text »common« is used in the sense of the people in a very general way.*

company Suntory. SUNTORY blue rose APPLAUSE, the first blue rose with nearly 100% blue pigment in the petals, was announced by the company on October 20, 2009, to go on sale from November 3. Paradoxically but perhaps exemplary, the plant production—growing, harvesting—was meant to take place in Suntory's key markets but was outsourced (the main production is in Columbia, South America) and the cut flowers were then shipped to worldwide markets. Fukuhara and Tremmel take this blue cut flower, an organism and its information plus its implications, to multiply and grow their own flowers using plant tissue culture methods. Everyday material such as kitchen utensils and easily available goods serve to develop DIY biotech methods, following ideas around forms of openness, bio-sharing, and possibly contributing to practices of de-mythologising science. Brought back to life, the plants are inserted and distributed in the public, in what the artists call »free spaces, where [the flowers] can grow and prosper« [6].

By its very nature Common Flowers / Flower Commons itself is a model of distribution. Featuring elements of a socially engaged and infused practice, the project has various manifestations. It provides a set of instructions. It becomes the headquarter or hub, issuing tissue cultured flowers for further growth and distribution. It is one nodal point in a decentralised system. It functions as a museum lab when presented as an installation in an exhibition or gallery space, e.g. Common Flowers / White Out project at the CODED CULTURES event in Yokohama, Japan, 2009, open for participation by visitors to »excorcis(e)« DNA [7].

6 http://www.common-flowers.org/ComFlow-Description.pdf [Accessed: Jun 10, 2010]

7 http://bcl.biopresence.com/journal/201/ [Accessed: Jun 9, 2010]

Common Flowers *at the* Nam June Paik Award Exhibition*, Cologne 2008, included a similar lab setup, an assemblage of useful things for flower production, alongside a bunch of blue flowers neatly arranged in a large glass vase on a gallery socket—the art object par excellence. Besides the setup as factory laboratory including test tubes, tools, tissue, flower material and soil, the project's online presence traces the history, links, and underlying strategies by the artists from its beginning. There are the common flowers growing in a flower commons.*

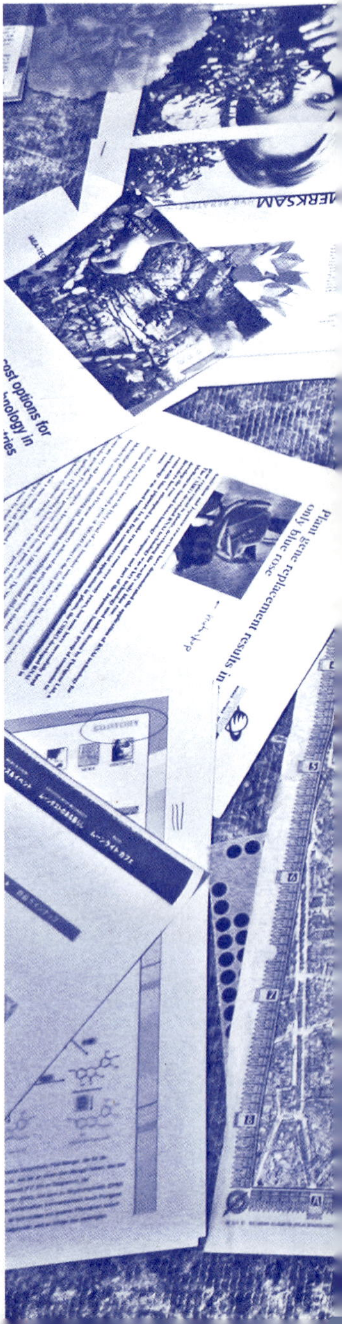

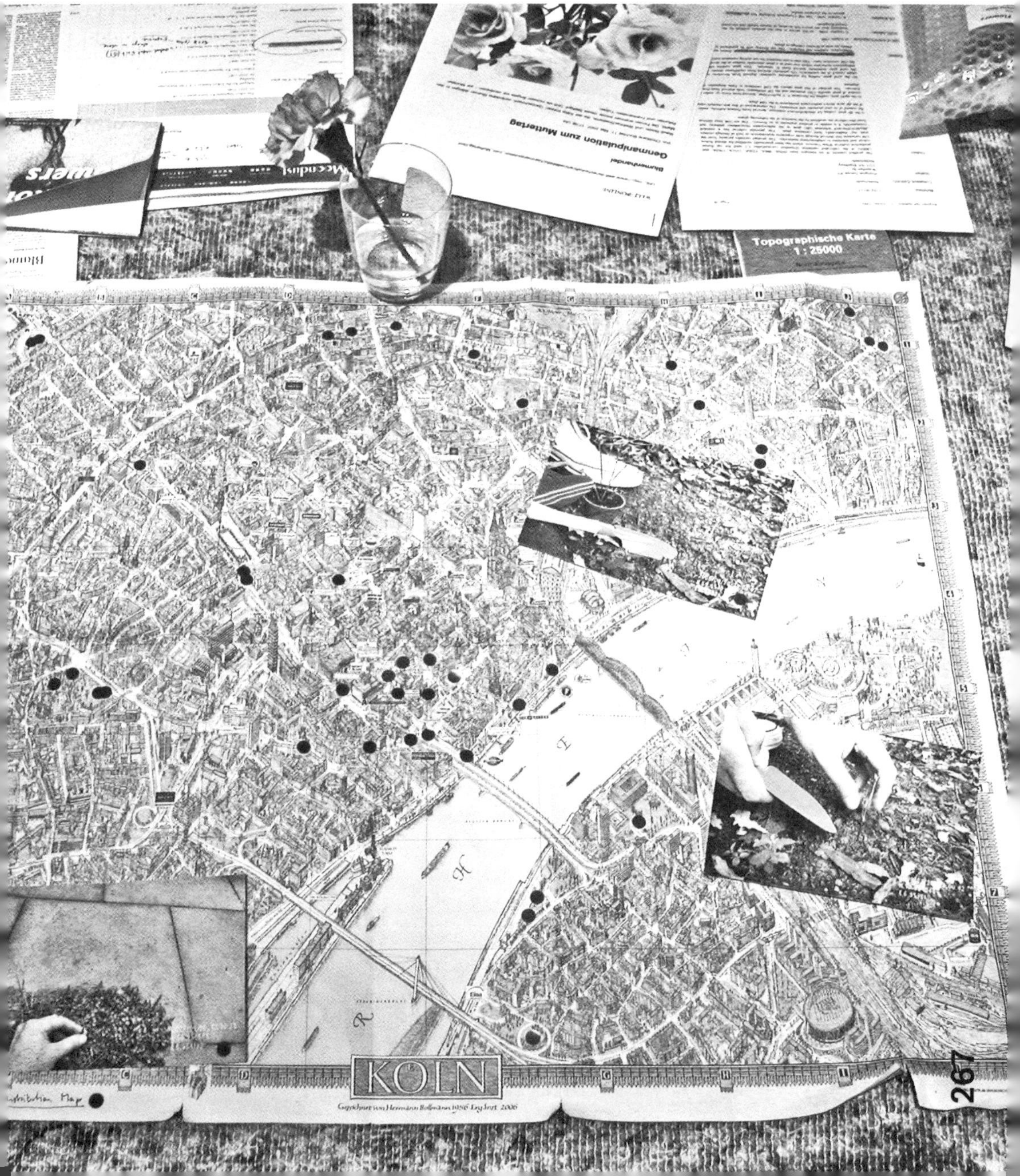

Fig. 2: Map of Tentative Flower Commons *in Cologne*

A Walk Around *Omotesando, Tokyo, reveals organic arrangements in the form of a potential eruption of a garden shop overloaded with plants and proliferating roots. This arrangement in urban space brings other issues into play: think of the relation of different plants and plant assemblages to a socio-political site, the various roles of plants in society and how they map the organisation of socialised space!*

A counter example to Common Flowers / Flower Commons *can perhaps be found in the investigations of a* botanical diaspora [8] *Austrian artists Lois and Franziska Weinberger undertake. Working with migrating plants as a poetic/political statement, they actively insert bio-waste, the residual, the overlooked, the out-of-order, the wildly growing, the foreign or immigrant into social space, and by doing so question the dynamics of nature and culture within that space. Utterly opposite to the weed (waste) with which the Weinbergers work, the flowers in* Common Flowers / Flower Commons *are a surplus (product) in socio-political space. Although, or precisely because they are naturalised, they propose everything else than a left-over or minor organism/thing that has to be kept at the periphery of society. Tom Trevor in his essay* Secondary Nature *insists that there is nothing other than a secondary nature, that a primary nature—a nature not yet cultivated—has been fully replaced by this secondary one. He says that* »[…] the starting point is a thoroughly cultured space; man made places in which the uncultivated, untamed ›weed‹ struggles to survive, sprouting in marginal zones on the edge of the city and thriving on the waste

[8] Trevor, T.: »Secondary Nature«. In: Weinberger, L. and F.: Home Voodoo. *pp. 19–37; p. 31. Bristol: Arnolfini, 2007*

products of human society. Nature and culture overlap in these sites, on the periphery of social space. As the curator Catherine David has said, ›Nature in the post-industrial era is a secondary nature, a second-hand nature, a post-cultural nature—and a post-history nature, the 'dopo storia' that Pasolini evokes in his texts in the 1970s—'ruins' (vacant lots, post-industrial wasteland, waste dumps, etc.)‹«[9]. *In the sense of this secondary nature, the blue flowers might be the visual and conceptual incarnation of the non-peripheral, the non-foreign, the other-than-ruins. No waste. They are that which can be mastered and regulated. As the weed does, they contribute to a secondary-ness albeit in a contradictory way. Within the parameters of the secondary nature they are the opposite of weed (waste). But if diaspora means a removed, dislocated, deterritorialised common identity, this artificial common (artificially produced or artificially created common) embodied in the* Common Flowers *might also indicate a diaspora, if not, at least, the diasporic. Distributing the blue flower—its* code *and information—among the common, the people, the general public, it returns to an unstable place where, similarly to Weinbergers' immigrated wild plants, it* »gives way to a precise botanical [in the case of the blue flower even more so biotechnological] system«[10]. — *A variant of the »botanical diaspora«?*

[9] *Trevor, T.: Ibid. (see note [8]), p. 22*

[10] *Weinberger, L.: quoted in Trevor, T. (see note [8]), p. 22*

Further Complications. *Further complications when the above diagrammed power structures itself are put into question—disclosed as a device to continue narratives of sovereignty and forces within social space* [11] *. Might it be obligatory, a necessary detour here to dislodge the common flower from organised, governmental domains? To find a niche to transform this marginalising, pessimistic, yet present state into something else?*

[11] *There is an interest in freeing the debate from legacies of Henri Lefebvre's analysis of socially produced space, within which* »state-imposed normality makes permanent transgression inevitable«. *Lefebvre, H.: quoted in Trevor, T. (see note* [8] *), p. 26*

In Means without End: Notes on Politics *Giorgio Agamben writes of a form of politics that potentially exceeds the system of state sovereignty* [12] *. He proposes a* *coming politics* *by returning to Michel Foucault's concept of* *biopolitics**, re-activating and clarifying the concept's forming elements. Agreeing with Foucault that life now is intrinsically linked and subordinated to politics (governmental principles and states) and thereby bio-political—Foucault:* »what is at stake today is life« [13] *—Agamben points out a lack of decisive definitions here. In order to trace the biopolitical, further models of the political and possible exit strategies through these other politics, one has to clarify what one means with biological life by defining its very concept. Without going into historical details and their time and space trajectories, Agamben proposes an agency in, or with what he calls »form-of-life«; this is a proposal for abandoning the exclusion and isolation of naked life from political power, i.e. the context of the forms of life.* »The form-of-life

[12] *Agamben, G.: »Part 1, Form-of-Life«. In:* Means without End: Notes on Politics. *pp. 3–14. Minneapolis, London: University of Minnesota Press, 2000. Agamben introduces the term* form-of-life *(p. 3) to explore* »life that can never be separated from its form, a life in which it is never possible to isolate something such as naked life« *(pp. 3-4).*

[13] *Foucault, M.: quoted in Agamben, G.: Ibid., p. 7. On the biological life—political life, see especially pp. 7–9. For Foucault's detailed analysis of biopower and biopolitics see: Foucault, M.:* The History of Sexuality, Vol. 1: The Will to Knowledge. *London: Penguin, (1976) 1998*

defines a life—human life—in which the single ways, acts, and processes of living are never simple facts but always and above all possibilities of life, always and above all power. Each behaviour and each form of human living is neither prescribed by a specific biological vocation, nor is it assigned by whatever necessity; instead, no matter how customary, repeated, and socially compulsory, it always retains the character of a possibility.« [14]

[14] *Agamben, G.:Ibid., p. 4*

And, »A political life, that is a life directed toward the idea of happiness and cohesive with a form-of-life, is thinkable only starting from the emancipation from such as division [biological life as the secularised form of naked life, divided from the political life], with the irrevocable exodus from any sovereignty« [15] *. The coming politics then are not only a way of silencing sovereignty but of undermining its very constitution. Transforming the constitutive elements of the biopolitical, the coming politics resist to distinct between different forms-of-life, but rather affirm the form-of-life as a multiplicity. Double political, form-of-life activates the passage from the biopolitical to coming politics by discontinuing the strategies it has brought to light.*

[15] *Agamben, G.:Ibid., p. 8*

With the common flower project, BCL avoid governance. Perhaps they add another layer to an authorial system. After all, the artists offer instructions —allowing whatever and wherever growth can happen, introducing irregularities into a governing system, abandoning models of hyper-regulation by modes of sharing and distributing, pointing to imaginary contact zones, leaving a multitude intact. It might be precisely this attitude, the artists' methodology of affirming a concept of the common inherent to a coming politics on which Agamben further notes: » [...] in question [here] is always experience of a common power. Community and power identify one with the other without residues because the inherence of a communitarian principle to any power is a function of the necessarily potential character of any community. [...] We can communicate with others only through what in us—as much as in others—has remained potential, and any communication [...] is first of all communication not of something in common but of communicability itself« [16] .

[16] Agamben, G.: Ibid., pp. 9–10. See also Jean-Luc Nancy's elaboration of community and being-with and the relation to the multi- and communicability. Nancy, J.-L.: »An Exchange, Jean-Luc Nancy and Chantal Pontbriand«. In: Morgan, J. (Ed.): Common Wealth. pp. 111–119. London: Tate Publishing, 2003

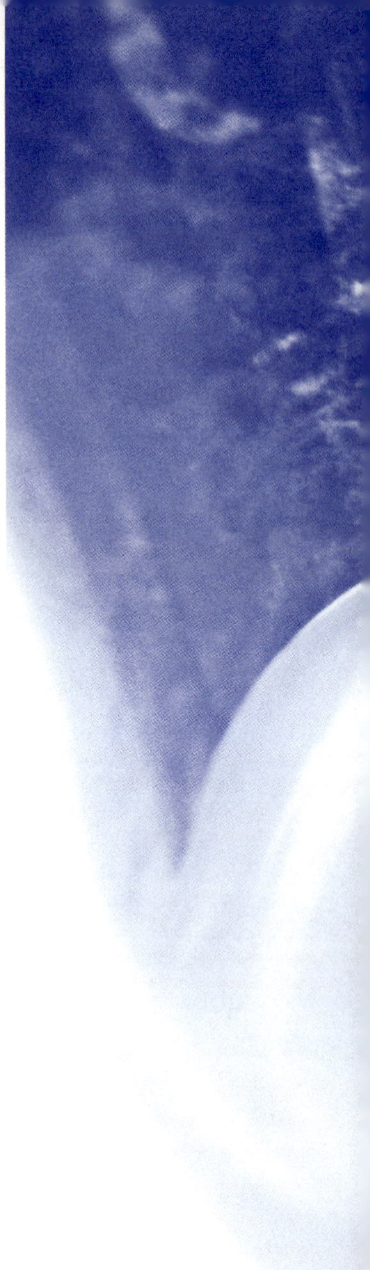

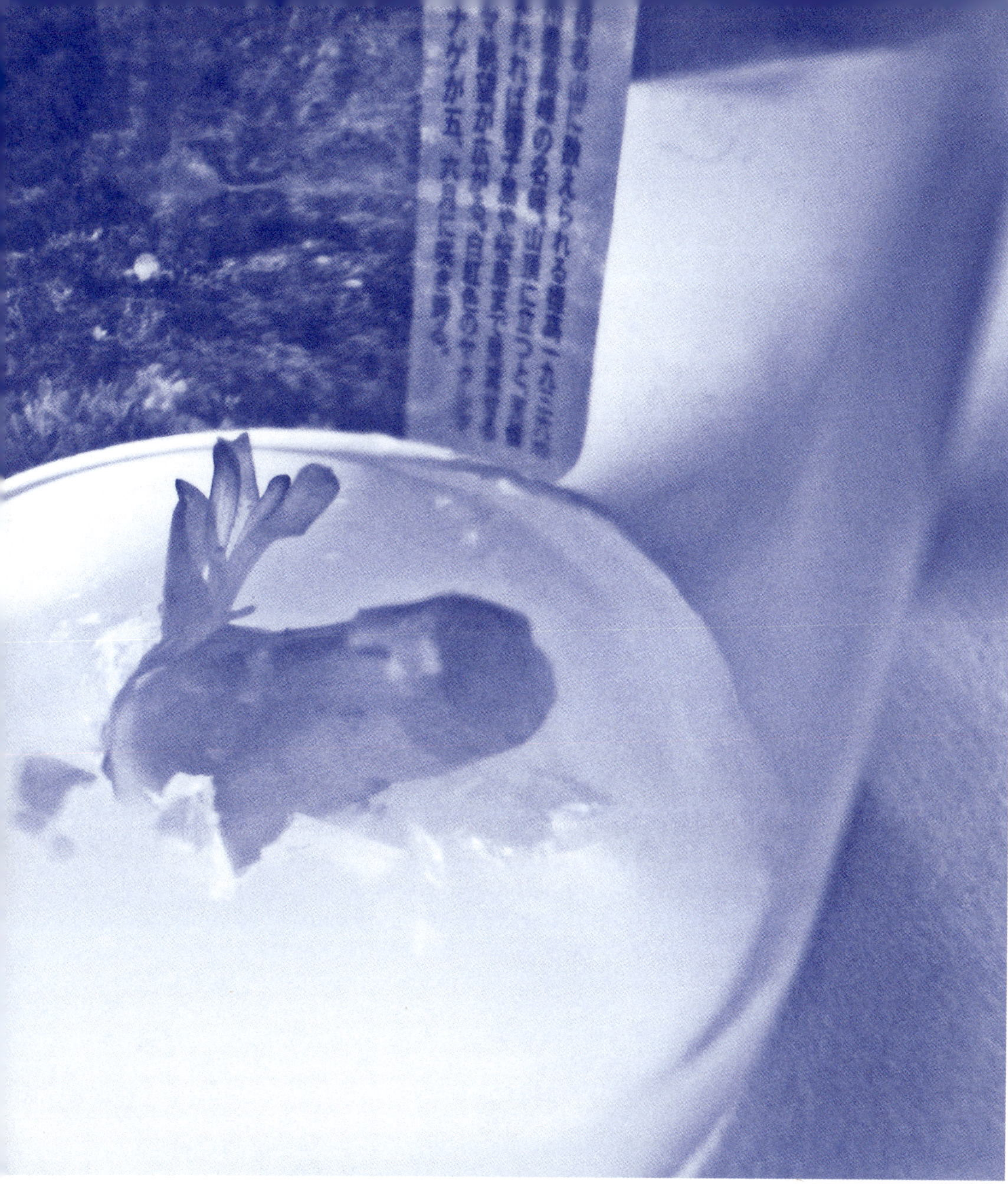

Fig. 3: Developing carnation tissue culture

***It is* DIY** *I keep returning to, not just as a practice in itself but as a measurement for our relation to the scientific, knowledge and the redistribution of media economics. The bio-hacking (hacking biotechnology) exerted and acted out by Fukuhara and Tremmel through bio-tech-DIY, speak of an interest in a reformation of established technologies and systems, of working with a biological resistance, of DIY as a self shaping process. But there seem to be many myths here: the myth of hacking to possibly penetrate and subvert dominant corporate environments* [17] *; to confirm that sharing and open code, e.g. open source is the preferred, the democratic, politically and ethically correct way to go* [18] *; to add a revolutionary flavour to current media practice; to add a revolutionary flavour to the discourse of knowledge linked to science and progress. Should one bind bio-hacking to a sort of flattening of scientific revelations? Should one follow* Critical Art Ensemble's (CAE) *statement in relation to the rhetoric of biotechnology in the public sphere* [19] *?*

[17] *On hacking and revolution, or the hacker as class, see: Wark, McK.:* Hacker Manifesto. *Cambridge, Mass. / London: Harvard University Press, 2004*

[18] *For a discussion on open source that* »fetishes all the wrong things« *where the opposition between closed and open is flawed, and alternative logics of control, see: Galloway, A. R., Thacker, E.:* The Exploit, A Theory of Networks. *pp. 124–126. Minneapolis / London: University of Minnesota Press, 2007*

[19] *Critical Art Ensemble, »The Promissory Rhetoric of Biotechnology in the Public Sphere«. In:* Molecular Invasion. *Chapter 2. New York: Autonomedia, 2002. / In* Digital Resistance. *Chapter 3. New York: Autonomedia, 2001*

Writing on a rhetorical failure, this art collective points out that there is no escape for any scientific discovery—essentially miraculous—to be assimilated into the system (pancapitalism) [20] *. What are the consequences for an artistic practice that addresses such propositions?*

[20] *Critical Art Ensemble: Ibid. (see note* [19]*), p. 57*

In various ways BCL*'s work situates itself within the legacies of the* Wiener Gruppe, *mentioned by the artists in an interview with the author, and of the artist and political activist Gustav Metzger. Especially Metzger's investigations in the early 1960s around* Auto Creative Art *and* Auto Destructive Art *share aspects emerging in the processes undertaken by Fukuhara and Tremmel. Think synthesis of science, computer, art, growth; technology and artwork as agent; format of manifestos; rupture in the socio-political and economic sphere; art/science as ambivalent singularity (check out* Liquid Crystal Environment *(1965, remade 2005) for this strange crystallisation of art into science and vice versa); artist-activistscientistmediahackermentality? The economic, social and cultural conditions when Metzger wrote his* Manifesto Auto Destructive Art *(1960), and* Auto Destructive Art Machine Art Auto Creative Art *(1961)* [21] *might have changed, but today's environment (in a general sense) can be seen as a continuation and exploitation of these previously laid-out globalised states.*

[21] *http://www.luftgangster.de/audeart3.html; http://www.luftgangster.de/audeart4.html [Accessed: Jun 16, 2010] The quotes that follow are from these sources. Two further sideway-references to BCL's practice: Macrolab's self-contained insular systems, http://makrolab.ljudmila.org/ [Accessed: Oct 31, 2010]; and Japanese artist and researcher Akihiro Kubota who interestingly explores art and generative media, http://dp.idd.tamabi.ac.jp/bioart/ [Accessed: Jun 16, 2010]*

Metzger: »Auto Creative Art is art of change, growth movement« *(1961);* »Auto Destructive Art is the transformation of technology into public art.« »Auto Destructive Art is art which contains within itself an agent which automatically leads to its destruction within a period of time not to exceed twenty years. Other forms of auto-destructive art involve manual manipulation. There are forms of auto-destructive art where the artist has a tight control over the nature and timing of the disintegrative process, and there are other forms where the artist's control is slight.« *(1960);* »Auto Destructive Art and auto creative art aim at the integration of art with the advances of science and technology. The immediate objective is the creation, with the aid of computers, of works of art whose movements are programmed and include self regulation. The spectator, by means of electronic devices, can have a direct bearing on the action of these works.« *(1961)*

Related to BCL, Metzger's landscape of interest might bear different objectives with his focus on the auto destructive power of a work of art (creative = auto destructive). Indeed it is—literally and conceptually—a seed of proliferation (of flowers, things, ideas, ideologies) the artists are after; anti-ephemeral in some ways, they create a flourishing archive in the present. It might be the disintegrative force the two practices share, the affective quality of dispersal, dissolution, the non-regulated and the self-regulated—where the work itself becomes the inventive and discreet regulator of a system in which it is marginalised or from which it is removed.

Writing on Common Flowers / Flower Commons, *it appears that the questions and actions laid out above are both relevant to and at stake in* BCL*'s project. If there is a code inherent to their practice, it might be accurate to call it a deviate of, or perhaps a contemporary take on the Situationists'* détournement.

But to pin down their activities to a work around the spectacle of images / media / economics and tactical critique is not entirely sufficient to give their actions their proper site. To me, BCL *do two things: first, they embody a desire for a movement from aesthetics to the (bio)political—questioning the very ability for that movement. Second, within the ordered and controlled space they are operating in, and working against, they create a second kind of order, a* DIY *order.* BCL *manage to provide the tools for a silent, indirect, dispersed, maybe more efficient hacking, opposed to hacking that loudly and violently breaks codes.* BCL *manage to give space to imagine a subversion, which is only possible by including people as actual and virtual agents. Imaginary agents operate among the common.*

Writing this text, I re-visit Tokyo; the little planting pots around the modest Japanese houses, the flowers never opulent, rather rhizomatic, a thing in between the weed and the hyper-flower.

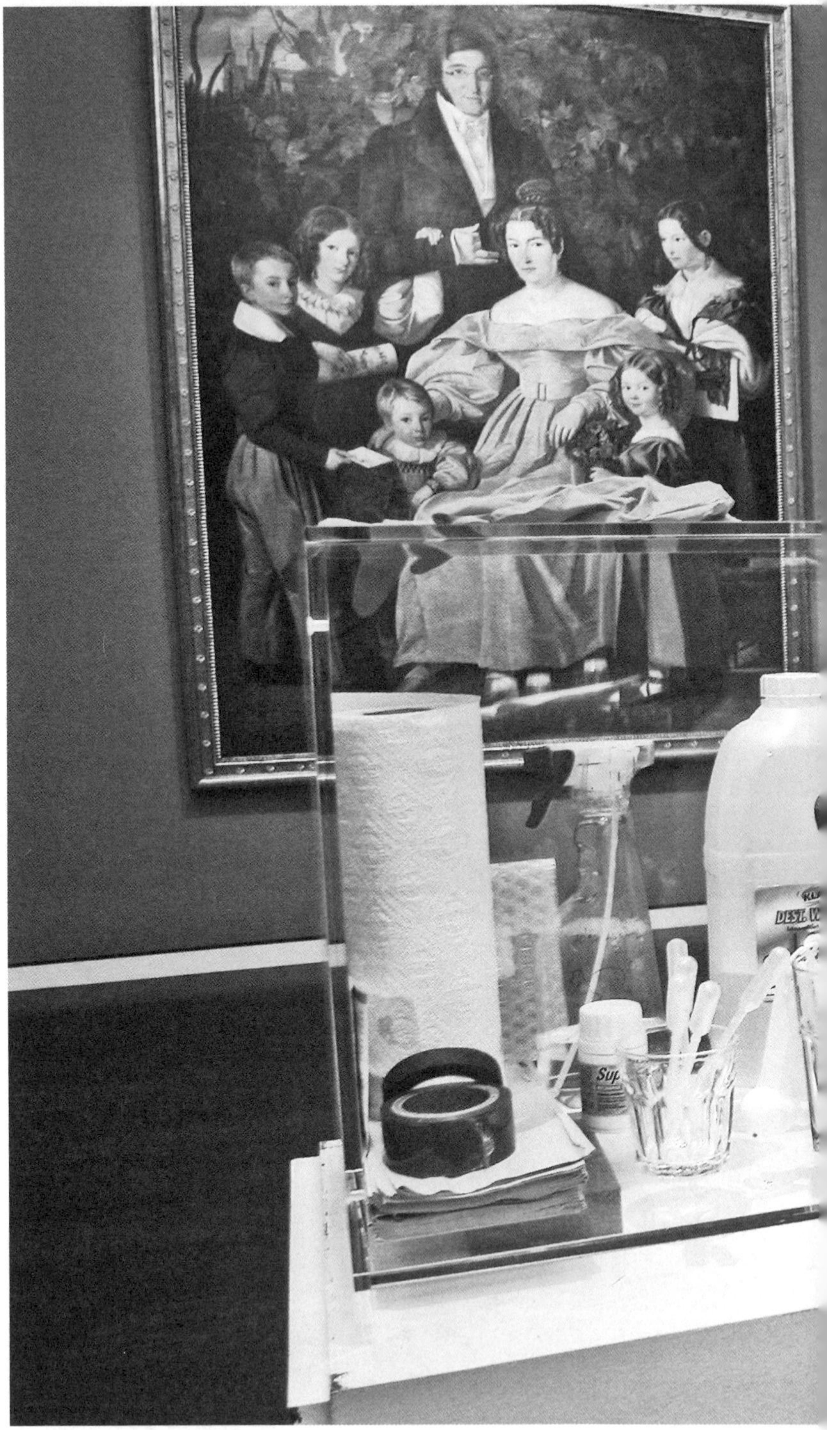

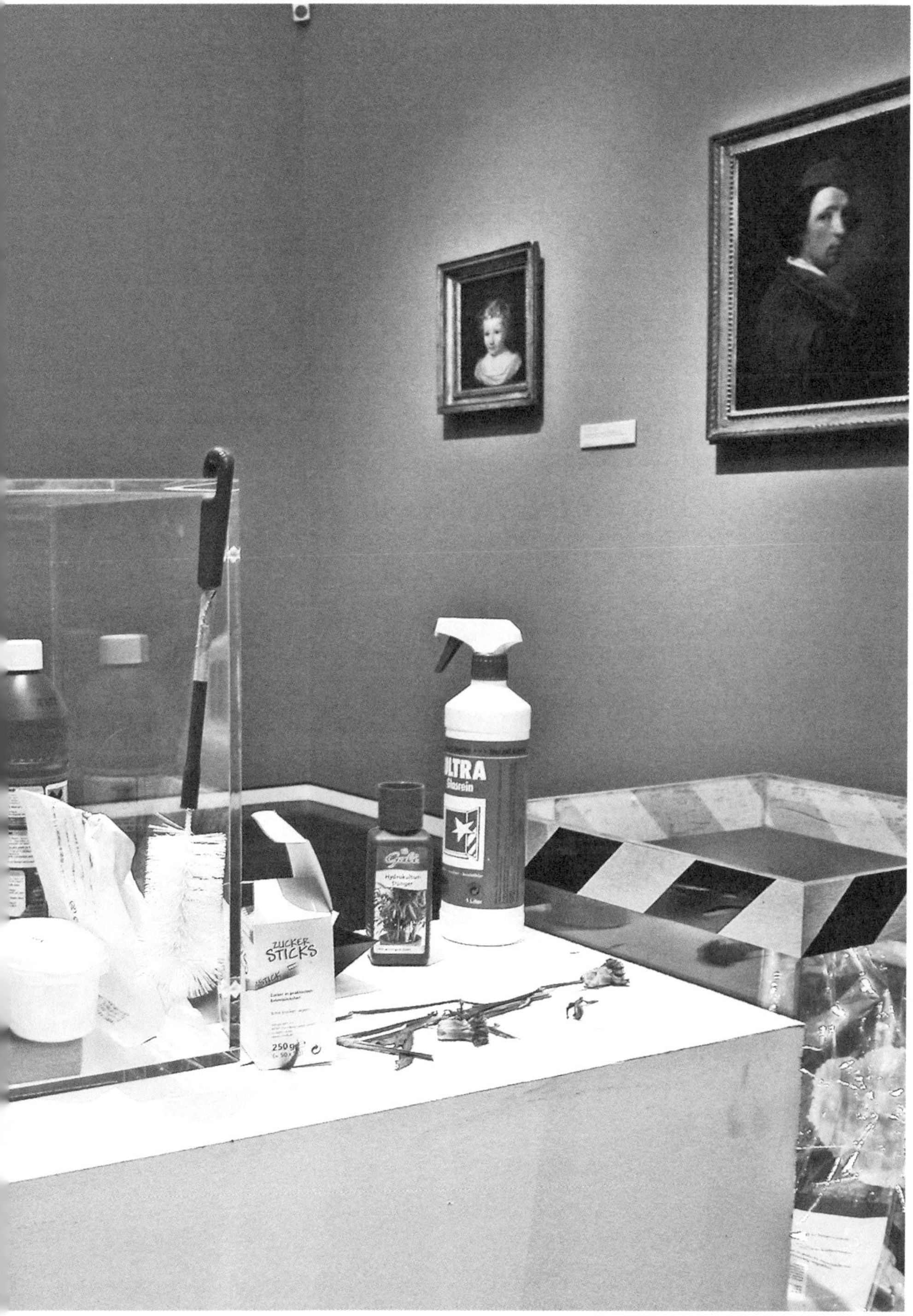

Fig. 4: DIY Plant Tissue Culture Lab *installed at the* Wallraf-Richartz Museum *in Cologne*

Ludic Chindogus as Erotic Toys— Pleasure, Play, and Politics Beyond Materialism

MARGARETE JAHRMANN

This paper introduces a number of conceptual key terms around the art and politics of play, as Jouissance, Playsure Politics, Ludic Chindogu Interfaces and Ludics. The joyful and even erotic play with the technological Chindogu (Kawakami 1995) as an artifact is understood as a way to gain an immaterial perspective on Ludic Interfaces as political tools, which can be identified as seminal practice for the development of a critical consciousness through play. Jouissance as discussed by Julia Kristeva (Kristeva, 1984) and Slavoj Žižek (Žižek, 2005) is useful as technical term from cultural studies and in particular from the perspective of political theories, in order to emphasize the quality of enjoyment and erotic attraction in the agency dimension of play with an object. The contemporary slave and master relation of players in everyday life and their relation to their technological objects can be identified throughout the paper as related to concepts of play and desire as driving forces for social agency in everyday life that really matters! The emergence of Ludics as art form is informed by the practice based research in the Internet of Things, expressed in Urban Games and Gamefashion. The methodological activist practice of Ludics was academically discussed in the author's doctoral thesis, submitted at the Centre for Advanced Inquiry in Integrative Arts, University of Plymouth, UK. A selected number of case studies of activist interventions and exemplary activist artworks of the genre of game arts give evidence for the anthropomorphisation of political Ludic Interfaces of everyday life in a contemporary ubiquitous Ludic Society.

Introduction and Overview

Our contemporary society appears to be heavily determined by ubiquitous technologies and smart toys with playful interfaces, including so-called smartifacts. Smartifact *is a term first coined by researcher Harry Vertelney at Apple Computers Corporation in the 1980s to refer to new forms of software based agents. Smartifact is used in this article to connote the fictional concepts, as described by writers of the* Cyberpunk *genre, as Bruce Sterling (Sterling, 2005). According to observations of developments of consumer technologies over the last decade, the material affordances of these objects, as Miller (Miller, 2006) describes them in the second wave of material studies, increasingly influenced the social design of urban spaces, private life, and the role of the self. Despite the factual presence of technological objects, critical theory in interaction design studies barely questions this technological materiality. The actual discourse mostly ignores the political brisance of the influence of technological objects on individual and social life. By contrast, game and play cultures offer a significant political commentary on these kinds of developments.*

Since the late 1990s, the new genre of game art started to mirror these cultures. This newly constituted field of artistic intervention embraced the increasing presence of playful interfaces, although it ignored its inherent political potentials in activism and social design. However, new forms of critical intervention in roleplay, creative work and text began to emerge from the play with technological gadgetry in everyday life. In particular, this critical creative work, found in the deviant fields between irony and subversion in activist and arts avant-garde provides evidences for the development of the idea of play politics, elaborated as ironic Playsure Politics.

This paper and the supporting research practice aims to provide models for further interventions into the conditions of technological artifacts, in order to develop a political consciousness about the master-servant relation to machines in the internal dynamic of the player. In addition, it will suggest a theoretical framework, Ludics, *for the field through the integration of anthropological concepts of play, pleasure and enjoyment in relation to practical examples of subtle erotic forces in play with absurd machines. The critical analysis of technological objects serves as a catalyst for a new socio-political theory of art and playfulness as a research question of urgency in contemporary ubiquitous computing worlds. The argument is elaborated through the following key terms of Ludic practices.*

1 *Key Terms of Ludics Practice*

Ludics as practice led research aims to offer a model of playfulness studies, which overcome the lack of pleasure, politics and material consciousness in games studies of the last decade, as introduced by Juul (Juul, 2003) , Frasca (Frasca, 2001) or Pias (Pias, 2000) . With a survey of the dominant understanding of playfulness in the current electronic culture, it theoretically grounds subversive practices in play as political activism of everyday life. It is a model that subjects this to a critical evaluation relative to:

1. A critical assessment of playfulness as distinct from game studies in historic and contemporary theories and its synthesis as a particular dimension of political agency.

2. The classification of technological materiality by an in-depth survey of cases of the anthropomorphization of technological objects and the consequential introduction of the new category of semi-synthetic play.

3. Ubiquitous play as condition of social networks, based on recent activist evidences and examples of contemporary activist arts.

4. A multifaceted evaluation of affordances of play in smartifacts *and* Ludic Interfaces*, elaborated in a comparative analysis of proto-computational historic artifacts and the introduction of a material consciousness.*

5. Political subversion and synthesis in arts, presented as a theoretical narrative of cases of subtle erotic in roleplay as precedents of contemporary play with the self in networked Con-Dividualities.

6. Historic evidences of Ludic Interfaces *and political roleplay; the case studies show the power of playfulness as a consciousness strategy, when it is synthesized with theoretical concepts for a new understanding of politics in everyday life and technologies.*

7. Case studies of the author's artworks have contributed to the emergence of a new methodology of playful intervention and agency, which is coined as Ludics.

Fig. 1: Ludic Society Club Badge. *Homage to »pataphysics«. Tucson Arizona, 2006*

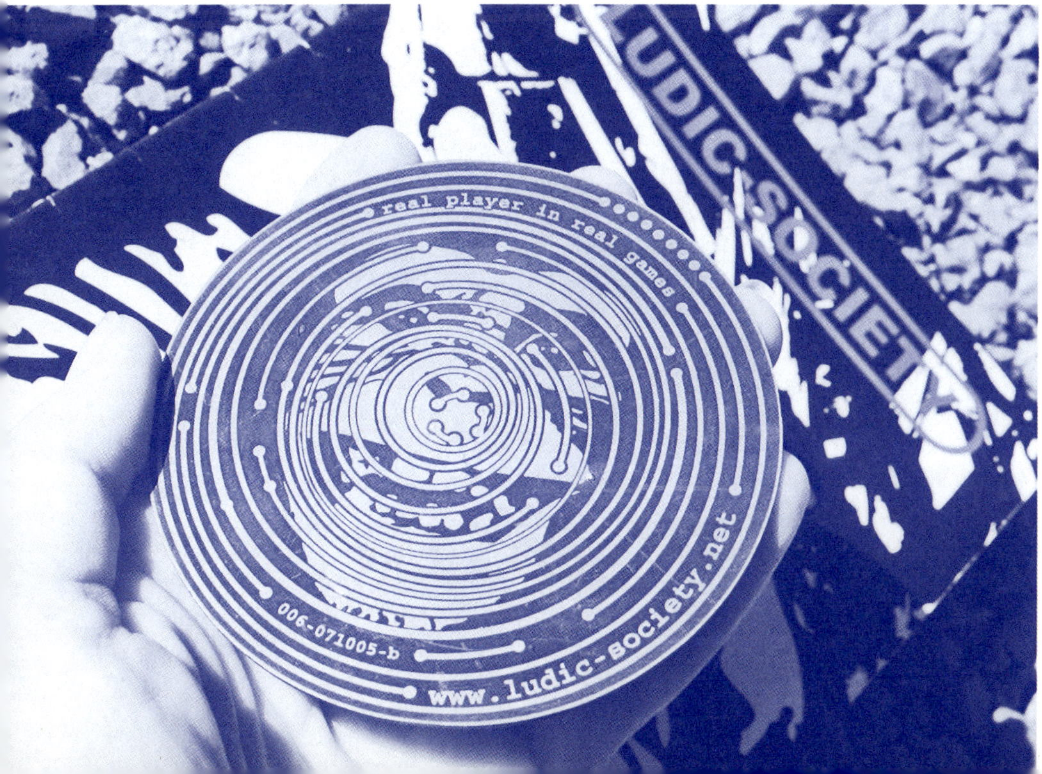

The practical and theoretical solution, coined as Ludics, *emerged as methodological platform from practice led research in the artworks of the author. This framework identifies art practice as a discrete field of research, and thus introduces a classification of methods according to a theoretical model of* Ludics. *This consists of the categories of conceived, perceived, and lived agency, which support a methodological framework of play politics, agency, and mutual information of theory and practice.* Ludics *aims to provide a conceptually informed toolbox of strategic interventions, capable of generating a new form of practical research.* Ludics *in its full potential can be understood as a new concept, which was strategically introduced by the invention of the* Ludic Society *as arts project and playful research affiliation in 2006.*

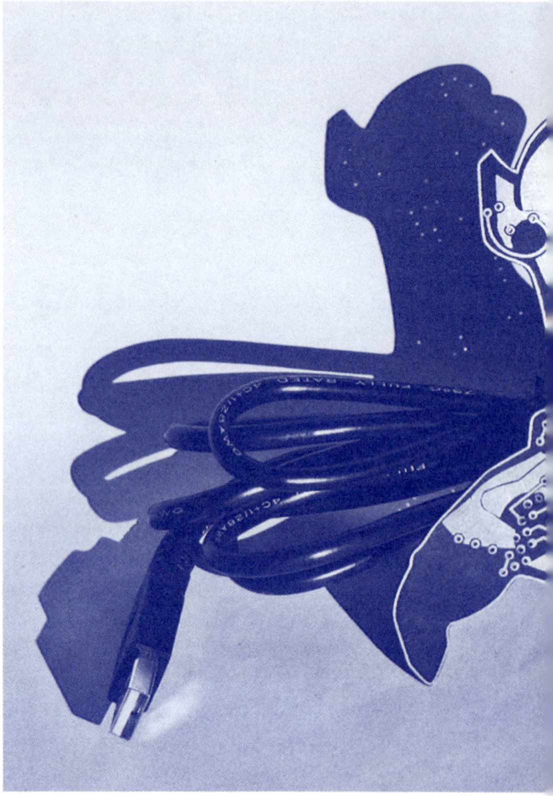

Fig. 2: Max Moswitzer / Margarete Jahrmann: GoApe Chindogu, New Bachelor Machine. *Madrid: ARCO, 2007*

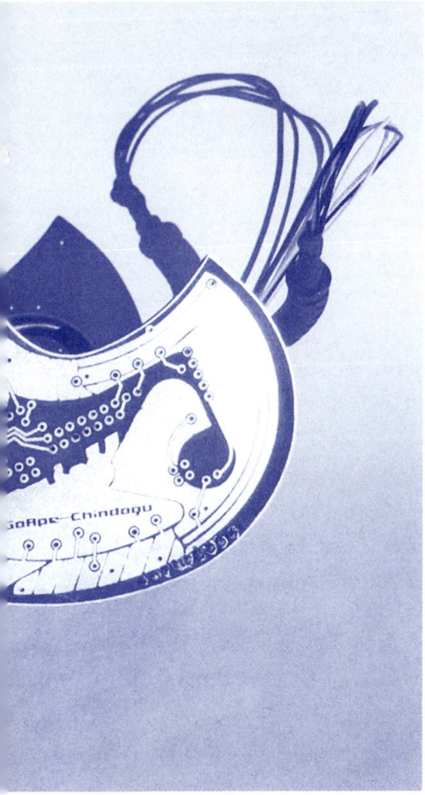

2 Ludic Chindogus

Chindogu *describes a state of mind that is based on pleasure, attraction and amusement in regard to technological artifacts. Kawakami (Kawakami, 1995) described the philosophy of Chindogus in Japan as a subversive practice in order to reach a particular consciousness in regard to useless objects. In the Western Hemisphere* Critical Arts Ensemble *(CAE, 1996) published fake advertisements of useless technologies. This addresses a particular kind of absurd technological object, which becomes a toy for amusement and joy, only by changing the attitude towards the object's materiality. This particular pleasure gained by the existence of the artifact contains a dimension of subversive attraction, which is very much bound to the arts practice of the author.*

Moreover, the author's engagement with certain aspects of computer technologies, interface cultures, network communities, online environments and play culture over the last decade integrates these two dimensions in a new form of Ludic Chindogus, *called* New Bachelor Machines, *in which philosophy and art practice converge. In* Ten Tenets of Chindogu *Kawakami refers to the real satire aspect of analogue gadget industries. He argues:*

»Every Chindogu is an almost useless object, but not every almost useless object is a Chindogu. In order to transcend the realms of the merely almost useless, and join the ranks of the really almost useless, certain vital criteria must be met. It is these criteria, a set of ten vital tenets that define the gentle art and philosophy of Chindogu« *(Kawakami, 1995)* .

Joy and pleasure are evoked by their appearance, which for them exists. It is obvious that their use is not the main target of invention. They are symbolic artifacts, toys between arts and amusement in a social configuration, which ironically mirrors associations, establishing power structures. Despite this, technological and other Chindogus are discussed and collected in playful societies. The association around the investigation of Chindogus expresses a particular interest in the gadgets used in everyday life for the deliberation of amusement. As part of this amusement of objects, a word play between »thing« and »penis« can be identified in the term »Chindogu«. The association reflects on erotic dimensions 1 . The inherent dimension of anarchy, found in sexual enjoyment combined with uselessness, is also expressed in the Chindogu manifesto: »Inherent in every Chindogu is the spirit of anarchy. Chindogu are man-made objects that have broken free from the chains of usefulness« *(Kawakami, 1995)* .

1 *This is what the editors of the website of the International Chindogu Society state:* »Well, dogu is Japanese for ›tool‹ and chin is Japanese for ›weird‹ (not to be confused with the Japanese for ›penis‹, which is also chin). Thus, a Chindogu is a weird tool. Likewise, chinchin is a weird penis. However, under no circumstances is Chindogu ever a penis tool. At least not yet!« *http://chindogu.com/chindogu/ [Accessed: Jan 12, 2010]*

The aspect of freedom merges in the useless object with the Jouissance of erotic attraction. In the case of the Chindogu, as described by Kawakami, the gaze on useless objects follows a path of »fetishisation«, as an ironic arts-oriented project.

Nevertheless, it uses means of expressing politics as the manifesto. Ten Tenets of Chindogu *is written in this style. It claims that, similarly, in sports Chindogus are not only collected, but also produced. In paragraph two of the manifesto it states:* »A Chindogu must exist, you are not allowed to use a Chindogu, but it must be made« *(Kawakami, 1995)* .

The main difference of the gadget of everyday life is, according to the manifesto, found in its intentional uselessness when creating the object. Uselessness is defined as a joyful quality in analogue technological gadgetry, according to paragraph one of the manifesto. This means that when looking at a device you cannot imagine its use at the first glance, but enjoy its aesthetic beauty of absurdity. This attraction of uselessness follows an attitude of enjoyment in relation to devices and the machines of technological cultures [2] *. Similar to an erotic toy or a fetish, the joy of the existence of the object replaces its use and function.*

[2] *Chindogus inherently contain* Play affordances*. This term is suggested to be used in this paper in order to describe a theoretical and technical aspect of material studies within the field of contemporary technological interfaces. It draws on affordances as expression from theories (Gibson, 1977) and psychology, as an action that an individual can potentially perform in his or her environment. In this thesis, it is identified by a comparative analysis of technological artifacts and objects of contemporary everyday life that require practices of play as technique of interaction.*

An erotic pleasure gained by the look on hermetic machines is expressed as experience of technologically determined life in Western industrial culture. The understanding of Jouissance *as dimension of play is supported by the conception of the absurd artifact as tool for critical enjoyment by play. The element of pleasure by the presence of uselessness gives the individual player the ability to feel free to critically take position. By subversion of functionality, certain useless objects offer a solution to circumvent the materialist approach of capitalist society. In a simple roleplay, the master-servant relation between the object and the subject is switched. This shift enables a more profound political activism that goes beyond pre-defined boundaries of subject-object relationships. Enjoyment and amusement, caused by the absurdity of technological objects of everyday life, are identified as key element in agency. The* Chindogu *is identified in this analysis as crucial vehicle of* Jouissance *practices. This argument is grounded on a literature survey about useless objects of the 20th century.*

Most importantly, the concept of Chindogu *can be used to introduce uselessness and erotic attraction to technological fetish objects connected to play, as a subversive quality to critique hegemonic power conditions. In the technological dominance by the production chain of objects, the idea supports the development of a* European Chindogu *with a clear political interest, in contrast to the Japanese understanding of pure amusement through joy and erotic attraction.*

Apart from a recent hype based on a view on the Asian gadget, simultaneously to the rise of the concept in Japan, in 1995, the American group of artists Critical Art Ensemble *spoke about* The Technology Of Uselessness, *addressing an activist program against technological dominance by publishing newspaper advertisements about useless technologies. The arts activists argued:*

»The expectation that technology will one day exist as pure utility is an assumption that frequently surfaces in collective thought on the development of society and social relations. [...] Having once left the production table, the technology that lives the godly life of state of the art uselessness has no further interaction with humans as users or as inventors; rather, humans serve only as a means to maintain its uselessness. The location of the most complex pure technology is no mystery. Deep in the core of the war machine!«
(Critical Art Ensemble, 1994)

This is juxtaposed with another radical position on Jouissance *and uselessness, which is taken from contemporary European cultural history of political scholars such as the Viennese philosopher Robert Pfaller (Pfaller, 2003) . He coined the term* Interpassivity *(Pfaller, 2000) to describe the uselessness of the imperative interactions of certain technological interfaces relating it to the erotic attraction of technological objects. Interpassive consumption machines and the placeholder function of technology for enjoyment form the anchor points of his analysis. The subtitle of his study,* Distributed Enjoyment, *refers to the delegation of* Jouissance *in objects, which substitute sublime sexuality into technologies. The motive of substitution and enjoyment is further elaborated in Pfaller's declaration of a rising emphasis on pleasure reached by technology's cultural domination as a fetishisation process (Pfaller, 2002) . By a critical analysis of the phenomenon of* Chindogu, *a philosophical strand of playfulness and enjoyment can be touched, which is—again not surprisingly—embracing the dimension, sexual enjoyment and politics, in playful* Jouissance.

3 *Jouissance*

The important third dimension of play is affective and described as the concept of Jouissance [3] .

[3] Jouissance *is often defined psychoanalytically and culturally:* »The usual English translation ›enjoyment‹ does not carry the sexually orgasmic connotation of the French term, it does add to the idea of taking pleasure in something. In Lacanian circles, Jouissance is distinguished from pleasure (plaisir) in that the latter indicates simply the search for psychic balance (homeostasis) through the release of tension, whereas the former is supposed to be in a perpetual state of and in violation of the pleasure principle. There is thus an implicit analogy drawn between demand and desire (see transgression). Julia Kristeva offers a slight development and a bit of word-play: she uses plaisir for sexual pleasure and Jouissance (or j'ouïs sens, ›I heard meaning‹) as total joy due to the presence of meaning.« *http://www.arts.ouc.bc.ca/fina/glossary/j_list.html [Accessed: Mar 6, 2009]*

This section will define the theoretical concept of Jouissance *as subversion through the erotic dimension in play.* Jouissance *as political idea is informed by the origin French »jouir« or »to enjoy«. In order to introduce the conceptual entanglement of play and the* Jouissance *meaning »French for pleasure«, the trust of playfulness as a creative drive is used to identify the agency potential of concept for a new form of play politics.*

According to the Oxford English Dictionary (Oxford English Dictionary, 2009) Jouissance *is defined as* »The possession and use of something affording advantage in the sense of enjoyment«. *Lacan introduced Jouissance in his critique of psychoanalysis as a theoretical concept. In his famous* Seminars XX *at the University of Paris, Lacan (Lacan, 1972) suggested the use of the term for a sophisticated form of pleasure, which was informed by the*

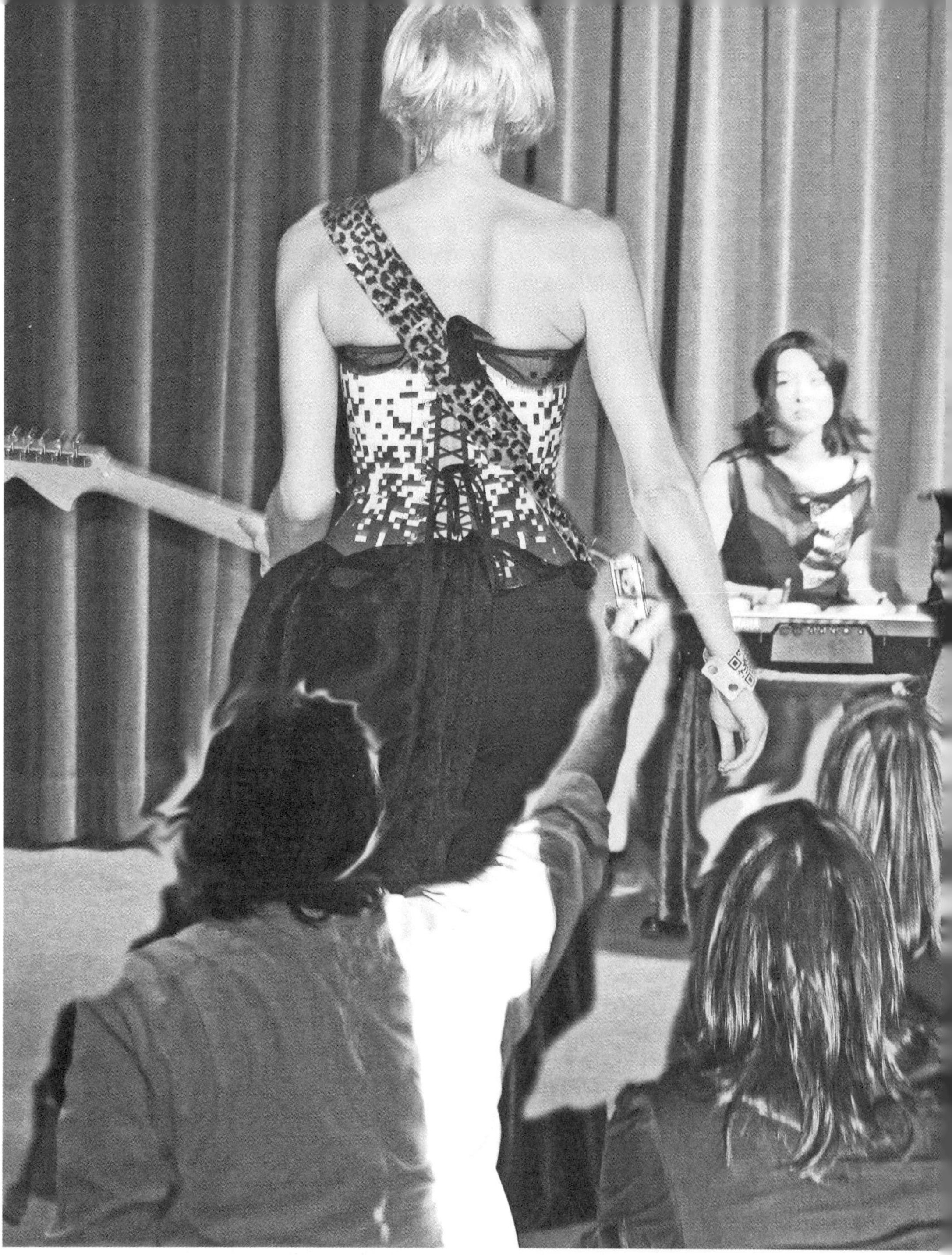

Fig. 3: Margarete Jahrmann collab. Boudoir & Who Killed Bambi: Jouissance Corsage—Virtually transparent/Mediology Performance. *Wien: Volkstheater, November 2009*

relationship between objects, subjects and the creation and shifts between different aspects of enjoyment and the desire of the self with its complex appearances. By analyzing this form of joy, Lacan constantly refers to Hegelian dialectics of »a master and a servant« relationship. The »master and servant relationship« as described in the theoretical object is produced out of the enjoyed or obsessive relationship between subject and object. The Lacanian desire for »plus-de-jouir« *(Žižek, 1992)* *can be understood as a wish for more enjoyment through play, which is tied to the object. Lacan suggested that the object of desire as an »objet petit a«* *(Lacan, 1972)*, *constitutes enjoyment, which nowadays particularly includes the technological object. This is a reminder of the frame of technological materiality, where the bond to materiality is substituted with the surplus of enjoyment by play. According to the literature survey, free play appears as associated with* Jouissance, *desire and pleasure. Drawing on the idea of free play, this divide can be unmasked as pure construction of hegemonic suppression. The thinking framework of pleasure and play is based on concrete ideas of structural processes in society as dimensions of aesthetic education and enjoyment. In this argument, the anti-thesis of reason and sensuality is dissolved in a practice of identification with a political driven desire for »freeplay«. Derrida* *(Derrida, 1978)* *introduces the idea of freeplay:*

> »And, as always, coherence in contradiction expresses the force of a desire. The concept of centered structure is in fact the concept of a free play based on a fundamental ground, a freeplay, which is constituted upon a fundamental immobility and a reassuring certitude, which is itself beyond the reach of the freeplay« *(Derrida, 1978)*.

This section's observations of a pragmatic real politics of play and enjoyment in network technologies are supported by an analysis of the Jouissance *concept by the political philosopher Slavoj Žižek* (Žižek, 2005)*, who newly interprets and draws on Lacan. He discusses a conscious form of enjoyment in contemporary real politics. This theory emphasizes the pleasures of popular culture and popularity, particularly in how Žižek declares joy and sexual pleasure as political. According to Žižek, the »other« and »violation of constraints« and »limitations« take an important role in* Jouissance.

Enjoyment becomes paradoxical if it is combined with the necessary transgression or violation of constraints. Žižek talks about the obscenity of Jouissance*, emphasizing the concern of fetish theories in relation to sovereignty. In that sense, he approaches the politics of* Jouissance *masked in popular culture. The force of the desire for freeplay opens up the discourse into political efficacy. Accordingly, freeplay can be identified as the key element in understanding the mental aspects of play and* Jouissance *as crucial for political agency. This section considers an idea of enjoyment in play for political aims. It draws from a popular orientation of a political theory on enjoyment, also towards a critical dimension of popular play in the »* Funware *« of present social network technologies.*

In present times, comparably, smart objects and multiple selves infiltrate popular culture, as the following supporting evidence in art activism's subtle enjoyments of play with the self will demonstrate. Corresponding to the observations of political roleplay in activism, art will be presented in the last section. Accordingly, a literature survey of cultural studies scholars such as Žižek (Žižek, 1992) *or Kristeva* (Kristeva, 1984) *suggests that the shift to subjectivity, identity and playfully taken roles for political agency is closely tied to material affordances of contemporary technological materiality. However, it does go beyond its constraints in terms of mental effects.*

Playful arts practice, as one of the few remaining kinds of self determined work, is identified in this section as a particular form of enjoyment, based on contemporary concepts of obsession and Jouissance. Jouissance *is useful as technical term from political theories to emphasize the quality of enjoyment and erotic attraction in the agency dimension of play, related to desire as driving force for political agency.*

4 Playsure Politics

In this key term of the paper, Playsure Politics *is understood as erotic pleasure in play caused by the materiality of technological objects, which appear increasingly useless, according to market mechanisms. This directs the focus towards the aspects and relevance of politically conscious subversive erotic joy and pleasure. In short,* Jouissance *is related to the immaterial qualities of attraction regarding the technological object.*

Politics is historically up to date with the discourses of political theories considered as antipode to play. This angle supports the bridge between play and politics through historical examples in the materiality and cultural theories of politics and agency, as a politics of play. In a survey of historical sources of a political use of playfulness, combined with an analysis of the current practices of play and the self in art activism, this relation extends the analysis into the mental conditioning and quality of playfulness in the player. This is where the concept of Jouissance, *political conscious enjoyment as a subversive agency, informs a politics of play. Evidence of play and joyful activism exemplify the connection of joy and politics, according to a theoretical clarification of the* Jouissance *concept in relation to play. According to particular practices in electronic and networked life, the play with Chindogus includes the absurd technological gadgets of everyday life. The effects and strategies of agency by play developed in these activist plays can be subsumed under the term* Playsure Politics. *Things in society as constituting elements of thing politics, serve as inspiration for the suggestion of this paper, which is the idea of a politics of »playthings«. The concept will draw on three categories of Latour:*

a. politics is no longer limited to humans and incorporates the many issues to which they are attached;

b. objects become things, that is, when matters of fact give way to their complicated entanglements and become matters of concern;

c. assembling is no longer done under the already existing globe or dome of some earlier tradition of building virtual parliaments (Latour 2005) .

This listing opens possible comparisons to technology and synthetic objects in the context of contemporary play cultures. In view of that, it can be said that objects become things, in the moment when their complex relations replace facts. If thing politics is as well regarded in a relational way, it brings efficacies of things and play into the field of view. This perspective directly results from a shift of focus from an understanding of politics as intentionally organised agency towards an experience of politics as constant intervention inherent to the affordances of technological things. The new contemporary form of ubiquity enforces this dimension of political agency, from nation states towards conceptual forms of social life. By acceptance of the political reality and social efficacy of things, technological objects and play are put to centre stage of a material consciousness and the artist as activist roleplayer.

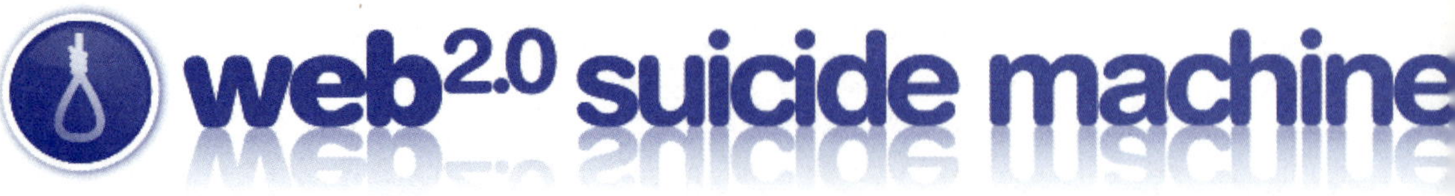

Fig. 4: moddr_: Web 2.0 Suicide Machine, *2010*

In reference to the description of the role of the artist as an activist player in the media, the 1990s genre of net art can be compared to actual playful arts practices in game arts and interventionist fine arts. In very recent forms of art dealing with web 2.0, similarities can be observed towards interventions in real-life social systems and in activist roleplaying. According to observations of roleplaying in popular electronic social network applications, a subversive dimension of roleplay activism can be observed in web 2.0 (the participatory form of the web on social platforms). Critical but joyful art can be increasingly found in these platforms, which represent a contemporary form of roleplaying from the perspective of this section. For example, the ironic Web 2.0 Suicide Machine, *2010, by the art group* moddr_ *exploits the enjoyment of destruction and intervention of big company structures in social web services. The service deletes individual accounts in web 2.0 social networks and calls this script based action* suicide of the online self. *It draws its brisance from the relational structure of standardised social online environments and the double bind of such art work. It only gains content if it is communicated through further reporting in the realm of the mass media. In this case, play and pleasure, the roleplay of the artist as liberator from the suppression of big companies of social intercourse merge against capitalisation of friendship and love. This does not mean that the artists who created the work deleted their appearance from the social web or did not capitalise personal friendship and love for their own career. By contrast, they forced their social web online appearance into the extreme, in the communication of roleplay, in blogs and news feeds and exploited personal relations.*

This section identifies such contemporary interventions into the funware *of social networks as practices of roleplay, which adapts existing consumer technologies for political intervention, like classical net art of the 1990s minor media operations. By applying these political lines of thinking with the investigation of consumer practices, Fiske called the results* »micro politics of everyday life« *(Fiske, 1989)* . *Considering requests for minor interventions, the contemporary roleplay of the artist in the electronic realm can be redefined. The curator Andreas Brockmann (Brockmann, 2001) introduced the term* Minor Media Operator *in order to describe an artist as an activist figure, similar to a political roleplayer. The focus on minor interventions by artists appears to be crucial in terms of efficacy.*

In that sense, performing playful arts in electronic networks has its effects. With the start of the network arts scene in the mid 1990s the term Minor Media Operator *was inspired by the trust in the efficacy of minor interventions on power structures generally inherent in technologies. As a method of roleplay, the concept of* Minor Media Operator *introduces the artist as equivalent to the attractive public intellectual.*

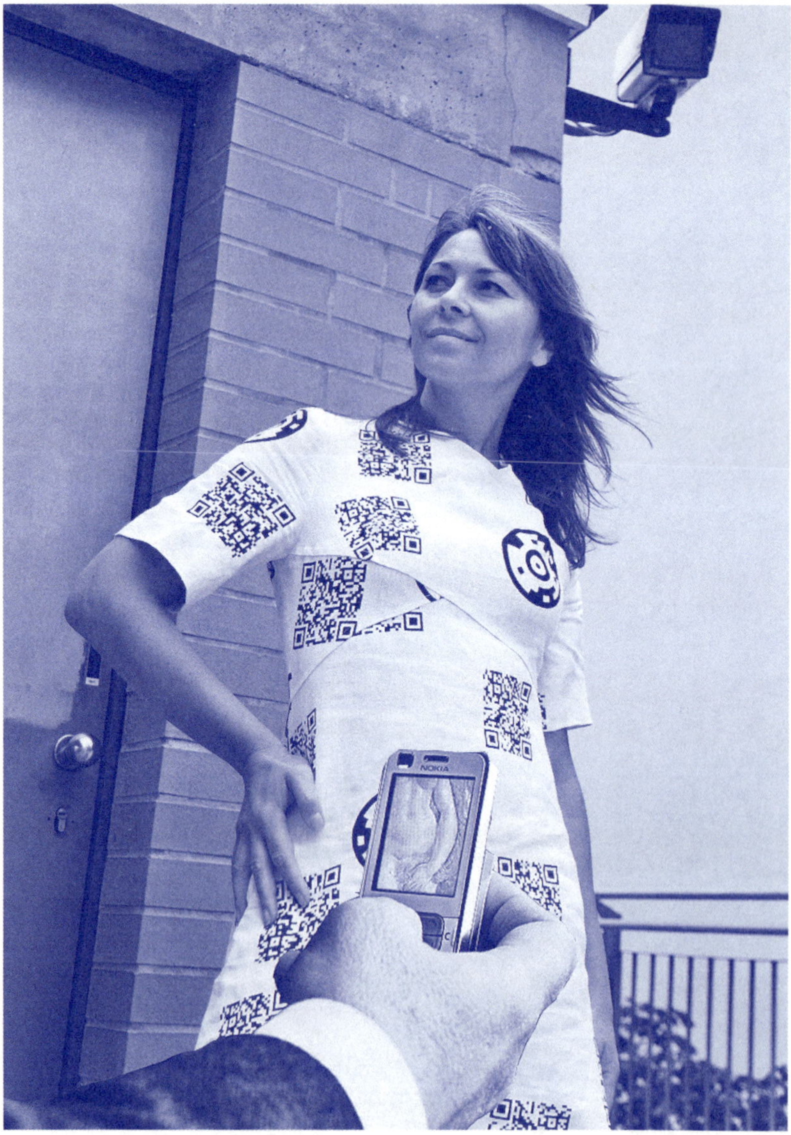

Fig. 5: Margarete Jahrmann: Semacode Dress, Urban Camouflage Performance. *Xian: Digital Arts Week, 2010*

Evidence of Political Role Play in Activism—Subversion and pleasure in play with the self as a political strategy

This section closes by giving an overview on various approaches to play related political activism, in particular the play with fictional identities, activist art, and its criticisms. In the course of this analysis, a dimension of Jouissance *is pointed out. It is tested by an analysis of practices in art activism as fake roleplay. These tactical interventions will be discussed as the most effective and powerful strategies for intervention in electronic networks. The pleasurable enjoyment of the play coupled with the self is analysed in this section in order to demonstrate how it transcends materiality of play affordances. Considering these observations, contemporary practices of play with technological materiality, can be newly interpreted. However, these practices of political roleplay demonstrate how to become active and conscious by using a dimension of play and lust, gained in the inter-play of the self, the object, and the other.*

The pleasure gained by play with the self is important as a motivation for agency. According to the following case studies, the political practice of the activist's roleplay is driven by enjoyment of the new meaning introduced in regard to agency. According to the literature survey on activism, Umberto Eco *(Eco, 1967)* *coins the expression* Semiological Guerrilla *(Eco, 1967)* *to describe this shift of meaning in communication. This term describes a practice of inter-play of objects, meaning and subjects. Eco argues:* »The battle for the survival of man as a responsible being in the communications era is not to be won where the communication originates, but where it arrives« *(Eco, 1967)* .

Semiological Guerrilla *tactics invert the communicated messages; in the moment, they arrive at a public audience and are enjoyed by roleplay practices. In these cases, fictional identities are invented as a cover or a mask for political and activist purposes. The art work evidence —— like* Semacode Dress, *2010. [...] The Urban camouflage dress never shows reality on digital camera displays. It introduces particular Sema code-fashion-patterns as urban dress code, which makes the wearer invisible for digital eyes. The fashion series conceptually aims to trickster mobile phones and surveillance cameras. [...] Similar to El Subcommandante Marco's wool-mask, this piece of clothing makes the wearer invisible for electronic cameras of mobile gadgetry, as phones, which are increasingly used for surveillance purposes —— displays how political roleplaying, as an avant-garde arts practice, allows one to develop an understanding of the joyful agency mechanisms of play politics.*

Ludic keyterms are informed by cultural and historical studies, anthropological and political theories, the arts and technical language. Ludics as newly coined term can be identified as the most challenging concept, particularly in the way it is introduced and applied, in order to enable further analysis of the intersection of philosophy, anthropology, everyday life, play, politics and art.

References

Broeckmann, A.: »Minor Media—Heterogenic Machines«.
In: Chimères *No.42. Paris: Printemps, 2001*

Critical Art Ensemble: The Technology of Uselessness.
New York: Ctheory, 1994

Derrida, J.: »Structure, Sign and Play in the Discourse of the Human Sciences«.
In: Bass, A. (Ed.): Writing and Difference. *London: Routledge, 1978*

Eco, U.: Towards a Semiological Guerilla Warfare: Travels in Hyperreality.
London: Picador, 1987

Fiske, J.: Understanding Popular Culture.
London: Routledge, 1989

Frasca, G.: »Videogames of the Oppressed: Critical Thinking, Education, Tolerance, and Other Issues«. In: Harrigan, P., Wardrip-Fruin, N. (Eds.): First Person. New Media as Story, Performance, and Game. *Cambridge, Mass.: MIT Press, 2003*

Gibson, J.: »The Theory of Affordances«. In: Shaw, R., Bransford, J. (Eds.): Perceiving, Acting, and Knowing. *New York: Lawrence Erlbaum Associates, 1977*

Heidegger, M.: Die Frage nach dem Ding: zu Kants Lehre nach den Transzendentalen Grundsätzen. *Tübingen: Niemeyer, 1984*

Juul, J.: »The Game, the Player, the World: Looking for a Heart of Gameness«
In: Copier, M., Raessens, J. (Eds.): Level Up: Digital Games Research Conference Proceedings. *Utrecht: Utrecht University, 2003*

Kawakami, K.: 101 Unuseless Japanese Inventions: The Ten Tenets of Chindogu.
New York: W.W. Norton & Co, 1995

Kristeva, J.: Revolution in Poetic Language.
New York: Columbia University Press, 1984

Latour, B.: Science in Action: How to Follow Scientists and Engineers through Society.
Berkshire: Open University Press, 1987

Pfaller, R.: Die Ilusion der Anderen. Über das Lustprinzip in der Kultur.
Frankfurt a.M.: Suhrkamp Verlag, 2002

Pias, C.: Computer Spiel Welten. *Dissertation.*
Weimar: Bauhaus- Universität Weimar, 2000

Safo, P.: Sensors: The Next Wave of Innovation.
New York: ACM, 1997

Senneth, R.: The Craftsman.
New Haven, London: Yale University Press, 2008

Sterling, B.: Shaping Things.
Cambridge, Mass.: MIT Press, 2005

Žižek, S.: Mehr-Genießen. Lacan in der Populärkultur.
Vienna: Turia und Kant, 1992

Urban Playgrounds, Alternate Games— on Urban Play, ARGs, and Psychogeography

VERENA KUNI

To the Core of the City? This Way, Please: Down the Rabbit Hole. Let us Explore its Hidden Structures, its Inner Guts. And then Let us take over the System ...

This may be the promise. However, meanwhile most of what comes up under the charismatic umbrella term Alternate Reality Games *does so thanks to investment of major brands. With* Interactive entertainment *as the main tag, with a* Puppet Master *leading proactive consumers to the next trendy sellout* ARGS *are being considered, researched and developed as* »a medium for lifestyle, marketing and advertisement«.

Sure, this is not a game. Yet, this is not what you'd expect from something called »alternate«? You think whatever might be considered as the potentials of collective intelligence and collective creativity could take another direction? Like, in example, towards new ways of research and new ways of taking action in urban space? Okay. Perhaps all you have to do is just to try a little harder. Watch out for the Rabbit Hole. Enter the Game. And find your way to play ...

1

1 *Departing from a brief introduction into the field in focus —urban playgrounds—and into possible approaches to it offered by different games played in this field, the following essay will take a closer look at ARGS. However, rather than giving a survey of what has been so far developed and released within this (sub-)genre of contemporary gaming, the aim is to dig deeper into ARGs from a methodological point of view—and to propose some thoughts on the potentials (and problems) of ARGs and ARG-related features as a tools for collective/networked research and action in urban environments.*

CURRENTLY PLAYING: ~~CC VIENNA~~

CURRENTLY PLAYING: UPLAY EVERYWHERE

This is (not) a game. This is (not) a text. This is a code. And: yes, indeed: play has already started. »Oh dear! Oh dear! I shall be late!« True. But don't worry: You can always join. Moreover: It has probably not ended whenever you may think it's finished. It is not. Thus, feel free to

ENTER: UPLAY

Anytime. EVERYWHERE.

~~C IS FOR~~ ...

CARRIER
CERTAINTY
CHANCE
CHOICE
CITY
CLOSURE
CODE
COLLABORATION
COMMONS
COMMUNITY
COPY
CORPORATE
CRAP

CREEPY

CREATIVITY

CULTURE

...

Make your choice!

As often, it makes sense to start with very basic definitions. Code *can be defined as a rule, a set of rules or a set of instructions for translating information into another form or representation. However, code may also be the carrier of information itself. This can render dealing with code somehow complicated. It can be a problem. It can be a potential. Play is one option to test the limits of the latter. However, playing with code is also a risk.*

Culture *can be defined as a set of codes shared by those who belong to this culture, providing a framework for everyone who deals with it. Thus, to act and to deal with(in) culture, you will need to know the code—how to read and understand the code, and how to use it. That's why people ask for rules, why they ask for instructions. And that's why modes of communication and representation matter. However, obviously rules and instructions are not only coded, but come as codes as well. Moreover, not only the former but the latter can likewise be true for representation. The crucial questions are: What is operated here, by whom and how?*

~~*D IS FOR ...*~~

DANGER
DAMAGE
DATA
DEBATE
DECISION
DEFINITION
DEFENSE
DELETION
DENSITY
DESIGN
DETAIL
DEVELOPMENT
DEVICE
DIFFERENCE
DISPLAY
DONATION
DONE
DOUBLE
DRAG
DRAMA
DURATION
DUTY

...

Make your choice!

Given the political dimensions of this question it may indeed seem risky, if not inappropriate to think about options for play with(in) this system: to play with codes—rules, instructions, and re-presentations. Yet this is exactly what is offered by projects claiming urban space as playground—contemporary cityscapes under the conditions of globalization as zones of conflicts and clashes between codes of different social, political, historical, ethnical, religious etc. origins are predestined for this very kind of play. The point is of course: How and by whom is the playground as well as the play itself defined? What is being played? Is it a game? If this is not a game, but a(bout) play: what is the difference?

Definitions of game(s) and play are multiple and may vary according to the set of theories and practices they are built upon. This makes it considerably difficult to briefly sum up something like »universal basics«. However, focussing on the difference between game(s) and play allows sketching down some of the more relevant characteristics at least.

A game is usually considered as an activity taking place within a defined framework. A game has rules. A game separates those who play from those who don't. A game is located in space and time within fixed dimensions. A game has a starting point, and it has an end.

Play*, in contrast, may share some or all of these features or not. Play is not necessarily situated within a defined framework. Play does not necessary follow a stable set of rules. In play, borders between players and others—those consciously playing and others who are unconsciously or involuntarily involved—may dissolve as well as the dimensions of space and time. Play does neither need a previously fixed starting point nor an end.*

This fundamental openness—in terms of not being restricted and pre-defined in the way games necessarily are—is obviously a potential, and a problem of play. Above all, the very tension between the former and the latter can prove as its most important quality.

~~G IS FOR ...~~

GAME
GADGET
GAIN
GATEKEEPERS
GAZE
GEAR
GEM
GENDER
GENE
GENEROSITY
GENRE
GIZMO
GLITCH
GLOBAL
GO
GOAL
GONE
GOSSIP
GRAVITY
GREED
GUARANTEE
GUESS

...

Make your choice!

Yet there are—and probably there have always been—also games stressing the rather narrow, traditional definitions of the genre. Games that tend to transgress borders, games that bend towards more open, process oriented forms of play. And not by chance it's exactly these kinds of games being played on likewise expanded urban playgrounds, encompassing not only cityscapes as architectural and social agglomerations, but related mediascapes as well.

Their denominations are already telling: Urban Games, Live Action Roleplaying, Pervasive Games, Alternate Reality Games. *So are the related definitions, however instable and debatable they may be.*

Urban Games*: Games that take place in urban environments and use the cityscape or certain parts of it, rather than distinct areas officially dedicated to games and sports as playgrounds.*

Live Action Roleplaying*: Games that take place in realtime and in real space everyday environments, using the latter as playgrounds for game community based performance and play.*

Pervasive Games*: Games that transgress and transcend different layers of experience.*

Alternate Reality Games*: Games that create shared experiences of alternate realities.*

For good reasons these terms—widely in use, yet connected to a whole range of varying definitions, theories and practices—have to be handled with caution: above all, as defining games in theory is one thing, subsuming a specific game under one of these categories in practice is another. The same is true for talking about games on the one hand and experiencing a game on the other. Nevertheless, they can be helpful for further clarifying what are the issues here: What are the specific potentials—and problems—of playing (with) alternate realities in urban spaces?

~~*U IS FOR ...*~~

U-TURN
UBIQUITOUS
UGLY
UNCANNY
UNDEAD
UNDERGROUND
UNDONE
UNITARY
UNSUSPECTED
UPLAY
URBAN
USE
UTTER
UTILITY
UTOPIA

...

Make your choice!

Urban Games are historically and conceptually related to the traditional genre of street games, with which they share not only the playground—public streets and spaces—but also their main characteristics: A game takes place within a fixed setup of time and space, of rules, and players. Physical and strategic skills, movement and competition are usually core elements, as well as teamplay. Urban Games may relate to digital media culture and may also include the use of media—however not used as playgrounds in their own rights. Even the urban playground itself is rather neatly defined as a stable field than something to explore. For the time of the play, players may adopt a role and behave according to it. However, usually this role is rather functional than inviting to further develop it in more elusive processes of interaction with other players. In contrast to this, the latter is a key element in Live Action Roleplaying. Players may develop not only their role, but the storylines of play as well, and this process may be either directed or open. Again, the games will usually take place in public space and within a predefined terrain, but not necessarily in urban environments.

Moreover, time is used in a different way, as it has to keep with the development of the storyline and vice versa. However, usually there's not only a starting point, but also an end. And while the games may relate to digital media culture and also may include the use of media, again these are not used as playgrounds in their own rights. Actions and items in one reality represent actions and items in another one—but there's no exchange between them.

Exactly this is the most important feature we find in Pervasive Games, as well as in ARGS. Pervasive Games are built upon the basic concept of blurring the borders and boundaries of and between different real and virtual spaces, and they strongly rely on networked media to define and develop their playgrounds.

Now, how do they do so? And what is the difference between Pervasive Games and ARGS? [2]

2 As Pervasive Games and Alternate Reality Games share the mentioned core features, and as one more general layer these very features could be aptly described as mandatory for »pervasiveness«, it is indeed possible to subsume ARGs as a sub-genre of Pervasive Games. Just as we may find the majority of Pervasive Games created for and being played in urban environments—thus giving a reason to subsume them as a special sub-genre under the roof of Urban Games. However, not only it makes sense at this point—as we are looking at the very specifics of the mentioned genres—to look for the differences rather than for the commonalities. Also as we want to ask to dig deeper into and to discuss the specifics of ARGs respectively it is necessary to separate the latter from Pervasive Games in a more general perspective.

~~P IS FOR ...~~

PARTICIPATION
PERSONA
PERVASIVE
PILOT
PLAY
PLAYGROUND
POLITICS
POSITION
POTENTIAL
POWER
PRACTICE
PRESET
PREY
PRIVACY
PROBLEM
PROPERTY
PSYCHE
PSYCHOGEOGRAPHY
PUBLIC
PUPPET MASTER
PUZZLE

...

Make your choice!

Pervasive Games combine »physical presence and virtual experience«, and vice versa. To do so, they combine movements in, and explorations of, physical spaces with extensive use of networked media technologies; they strongly rely on mobile interfaces and gadgets—especially locative ones. Which means technology is mainly used as a game tool enabling players to proceed physically in physical space, to communicate with other players in virtual space—and, in case, also to move and/or control movements of their avatars in the latter. Both physical space(s) and virtual spaces are continuously connected, but for individual players the data exchange between them is not necessarily under full control. Moreover, not only for non-players, but also for players it is not necessarily clear who is a player and who is not. Players are usually informed about the start and the end of the game. The rules and the goal of the game are communicated in advance. While exploring both the physical and the virtual parts of the playground can be understood as important part of the game, the playground as such will be rather defined in advance than remain undefined during the play.

Last but not least, the gameplay may be based on a narrative that explicitly invites to explore the physical space with the means of ubiquitous computing, and players will not necessarily know the full story. Yet the narrative itself will not only be rather set and determined in advance than being further developed during the play and according to player's actions. While it may embrace virtual as well as physical space, and define their relationship, throughout the play it won't be stressed as one of the core mechanisms of the game—but rather provide a stable frame.

~~*A IS FOR ...*~~

ACTION
AFFINITY
AFFLICTION
AGGRESSION
ALTERNATE
ALTERNATIVE
AMBIGUITY
AMBITION
ANECDOTE
ANOMALY
ANTICIPATION
ANTINOMY
ANXIETY
APPARATUS
ARRANGEMENT
ART
ARTIFACT
ARTIFICIAL
ASPIRATION
ASSEMBLING
ATTRACTION
AUGMENTED
AUSPECIES

...

Make your choice!

In contrast to this, Alternate Reality Games *may well be based on presets in many ways. However, these are not communicated to the players. Players—or those who want to take part in a game—may perhaps not even know exactly during the first phases if the game has started already or not. Everything has to be explored, and every element may undergo various transformations during the play. Almost always there will be alternatives, and with them the task to find out which decision will lead to the next level of the game. Moreover, at each point it may even be a core part to find out what the task is, and what the alternatives are to decide between. Last but not least, for in many games and on many game levels solving the task will be only possible as a collaborative project involving active exchange between players, finding out with whom to collaborate will be part of the process as well.*

Thus alternate realities may unfold not only within the narration, but rather on almost every layer and around almost every element of the play. Like in Pervasive Games breaking down borders and boundaries of and between physical and virtual spaces is nodal. This process itself is initiated by a whole variety of different mechanisms and interfaces: It is run on the level of technology, media, semantics, and interactions. Everything could be part of the game. Everything could be part of its code. We could say: Above all, it's the code that matters. As it does in coded cultures anyways. Everywhere. At all times. This is exactly the point—and this is where the »A« comes into play. If »A« is for »Alternate«—what exactly does this mean? Simply put and taken literally, »Alternate« could be translated into »alternative interpretation«—i.e. an alternative interpretation of a given code. This process, however, does not necessarily need an altered code. Thus creating alternate realities will also not necessarily afford manipulations of what is usually perceived and communicated as (a) reality [3].

[3] As a matter of fact, speaking of (a) reality on a rather general level may be problematic enough. A minimalist definition might tell us reality consist of what is real i.e. in contrast to what may be appear as or considered as being real. Everyday experience not to speak of specific experiences i.e. in the context of playing a game gives reason to doubt that reality can be aptly defined by excluding appearances and considerations. Reality does not only consist of physical things to knock on.

Alternate Reality Games definitely will—and by definition aim to—alter what is perceived and communicated as reality, be it by manipulating the way players read and interpret existing codes, or be it by inserting codes that are created only for the sake of play.

Alternate Reality Game

»A cross media game that deliberately blurs the line between in-game and out-of-game experiences« *(Gosney, 2005)* .

»A game of sorts« *(Szulborski, 2005)* .

»An interactive narrative that uses the real world as a platform, often involving multiple media and game elements, to tell a story that may be affected by participants' ideas or actions« *(Wikipedia, 2010)* .

Now, how would we call a reality that is manipulated this way? Correct: We would call this reality an augmented reality. Existing codes are being enriched.

But what about the definitions of »Augmented Reality« we are usually dealing with in contemporary media culture? These definitions will tell us that an »Augmented Reality« is based on the perception of a physical space to which additional information is being added in real time by technological means.

Obviously, this is a rather reduced understanding of the possibilities at hand to augment reality. The more recent developments in information and communication technologies, in interface and device design have already led to a whole variety of options to more or less seamlessly integrate augmented reality applications into everyday life. These enrich and alter our reality in many ways, and the more they become part of our every life experience, so do the enrichments and alternations. The borders and boundaries between non-augmented *and* augmented *melt down to become permeable in both directions. Which is exactly the experience we can make in Pervasive Gaming, exactly what is happening in Alternate Reality Games.*

However, while the latter may use whatever technology is at hand, and preferably indeed the very technologies that most people will already take for granted, they will not necessarily have to rely on technology to alter reality (or: realities) for the players. Far more important is another element and another tool: Human psyche—and psychology.

~~E IS FOR ...~~

EASY
ECHO
ECONOMY
ECSTASY
EDGE
EFFORT
ELUSIVE
EMOTION
ENDS
ENDURANCE
ENERGY
ENVIRONMENT
ERRANT
ESCAPE
EVOLUTION
EXIT
EXPERIENCE
EXPERIMENT

...

Make your choice!

Now if »P« is not only for »Pervasive« and for »Play«, but also for »Psyche« and »Psychology«, this may be the right moment to talk about what is perhaps the most decisive element in any game: experience. It's the experiences we make, in life as well as in play, that constitute our reality —and that may alter our reality as well.

To a certain extent, this is or can be true for any kind of games. However, the question is of course which kind of experience is made during play—and if it is part of the games' purpose to generate and to direct specific experiences to be made. As we might already guess, for Alternate Reality Games generating and directing specific experiences is nodal. This is obviously one of the core potentials as well as one of the core problems of Alternate Reality Games. Manipulating people's experiences and altering their realities may be easier than you might expect but it is for sure not something to be taken easy. It has to do with power, and thus is a question of politics and ethics.

In Alternate Reality Games this power—and the related responsibility—is usually in the hands of those who create, develop and direct the gameplay. There's also a telling term for this position: The Puppet Master. However, the power position of the Puppet Master should not be overrated though. Not only does s/he not know enough about the dispositions individual players bring into play—moreover, ARGS are multiplayer games that strongly rely on the dynamics carried in by various collaborations of and interactions between the players—and these dynamics, as well as their outcomes, can hardly be kept under full control. Due to multiple uses of a whole range of different sites and/as interfaces and places for communication and interaction, and due to the necessity to keep the boundaries between everyday experiences and purposefully initiated experiences pervasive, the playgrounds of Alternate Reality Games can hardly be kept under full control.

Let us return to the part of the playground we are especially interested in: urban space.

~~*S IS FOR ...*~~

SAFETY
SCANDAL
SÉANCE
SEEING
SEPARATE
SIBLINGS
SIGNS
SITUATION
SOLUTION
SPACE
STABILITY
STAGE
STORY
STRATEGY
STRENGTH
STRESS
SUBSTITUTE
SUPERFICIAL
SURPLUS
SURVIVAL

...

Make your choice!

What we can learn from any game stressing pervasiveness, and especially from Pervasive Games and Alternate Reality Games, is that to a certain extent today's urban spaces are per se augmented and pervasive. They are soaked and impregnated by a whole range of technologies, and experiencing physical space is almost impossible without experiencing mediated space at the same time. Moreover, this is not a phenomenon limited to digital and network media technologies. While these have for sure enhanced, augmented and multiplied experiences of pervasiveness, and probably also sharpened our sensibility for these experiences, quite similar observations could be made for earlier media technologies.

The reason for this is clearly that experiencing space is not only a question of physical conditions. Every movement of our body is at the same time a movement of our mind. Our experience is also, or even primarily, a psychical one. Moreover, also social conditions come into play. »P« is also for »Persona«: The role(s) we come to be, becoming our personality, are built upon reflection, interaction, and exchange. The presentation of self in everyday life has multiple stages, sets, and playgrounds. Indeed, we all play. Anytime. Everywhere.

In turn, space, and especially public space, is not only structured by individual actions and experiences, but by collective actions and experiences as well. Interactions take place. Anytime. Everywhere. Thus we are dealing with a field in continuous transformation.

Obviously, mapping this field only with the means of topography won't return the data needed to deal with it. To play with the code, we have to understand it. We have to know about the story behind it. It's the story that enables us to read the signs.

One of the techniques developed to gain a deeper understanding of urban space as a complex system of dynamic codes is Psychogeography.

~~I IS FOR ...~~

IDEA
IDENTIFICATION
IDENTITY
IDEOLOGY
IGNORANCE
ILLEGAL
ILLEGIBLE
IMAGE
IMAGINATION
IMPATIENCE
INCEST
INDIVIDUAL
INFECTION
INFINITE
INFORMATION
INFRINGEMENT
INSIDE
INTENSITY
INTENT
INTERFACE
INTIMACY
INVESTIGATION
INVESTMENT
IRRATIONAL
ITEMS
ITERATION

...

Make your choice!

Draw a straight line on a map. Walk it. Draw a circle. Walk it. Throw dices whenever you reach a crossing. Choose your direction based on the result. Turn to the left whenever you reach a red traffic sign, turn to the left whenever you reach a green one. Ask strangers for suggestions where to go. Try to listen to and/or sense the faint vibrations of the subway. Follow them. Read the signs in the streets. Follow them. Get lost. These are only some of the techniques Psychogeography proposes to walk a city. On the first sight they may seem, above all, deskilling. True. But that's the basic trick—a considerably simple one. Yet there are good reasons to test it. A considerably difficult task, yet there are good reasons to try. For generally our movements are directed. Directed by what we would call our free will. However, this so called »free will« is usually following presets. Tasks. Duties. Plans. Consciously made up or not.

Psychogeography

»The study of the precise laws and specific effects of the geographical environment, consciously organized or not, on the emotions and behaviour of individuals« *(Debord, 1955)* .

»A study of how and why we mediate reality with the contents of our psyches. Culture is not automatically adaptive to or even accurately perceptive of the real social and physical world« *(Stein, 1987)* .

3

3 It's definitely not necessary here to enter more general debates about the existence or non-existence of »free will«, be it from the background of traditional philosophy or be it from the background of more recent developments in neuropsychology. However, it could be mentioned that the emergence of the genre may aptly be discussed in a broader framework of media sociology and psychology. A.o. for it is for sure not by chance we find this emergence in times of heightened attention towards self staging, enforced self reliance and the suggestion of an overall gautonomy h of the individual—which may nurture the need for moments of release by the way of delegation of power to others—or, looking at the growing density of networked information and communication systems, of a heightened sensibility against the latter —which may nurture anxious feelings of living in a completely supervised environments and, in case, an affinity for conspiracy theories. These conditions will of course at first sight point us towards a game genre like ARGs. Yet it would likewise make sense also to rethink certain characteristic elements of Psychogeography the invitation to delegate decision processes to chance, the preference of erratic strategies against planning, and a state of mind that is prone to read whatever kind of sign as meaningful from this very background as well.

~~R IS FOR ...~~

RABBIT HOLE
RACE
RADICAL
RAGE
RANDOM
RATIO
READYMADE
REALITY
RECALL
RECIPROCITY
RELATIVITY
RELEASE
RESEARCH
RESISTANCE
REVENGE
RIDDLE
RISK
ROLE
ROLEPLAY
ROOT
RUIN
RULES
RUN

...

Make your choice!

For this very reason Psychogeography starts with erasure of presets—this is, of course, only an expedient. The goal is sensitization: Becoming more sensitive towards what usually is somewhat beyond our radar and radius of attention. Thus, walking a city, opening the senses and opening the mind for the city itself should enable us to get deeper insight. A next step may then focus a research topic guiding the attention, and with it the walks. Moreover, at this point—be it for the preparation, be it during the performance, be it for the documentation, be it for the analysis of the walks—other methods and techniques may be introduced and combined with each other: methods developed in academic fields—i.e. cultural studies, anthropology, sociology, psychology, psychoanalysis, architecture and urban development—as well as methods and techniques developed in the arts. Now if research comes into play, what about play itself—and what about play as in »playing games«, Alternate Reality Games respectively? One might argue that play should be »a free activity standing quite consciously outside ordinary life as being not serious«. *According to this definition, play would necessarily exclude serious research activities just as some more traditional concepts of science and scientific research might claim serious research activities would necessarily exclude play. However, already on a more general layer there are good reasons to call rigid concepts of this kind in questions.*

Not only can play per se including play as a free activity embed features and formats of teaching and learning, skill development and skill sharing, information retrieval and knowledge building. Also does research sometimes take place on a playground and deliberately embrace playful and play-like strategies. Moreover, as already stated above, pervasive play breaks down the borders between whatever may be considered as inside and what may be considered as outside the game, the gameplay and the playground. And especially ARGs may involve tasks that imply the necessity for doing research, or to apply methods and strategies usually applied in related fields of profession.

Psychogeography in turn is not only strongly built upon and per se includes ludic elements, playful strategies and techniques of play. Moreover, blurring the boundaries between a functional access and a ludic attitude towards the field of research, between whatever may be considered as inside and what may be considered as outside is nodal.

Thus, not only we may aptly add game studies, game design and play—including the notion of play as in »playing a game«—to the set of methods and techniques we may use for psychogeographic research. It definitely makes sense to add Alternate Reality Game studies, ARG design and ARG play, and to connect the approaches of Psychogeography with those taken by ARGS.

~~T IS FOR ...~~

TACTIC
TACTILE
TAKE-OVER
TALE
TARGET
TASK
TAXONOMY
TECHNIQUE
TECHNOLOGY
TENACITY
TEMPTATION
TERMINAL
TEST
THRESHOLD
TOOL
TOPIC
TOPOLOGY
TRACK
TRAGEDY
TRANSCENDENT
TRANSMEDIA
TRAP
TREMOR
TRICK
TROPE
TROPHY
TRY
TUNE
TWILIGHT

...

Make your choice!

Now how can we bring what was sketched out so far in theory into practice? Could Alternate Reality Games indeed work as tools for psychogeographical research? If so, how?

To answer this question, let us first quickly resume what connects the concepts of Psychogepgraphy and of Alternate Reality Gaming from a methodological point of view: Both are challenging the strict separations between serious and not serious activities, between inside and outside, between physical and virtual realities, images and imaginations. Both invite to break with certain presets and to embrace alternate perspectives instead.

How do they do so? For Psychogeographic research—apart from stressing walking as a physical and at the same time psychical movement—the ludic approach is a key element. In turn, in Alternate Reality Games many challenges come as puzzles—riddles that need individual as well as collective research, including tracing and tracking, data retrieval and analyses, experiments, problem solving. This may look, at least at the first glance, like a mirror inverted relation rather than a parallel in methods. However, we have of course to take in account that the challenges in ARGS are themselves part of the games. Thus, in a more accurate ascertainment we would have to admit that ARGS—in comparison to Psychogeography—tend to refer to rather sophisticated forms of play. But then we have another key element to deal with, and this time there seem to be good arguments to prefer the somewhat straight and simple ludic approach of Psychogeography: Delegation. In Psychogeography, delegation is inserted by the way of low level game-like rules, i.e. when the decision between turning left or right is made by the way of throwing a coin or when the pathway is determined by a circle drawn on a map. In ARGS, delegation means following rules and directions fixed by a Puppet Master.

Yet at a certain point proceeding in psychogeographic research will demand to leave the rather simple levels of play. In contrast to that, a Puppet Master—or maybe better: the person or the team who develops and directs the game—may have to react to the inputs of the players and to keep up with the interactive dynamics of play. Nevertheless, at least conventional ARGS usually afford to be led to more or less foreseen results.

What a pity. For at the same time, ARGS —and this it at least for the more prominent ones, be them developed for major companies or, as over the last years in growing numbers, by independent game designers—have been proved to be a genre with great potentials in relevant fields like collective problem solving, skill sharing and knowledge building, and even in social, ethical and political consciousness raising. Whereas Psychogeography may have faced a revival especially in artistic circles, and within these circles and beyond it may have gained importance as a tool for urban research. In the field of psychogeographic research, major achievements have been made and further leading potentials have been developed with the help of »new« information and communication technologies. Nevertheless, we must not forget that art—even public art—has a rather limited public, compared to what is today considered as a multiplayer pervasive online game.

Not to mention the possible »bandwidth« and level of activity ARGS can gain—especially when being played primarily on popular platforms. Thus, if »A« is for »alternate« and for »augmented«, and if »P« is for »Psychogeography«, »pervasive« and »play«, then—at least when seen from a methodological perspective—bringing both potentials together may be a promising option indeed. Coded cultures will provide a perfect framework, and perfect playgrounds anyway. For ARGS, as the genre is still missing in major parts a really creative perspective that would not only solve the Puppet Master problem, but also make more and better sense of its cultural potencies and powers. And for Psychogeography, to widen not only its spectrum of techniques

and strategies but also the spectrum of its technological as well as social tools according to the potencies and powers of current information and communication media would definitely strengthen its cultural and political impact—probably also open new perspectives for future research and action in urban environments. Thus, why not unite these forces—be it by designing ARGS built upon the setup and moving within the framework of a psychogeographic research and/or be it by enhancing psychogeographic research with the more sophisticated ludic elements, techniques and technologies of ARGS. The playgrounds are there. So are players. What if the game has already started? Play is open. It's up to you to follow this rabbit. Or another one. At any time.
Everywhere.

References

Avedon, E.M., Sutton-Smith, B. (Eds.): The Study of Games.
New York, London: John Wiley & Sons, 1971

Caillois, R.: Man, Play and Games.
Urban, Chicago: University of Illinois Press, 2001

Coverley, M.: Psychogeography.
London: Pocket Essentials, 2006

De Certeau, M.: The Practice of Everyday Life.
Berkeley: University of California Press, 1988

Flanagan, M.: Critical Play. Radical Game Design.
Cambridge, Mass.: MIT Press, 2009

Gosney, J. W.: Beyond Reality. A Guide to Alternate Reality Gaming.
Boston: Thomson Course Technology PTA , 2005

Harrigan, P., Wardrip-Fruin, N.: Second Person. Role-Playing and Story in Games and Playable Media. *Cambridge, Mass.: MIT Press, 2007*

Home, S.: The Assault on Culture. Utopian Currents from Lettrisme to Class War.
Edinburgh: AK Press, 1991

Home, S.: The House of Nine Squares. Letters on Neoism, Psychogeography and Epistemological Trepidation. *London: Invisible Books, 1997*

Huizinga, J.: Homo Ludens.
Boston: Beacon Press, 1955

Knabb, K. (Ed.): Situationist International Anthology.
Berkeley: Bureau of Public Secrets, 1981

McGonigal, J.: This Might Be a Game. Ubiquitous Play and Performance at the Turn of the Twenty-First Century. *Ph. D. Dissertation. Berkeley: University of California, 2006*

Montola, M., Stenros, J., Waern, A. (Eds.): Pervasive Games. Theory and Design. Experiences on the Boundary Between Life and Play. *Burlington: Morgan Kaufmann, 2009*

Plant, S.: The Most Radical Gesture. The Situationist International in a Postmodern Age.
London: Routledge, 1992

Sadler, S.: The Situationist City.
Cambridge, Mass.: MIT Press, 1998

Salen, K., Zimmerman, E. (Eds.): Rules of Play. Game Design Fundamentals.
Cambridge, Mass.: MIT Press, 2004

Schell, J.: The Art of Game Design. A Book of Lenses.
Burlington: Morgan Kaufmann; Axminster: Triarchy Press, 2008

Self, W.: Psychogeography. Disentangling the Modern Conundrum of Psyche and Place. *New York: Bloomsbury, 2007*

Smith, P.: Mythogeography. A Guide to Walking Sideways. *Axminster: Triarchy Press 2009*

Sonvilla-Weiss, S.: (IN)VISIBLE. Learning to Act in the Metaverse. *Vienna, New York: SpringerWienNewYork, 2008*

Stein, H. F.: Developmental Time, Cultural Space. Studies in Psychogeography.
Norman: University of Oklahoma Press, 1987

Stein, H. F., Niederland, William G. (Eds.): Maps from the Mind. Readings in Psychogeography. *Norman: University of Oklahoma Press, 1989*

Sutton-Smith, B.: The Ambiguity of Play. *Cambridge, London: Harvard University Press, 1997*

Szulborski, D.: This is Not A Game. A Guide to Alternate Reality Gaming. *Macungie: New-Fiction Publishing, 2005*

v. Borries, F., Walz, S. P., Böttger, M. (Eds.): Space Time Play. Computer Games, Architecture and Urbanism. The Next Level. *Basel: Birkhäuser, 2007*

ARGology. About Alternate Reality Games
http://www.argology.org/

avantgame—ARG design and research by J. McDonigal
http://www.avantgame.com/

Bureau of Public Secrets
http://www.bopsecrets.org/

The Situationist International Text Library
http://library.nothingness.org/articles/SI/

unfiction. Alternate Reality Gaming
http://www.unfiction.com/

From Somebody's Desire to Everyone's Responsibility

YUKIKO SHIKATA

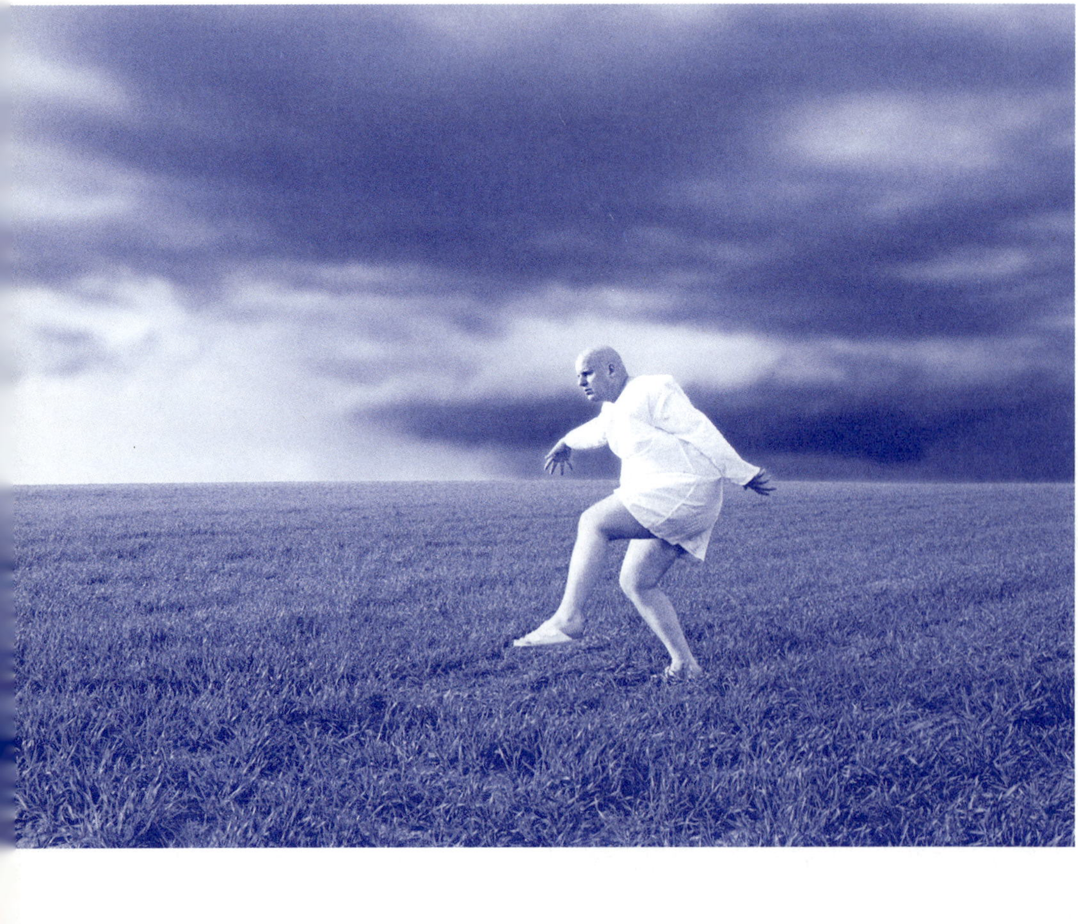

1 *The Monstrousness of the Abyss*

Let me start with my conviction that UBERMORGEN.COM*'s peculiar singularity and »monstrousness« is apparent from their profile, the atmosphere they create and their actual projects. This struck me when I first encountered them. The impression of depth, of an unfathomable abyss, so to speak, made a great impact on me and has remained with me to this day.*

I first met Hans Bernhard and lizvlx in 2002 on the occasion of Kingdom of Piracy (KOP) *at* Ars Electronica*, Linz, as artists and one of three teams of curators of the project.* ***UBERMORGEN.COM*** *was represented at* ***KOP*** *with the work* Injunction Generator*, an online conceptual work demonstrating the practice of* digital actionism*. Hans, having suffered »a manic episode (bipolar affective disorder)« half a year previously, was obviously still struggling to get his eyes and his mind into focus and lizvlx looked like an alien with her vivid pink hair and her eccentric outfit.*

Hans' health has improved since. Now Hans and lizvlx both look healthy and have two daughters but as far as their artistic activities are concerned they are as radical and »monstrous« as ever.

What does their »monstrosity« consist in? You could say it is the perspective of those who have looked into the world's abyss—at the reverse side of everyday life, the borderline between life and death—or of those who have elected to observe society from a point of view located in the realm of so-called non-human existence. The making of this perspective includes in Hans' case the experience of the above mentioned manic episode induced by overdosing for ten years on »the internet & tech (digital cocaine), mass media hacking, underground techno, hardcore (illegal) drugs, rock & roll lifestyle and net.art jet set (etoy)« [1].

[1] UBERMORGEN.COM, on »PSYCH|OS«. In: open nature. Exhibition catalogue. Tokyo: NTT Inter-Communication Center (ICC), 2005

The concept of the human being (in socio-political, physical and psychological terms), endowed with will and rationality as defined by European Modernity is no longer valid for them—they have bravely abandoned it in favour of a perspective of »out of human«. From a horizon that extends beyond the mainstream interpretation of the meaning of society they have been reminding us of the necessity to redefine our relationship with the world. For their persistent societal interventions UBERMORGEN.COM make use of their keen sense of the accelerating speed at which the information environment is evolving. Transcending the traditional limitations of »art« as a profession, they penetrate into a no-man's land that artists are banned from entering as a rule by modern society. By disclosing the blind spot of technology sanctioned by society they try to open the no-man's land to the public through their projects as a unique social and physical experience. Hacking into the public spheres in the name of art, UBERMORGEN.COM make use of *conceptual, informational and physical strategies. Their art, in other words, works in the twilight zone where the very concept of art is becoming meaningless. In addition to this there is the intriguing question whether we should view humanity—the driving force behind the development of societal and technological systems, which invariably ends up being driven rather than in control—as the most uncanny entity of all? Can we think of the human being as the biggest and the last abyss?*

UBERMORGEN.COM tries to show us—the naïve innocents—the desire and the behavior of humanity by taking up a position in the realm of the unknown, on the border between the human and the non-human.

In Greek tragedy, a deus ex machina *suddenly appears when the characters of the play have made such a mess of things that, as far as they are concerned, there is no longer a way out. The deity puts them on their feet again, so to speak, and enables them to again get on with their lives. In other words, in Greek tragedy people keep a low profile and let the god—the superpower—get on with the job of saving them and the world. In the age of digital networks, however, no deity is in sight to lend a helping hand and we are confronted at all times with too many complex problems for which no single solution will suffice. In addition to this, we are by no means passive, we are busy producing and accelerating the problems that beset us and at the same time we shift the responsibility to others and to society as a whole: a complex vicious circle is in operation.*

Through their projects, UBERMORGEN.COM *exaggerate and disclose the complex problems for us so that we may confront them. They resort to shock treatment for us to become aware of the dilemmas we are caught in, in an age that must muddle through without help from a* deus ex machina. *We need to be galvanized into thinking and acting on our own. The stage* UBERMORGEN.COM *prepare for this is tilted towards comedy and they themselves also tend to assume objective roles that draw heavily on the outrageous potential of comedy for their quixotic adventures in 21st century society.*

Comedy and tragedy are, after all, two sides of the same coin. The same event could be interpreted as tragedy for someone at its centre and as comedy for people outside. Even if the event ostensibly contains comical foolery or fun, it could still be interpreted to harbour tragedy on a meta-layer. Regardless of whether we are dealing with comedy or tragedy, the introduction of unexpected events highlights our different desires and patterns of behavior, individual and societal stupidity, reshuffles traditional feelings and morals and makes us ask fundamental existential questions concerning ourselves and the world. UBERMORGEN.COM *puts the focus squarely on the potential of the human being as an agent for change and a better world.*

The theater operates fictional, artistic frames and the audience is stimulated through the willing suspension of disbelief. But some modes of artistic expression exclude existing fictional frames and connect directly to the real society for active intervention. Ostensibly seamless interpenetration between fiction and reality is the unique hallmark of UBERMORGEN.COM, *and freeing both from traditional limitations is indeed thrilling.*

At the same time this is a risk-fraught business, potentially involving the artists coming to grief in both physical and mental terms. UBERMORGEN.COM *have been developing their projects before this backdrop.*

2 From Blurring the Content/ Ground to Research

UBERMORGEN.COM*'s projects that are representative of their bold experiments with the borders traditionally separating art and society and the virtual and the real in the* post-web 2.0 *age include* EKMRZ *Trilogy:* GWEI—Google Will Eat Itself *(2005),* Amazon Noir—The Big Book Crime *(2006) and* The Sound of eBay *(2008), realized together with Alessandro Ludovico. All are program based hacking projects targeting various companies' web-based programs (such as Google's* Adsense *and Amazon's* Search Inside the Book *function).*

As the proper domain of these projects is the internet, it is difficult to display them to advantage in the exhibition format. A code based process as artwork is reminiscent of conceptual art and, in the way an algorithmic process is applied via the internet, of instruction art and of 60s action art. These projects raise issues concerning power relations within the economic system as well as fundamental questions on the role of art by making the real economic network that is driven by people's desires a venue for art.

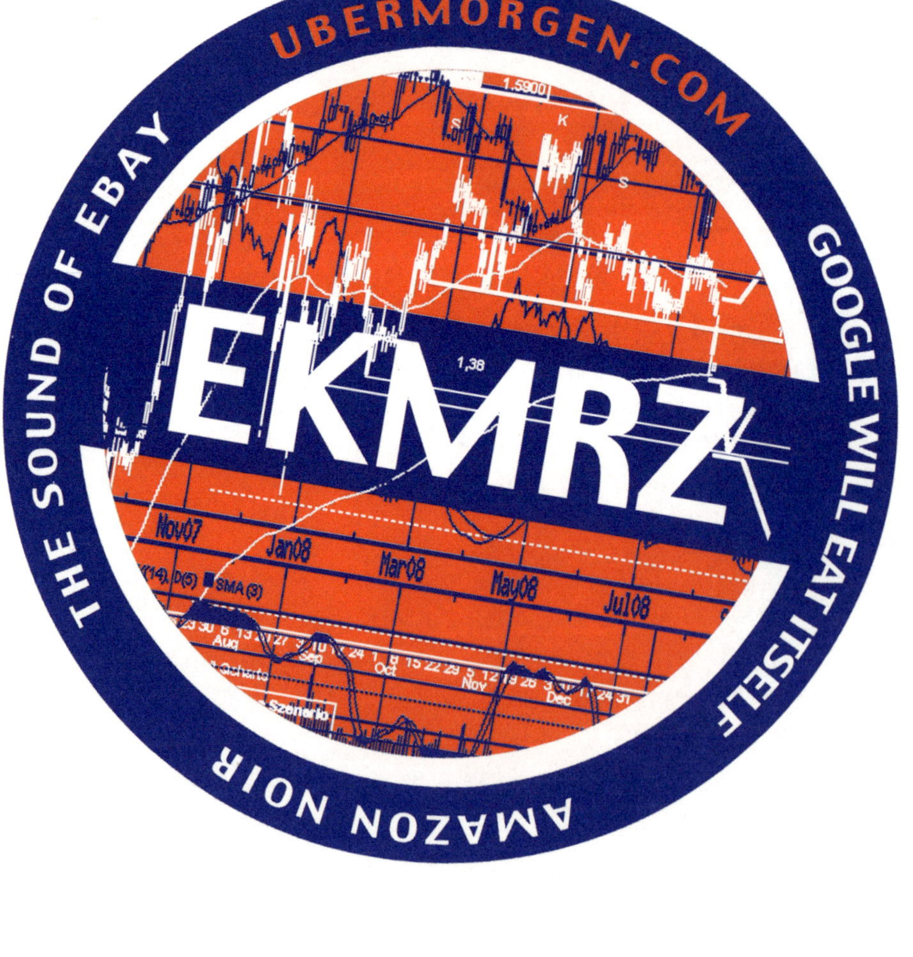

These projects also showcase contemporary problems concerning Cannibalistic Systems *that devour each other. In a feedback loop desire is driven automatically to produce new desires. In this state it is impossible to say with whom desire originates because it is in fact created in the network and each individual desire is just one of the nodes of networked desire. An algorithmic* desiring machine *is in operation behind it. The log of each person is stored and analyzed and new services are recommended according to that analysis, thus calling the next generation of desires into being.*

UBERMORGEN.COM identifies this latent vulnerability and the potential to hack into it as a medium for art (cannibalistic feedback). Far beyond the static relation between the ground and the contents in modernist painting or conceptual art, it is a dynamic intervention by the codes in the networks where the border between the ground and the content is blurred.

In their activity over ten years, UBERMORGEN.COM have gradually shifted their emphasis. As they themselves see it, they started out in 2000–2003 with »superficial spectacular work« (such as Injunction Generator *and* Vote-Auction*), moved »to more conceptual work« utilizing the internet (such as the EKMRZ Trilogy) in the years 2001–2008, and from 2008 they have been focusing on* »more research based work... looking at topics, images and material in which we have a serious interest. It functions as the basis of the project and from there we publish images, sounds and networked data for online, museums and galleries« [2].

[2] All quotes in this paragraph are from the E-Mail from UBERMORGEN.COM on May 7, 2010

Also according to **UBERMORGEN.COM**, *they have moved on over time* »from actionism, conceptual, (com) passionate approach to make more actual things« [3]. *Most of their works are regarded as »political, aggressive action art«, not least because of their intention of provocatively getting involved in actual socio-political contexts, such as the US presidential elections (Vote-Auction) and real-world companies like Google, Amazon and eBay. Their real goal is even more ambitious than that. They have been dealing with issues underpinning these phenomena—the complex machinery consisting of mediated reality, the power structure in the internet age, the desires and emotions of people—by taking up positions inside and outside of that machinery and by doing so not as activists but as artists. They do not engage in propaganda for propaganda's sake but raise serious questions how power and the media work and how art can hack the blind spots.*

[3] *skype meeting with* **UBERMORGEN.COM** *on May 19, 2010*

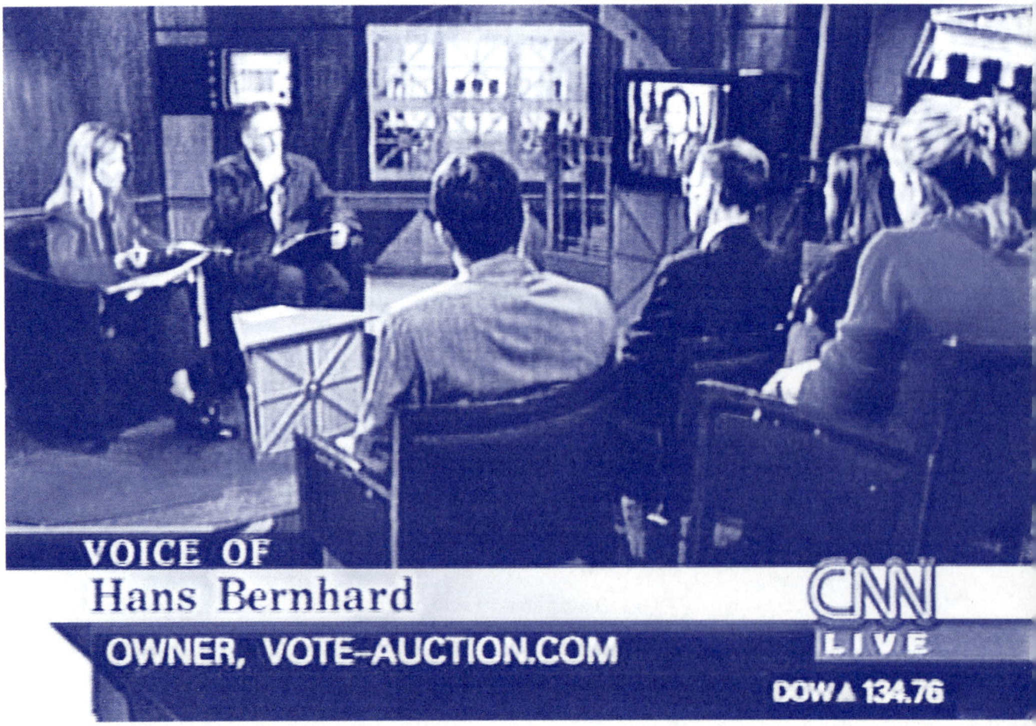

3 *Superenhanced: Human Vulnerability and the Potential to Fight Back*

»We are neither the politician, nor the journalist. We neither declare the truth, nor present the answer. As artists, we have been researching the complexity of reality and asking questions. And the research aspect is getting stronger and stronger in the latest projects« [4].

[4] *skype meeting with* UBERMORGEN.COM *on May 19, 2010*

Superenhanced *is among the first* UBERMORGEN.COM *projects after they started to focus on research. At the core of this project is a notoriously asymmetrical power relationship—the kind of imbalance of power that exists between interrogators (presumably some sort of government agency) and the prisoners targeted for interrogation.*

This project consists of different formats, one of them being the Superenhanced Generator, *which is interrogation software designed to identify potential terrorists and other potentially dangerous persons. The software forces the user to reply to many questions, seeking to elicit admissions of guilt. The software automatically double checks answers and optimizes further questioning via E-Mail and Facebook to continue the session. In an age marked by the exponential rise of stored information,* Superenhanced Generator *puts before our eyes the very real danger of people being handed over to machines for questioning.*

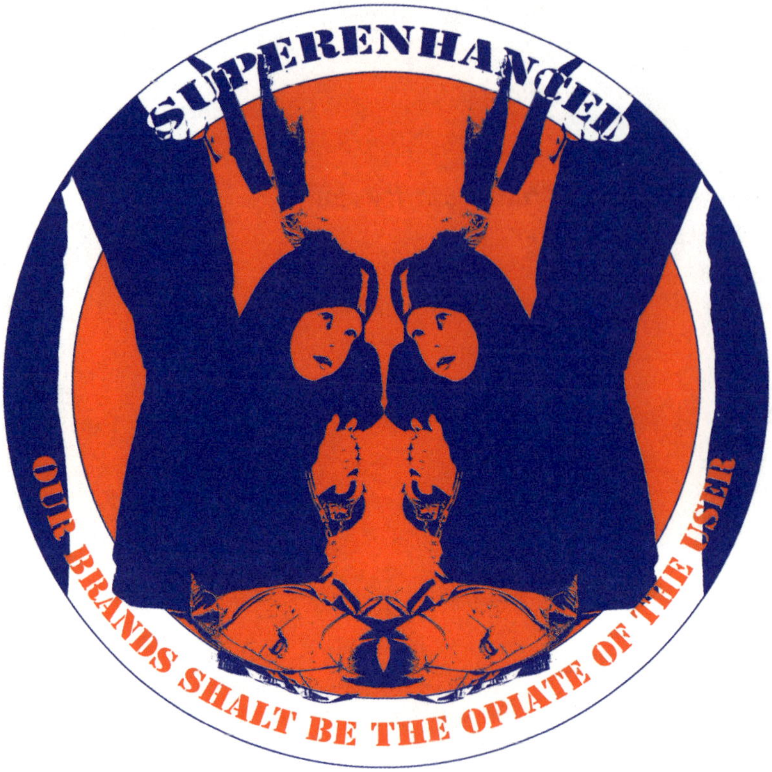

The purpose of interrogation is to identify potential enemies, in this case presumably non-Americans and non-Europeans, for further processing, in an effort to protect the power and dignity of the governmental body.

Enhanced Interrogation *is designed to make persons subjected to it disclose their political and religious views, which can then be used to construe the profiles of potential terrorists. For the same project,* UBERMORGEN.COM, *never averse to shock tactics, use photographs and videos showing small children—in fact none other than their own two daughters—with heads covered with black plastic bags and hands bound together, What are these shocking pictures supposed to be telling us? One inter-*

pretation that seems possible to me is that UBERMORGEN.COM*, by casting children as terrorists, remind us of the time when the terrorists themselves were children. What binds us together, even with terrorists, is our common humanity, which is another way of saying that human rights are inalienable rights that even terrorists are entitled to. The abuse images raise many reactions reflecting the social, mental states of each audience, and making them emerge for open discussion is the strategy of* UBERMORGEN.COM.

Governmental interrogation facilities such as military bases are top secret, strictly controlled areas where security, discipline and hierarchy are all important. Human rights do not apply for prisoners held in these facilities and torture, illegal in the best of cases, depends for its severity on the person in charge and on the contingencies of the situation. Superenhanced *deals with what is liable to happen in a situation in which one party, a human automaton, unthinkingly obeys commands, without taking responsibility for their actions, and the other party is utterly defenceless. Deprived of legal protection, prisoners are exposed to the full hardship of the* State of Exception *as described by Giorgio Agamben.*

As part of the project, UBERMORGEN.COM *invited Chris Arendt, a former Guantanamo Bay Prison guard, to Vienna, where he not only gave a presentation at the UM Salon but lived at Hans and Livlx's house for two months as a research object and part of the family.*

The project provides vivid testimony to what totally asymmetrical power relationships may give rise to, particularly where the person in power is shielded by what is called national interest *and where the alleged need to defend national interest wipes out all considerations of justice and of the life and dignity of the prisoner ... Taking up their stance in the twilight zone between what is legal and what is not, what befits a human being and what does not,* UBERMORGEN.COM *make us aware of the difference between »what exactly is happening« and »what might potentially happen« to spur us into responsible action.* Superenhanced *puts the focus, on the one hand, on the ease with which power corrupts human beings, given a suitable power structure, and, on the other, it shows there is still a potential left to fight back.*

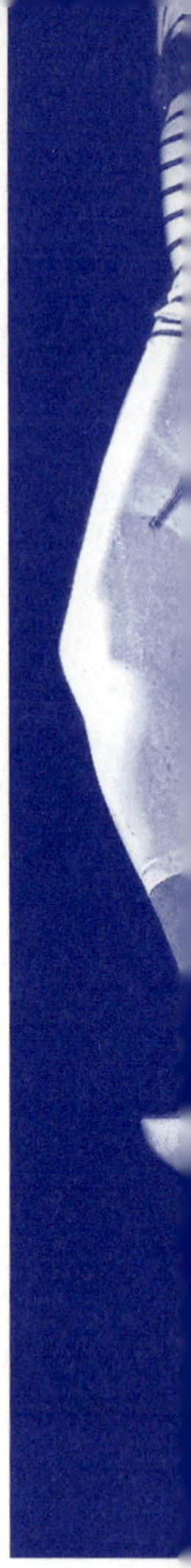

WOP
POW
By

New York - Paris - Mogadischu

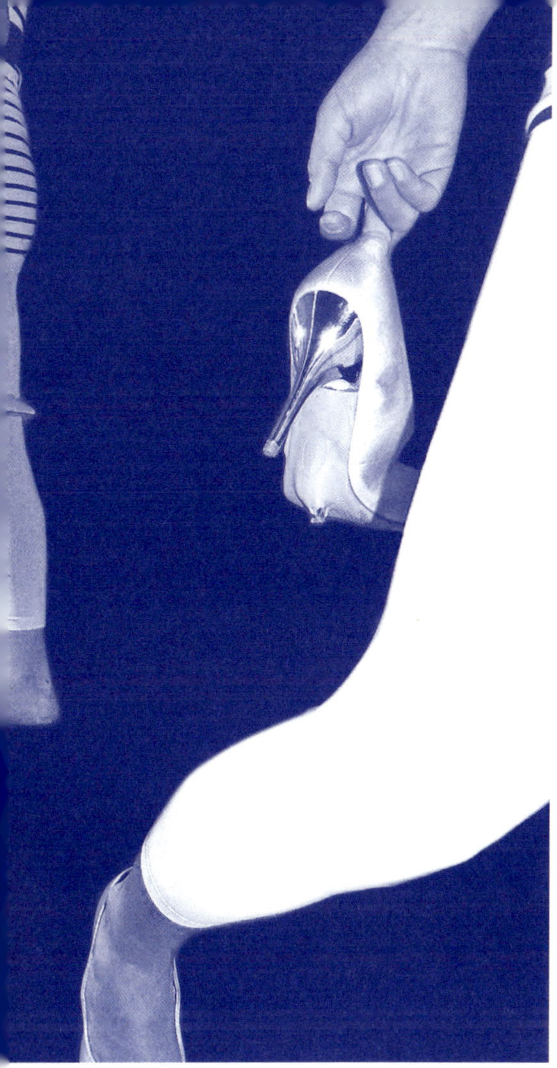

4 WOPPOW & UGI: Desire and the Market

UBERMORGEN.COM has started to tackle issues concerning our daily lives in their most recent and still ongoing projects, WOPPOW *and* UGI—UNIVERSAL HEALTH.

WOPPOW *establishes a connection between* haute couture *and the Somali pirates. The story of African French designers relying for inspiration on the fashion sense of Somali pirates and their use of vivid colors highlights the confrontation between the former colonizing country and its ex-colonies, between rich consumer societies and poverty-stricken developing countries, the fashion industry intent on selling »dreams« and real piracy as well as the entangled post-colonial structure: African French designers looking for the thrills of exoticism copy the pirates' outfits to survive in the fashion business.*

It is highly ironical that the clothes worn by pirates, people outside the confines of the law and outside the traditional economy, should be copied by the highly developed fashion industry. Who is robbing whom? The fashion industry (always and everywhere on the prowl to commit theft in the name of the creative touch) and the pirates, who scrape a hazardous living on the border between life and death (the market would find it cool) emerge with their roles reversed—the former stands for sin, the latter look sacred. In what amounts to a major scoop, UBERMORGEN.COM have opened a hidden door to show the complex relations in an economy-driven society by connecting French fashion and Somali pirates.

The project also raises questions on the concepts of creation and copyright in the fashion business, which actually lives by pilfering everything and anything, and how these concepts are supposed to survive in the 21st century, in an age of shared information. How do the tectonic shifts occurring in the exchange of information—the Wiki culture and Content-for-Free Revolution *happening everywhere—affect the fashion business and the concept of creativity in the fashion world?*

Another ongoing project, UGI—UNIVERSAL HEALTH, *focuses on the health industry, on people »dying to be healthy«. The obsession with health is a fundamental issue that is in itself by no means new. What is new is the scale on which the masses subscribe to the wish to be healthy, which is a product of the progress of medical science and technology, and the encouragement of sports in modern Europe, especially in the 20th century.*

The concept Universal Health*—with abstract and violent overtones—has excluded the oppositional concept »unhealthy« and stands for the unrealistic desire to be in »perfect health«, to »get back to the real (natural) me«. As is the case with the »search for the self« or for »perfect happiness«, there is no definitive answer or real goal, and the industry tries to manipulate people's expectations by promoting new products.*

As living beings, we are all headed towards death, and the body, being in a state of continuous change, is unlikely ever to attain »perfect health«. The health industry, seeking to return »healthy« profits for its capitalist entrepreneurs, is doing everything in its power to make people take an obsessive interest in their health. The human body and mind are mapped and colonized by the health industry. And in the 21st century this colonization is speeded on its way into our body by nanotechnology. Organ transplants are used to stave off imminent death and genetic engineering helps us detect potential diseases. Market driven medicine has produced a new map of colonization with a sharp divide between rich and poor. It is now a matter of routine for our biological data to be logged, data based, networked and used also for potentially ominous reasons. At the same time a movement is gaining in strength to make drugs more readily available to poor countries in the form of generic drugs, associated with the free movements of our age.

Being aware of the current situation, UBERMORGEN.COM *critically present* UGI—UNIVERSAL HEALTH. *The project turns on the roles of fundamental desires and of the market as regards how people's daily lives are shaped. Health, which bears directly on the way people lead their lives and on their life spans, is most acutely felt in its absence. And the market works not only by targeting the sick or the physically inferior, it boosts everybody's desire for health. Medical science here comes to resemble religion: both are results of people's vulnerability and their desire to believe in something that will alleviate that sense of vulnerability.*

Medical, technological and economic progress offers innumerable promises of cures and beauty treatments to people whose first concern is eternal health and beauty. The medical business is deeply involved in the tautological structure of capitalism. UGI *critically and humorously deals with the relation between society and human nature—the absence of responsibility for others. The question is how to escape from the endless loop of market driven desire.*

5 **Get Out of It and Take Responsibility**

Interrogation, torture in specially controlled facilities, fashion, pirates, medicine ... At a first glance, the topics UBERMORGEN.COM deal with in parallel seem far apart, but from the viewpoint of human desires and their manipulation by market forces in the networked society we begin to see some common ground. One point all topics share is the emphasis on »responsibility«. In our society, the individual's responsibility is suspended and the networked desire is rapidly accelerated in feedback loops.

The lack of responsibility is especially visible in the asymmetrical communication system that used to enable a small number of actors—governments, TV, industry, business—to monopolize information fed to a mass public in a model that was established and developed in the 19th and 20th centuries. In the mid-90s, the internet enabled people to communicate with each other on a global scale. In the late 90s, open source movements and P2P networks arrived and in the 00s web 2.0 (blog, SMS, twitter ...) drastically activated interactive communication. Now anyone who is literate and has a modicum of computer savvy can not only access the vast information storehouse of the internet but comment on a topic of their choosing for further interaction.

The rational notions of »the self« or »the public sphere« that were promoted from the days of European Modernity—by J. Habermas for example—cannot be applied anymore since the end of the 20th century. The world is shifting away from the grand model of socio-political and technological systems that used to inform the mass media based society. The very word »public« is acquiring a new meaning in that the autonomous individual constitutes the »public« by way of dynamically interacting with other autonomous individuals. Here »each individual« does not refer to the »isolated self«, but to the »connective self«, which actively shares information with others and co-operates with them.

We have to bear in mind that, just as the internet itself is an American invention, most networked services are today developed and provided by US companies and organizations. We have to utilize the system for active interaction to create new cultural value that transcends national interests and considerations. A level playing field also with regard to communication, new ways of collaboration to produce new systems and creations, the direct distribution of data through the internet, networked individuals: all these combine to create the new »public sphere« and »cultural value«, which will lead in the end to new »economic value«.

The 21st century is seeing the rise of a share-based culture both with regard to software and hardware. DIY-based communities and collaboration are spreading. The development of life and environmental sciences in addition to IT will further enable us to collaborate on a number of issues, including ones that are notoriously difficult to tackle —issues relating to life and death, brain, consciousness, etc.

The issues UBERMORGEN.COM specialize in usually raise the question how information in fields that used to be off limits to the public can be made accessible. Their strategy is clear and provocative. First, the ways in which they choose to disclose sensitive information is usually eccentric and apt to create a shock. Hypnotically repetitive on some occasions, they entice their audiences into the realm beyond good and bad, beyond existing law and ethics, which means we get strongly involved in the issue psychologically. And, finally, they leave us thinking about the underlying problem and the meaning of the project. Their way of making people involved derives from their commitment to research on the controlled slave status—hypnotized ecstasy, sweet inaction, paralyzed responsibility.

5 *skype meeting with UBERMORGEN.COM on May 19, 2010*

»People need authority, authority machines, authority without responsibility« 5 *. What UBERMORGEN.COM seems to be wary of more than anything else is the irresponsible exercise of authority. Taking on the manipulative effects of the huge hybrid authority machine of late capitalism and the internet, they seem to count on help from the autonomous networked machine, in which each person is a node ready to get connected and contributes their share to collective responsibility.*

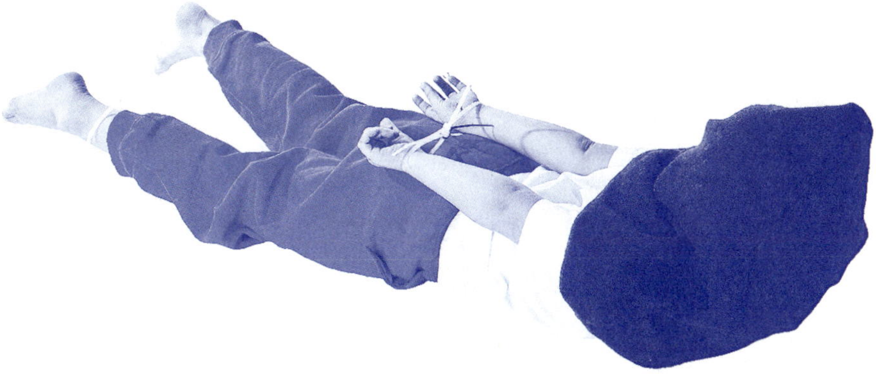

formational Materialism
Digital Dissemination Systems
Playful Interfaces
Iconocracy
propagation of Common Flowers and as a way to release the flowers into the environment. D… national legislation, the deliberate … is considered illegal; but in cases where permissions are granted, it has to be considered legal.
Project Worlds
rrogation
ect Worlds

4

Cannibalistic Systems
Salaryman
Edo's Formulation
Decoloniality of the Digital Mode
DIY Flowers
Information Prochronism
Co-Evolution
roleplaying in the history
Playful Interfaces
Datsu-Sala
Alternate Reality Game
Digital Actionism
Futuristic Hyperb…
Technological Determinism
Societal Plants
practices and acti…
Post-Humans
Culture of Control
Diaspora
Playfulness
Distance
Depoliticizatio…
Mit… Device Art
Bio-Sharing
Evolutionary Anthropology
Human Computing
Creativity
Playfulness
Collective Intelligence
Pervasive Game
…duality
…vailable flowers
Smartject
…rs are a strategy to make aware of developments in bio-science … ation to ethics, and the definition of the public and socio-poli…
Playsure Politics
Art and Knowledge Transfer
Bio-Hacking
Necropolitics
Smart Populations

Glossary

Difference

Radical Hardware

We refer to cannibalistic syste… referential and self destructing processes. Remarkably, the self cannibalizing object i… itself. Such systems can be purely conceptual or actual implemented processes targeted a… ifference between purely … systems and mixed systems of auto-c… …e Google Will Eat Itself project … …ibalism and par… pragmatic conceptual piece.

Cyber Modernity

Cool Hunting

Culture of Play

Information

Media Art

Homology: Serial / Phylogenetic

Biopolitics

Lusory Attitude

…ve Slow Food

…Politics

Ludics

Chindogu

Closure of Information

Interpassivity

Difference

Media Geijutsu / Media Aato

Observation Technolog…

Tokusatsu

Zero Interface

Cloud Computing

…etishism

Signs

Realm of Action

Tokyo's Urbanizat…

…d by Yoshihiro Tatsumi … by other se… who wanted t… …ildren's entertainment. Important …s protest, subcultural rebellion. showcase for Gekiga was the …ga magazine Garo, founded in …suichi Nagai (1921–1996).

Enhanced Interrogation

CAM

Digital Cocaine

cognitive Capitalism

Chindogu

Artistic Research

Jouissanc…

Art Product

Global Brain Scapes

Meta-Codes

…des

Flower Commons

between botany (plant s… (migration or movement … …amiliar territory). Migrating …istic investigations. …ople, open and closed borders, borderland, social and biological and (horti)

Play Affordances

…nterface

and Knowledge Transfer

Code

Japan Cool (or Cool Japan)

Biopolitics

Funware

Highscore Cultures

Laws of Cool

Bionomical Feedback

Negentropy

Collective Experimentation

Cyber Modernity

Ludic Interface

Proto-Culture

…originally meant urbanites (typically males) with a strong commitment to one particular hobby. The cultural genesis of this »otaku« commitment is often described by decade of birth.

Intellectual Capital

Cybernetic Turn

Glossary

Alternate Reality Game *Kuni, 311*

Games designed to create shared experiences of alternate realities. Pervasive Games are built upon the basic concept of blurring boundaries between real and virtual spaces, strongly relying on networked media. As Pervasive Games and Alternate Reality Games share core features, it is possible to subsume the latter as a sub-genre of **Pervasive Games**.

Art and Knowledge Transfer Reder, 54

In artistic work, in particular, this can be exemplified while keeping sight of the singularity that so often eludes science. This has been the focus of many of my own research projects on *Art and Knowledge Transfer* at the University of Applied Arts Vienna, which seek to illustrate such processes. Here the explicit subject is »artistic research with artistic means« that is, an expressly »different research«—like essays—as an alternative to any »officially approved« development just oriented on financing interests.

Artistic Research Reder, 55

Both science and art are governed by project worlds and project work in an exemplary sense. They are dependent on operating systems, well-established settings and institutions. This is how Bruno Latour notes in *Pandora's Hope. An Essay on the Reality of Science Studies* (Latour, 1999) that a »no-man's land« emerged between cultures that have hardly any more contact, because the »hard« natural sciences and technology and the »soft« humanities/literary studies only sporadically embark upon interdisciplinary projects.

Art Product Kusahara, 139

Art product is a commercial product that is conceived and realized by an artist as a part of his/her artistic activity. In the Western art tradition it has been considered wrong for an artist to commercialize an artwork although avant-garde artists such as Marcel Duchamp already made such attempts. Japanese artists such as Takashi Murakami have produced art products, challenging the Western art paradigm.

Bio-Hacking *Gfader, 264*

A form of hacking that deals with the understanding and consequent modification of biological systems, or, as one might say, biological programs. Elegantly executed, hacking is potentially discreet; BCL says: »A small gesture with a big outcome«. *The aim: to regain power over our shared biological destiny.*

Bionomical Feedback Chen, 196

As long our mode of perception relies on physical receptive organs, the flux of data we face daily is forming biological feedbacks to our body. At the same time, numerous lifelog systems are capturing and converting biological phenomena to digital data: another question remains to explore what is the bionomy specific to digital data, and its correlation with the physical bionomy.

Biopolitics Gržinić, 124

The terms *biopolitics* or *biopolitical* refer to what on one side Michel Foucault described in the 1970s as governmental regulation of populations through biopower (the political power that resides on all aspects of human life) and is predominantly taking place in the First Capitalist World, and on the other what Giorgio Agamben defined in the 1990s the biopolitical as a way of life that is imposed again in the First Capitalist World according to which what matters is mode-of-life, good life and subjects as brands. In the other worlds, Third and Second Worlds, on the contrary what is reinforced is necropolitics, structures of slavery, naked life and brutal expropriations. In the 2000s biopolitics and necropolitics co-exist at once, shoulder to shoulder, in different parts of the world.

Biopolitics *Gfader, 270*

The intrinsic link between bio (life) and politics. First introduced by Michel Foucault. Linked to debates of governmental principles, local and global orders, chaos, multitude and reduced forms of life. An abstract term informing our current occupation with matters of life, the state, everyday (em)power(ed) systems. Follow Foucault, subvert Foucault, transform Foucault. Read Agamben's Means without End: Notes on Politics; The Open: Man and Animal.

Bio-Sharing *Gfader, 264*

A derivative of bio-hacking. Based on the assumption of distributing and therefore sharing biological information and codes among the people, the common. Underlying are ideas of revealing biological and communicative systems of plants, in the context here the system blue flower.

Botanical Diaspora *Gfader, 268*

suggests a symbiotic relationship between botany (plant sciences, plant biology) and diaspora (migration or movement of a group of people, a community, away from their homeland or familiar territory). Migrating plants can form the starting point for artistic investigations. Relevant considering the movement of people, open and closed borders, borderland, social and biological and (horti)cultural peripheries.

CAM Faßler, 78

The approach of *Co-Evolutionary Anthropology of the Medial (CAM)* is based on the firm conviction that the open differences between genetic determination, morphogenesis, and neurophysiology are the non-intentional resources for cognitive differences, human intelligence, and human self organisation. All formats of couplings are considered as conditionally determined and therefore strictly bound to selective interactivities which happen between biotic and a-biotic conditions.

Cannibalistic Systems *Shikata, 341*

We refer to cannibalistic systems/auto-cannibalistic systems as self referential and self destructing processes. Remarkably, the self cannibalizing object is not aware of its action and therefore is unable to stop eating itself. Such systems can be purely conceptual or actual implemented processes targeted at system weak-points. The difference between purely cannibalistic systems and mixed systems of auto-cannibalism and parasitic systems can be not worth mentioning. One prime example is the Google Will Eat Itself *project (http://gwei.org) using both auto-cannibalism and parasitic behaviour in one pragmatic conceptual piece.*

Chindogu Russegger, 23

A Chindogu or »un-useless object«, as introduced by Japanese Inventor Kenji Kawakami, is a modified everyday life gadget. The modding culture behind it is more a critical art-form or attitude than a serious attempt. By inventing special solutions for minor problems, a gadget solves them by creating several new problems. This is why the Chindogu cannot be defined as useful or useless and why it carries the undecided meaning of (un-)uselessness.

Chindogu *Jahrmann, 281*

Chindogu (Kawakami, 1995) describes a state of mind that is based on pleasure, attraction and amusement in regard to technology. Kenji Kawakami described Chindogus as almost useless objects. In Ten Tenets of Chindogu *Kawakami refers to the real satire aspect of analogue gadget industries. He argues:* »Every Chindogu is an almost useless object, but not every almost useless object is a Chindogu. In order to transcend the realms of the merely almost useless, and join the ranks of the really almost useless, certain vital criteria must be met. It is these criteria, a set of ten vital tenets that define the gentle art and philosophy of Chindogu« *(Kawakami, 1995)* .

Closure of Information Chen, 176

The enclosure movement of information, as represented by lobbying activities by proprietary software enterprises accelerated in the late 1990s, is today moderated by the pervasion of open source software and open contents. See Boyle, J.: *The Second Enclosure Movement and the Construction of the Public Domain.* (http://www.law.duke.edu/pd/papers/boyle.pdf)

Cloud Computing Chen, 162

Formerly called *Webware* or *SaaS*, cloud computing has become the standard scheme for today's computing. The data and the algorithm codes are now in the *cloud*, no longer in local storage: this transition has permitted important development and pervasion of computing virtualization in both enterprise and consumer areas by such companies as Google or Amazon.

Codes Faßler, 71

Codes are cognitive and expressive actions and micro-programs. Codes are the key virtual for all human-environment-interactivities. They are micro-archives, with which human beings manage interrelations of invention, convention, consuming, storing. With codes we create content. Therefore codes make distinction certain. Culture is an invented format, through which this coded certainty becomes self evidence—or identity. Consequently I use culture as an interface, neither essence, nor continuity. Culture is a market of compilers for finished differences, a heterarchy of distribution rules for legalised differences. Culture administrates the logics of differences; it is like the home of virtual supply chains.

Code *Gfader, 269*

There are technological, cultural, social and technical codes waiting to be deciphered, studied, reinterpreted, hacked. BCL says: »Coding is active participation«.

Co-Evolution Faßler, 71

As the researches on the evolution of cells, organisms, cell-stress, and organic self organisation show us: we cannot think about evolution as a selective and creative process on its own. As far as evolution takes place in cells and complexities, this is always part of cooperation, competitiveness, coordination and self protection. Within these networks rules beyond the genetic determinations emerge and influence the expression of genes (or brain, or group). These rules are called »epi-genetic rules« (Ch. Lumsden). They are the fundament of what is called cultural co-evolution: Always expect the unexpected!

Cognitive Capitalism Gržinić, 117

At the center of the digital mode of production that corresponds to the present financial capitalism stays knowledge being elaborated through new media and digital technology into knowledge dissemination and storage systems. The digital mode of production is connected to knowledge production via Information-Communication-Technology (ICT), forming as well what is known as cognitive capitalism. In the time of global capitalism the capacity of digital networks, platforms and circuits to unlimited exchange while producing and disseminating content through circulation of information is remarkable.

Cognitive Slow Food Faßler, 71

This term focuses the differences between flow and selection, between augmentations of digital connectivity and time. The brain needs to select and model information clusters. Cognitive meaning derives from the emerged linkages made among the highly parallel streams of information with others distributed throughout the cortical system in a vast associational network enriched by feedback and re-entry loops from the body, its surroundings and internal figurations. The fast food of data streams or escape velocity of information becomes important for life by slow cognitive reorganisation of options.

Collective Experimentation Reder, 53

»Collective experimentation with what humans and non-humans can tolerate or renounce.« As Bruno Latour concludes in *We Have Never Been Modern* (Latour, 1993) it would be false to speak of a failure of modernity since »modernism« was not an illusion, but an active performing [...] *»If we do not change the common dwelling, we shall not absorb in it the other cultures that we can no longer dominate and we shall be forever incapable of accommodating in it the environment that we can no longer control. [...] Neither nature nor the others will become modern. It is up to us to change our ways of changing«.*

Collective Intelligence Gržinić, 119

In cognitive capitalism, as it is developed among others by Michael Hardt and Antonio Negri, we see highly digitalized and virtualized »network societies«. The outcome of this networking is a »General Intellect«, a collective intelligence so to say, that refers to a set of knowledge, competencies, linguistic uses, and ways-of-doing-things, more or less available to »everybody«. The way of capturing information goes through creating databases (in relation to hardware) and tools (in relation to software) for their usage. The general intellect or the collective intelligence is therefore a huge knowledge storage system. The biggest struggle today is on the level of keeping it free and accessible to everybody, as capitalism insist on its privatization and instrumentalization for power and profit.

Coming Politics *Gfader, 270*

Giorgio Agamben's liberating attempt to define politics yet to come. Based on life towards happiness and multiple forms of life without isolating naked life. A complex, rich proposal and term. Includes potentially all politics which suggest a different, non-reductive ground for describing and acting out the political and political life, non-statist politics.

Common Flowers *Gfader, 263*

Do flowers propose being common, are they always shared by all or many? How are flowers common or non-common? Genetically modified flowers, purposefully purely aesthetic, are a product. There are attempts to make the underlying code of these organisms, the function of specific genes, available to the common.

Con-Dividuality *Jahrmann, 284*

is used in order to describe a particularly political practice of activism, which is informed by a subversive avant-garde tradition of roleplaying in the history of mechanisation. In the interpretation of this thesis it refers to the altered concept of the self and representations of multiple and collective selves in relation to social networking practices and activism.

Conditioned Production Faßler, 71

No idea, no artifact, no thing that thinks has metaphysical reasons. The world—as we know it—exists as handcrafted model, is cognitive abstraction, cognitive artifact, packed information, or in a radical sense a mixed and changing construction. The conditions for that are manifested in laws of nature and laws of invention. That is what I call: conditioned determinations. These conditioned determinations are rebound to the accelerating relations between inventing—conserving—applying—irritating—changing—and new inventing, or let me say: to the artificial.

Cool Hunting Russegger, 28

Cool hunting would describe the eager search for new and emerging ideas, projects or things within the pop-cultural terminology of »coolness«. The attitude can be described on the one hand as an unemotional detachedness to happenings and on the other hand as a contemporary commitment to the greater cultural root of developments like »cool« media, digital media, computer based communication systems and artifacts.

Culture of Control Yoshioka, 108

With the infiltration of digital technology into many parts of social as well as personal life, we have aquired a habit of organizing everything according to terms like »programming«, »execution«, »errors«, »(numerical) evaluations« etc. This seems to form a »culture of control« in which we develop technological attitudes towards life.

Culture of Play Kusahara, 153

Culture of asobi, or culture of play, is a Japanese tradition. Since playfulness was highly appreciated, culture of play developed in many levels. Cultural games such as *hyakunin-isshu* represents culture of play. *Kosupure* is another example.

Cyber Modernity Faßler, 75

This term notes the transformation of all concepts of modernity into a subroutine of complex cybernetic structures. Modernity, based on more or less linear rationality, figured in typocracy, the exclusive power of the alphabetic order of written texts, was re-engineered by information-flows, data, matrices and intelligent visualisation. In contrast to old-school modernity of one society, based on national economies, institutions and technologies, Cyber Modernity is globally based on Cybernetic Turn, Iconocracy.

Cybernetic Turn Faßler, 75
This refers to the technological, epistemological, cognitive and communicational change, that was initiated by the MACY-Conferences in the 1940s, J. v. Neumann's Computer-Architecture, C. Shannons mathematical Bit-Model, and N. Wieners *On Cybernetics*. It transformed the ideals of symmetric, static, or linear systems into the open world of dynamics, recursive interactions, non-linear and asymmetric status. The 1st Turn focussed on control. The 2nd Turn, connected to individuals like E. v. Glaserfeld, H. v. Foerster, P. Watzlawick underlined the interrelation and self organisation (autopoiesis) of any material organisation (not only organisms).

Datsu-Sala Yoshioka, 106
Means a person who has gave up, or an action to quit, the life as Salaryman and to pursue a freer, or more independent occupation like an entrepreneur, a shop owner, a farmer and so on. Most businessmen in Japan seem to imagine (or at least fantasize) about going Datsu-Sala, psychologically compensating hardship of their real life.

Decoloniality of the Digital Mode Gržinić, 120
Although a lot is said about the world at hand in global capitalism because of new media technologies, it is becoming obvious that a lot of new digital ideas are wrapped into old grammars of power and hegemonic relations. The decoloniality of the digital mode of production asks for the possibility to develop alternatives in the digital realm that will offer new possibility for common ownership as general intellect, participation and justice in terms of distribution of technology and knowledge. The idea of decoloniality of the digital is connected with a parallel process of decoloniality of knowledge and the social and political developed by Anibal Quijano, Catherine Walsh, Lewis Gordon, Walter Mignolo.

Depoliticization Gržinić, 127
Today global capitalism functions with two processes developed by Santiago López Petit. On one side it is represented by the War State, that is—in its verticality—functioning by way of force, violence, fear, therefore it is a pure fascist state. However, it would be too simple if we would use historical fascism for its naming, because we would fail to emphasize what the major logic of dominance in the world today is, and this is the logic of war. While, on the other, there is also the neoliberal context of the autonomy of individuals, which is the neoliberal freedom of having rights to just be an individual brand. This situation sterilizes the »Other«, evacuates the conflict from public space, neutralizes the political and produces a condition of life that is called depoliticization.

Destructive Creativity Russegger, 28
Based on the innovation paradigm of »creative distruction« by Joseph Schumpeter, destructive creativity focuses on artistic outcomes not directly related to economic innovation or even opposed to entrepreneurship. This destruction can be observed for example in the theory of Iconoclasm or vandalism since the French Revolution (e.g. Gamboni, 1997).

Device Art Kusahara, 137
Device Art is a form of art in which the device itself is content. The mechanism represents the theme of the piece. Content and tool are no longer separable. Artworks are often playful and can sometimes be commercialized into devices or gadgets for use in everyday life. Refined design and playful features are traced back to the Japanese tradition of appreciating tools and materials.

Difference Faßler, 71
Difference is the basic key for any kind of living cell or system. If a cell tries to »survive« as specific bio-chemical difference in environment, or complex systems of any kind: all try to keep the difference, build membranes, frontiers, corridors of inclusion-exclusion, forms and significance. Difference is self defense and the space for creativeness between information as signal and information as sign. In the spaces of difference humans create distances to signals as first impressions, and formalize signs, codes, forms, figures as accidental gifts *»from the phenomenal world to the human brain-in-formation«* (B. M. Strafford).

Digital Actionism Shikata, 335
Digital Actionism is the contemporary combination of the traditional Viennese Actionism and radical online and mass media projects. At the center of the action is the human body serving as a thin membrane through which data and information flows. The digital actionists' body is in the eye of the hurricane where it is quiet and calm while the storm is tearing down the environment. The respective body is affected psychologically. The reach and frequency of Digital Actionism can be vast (compare Vote-Auction, *500 Million Audience). Digital Actionists can be educated by actual Viennese Actionists and their offspring.*

Digital Cocaine Shikata, 336
The myth of the pop star and the construction of a fascist global uber-corporation was the driving force behind Hans Bernhard's work between 1994 and 1998. The fusion of drugs and technology was blended with results of the analysis of Andy Warhol, Archigram, Futurism, Michael Milken, Michael Jackson and contemporary boy groups such as The Backstreet Boys. These extreme 2–11 day adventure trips into the unknown realms of cyberspace are called »Digital Cocaine«; combining chemical drugs and techno-reality into an almost deadly mix of excitement, danger and thrill. The consequences can be grave and in Hans Bernhards case led to a mental illnesses best described in the UBERMORGEN.COM project Psych|OS.

Digital Dissemination Systems Gržinić, 129

The capitalist system sees its salvation in ICT and on further capital accumulation based on digital dissemination systems. Behind the knowledge digital dissemination systems lays the myth of salvation from the crisis and bankruptcy produced by financial capital that started to be poignantly visible from 2008 on. The question that is posed is whether global dissemination knowledge systems are really possible as free systems of access and exchange? As dissemination systems initially promising freedom are more and more controlled and banned today.

Distance Faßler, 75

Distance is the mode, to keep a difference fruitful. Distance, as a human tactic for hunting and creating, could be understood as the creation of unmarked spaces (H. Spencer), which carry the chance to place an indirect, conditioned »something« as an additional world dimension.

DIY Flowers *Gfader, 264*

are seen as a counter model to commercially available flowers. Do-It-Yourself flowers are a strategy to make aware of developments in bio-science and genetic modification, their relation to ethics, and the definition of the public and socio-political grounds. Artists and activists already investigate in DIY flowers.

Edo's Formulation *d'Heilly, 222*

Edo (1603~1868) was created in resistance to modernity. It's completion closed Japan for ¼ millennia. When modernization infiltrated, Edo was undone. It was a medieval city, populated east of the castle, backed by the Pacific. It faced Japan's largest plain, with five roads leading to it, each dotted with check points, and execution grounds before its gates.

Enhanced Interrogation *Shikata, 344*

Enhanced Interrogation is the newspeak term adopted by the G.W. Bush government for torture. This terminology was re-introduced to prevent constitutional rights and international rights to kick-in and prevent the governement and its institutions and agencies (Military, OGAS/CIA, private corporations) to abstain from torture. But it was argued legally and implemented criminally from top down (president-torturer). The process is still ongoing under President Obama. Related terminology: Extraordinary Rendition (governementally ordered kidnapping to sites where Enhanced Interrogation is used, i.e. Bagram, Guantanamo, but also Syria, Egypt, Poland). This term is related to the UBERMORGEN.COM project Superenhanced *and* Torture Classics. *(www.tortureclassics.com)*

Evolutionary Anthropology Russegger, 11

Evolutionary anthropology is the study of the relation between social behavior and the evolution of hominids and non-hominid primates. It includes the anthropology of human evolution, the socio-cultural evolution of human behavior, the archaeological study of human technology and the studies of human genetics and changes in the human genome.

Flower Commons *Gfader, 263*

The shared physical places where Common Flowers are able to grow. Flower Commons act as a source for the propagation of Common Flowers and as a way to release the flowers into the environment. Depending on the national legislation, the deliberate release of GM plants is considered illegal; but in cases where permissions are granted, it has to be considered legal.

Funware *Jahrmann, 295*

can be identified as an indicator for the everyday presence of play in social life. Funware is the use of game mechanics in non-game contexts. According to the Game Designer Gabe Zichermann, Facebook »looks, feels, smells like a game«, *and he describes Yahoo Answers as* »a research game [and also] a status game«. *Facebook as a* »non-fiction« *game has* »so many more users, and hours spent on [it] than any comparable virtual world«. *It's easy to use, 2D, html. It has tangible benefits in real life. It's free without any hidden fees. It's fun, and he describes it as a* »socially-propagating story«, *and status, likening it to a* »fireplace mantle of trophies, except you don't need to invite people over to your house«. *Details available online from: http://www.worldsinmotion.biz/2008/02/funware_gaming_the_web.php*

Futuristic Hyperbolae Yoshioka, 100

The rhetoric favoured by the government, media and industry to impress (or dizzle) people by referring to radical technological innovations in the future, which can drastically change our society, or can cause fatal catastrophes.

Gekiga Manga *d'Heilly, 225*

A term coined by Yoshihiro Tatsumi (1935–) and adopted by other serious Japanese cartoonists who wanted to distinguish their work from children's entertainment. Important to post-1960s protest, subcultural rebellion. The leading showcase for Gekiga was the monthly manga magazine Garo, *founded in 1964 by Katsuichi Nagai (1921–1996).*

Global Brainscapes Faßler, 73

Using A. Appadurai's term of global mediascapes, with which he offers a new spatial- and ethnological concept, Global Brainscapes describe real-time relations and co-operations in a virtual space or sphere. It underlines the latent offshore situation of any net-integrated community status and individual participation.

Global Fetishism Gržinić, 120

Coded digitalized culture functions today, referring to Jonathan Beller, as if global fetishism of the First Capitalist World, that is in a constant search for the spectacle of Third World poverty, peculiarities, capitalizes on structures of desires that are in retrospect programmed, coded by the First World capital for the Third and Second World's labor. The digitally coded images of the Third and Second Worlds become an essential mechanism in the continued occupation and exploitation of the Third and Second Worlds; in addition to the creation of surplus value, there is the creation of surplus pleasure, or surplus desire—again in such products we see how profit is being subsumed as ideological digital mode.

Highscore Cultures Tarasiewicz, 213

Being digital in the global networks means accepting the highscore culture: you should have lots of »digital friends« (rendering the term friend inflationary) and participate in the sense of the interactive web 2.0 to feed the global networks and receive a score (reputation or a real quantification of participation, such as »badges« or participation levels). Users, driven by Statusangst (»status anxiety«) (de Botton, 2004) are trying to be as creative as possible and innovate as much as they can, to stand out of the masses with their creativity, to get better jobs and better digital profiles (see systems such as LinkedIn, Xing, Stack Overflow). The digital profile, the digital fingerprint becomes a form to quantify abilities, innovativeness, flexibility, adaptability, and self representation to make them comparable and measurable.

Homology: Serial / Phylogenetic Chen, 164

Homology is the result of the genetic manifestation within a living entity (serial) or between species (phylogenetic). Bateson describes the *»pattern that creates a pattern«*, an expression that can be echoed with Varela's *»process that creates the process«*; an internal connection between different parts that constitutes an entity leads to external connection between different entities as well.

Human Computing Tarasiewicz, 214

The web revolutions (such as web 2.0 and *crowd sourcing*) increased the computational power of the global networks with the human resource, a global, distributed human computing takes place worldwide. The term Human Computing is adding to the discourse of Social Computing (Surowiecki, 2006). See the distributed (hidden) data mining of Apple or other big players as example.

Iconocracy Faßler, 96

Iconocracy is a general term like Plutocracy, Gerontocracy and Bureaucracy. It describes a dominant and used structure of power. As distinguished from the power of money, age, and bureau this new global program integrates information, cognition, flexible communication and decision as well as individual preferences, expressions, poetics and experiments. Iconocracy might be associated with brandings, marketing, advertisement. I do not use this term as an economy critique. For me it describes the core knowledge technology of the 21st century.

Information Faßler, 73

Information is like the exclusive (semi-artificial) meta-matter, like an unobservable micro-monitor, which only in processes of expanding compositions and connections—are they visual, numeric, literal, kinetic, temporal, acoustic etc—leads to informational macro monitors which we are used to call interfaces today. Interfaces are the combinatorial surplus without which Homo Sapiens is not able to use and reflect his »self made« differences = information.

Information Bionomy Chen, 189

As argued in Chen's article, information bionomy designates the concept of understanding and engineering digital data's connection to physical life forms and exploring data autonomy. In cybernetic context, it is taking inspiration from Wiener's concept of computation as an autonomous system as opposed to the instruction based model of v. Neumann.

Information Prochronism Chen, 175

Prochronism as argued by Bateson is the accumulation of processes through time emerging to the surface of a living being, thus making its characteristics open to the external environment and other agents. This information can be compared with what Gibson calls *»affordance of an environment«*; the environmental pressure is reflected in its constituting elements i.e. living beings.

Informational Materialism Faßler, 83

No sign, no code, no norm can leave the conditions of the matter behind. That is the message of the Cybernetic Turn. No one can ignore neither biology nor the non-physical, and non-biological status of the virtual. Streams of information happen as material transformations, no matter how abstract or transcendent they are presumed.

Intellectual Capital Gržinić, 122

Corporations make profit from appropriating the general intellect, presented always as collaboration and cooperation, as networking. The source of wealth and making profit is no longer only labor-power, but rather the »intellectual capital« that is possessed less by individuals than by networks of individuals, and that is expressed in things like capacity for innovation, institutional know-how, etc. Knowledge, language, verbal skills and networking, down to life itself, and not only (we would say »less«) labor-power in the factories (mostly situated outside the First Western World) become sources of economic value.

Interpassivity *Fuchs, 254*

A notion developed by Rober Pfaller and Slavoj Žižek to describe the dialectics of active interactivity and a more passive approach of delegated enjoyment.

Japan Cool (or Cool Japan) Yoshioka, 107

A politically charged term to emphasize the superiority of Japanese pop culture products, especially Manga, Anime, games and other digital contents. It was coined after »Cool Britannia«, the phrase frequently used in media since the 1960s, especially in the 1990s. The phrase itself was originally coined as a pun for the song *Rule, Britannia*.

Japanese Visual Culture Kusahara, 137

Japanese visual culture is often discussed along Manga and Anime, but they are part of a much wider phenomenon and longer history that goes back to the 12th century or earlier scrolls. Thanks to more than two centuries of peace from the 17th to the 19th century, visual entertainment became an important part of urban life. Inexpensive woodblock printing technology was behind the widespread visual culture.

Jouissance *Jahrmann, 281, 292*

»The posession and use of something affording advantage in the sense of enjoyment« *(Oxford English Dictionary, 2009) . Lacan (Lacan, 1972) introduced Jouissance in his critique of psychoanalysis as a theoretical concept. In his famous* Seminars XX *at the University of Paris, he suggested the use of the term for a sophisticated form of pleasure, which was informed by the relationship between objects, subjects and the creation and shifts between different aspects of enjoyment and the desire of the self with its complex appearances. Jouissance in the sense of Kristeva (Kristeva, 1984) is used as technical term from philosophy, cultural studies and in particular from the perspective of political theories to emphasise the quality of enjoyment and erotic attraction in the agency dimension of play. It is related to concepts of play and desire as driving forces for agency.*

Laws of Cool Russegger, 27

The Laws of Cool, as described by Alan Liu in his analysis of knowledge work and the culture of information, are representing a socio-cultural movement in human self organization based on contemporary informationalism. Organized tribes of knowledge clusters are celebrating the cult of invention within the innovation paradigm of creative destruction. By this means the Laws of Cool are describing unstable codes of creative production departed from industrial production processes such as Fordism or Keynesianism.

Ludics *Jahrmann, 281*

Ludics as newly coined term can be identified as the most challenging concept, particularly in the way it is introduced and applied in this Ludic Society project (2006–2010), in order to enable further analysis of the intersection of philosophy, anthropology, everyday life, and art. The term Ludics (Jahrmann, 2006) is proposed, in order to describe a toolbox of play agency. As a synthesis of practice and theory, this coinage supports a framework for activities including a potential for new critical art works. It offers tactics for social and political intervention. Although it still draws on separate disciplines, it intrinsically integrates the arts practice as knowledge practice, oscillating between practical theory and theoretical practice. Examples for this kind of Ludics art are provided on www.ludic-society.net and www.konsum.net. The writing practice exemplified in a series of Ludic Society Magazines reveals, how a playful text can powerfully explicate issues deeply masked by technological materiality. The playful Ludic method subverts an ideological complicity with conventional attitudes in philosophy, arts, economics and technology.

Ludic Interface *Jahrmann, 281*

Ludic Interface is coined in this thesis as a political concept, which draws on a survey of historic evidence of proto computational devices, compared to the use of these objects as artifacts. The creative reverberation of these objects in particular moments in history indicate an extension of this term into the field of artifacts as tools for political agency.

Ludic Interface *Fuchs, 242, 246*

Interfaces conceived by artists, creative thinkers or hacktivists that are: playful, application-specific, rich in connotative power and surprise, custom-built, aware of regional and historic context, critical, and inviting co-creativity, user generated or user driven content (or radically opposing those possibilities).

Lusory Attitude *Fuchs, 249*

A notion developed by Katie Salen and Eric Zimmerman to describe the intensity a player demonstrates to interpret a situation or setup in a playful manner.

Media Art Kusahara, 136

Media art is a genre that encompasses artworks that consciously use or discuss about media technology, which is not limited to digital technology. It overlaps with contemporary art, and new media art. As the term started being used in 1980s, there has been a discussion whether earlier forms such as video art should be included in media art or not.

Media Geijutsu / Media Aato Yoshioka, 101

Accoding to the legal definition in Japan, Media Geijutsu (officially translated into »media arts«) includes film, Manga, Anime, games, and digital media arts. »Media Aato« is the Japanized word from English »media art« and often means new forms of artworks making use of computers in interactive ways.

Meta-Codes Faßler, 89

If human groups share the keys of space, time, understanding etc. they create a structure of coded heritage. Its function is, to enhance the communication by using inventions and conventions of former times. Such meta-codes like history, belief systems, like visual, audiovisual, numerical languages, institutional sets, samplings or hacking strategies, carry out specific dramaturgies of content. With these meta-codes human beings create a recognizable world—or to say the interface of the virtual. It is the transformation of meta-codes which certifies the irreversible change of systems, not a single code or a single program.

Mitate Kusahara, 145, 152

Mitate is a practice of seeing beyond what is shown or written. The term goes back to 8th century, and is widely used today in daily life. In art it is a mode of representing and reading, metaphor, association and guessing among others. For example, through mitate rocks and pebbles in a Japanese Zen garden are understood as representation of mountains and sea.

Necropolitics Gržinić, 124

Biopolitics is a horizon of articulating contemporary capitalist societies from the so-called politics of life, where life (it does not matter anymore, via Giorgio Agamben, if it's bare/naked life or life-with-forms) is seen as the zero degree of intervention of each and every politics into contemporary societies. But today capital's surplus value is based on the capitalization of death (in Latin: »necro«) worlds. In his text *Necropolitics*, Achille Mbembe discusses this new logic of capital and its processes of geopolitical demarcation of world zones based on the mobilization of the war machine. Mbembe claims that the concept of biopolitics, due to the war machine and the state of exception being one of the major logics of contemporary societies, should be replaced with necropolitics.

Negentropy Russegger, 19

As an enhancement of the concept of Entropy, Erwin Schrödinger coined the term Negentropy. It can be used to evaluate a level of complexity by the measurement of the degree of organization internal to any system formed by interacting components. The term has created confusion suggesting that information processes negate the »second law of thermodynamics« by producing order from chaos.

Observation Technology Chen, 165

The advancement of resolution of observation technology through history has not only affected technological development but also philosophical discussions. Today's dissemination of computing power and algorithmic tools has to be understood as part of phenomena that are altering humanity's condition of life.

Otaku *d'Heilly, 225*

Otaku subculture originally meant urbanites (typically males) with a strong commitment to one particular hobby. The cultural genesis of this Otaku commitment is often described by decade of birth.

Pervasive Game *Kuni, 311*

Games that transgress and transcend different layers of experience by merging »physical presence and virtual objects«. They combine movements in and explorations of physical spaces with extensive use of networked media technologies. Therefore they strongly rely on mobile interfaces and digital gadgets.

Play *Kuni, 309*

Play is usually considered as a joyful activity not necessarily situated within a stable set of rules or within a defined framework. In contrast to games, play does not need a fixed location in space and time or a starting point nor an end. Moreover, the rules of play are handled differently and also can change or be changed by the players.

Play Affordances *Jahrmann, 289*

Play Affordance is suggested as term in order to describe a theoretical and technical aspect of material studies within the field of contemporary technological interfaces. It draws on affordances as expression from design theories and psychology, as an action that an individual can potentially perform in his or her environment. In this thesis, it is identified by a comparative analysis of technological artifacts and objects of contemporary everyday life that require practices of play as technique of interaction.

Playful Interfaces Russegger, 16

A playful or ludic interface can be every interfaced experience by applying it as such. By this means the ability of playfulness is becoming a powerful tool and mindset for individuals, to overcome existing patterns and standards of culture, art, science and technology. The interface by this means is a frameset of inter(re-)action not limited to technology or media. It can be applied by everyone trying to intend a shift of perspective in a certain field of action.

Playfulness Tarasiewicz, 207

On the one hand, playfulness describes a practice of motivation in temporary electronic and digital art, as it can be found regarding Ludic Interfaces and also in Device Art, on the other hand it means the fun and the pleasure resulting from technical innovations. Playfulness occurs between Lo-Fi and High-Tech: *Toy Benders* (sound-bricoleurs converting toys) as well as artists, who assign ludic features to non-ludic environments, are included in the term playfulness, as are the gamers and bobos out there, using their playful devices as intended fetish objects (see Smartphones).

Playfulness Kusahara, 141

Playfulness is often observed in art as the top layer over a serious theme, irony, or satire. It plays an important role in interactive art as a work needs to look inviting. Playfulness is widely observed in Japanese media art. It is a keyword in understanding Japanese popular culture. It also has a long history that goes back to 12th century *Scroll of Frolicking Animals* or even earlier.

Playsure Politics *Jahrmann, 281*

Playsure Politics is understood as erotic pleasure in play caused by the materiality of technological objects, which appear increasingly useless, according to market mechanisms. This directs the focus towards the aspects and relevance of politically conscious subversive erotic joy and pleasure. In short, Jouissance is related to the immaterial qualities of attraction regarding the technological object.

Post-Humans Gržinić, 130

Global financial capitalism (re)produces itself through dysfunctional logics, through economic, social and political disruptions, propped up by science and new media technology. Science and technology are being implemented for the figuration, representation, mediation and rationalization of the crisis, new forms of coloniality, deep processes of racism, discrimination and exploitation. Such technologies are seen as a »consensual hallucination«, the new »final frontier« of an out-of-control realm where only »post-humans« will be able to live. In the meantime, those who sometimes are not even considered to be fully human are looking for discarded food in the immense garbage dumps on the outskirts of the big cities of Asia, Latin America, Africa, and Eastern Europe. This is becoming more and more visible, especially with the present crisis of the financial capitalism, across Europe and the US.

Project Worlds Reder, 51

The notion of projects worlds is going back to Daniel Defoe's text *An Essay upon Projects* (Defoe, 1697) in which he propagated the notion of »project« for the first time, describing in highly pragmatic terms the »project worlds« to be aspired to: *»Projects of the nature I treat about are doubtless in general of public advantage«* if they *»are built on the honest basis of ingenuity and improvement«* combining *»own advantage«* and *»circumstances of public benefit«*.

Proto-Culture Faßler, 77, 91

The term Proto-Culture locates codes in the heterogeneous fields of formative dimensions. Formative dimensions or formative fields are non-intentional aggregations of coded and prefigured form options. They could be used or not, be forgotten or being present at the actual offers for formative practices. Proto-Culture opens a temporal and creative difference between the ongoing inventions of imagination, fiction, sign and design on one hand and of institution, function, conventions and performative regimes on the other hand.

Radical Hardware Tarasiewicz, 209

With this term, I want to state works such as Device Art as well as works from the modding cultures, extended with a critical component and transformed into media arts. The artist STELARC is a good example for somebody using radical hardware (in fact, he is the incarnation of radical human hardware).

Radical Software Tarasiewicz, 210

I want to highlight the term radical as a positive attribute of new media arts (in terms of quality, not in terms of conformity)—radical software describes game interventions and »application art«. Radical software are neither pieces of software art nor educational games.

Realm of Action Reder, 52

The very reason that all talk of »public benefit« has been robbed of all meaning, thanks to its inflationary use and profit benchmarks, stock rates, election opportunities, market forces, efficiency and cost structures have come to govern our realm of action, as if there were hardly any more »deviating« freedoms—in Defoe's sense (1697!). For this very reason, voluntary corporate government guidelines and non-profit projects are now more necessary than ever before. How such voluntary action, unwritten rules, social behavior, cooperation actually plays out tells something crucial about the state of affairs and the necessity of general parameters.

Salaryman Yoshioka, 106

Japanese white collar businessman. Especially during the period of the post-war rapid economic growth (late 1950s–early 1970s), the word used to imply total devotion to work, suppression of personal feeling, and loyalty to a cooporation one work for, with a resemblance of *Samurai* in the Edo Shogunate or of a soldier in the time of war.

Signs Faßler, 77

A Sign is based on cognitive and communicational movements away from (direct, intentional or non-intentional) signals. The new inventions are signatures, which function is to combine material things, ideas, concepts and emotion. They filled the vacuum of the unmarked cognitive world with new brain products, which could stand for their own and transported the promise, to be intimately related with facts and figures: these brain products where signs. With signs indirect, artificial status fixings are invented. With codes indirect, artificial relations are created.

Smartject Russegger, 22

The theory of Smartject describes a phenomenon based on a new type of individuality in media intensive and mediamorph lifestyles, embedded in technologically highly developed areas and environments.

Enabled by project based cooperation and object based self organization, using smartifacts and trans-classical forms of media- and communication technology. The terminology was created for the Ph.D. thesis of Georg Russegger with the same title.

Smart Populations Russegger, 22

Smart Populations, as coined by Manfred Faßler, are Communities of Projects based on contemporary self organization and media integrated knowledge cultures. Attended by the shift of mediated self empowerment of humankind, smart populations are a counter theory to swarm intelligence and wisdom of crowds, based on anthropology of the mediated or medial.

Societal Plants *Gfader, 264*

It is obvious and important to trust the role and function of plants in society, in social space, in how social space is organised and reorganised. There are modest, opulent, rhizomatic and resistant plants, dying plants, hacked and hackable plants. There are all kinds of micro and macro communities and plants sometimes resemble such collectives.

Straight Interface *Fuchs, 246*

The notion has been coined by Mathias Fuchs to describe technically designed traditional interfaces as opposed to ludic interfaces. Fuchs describes the latter in suffering from being effective, universally applicable, highly predictable, globally available, and unaffected by regional or historic context and suggests that this makes them unappropriate for artistic, creative or politically motivated applications.

Technological Determinism Gržinić, 118

As early as the end of the 1970s, it had already been claimed by Christopher Lasch, that the notion of technological determinism—a kind of blind belief in technology—is at the base of all popular comprehensions of industrial and technological revolutions. Nevertheless, he argued, we have to be aware that new inventions, new processes and new applications of scientific discoveries do not put forward the changes in ameliorating production as well. When these inventions are used in the process of reproduction, then it is for the sake of the new organization of labor processes (read: even bigger exploitation through rationalizations and efficiencies).

Tokusatsu *d'Heilly, 225*

Live-action film or television dramas that make considerable use of special effects. Godzilla is probably the best known series in the kaiju, or monster genre, though there are many many important titles and genre such as superhero, mecha. Aesthetically roots in Kabuki transformations and King Kong man-in-suit-storming-around-a-miniature-set cinema.

Tokyo's Urbanization *d'Heilly, 223*

Phase 1: 1868~1945. Tokyo was created in replacing actual power (shogun) *with abstract power (the emperor), and emptying by half. At this point, Tokyo was 19% temples, 21% private property, and 60% public lands. Most of these were handed to powerful clans from South Japan, and young capitalists, to exploit in funding speculative experiments in modernization, and later, war.*

Phase 2: 1946~1991. At the end of WWII, Japan's urban centers had been bombed blank. As Japan's most viable economic center, Tokyo saw a flood of new inhabitants and the ensuing frenzy of consumer middle class creation lasted two generations. From the early 1980s, a combination of bad domestic policies and foreign intervention inflated, and devastated land asset values.

Phase 3: 1991~. Tokyo, the world's largest metropolitan conurbation in terms of population, GDP, individual land ownership, rail and other infrastructure … a highly functional and stable megacity with dramatically diminished levels of individual disposable income, saw rampant middle class consumerism shift to a DIY, deflationary back-to-basics cultural model.

Urban Game *Kuni, 311*

A game taking place in urban environments and using the cityscape or certain parts of it, rather than distinct areas officially dedicated to games and sports as playgrounds. Urban Games are historically and conceptually related to the genre of street games, both using public streets and spaces as a playground and taking place within a fixed setup of time and space, of rules and players.

Zero Interface *Fuchs, 256*

The notion has been developed by Christiane Paul and describes interfaces that are reduced to a level of minimal possible interaction.

Index

D

E

F

G

H

Biographies

Bernhard, Hans / UBERMORGEN.COM

Hans Bernhard (USA/CH/AT, *1973) is a Swiss-American writer, actionist and digital artist working in the field of media hacking, txt-modification, conceptual art and net.art. Living and working in Vienna and St. Moritz. Since the mid-1990s, he has been a frequent speaker at conferences and universities worldwide, and has exhibited his work in venues such as Laboral Gijon (Spain), SFMOMA (USA), ZKM (Germany), New Museum New York (USA), Museum of Contemporary Art Tokyo (Japan), MOCA Taipei (Taiwan) or MUMOK Vienna (Austria). Hans Bernhard is a co-founder of *etoy* (www.etoy.com). He studied visual communication, digital art, and aesthetics in Vienna (Weibel), San Diego (Manovich), Pasadena (Lunenfeld), and Wuppertal (Brock). Hans Bernhard weighs 130 kg (290 pounds), is keen on attention and gets a new haircut in every city he travels to.

Chen, Dominick

Born 1981. Graduated from *UCLA* (Design/Media Arts) in Apr 2003. MAS in Interdisciplinary Information Studies from the University of Tokyo in Mar 2006. Researcher at the NTT InterCommunication Center [ICC] (Tokyo) from Nov 2003 to Mar 2006, directing *HIVE*, ICC's open video archive (http://hive.ntticc.or.jp/). From Mar 2006, Board Member and Public Lead of *NPO Creative Commons Japan*, consulting license adoptions, directing and producing application-driven open content projects such as *AudioVisual Mixer for INTO INFINITY* for iPhone (2009–). Produced and developed the *TypeTrace* art project (http://typetrace.jp), a key-logger software for creative purposes, since Aug 2006 and exhibited in diverse venues. Awarded the *Super Creator* prize from the Information Technology Promotion Agency, Japan (Apr 2009). Co-founded *Dividual Inc.*, a web service venture since Apr 2008, directing development of mobile digital community *Rigureto* (www.rigureto.jp).

d'Heilly, David

David d'Heilly has been based in Tokyo and New York, and working in the arts and journalism between Asia, Europe and the U.S. for the past 20 years. His writings have been published in eight languages, in periodicals including *Studio Voice* (Japan), *Wired* (US), and *the Economist Intelligence Unit* (UK). He has acted as producer, director, editor, etc. on numerous film and television productions in seven countries. His first media art curations were for ICC's *On the Web* in 1995. He has since curated and produced art projects internationally, including one using 113 venues throughout metropolitan Stockholm, the only ever staged on the world's busiest train line, the *Yamanote* (Tokyo), and at PS1/MoMA (NY). He has taught at two universities, Zokei, and the Tokyo University of Fine Arts and Music. Current projects include a book detailing Tokyo's urbanization, an exhibition of original development drawings from seminal anime, and a multinational television co-production about feminism.

exonemo

Artist unit comprising Kensuke Sembo and Yae Akaiwa. Since 1996, exonemo presented experimental website productions, installations, and live performances by the equipment of their own making, crossing over various media, software/hardware and digital/analog. In 2006, they won the Golden Nica Award of Ars Electronica in the category of Net Vision. While participating in many exhibitions and festivals at home and abroad, exonemo keep extending its wide-ranging activities, such as managing the Tokyo chapter of »dorkbot«, a worldwide community that is »doing strange things with electricity«. exonemo is based in Tokyo and at exonemo.com.

Faßler, Manfred

Manfred Faßler is Professor at the Goethe University Frankfurt a.M. He has published a variety of books and numerous articles with the focus on Media Theory, Media and Cognition, Human-Media-Inter(Re)Action, Digital Network, Cybernetics 2nd Order, Binary Media and Cultures, Communication, Visuality and Media Evolution. He was professor, researcher and lecturer at several national and international Universities such as Freie Universität Berlin, Uni. Kassel, Essen, Basel, São Paolo, Milan, University of Applied Arts Vienna and many more. Further personal information: www.fame-frankfurt.de / www.uni-frankfurt.de/fb/fb09/kulturanthro/staff/fassler_home.html

Fuchs, Mathias

Musician, game artist, theoretician of new media. Mathias has pioneered in the field of artistic use of game engines in various game art installations. He started the first European Masters Programme in Creative Games at the School of Art & Design at the University of Salford in Greater Manchester. Creative Games is a discipline on the borderline of games, art and critical discourse. Mathias is currently leading the development a Joint European Masters programme in Ludic Interfaces. He is a Senior Lecturer at the University of Salford and Programme Leader in MA Creative Technology and MSc Creative Games. He created and publicly showed sound and media installations in Vienna, London, Mexico City, Tokyo, Helsinki, Stockholm, Norwich, London, Cairo, Vancouver, Paris, and Providence. Commissioned work for ISEA94 and ISEA2004, resfest, Ars Electronica, PSi #11, futuresonic, EAST, the Greenwich Millennium Dome. Creative games for museums, urban planning and theatre performances. http://creativegames.org.uk

Fukuhara, Shiho / BCL

received a BA(Hons) in Fine Art from Central St Martins and an MA in Interaction Design from the Royal College of Art in London. Shiho was participating at *Le Pavillon* at the Palais de Tokyo in Paris in 2004, and was invited to IAMAS (Japan) in 2005 as an Artist-in-Residence. She was also an Artist-in-Lab at ISEA2008 in Singapore, and again an Artist-in-Residence at AmbientTV in London (2009). Her works have been shown internationally, including ISEA (2008 & 2010), Ars Electronica (2009), the Japan Media Art Festival (2010). Together with Georg Tremmel she is a founding member of the artistic research framework BCL, in which she is investigating the relationships between art and science with a special interest in the social implications of emergent biotechnologies.

Gfader, Verina

is an artist and researcher based in London and Tokyo. Her interest is in the criticality of emerging practices, ethics and economies of art, with a particular focus on non-linearity, minor systems, and articulations of the democratic, active work. Studies in visual media, photography and fine arts. Projects include the essay »Nervous Light Planes«, (In: *Animation, an interdisciplinary journal, Vol. 3, No. 2.* SAGE Publications, 2008); *an InviTe For mAking OrnAmentS*, workshop initiated with Merce Rodrigo García, with a contribution by Japanese architects Kazuyo Sejima and Ryue Nishizawa/SANAA. London: Serpentine Pavilion/Café, 2009; and *DREAM READINGS between OLIVIA PLENDER and UNNAR ORN*, project coordinator. London: E:ventGallery, 2009.

Gržinić, Marina

Philosopher, artist and theoretician, lives in Ljubljana, works in Ljubljana, Slovenia and Vienna, Austria. She is Professor at the Academy of Fine Arts Vienna, and researcher at the Institute of Philosophy at the ZRC SAZU (Scientific and Research Center of the Slovenian Academy of Science and Art) in Ljubljana. Selected monographies by Gržinić are: Gržinić, M. (Ed.): *Re-Politicizing art, Theory, Representation and New Media Technology*. Vienna: Academy of Fine Arts Vienna / Schlebrügge, 2008. Gržinić, M.: *Une fiction reconstruite. Europe de l'Est, post-socialisme et rétro-avant-garde [Fiction Reconstructed. Eastern Europe, Postsocialism and Retro-avantgarde]*. Paris: l'Harmattan, 2005. Gržinić has been involved with video art since 1982. In collaboration with Aina Smid, she realized more than 40 video art projects (http://www.Gržinić-smid.si/). Gržinić is the co-founder and co-editor of *REARTIKULACIJA*, artistic-political-theoretical-discursive platform from Ljubljana.

Jahrmann, Margarete

Margarete Jahrmann is an artist, Professor for Game Design at the University of Arts Zurich and researcher on the *HERA* project *Pervasive Prosumer Plays/FLOW* at the University of Applied Arts Vienna. As an internationally renowned artist she exhibited worldwide in the last ten years (2010: *Digital arts weeks*, Xian; *Space Invaders*, FACT Liverpool; *game.Art*, NEMK Amsterdam. 2009: *Tales of Play*, Alta Tecnología Andina, Lima; *Enter_Act*, Kunstmuseum Aaros. 2008: ARCO/Laboral, Gijon; SESC/File, São Paolo. 2007: DIGRA, Tokyo) and received major media arts awards as the distinction in interactive arts Prix Ars Electronica 2003 and software arts award Transmediale Berlin 2004. 2006 she founded the international arts research association *Ludic Society* and since then edits the LS magazine. 2010 she submitted her doctoral thesis on Ludics: *The Art and Politics of Play* at the University of Plymouth, Caiia (Centre for Advanced Inquiry in Integrative Arts). Her research focus lies on Play as research method, political activism and subversion and hybrid forms of intervention by arts. She frequently curates and publishes in the field of electronic network arts and critical culture. http://www.ludic-society.net

Kuni, Verena

is scholar in the field of history and theory of art and media cultures and professor for Visual Culture at Goethe University, Frankfurt a. M. Since 1996 she is lecturing, researching and teaching at universities and art academies in Europe and beyond. From 1995 to 1999, she co-curated the video section of *Kasseler Dokumentarfilm und Video Festival*, where since 1999 she is director of the yearly interfiction summit for art, media, and network cultures. Her research is dedicated a.o. to transfers between material and media cultures; media of imagination and technologies of transformation; alternate realities; urban biotopes; DIY and prosumer cultures; games, play and toys as tools. She has published widely (in print and online) on contemporary arts and media, their histories and futures. http://www.kuniver.se

Kusahara, Machiko

Machiko Kusahara is a scholar in media art, digital media culture and media history. She is a professor at Waseda University, Tokyo, and holds a Ph. D. in Engineering from University of Tokyo. Since early 1980s she curated, juried, wrote internationally, and was involved in launching Tokyo Metropolitan Museum of Photography and NTT/ICC in Tokyo. Her publications include: »Presence, Absence, and Knowledge in Telerobotics Art«. In: Goldberg, K. (Ed.): *The Robot in the Garden: Telerobotics and Telepistemology in the Age of the Internet.* Cambridge, Mass.: MIT Press, 2000; *From Ukiyo-e to Mobile Phone Screens—A Japanese Perspective.* Migrating Images, 2004; *They Are Born to Play: Japanese Visual Entertainment from Nintento to Mobile Phones.* Art Inquiry, 2004; »Device Art: A New Approach in Understanding Japanese Contemporary Media Art«. In: Grau, O. (Ed.): *MediaArtHistories.* Cambridge, Mass.: MIT Press, 2007; »Device Art: Media Art Meets Mass Production«. In: Freyer, C., Noel, S., Rucki, E.: *Digital by Design.* New York: Thames and Hudson, 2008; »A Turning Point in Japanese Avant-Garde Art 1964–1970«. In: Broeckmann, A., Nadarajan, G.: *Place Studies in Art, Media, Science and Technology.* Weimar: VDG Weimar, 2009.

lizvlx / *UBERMORGEN.COM*

lizvlx (AT/CH, *1973) is an Austrian net.artist working in the fields of digital imagery, media actionism and programming. She studied both commercial sciences as well as fine arts in Vienna and now works out of St. Moritz and Vienna. Using technology, computers, and sculpture as media since 1994, she has exhibited her net.art works in venues like the Ars Electronica (Austria), the Konsthall Malmoe (Sweden), the NTT/ICC Museum (Japan), ARCO (Spain) or the Lentos Kunstmuseum (Austria). lizvlx was also a founding member of *194.152.164.137* and of *netznetz.net*. lizvlx is allergic to milk protein and enjoys changing hair colors.

Muneteru, Ujino

Japanese sound, sculpture and performance artist, born in Tokyo, May 7, 1964. Lives and works in Tokyo. Has exhibited and performed in Australia, Austria, Canada, China, Germany, Indonesia, Japan, Korea, New Zealand, Sweden, Switzerland, the UK, and the USA, at venues including Ars Electronica, The Barbican Gallery, Biennale of Sydney, Deitch Projects, Galleria d'Arte Moderna Bologna, Govett-Brewster Art Gallery,

Guandong Museum of Art, The House of World Cultures Berlin, The Mori Art Museum, the Nam June Paik Art Center, Selasar Sunaryo Art Space, and The Western Front Vancouver.

Reder, Christian

Born 1944 in Budapest. Studied at the University of Vienna (Social Sciences & Economics), consultant, writer, professor at the University of Applied Arts Vienna (Head of the Center of Art and Knowledge Transfer). Editor of the book series *Edition Transfer* at SpringerWienNewYork, co-editor of the newspapers *Volltext* (literature) and *Recherche* (science), Vienna.

Russegger, Georg

Georg Russegger is Scientific Manager of the research and development project *Ludic Interfaces* (www.ludicinterfaces.com) at the Interface Culture Lab, University of Art and Design Linz. Together with the association *5uper.net* he is artistic director of the *CODED CULTURES* festival (www.codedcultures.net) in Vienna. Georg Russegger received a Ph.D. in media- and communication-theory and did a Post Doc. at the Graduate School for Film and New Media (Tokyo National University of the Arts). His last book is titled *Smartject* and focuses on creative delineation practices in human mediated processes of self organization within complex media environments. As an artist he received a diploma in media arts at the University of Applied Arts Vienna and works under the alias Grischinka Teufl (www.datadandy.net). Since 1999 he is active in artistic and scientific fields based on the research about new artistic practices, mediaintegrated knowledgecultures and its greater impact on project design and individual self empowerment.

Shikata, Yukiko

Yukiko Shikata is a media art curator and critic based in Tokyo, specially assigned professor at Tokyo Zokei University, guest professor at Tama Art University. She has been curating many challenging projects at Canon ARTLAB (1990–2001), Mori Art Museum (2002–2004) and independently *Power of Codes* by Mischa Kuball (Tokyo National Museum, 1999), *Amodal Suspension* by Rafael Lozano-Hemmer (YCAM, 2003), *MobLab* (2005), etc. Selected exhibitions at ICC are *open nature* (2005), *Connecting Worlds* (2006), and *Light InSight* (2008). She is one of Int'l Advisory Boards of transmediale, ISEA2010.ruhr and curators of Shanghai eARTS 2009, juries of Nam June Paik Award and has worked as jury in many competitions including Prix Ars Electronica, UNESCO Digi-Art Prize.

Tarasiewicz, Matthias

(a.k.a. parasew) co-founded *5uper.net* and is one of the coordinators of *CODED CULTURES*. He was curating and producing various exhibitions and art-related events with 5uper.net (e.g. *CODED CULTURES*, 2004; *Cuisine Digitale*; *Playfulness*, 2008 and many others). Being active as a digital bricoleur/coder, researcher and technology theorist since the last millenium, Matthias is developing experimental media prototypes and creating projects on the intersections of media, arts, technology and science. He studied Visual Arts at the University of Applied Arts Vienna. http://parasew.com

Tremmel, Georg / BCL

studied Visual Media Art at the University of Applied Arts in Vienna and Interaction Design at the Royal College of Art in London, where he started his ongoing collaboration with Shiho Fukuhara. Their artistic collaborative research framework BCL has the mission to explore the relations, congruences and differences of biological and cultural codecs through artistic interventions and social research. The work of BCL has been recognized internationally by receiving numerous awards, fundings and exhibitions including a NESTA Creative Pioneer Award (2004), the Nam June Paik Award Exhibition (2008), an Honory Mention in Hybrid Art at Ars Electronics (2009) and an Honorary Mention at the Japan Media Arts Festival (2010). Since 2010 Georg is also a researcher at the University of Tokyo's Human Genome Center at the Laboratory of DNA Information Analysis, specializing on Visual Analytics and Information Visualization of Next-Generation Sequencing Data.

Yoshioka, Hiroshi

was born in Kyoto, in 1956. He studied philosophy and aesthetics at Kyoto University. He teaches aesthetics and art theory at the Faculty and Graduate School of Letters, Kyoto University. He was the editor in chief of the journal *Diatxt.* (Vol. 1–8), and the general director of the *2003 Kyoto Biennial* and the *2006 Ogaki Biennial*. He is the author of *Shiso no genzaikei: Fukuzatsukei, dennokukan, afodansu (The Present Tense of Thought: Complex Systems, Cyberspace, and Affordance Theory)*. Tokyo: Kodansha, 1997; (with Hisashi Muroi:) *Joho to seimei: No, kompyuta, uchu (Information and Life: The Brain, Computers, and the Universe)*. Tokyo: Shin'yosha, 1993; and many essays and articles on philosophy, art and media culture. He has also published translations of works such as Mark Poster's *The Mode of Information: Poststructuralism and Context*, Bruce Mazlish's *The Fourth Discontinuity: The Co-Evolution of Humans and Machines*, and Hal Foster's *The Anti-Aesthetic: Essays on Postmodern Culture*.

Wlodkowski, Michal

Michal Wlodkowski is one of the founders of *5uper.net*, coordinator of the festival *CODED CULTURES—Exploring Creative Emergences* and independent software designer. Since the founding of *5uper.net* he curated and produced various exhibitions, art related events and projects on the intersections of design, media, art and technology, among them *CODED CULTURES—Decoding Digital Culture* in 2004. Besides his engagement as an curator and artist, Michal Wlodkowski develops projects and researches in the fields of cybernetics and communication theory. He studied Communication Science at the University of Vienna, Digital Arts at the University of Applied Arts, Vienna and Ravensbourne College, London.

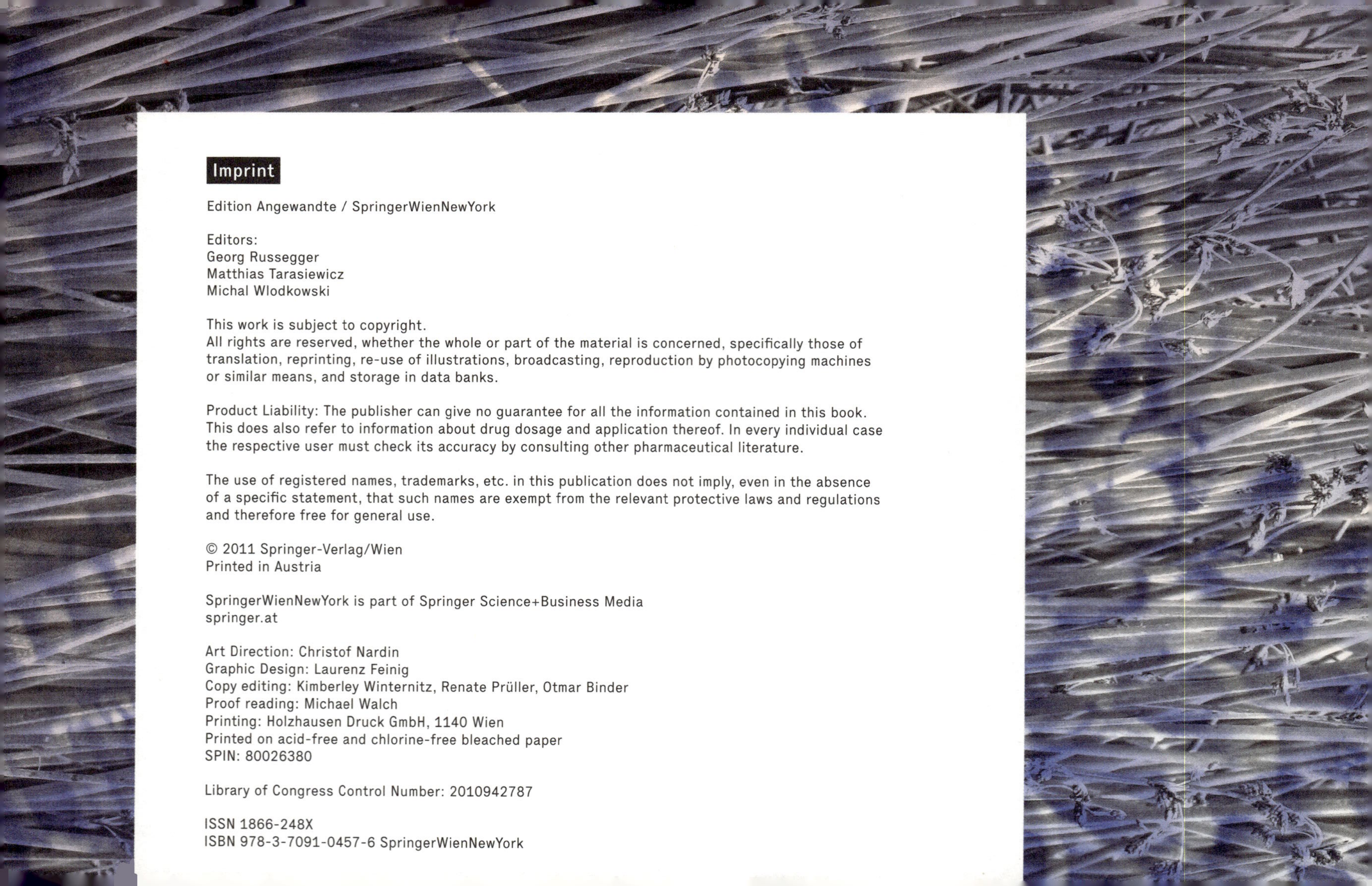

Imprint

Edition Angewandte / SpringerWienNewYork

Editors:
Georg Russegger
Matthias Tarasiewicz
Michal Wlodkowski

Printed in Austria

SpringerWienNewYork is part of Springer Science+Business Media
springer.at

Art Direction: Christof Nardin
Graphic Design: Laurenz Feinig
Copy editing: Kimberley Winternitz, Renate Prüller, Otmar Binder
Proof reading: Michael Walch
Printing: Holzhausen Druck GmbH, 1140 Wien
Printed on acid-free and chlorine-free bleached paper
SPIN: 80026380

Library of Congress Control Number: 2010942787

ISSN 1866-248X
ISBN 978-3-7091-0457-6 SpringerWienNewYork

Acknowledgements

This publication was possible through the support of different people, networks, communities, institutions, universities, public funds and sponsors. First of all we would like to thank all authors and participants for their great contributions and cooperation. We are grateful for the kind support of Kimberley Winternitz, Renate Prüller and Otmar Binder in proofreading and translating parts of the publication. Special Thanks are going as well to Laurenz Feinig and Christof Nardin for their fresh ideas concerning the cover and book design.

Without the strong support of the University of Applied Arts Vienna and in particular the rector Gerald Bast, Christian Reder and Anja Seipenbusch, who always support our projects and ideas so well, this project would not have been realized in this way. Also many thanks are going to Springer-Verlag especially to Angela Fössl, for the open mindedness in carrying out some new ideas in bookmaking with us.

Printed with the support of

CODED CULTURES · 5uper.net · Verein Stadtimpuls · WIEN KULTUR · di:'ʌngewʌndtə

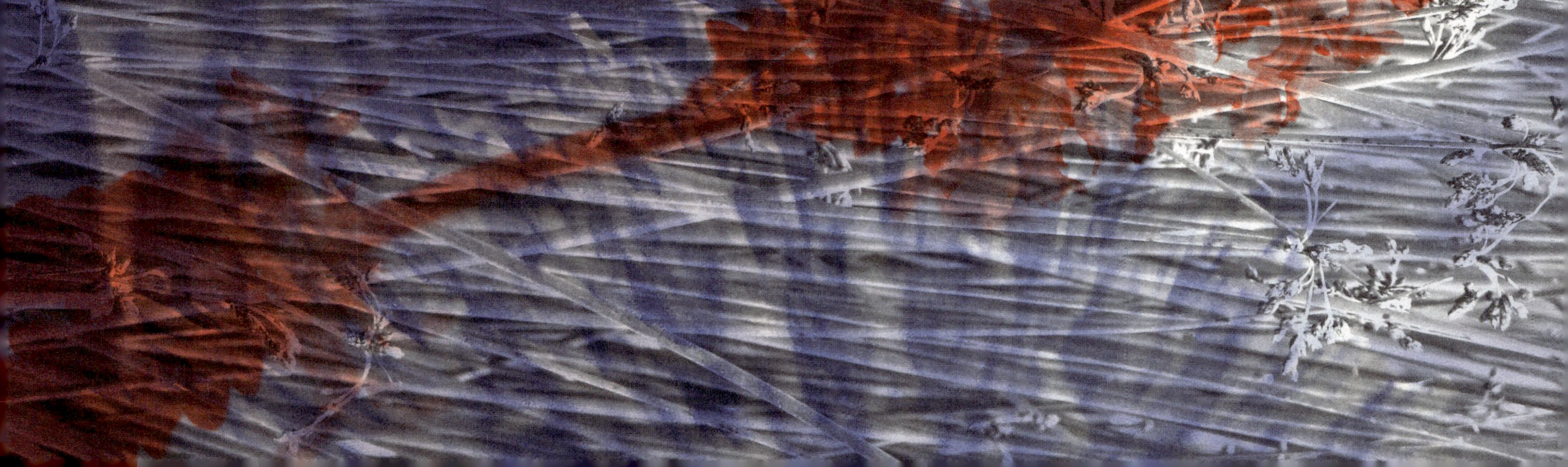

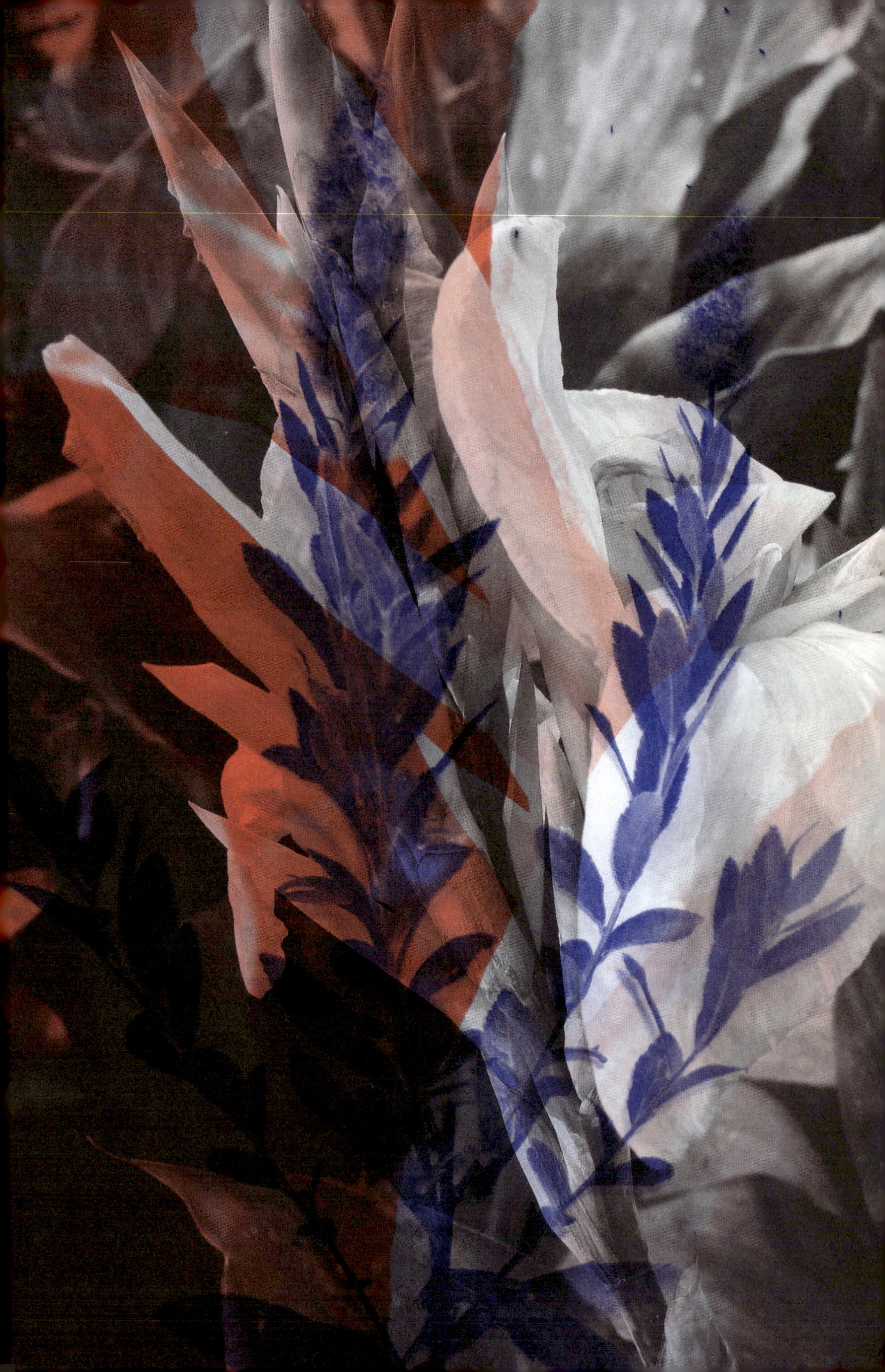

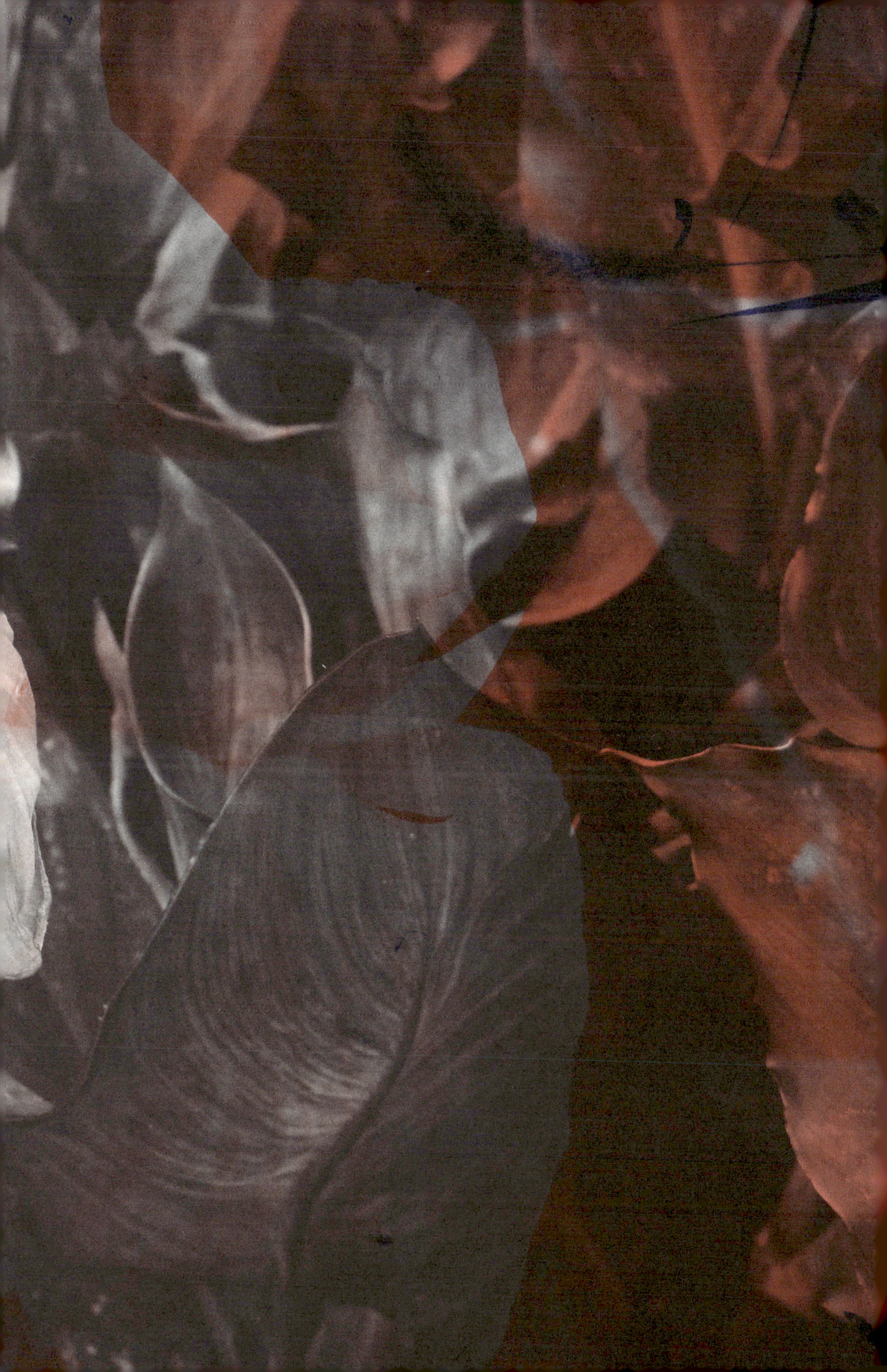

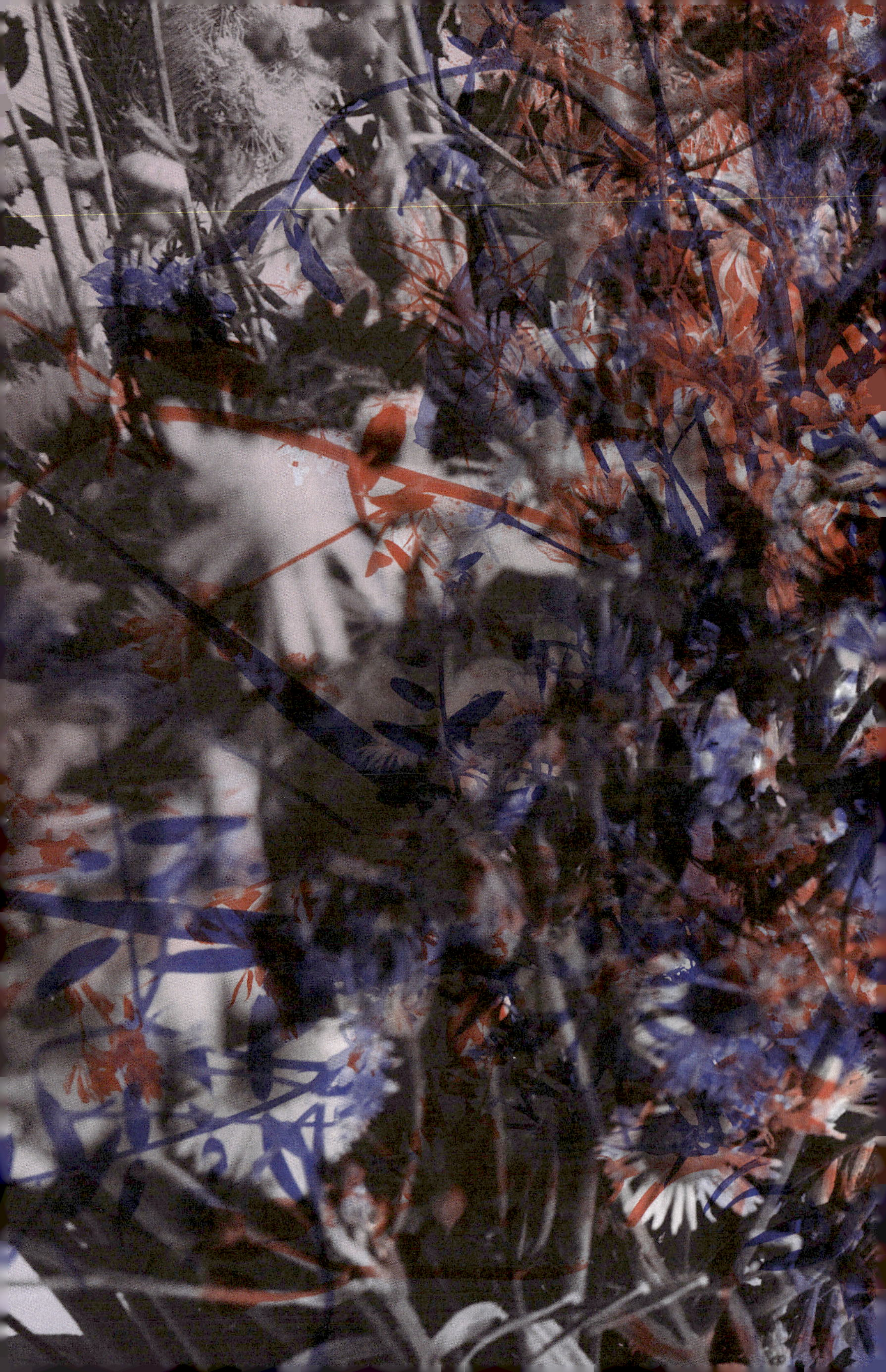